THE NATIONAL
GEOGRAPHIC TRAVELER

FLORENCE
&TUSCANY

THE NATIONAL
GEOGRAPHIC TRAVELER

FLORENCE & TUSCANY

Tim Jepson

Contents

How to use this guide 6–7   About the author 8
The regions 50–296   Travelwise 297–326
Index 327–33   Credits 334–35

Page 1: Farmhouse and
cypress trees near Pienza
Pages 2–3: The dome of
Florence's cathedral
Left: Young worshipers in
the Abbey of Sant' Antimo
near Montalcino

How to use this guide

See back flap for keys to text and map symbols.

The National Geographic Traveler brings you the best of Florence and Tuscany in text, pictures, and maps. Divided into three main sections, the guide begins with an overview of history and culture. Following are five chapters devoted to Florence and three to Tuscany, with featured sites selected by the author for their particular interest. Each chapter opens with its contents list.

The city and surrounding regions, and sites within them, are arranged geographically. Florence is divided into areas. A map introduces each area or region, highlighting the featured sites. Walks and drives, plotted on their own maps, suggest routes for discovering an area. Features and sidebars in the chapters give intriguing detail on history, culture, or contemporary life.

The final section, Travelwise, lists essential information for the traveler—pre-trip planning, special events, getting around, and what to do in emergencies—plus offers selection of hotels and restaurants, shops, activities, and entertainment.

To the best of our knowledge, all information is accurate as of the press date. However, it's always advisable to call ahead when possible.

Color coding

206

Each region is color coded for easy reference. Find the region you want on the map on the front flap, and look for the color flash at the top of the pages of the relevant chapter. Information in **Travelwise** is also color coded to each region.

Museo dell'Opera del Duomo

- 🄰 Map p. 54
- ✉ Piazza del Duomo 9
- ☎ 055 230 2885
- 🕐 Closed Sun. p.m.
- 💲 $$
- 🚌 Bus: 14, 23

Visitor information

Practical information for most sites is given in the side column (see key to symbols on back flap). The map reference gives the page number of the map and grid reference. Other details are address, telephone number, days closed, entrance charge in a range from $ (under $4) to $$$$$ (over $25), and nearest public transport in Florence. Other sites have information in italics and parentheses in the text.

TRAVELWISE

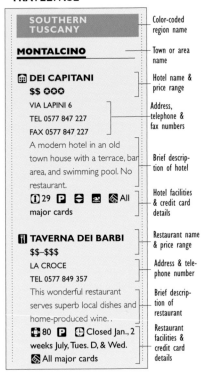

Color-coded region name

Town or area name

Hotel name & price range

Address, telephone & fax numbers

Brief description of hotel

Hotel facilities & credit card details

Restaurant name & price range

Address & telephone number

Brief description of restaurant

Restaurant facilities & credit card details

Hotel & restaurant prices

An explanation of the price ranges used in entries is given in the Hotels & restaurants section (beginning on p. 306).

FLORENCE AREA MAPS

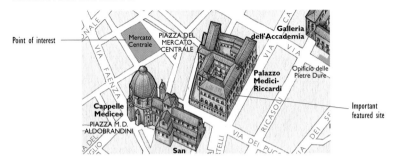

Point of interest

Important featured site

• A locator map accompanies each area map and shows the location of that area in the city.

WALKING TOURS

Walk route

Featured site (in bold) on walk route

Direction of walk route

Red numbered bullet links site on map to description in the text

Start point

Building outline

Point of interest not on walk route

• An information box gives the starting and ending points, time and length of walk, and places not to be missed along the route.

REGIONAL MAPS

Important featured town

Point of interest

Road numbers

Map reference

Regional capital

• A locator map accompanies each regional map and shows the location of that region in the country.
• Adjacent regions are shown, each with a page reference.

THE NATIONAL
GEOGRAPHIC TRAVELER

FLORENCE & TUSCANY

About the author

Tim Jepson has been a passionate and lifelong devotee of Italy, and of Florence and Tuscany in particular. Since graduating from Oxford, he has spent long periods of time living and traveling in city and region alike, including an idyllic summer in a vine-shaded house outside the little Tuscan town of Montalcino. Over the years he has written some 15 books on Italy, including several on various aspects of Tuscany, as well as numerous articles for the *Daily Telegraph, Vogue, Condé Nast Traveler,* and other publications. He wrote the *National Geographic Traveler: Italy.*

Now based in London with the *Daily Telegraph,* Tim continues to visit Tuscany regularly, and as a keen hiker and outdoor enthusiast, he takes a particular interest in the region's sublime countryside. He also revels in Florence and Tuscany's more sedentary pleasures—the food, wine, art, and culture—and hopes one day to indulge them all from a small Tuscan rural retreat of his own.

Tim has also worked on Italian programs for the BBC and commercial television, and his career has included spells in a slaughterhouse, on building sites, and as a musician playing piano and guitar on streets and in bars across Europe.

History
& culture

Drummer at the Siena Palio

Florence & Tuscany today

FLORENCE AND TUSCANY HAVE SUCH POWERFUL ARTISTIC AND HISTORICAL associations that it's easy to forget their significant role in the much changed world of modern Italy. Florence is a major central Italian city, a cosmopolitan and wealthy metropolis with considerable contemporary élan, while Tuscany is a region whose social and cultural traditions still find a powerful voice despite the changing face of its towns and countryside.

LOCAL LOYALTIES

Florence is the capital of Tuscany, but never confuse Florentines with Tuscans. In fact, never talk about Tuscans at all, except in the loosest sense, for most Tuscans are far more loyal to their local communities than to their region, never mind their country or regional capital. Italians generally retain prejudices that reflect their fractured history, and Tuscans are no exception. The Florentines and Sienese have been divided for centuries; so, too, the citizens of Lucca and Pisa, and the inhabitants of Arezzo and Cortona. This powerful sense of self-worth continues right down to the smallest village. The Italian word for it is *campanilismo*—the idea that your loyalties and worldly concerns extend no farther than the reach of your bell tower, or *campanile*. Modern mass media have produced a degree of cultural homogenization, but the weight of history and tradition still hangs heavy.

At first glance, these narrow loyalties might seem a force for reaction, an inward-looking approach that perpetuates division and stifles social and other progress. Tuscany's modern roots go back to the era of independent city-states, or *comuni*, and countless towns still jealously preserve symbols, buildings, and civic structures that reflect and recall past glories—towers, piazzas, statues, palaces, and imposing medieval walls. Tuscans literally inhabit their history. Yet it is Tuscany's skill to have incorporated its attachment to the past into a distinctive modern outlook, retaining the sense of belonging created by small town loyalties and a pride in the past that sustains a confidence in the present.

THE ECONOMY

The apparent conservatism and strong civic ties within communities also belie the considerable changes that have taken place in Tuscany since the end of World War II. In 1945 the region's economy was still predominantly agricultural, with a majority of workers little more than landless laborers or small-scale peasant farmers. Between 1951 and 1971 some 375,000 workers left the land, about 72 percent of the original agricultural workforce. Most moved into the myriad small businesses that provided—and continue to provide—the motor of an economic miracle that transformed Italy in less than a generation into one of the world's leading industrial powers. By 1991, the date of Italy's last census, just 4.7 percent of the workforce labored on the land, compared with 20.5 percent in commerce, 37.4 percent in industry, and 37.4 percent in service and other public or private businesses.

The Tuscan countryside is far from dead, however, for all the decline in numbers of agricultural workers. Some 52 percent of the region's available land is still given over to agricultural use. In some cases this means traditional crops—the great wheat fields of the rolling hills south of Siena or the sweeping vineyards swathing the slopes of Chianti and elsewhere. In others it reflects a willingness to turn the countryside into an arm of the tourist industry; *agriturismo* (farm-stay accommodations), for example, is booming. Elsewhere, new crops and European Union subsidies have been embraced enthusiastically, to say the least, with sunflowers, rapeseed, and flax, among others, adding new seasonal colors to Tuscany's pastoral summer palette. At the same time, a revolution in old industries, notably viticulture (wine producing), has seen an expansion of old markets, with Brunello di Montalcino wines and the so-called super

A postcard seller near the Ponte Vecchio in Florence. Money spent by visitors provides a livelihood for many Florentines.

Tuscan vintages revitalizing an industry once associated solely with the thin, acidic staples of Chianti and its close cousins (see pp. 272-73).

Although there is increasing pressure to relax planning restraints, the Tuscan propensity for preservation and conservatism—a pride in what the people have and what they had—has ensured that the countryside, one or two exceptions allowing, has remained largely undesecrated by wanton development or industrial-scale agricultural practices. To a

large extent, you can still gaze over Tuscany's vines, cypresses, olives, and terraced hillsides—all shaped by human hands for more than 3,000 years—and see the same landscapes used to such sublime effect in the backgrounds of Renaissance paintings.

LANDSCAPES

In the same way that Tuscany's towns and people display extraordinary diversity and individuality, so the region as a whole is a

patchwork of different landscapes and diverse character. To many visitors, the region may appear no more than the European artistic center *par excellence:* And no wonder, for in this regard it stands out even in Italy, the world's richest repository of Renaissance art and other works. Tuscany boasts over 270 individual museums and galleries, more than any other Italian region.

In Florence Tuscany has a capital whose artistic credentials need no emphasizing, while

Cypress trees such as these, near Pienza, have long been one of the most distinctive features of Tuscan landscapes.

Siena is widely acknowledged as Europe's most perfect medieval metropolis. At the other end of the spectrum, virtually every village, however small, has some artistic treasure—a Romanesque church, a faded fresco, a carved Madonna—that would be the envy of many European cities.

Yet Tuscany is also a region of major industries, as you'll see if you visit or pass through Prato, one of the world's leading producers of high-quality textiles; the chances are your "Made in Italy" clothes were made nearby. It's also a region of small and highly specialized industries, many of them based on natural resources and local skills that date back centuries: marble extraction around Massa and Carrara, furniture-making in Poggibonsi and fine glassware in Colle di Val d'Elsa, alabaster-working in Volterra, the fashioning of gold and jewelry in Arezzo. It is a region of major ports—notably Livorno, Italy's second largest—and myriad islands such as Elba, Capraia, Giglio, and Cerboli. It is also a region of beach resorts, particularly along the Versilian coast north of Pisa; plains (the Maremma in the southwest); spectacular mountains (the Alpi Apuane north of Lucca); extinct volcanoes (Monte Amiata); immense, ancient forests (the Casentino); wild, little-

visited uplands (the Mugello, Pratomagno, and Lunigiana); and the sublime and timeless landscapes—notably Chianti's woods and vineyards and southern Tuscany's villa-topped hills—with which the region is most closely associated. But, above all, of course, Tuscany is the region of Florence.

FLORENCE
In many ways, Florence, the Tuscan capital, epitomizes the region's contrast of old and

From the dome of Florence's cathedral visitors look out over the Campanile— the bell tower—and the streets beyond.

new, and the tensions and interplay between social and cultural traditionalism, the demands made on a modern region by its obligations to its heritage, and the pressures exerted by many millions of visitors. Then, of course, there are the Florentines. Social stereotyping is a dangerous game, but there's no

Gucci was founded in Florence, a place where art, style, and design are as important today as they were in the Renaissance.

escaping the fact that the average Florentine is a breed apart.

Dante (1265–1321), the great medieval Florentine poet, was in no doubt about his fellow citizens. They were *"gente avara, invidiosa e superba"* ("mean, envious, and proud"), and a Renaissance proverb described them as perpetual complainers, possessed of sharp eyes and bad tongues. Pride and arrogance are still charges leveled at Florentines by other Italians, a people who have well-rehearsed—and generally unflattering—stereotypes for inhabitants of all their major cities and regions. Walking around the city, you may indeed detect a rather haughty grandeur in the sleek, well-dressed Florentines parading their urbane streets with an obvious degree of self-satisfaction. But then who can blame them? After all, this is the city that nurtured the Renaissance; produced the likes of Dante, Michelangelo, Galileo, Machiavelli, and Leonardo da Vinci; invented French cuisine (see p. 20); rediscovered perspective; gave birth to many of Europe's greatest artists;

created the Western world's first chair of Greek; invented Italian as a literary language; created the basis of banking and thus capitalism; and invented opera, the piano, eyeglasses, and much more.

The past sits easily with modern Florentines, who, far from feeling overshadowed by their history, still bask in its glory, confident that the qualities that stood the city in good stead for 2,000 years—genius, diligence, verve, flair, hard work, vision—are qualities that still pertain. Florentines are generally dignified and decorous; you would never confuse a Florentine, for example, with his or her more boisterous Neapolitan cousin. They are also often cultured and civilized—another legacy of their illustrious past.

Fashion

If you suspect that the Florentines' sense of self-satisfaction is misplaced, then look no further than the city's continued strengths in such areas as fashion, design, and craft for proof that at least some of the traditional virtues still flourish. Young and old alike in Florence are testimony to the importance of fashion, displaying their finery as if on some giant catwalk. The notion of *bella figura,* of

cutting a beautiful figure and not making a fool of yourself, is an important one. Even the cynical statesman Niccolò Machiavelli (1469–1527) was moved to observe that the Florentines' main preoccupations were to appear splendid in apparel and obtain a crafty shrewdness in discourse.

Young people may dress informally, but their running shoes are invariably immaculate, their jeans are spotless, and their polo shirts and sunglasses sport the requisite designer labels. Older Florentines tend to prefer subtle and more sober clothes, blending a tweedy English classicism with dashes of designer and Renaissance ostentation.

Milan may now have the fashion shows and big names, but Florence is not without its own stars, not least Gucci, whose empire was founded in the city three generations ago, and Emilio Pucci, whose dramatically dyed silks caused a sensation in the 1950s, and whose designs have recently found a new place in the hearts of fashion *cognescenti*. Florence is also the headquarters of the company founded by one of the most famous shoemakers, Naples-born Salvatore Ferragamo, who emigrated to the United States at 15 and proceeded to design shoes for the likes of Greta Garbo,

Vivien Leigh, and Gloria Swanson. Today, the company still makes clothes, shoes, and accessories at its Florentine base.

The crafts tradition
Such items find a natural home in Florence, not least because of its powerful traditions of art and crafts and its many artisans' workshops. Street names across the city bear witness to the countless trades once practiced in them—Via della Spadai (Street of the Swordmakers), Via dei Fibbiai (Street of the Bucklemakers), or Via degli Arrazzieri (Street of the Tapestry-makers). You may no longer be able to pick up a sword in downtown Florence, but other examples of the artisans' craft reveal themselves at every turn. Leather, for example, is everywhere, whether as chic Gucci loafers, fake designer handbags (fakes are everywhere on Florence's streets), or the countless belts, shoes, and jackets of the city's San Lorenzo market. Marbled paper is another specialty, as is jewelry, which you find in little stores across the city, but especially on the Ponte Vecchio,

A break for ice cream, or *gelato*, is an essential part of the Florentine day.

the jewelers' traditional Florentine home. Across the bridge, the old blue-collar Oltrarno district contains many shops and workshops, from tiny ateliers jammed into the backstreets to the grand antique shops of Via Maggio. Similar workshops greet you in Via della Porcellana or around Santa Croce, where doorways are a jumble of dismembered chairs and half-finished tables, and the air is heavy with the scent of varnish and wood glue.

Problem areas

These images of past and present united in perfect harmony are not the full picture, of course, and no one would pretend that Florence is a city without problems. While family and social ties are stronger than in many places, drugs, homelessness, and unemployment are problems here as they are in any major metropolis. You would not want to spend time in the city's Cascine park after dark, for example, nor engage in conversation with many of the characters who hang around the railroad station in the small hours.

Other problems are more subtle, but no less invidious. One of the most obvious is the sheer number of visitors to Florence. No one can quite agree on a precise annual figure—it runs to many millions—but a glimpse at the lines outside the Uffizi art gallery or at the battalions of backpackers slumped outside the city's cathedral, suggest the number is often more than the city and its inhabitants can comfortably bear. Visitors create wear and tear on the city's infrastructure and on its fabric, and in a city like Florence, where the fabric is often the irreplaceable artistic legacy of centuries, the impact is all the more damaging. The demands of visitors and the need to preserve buildings and works of art also impose a huge financial burden on the city council.

Florence often does not help itself. Pollution is a problem, though not as much of a problem as it is in Rome or Milan. Much of it is caused by the Florentines' passion for cars—there are 2.7 cars for every Florentine family—the majority of which, at least, have been banned from the city center since 1988 (but only after considerable controversy). Other problems can be laid more squarely at the visitors' door, notably the replacement of neighborhood food stores by souvenir stores,

Festivals such as this one in Montalcino recall Tuscany's medieval past.

the workshops edged out by high-rent boutiques, and the traditional *trattorie* sacrificed to the gods of fast food.

DAILY LIFE

Despite such modern problems, however, Florence and Tuscany continue to draw strength from, and retain their links to, the past. City stores and businesses may now work through the day, but in the countryside and the smaller centers, the *siesta,* or post-lunch shut-down, is a still a mainstay of the day: Most churches, museums, and stores close, with life returning to the drowsy, deserted streets about 4:30 in the afternoon. Soon after that it's time for another ritual, the *passeggiata,* the early evening parade that sees a town's inhabitants, old and young, promenading along the main street, talking, flirting, courting, catching up, sipping an *aperitivo,* or simply watching the world go by.

FESTIVALS

Such displays emphasize the Tuscans' sociability. This is given fuller rein during Tuscany's many festivals and historical pageants, events that combine the locals' love of drama and spectacle with yet another chance to relive and reevaluate their past. At one extreme are the big set-piece pageants—of which Siena's Palio horse race is the most renowned—and at the other a huge range of small village fiestas, or *sagre,* which you'll inevitably stumble upon in the region's more rural backwaters. Many events have a religious raison d'être—to celebrate Easter or a saint's day; others are held for gastronomic reasons—to celebrate the wine harvest or a local specialty; and others, such as Florence's Maggio Musicale, have obvious cultural associations. Virtually all involve an immense amount of pageantry, with processions, fireworks, medieval dress, and copious amounts of food and drink.

Don't make the mistake, however, of imagining that such events are either for the benefit of visitors or fossilized ceremonies perpetuated for reasons of sentiment and spectacle. As in most walks of Tuscan and Florentine life, history, in one guise or another, is never far from the surface. For the past, in this part of the world at least, is a vital part of both the present and the future. ∎

Food & drink

One of the fruits of Tuscany's continued attachment to the land is the region's superb food and wine, a range of excellent ingredients contributing to a cuisine and variety of wines that are as good as any in Italy. Eating is a passion for Tuscans, and one that visitors can easily share. Lunch on a vine-covered terrace and dinner under a starry Mediterranean sky should be experiences as memorable as visits to the best museums and galleries.

FOOD

Much Tuscan food was based on peasant traditions—the so-called *cucina povera,* or "cuisine of the poor"—and dates from a time when poverty was the great culinary mother of invention. Other Italians still call Tuscans *mangiafagioli*—"bean-eaters"—an unfair appellation, but one that hints at the region's simple staples. Not all the food, though, has humble roots. Florentines are quick to tell you, for example, that they invented many of the great dishes of French cuisine, a claim they trace back to the marriage in 1534 of Caterina de' Medici to Henri de Valois, the future king Henri II of France. Caterina is said to have blanched at the idea of foreign food, and she made certain that she was accompanied to France by a retinue of Florentine chefs. Hence, say the Florentines, the presence in France of such modern-day "French" staples as canard à l'orange (duck in orange sauce), a simple variation of the Tuscan *papero alla melarancia,* and the famous Gallic vol-au-vents, still found in Florentine pastry shops as *turbanate di sfoglia.* Caterina also introduced the French to two essentials of the modern table—the fork and the napkin.

Today's Tuscan food contains plenty of sophisticated dishes that wouldn't disgrace the tables of restaurants in London, Paris, or New York, but for the most part the region's cuisine is a rural one based on the area's simple staples: Mouthwatering hams, cheeses, robust pulses, wild leaves, hearty soups, pastas, piquant salamis, grilled meats, fresh fish, seafood, and—of course—superb olive oil. Better still, most of this food is seasonal and locally produced, and it only appears at the time of the year it is grown. Visit during a few limited weeks in spring, for example, and you may be lucky enough to find tiny spears of wild asparagus on menus. Later, cherries will be in the shops, then apricots, and then peaches. In fall it is the turn of figs, field-fresh mushrooms, and plump, gold-green grapes. Rarely in a Tuscan market or food store *(alimentari)* will you find the year-round supply of vegetables and imported fruits found in northern European and North American supermarkets.

But if seasonal produce changes, the course of Tuscan meals remains inviolate. Breakfast is a simple coffee and croissant *(una brioche* in Italian). Lunch and dinner begin with starters or *antipasti*—literally "before the meal." These may include *bruschetta,* a rough slice of toasted bread rubbed with garlic and olive oil and topped either with tomatoes or a simple grind of salt and pepper. Often they will include a variety of hams and salamis served with saltless bread, or tiny crusty toasts *(crostini)* topped with olive paste, chicken liver pâté, or other savory garnishes.

You won't be expected to order every course, and at lunch most restaurants won't mind if you order just a first course and salad. First courses make less use of pasta than in many parts of Italy, tending instead toward soups such as minestrone (a rich ham and vegetable soup), *zuppa di fagioli* (bean soup), and the common *ribollita* (literally "reboiled"), a rich bean and cabbage soup that used to be reboiled and served on successive days. Another common first course is *pappa al pomodoro,* bread or croutons cooked in an herby broth and mixed with sieved tomatoes. Classic pastas include *pappadelle alla lepre* (noodles with a hare sauce), while the undisputed king of the main dishes is *bifstecca alla fiorentina* (Florentine beefsteak). Among the cheeses, look out for regional sheep's milk cheese (pecorino). Desserts include obvious Italian winners such as *gelato* (ice cream), but

The Mercato Centrale in Florence sells local produce in season.

also try some of the many regional specialties, especially the *panforte* of Siena, a rich cake of cocoa, walnuts, spices, and crystallized fruit made to a 13th-century recipe.

DRINK

While you can eat well morning, noon, and night in Tuscany, you can also drink well whatever the time of day and whatever the season. Good coffee is a given in almost every bar and café, from the breakfast cappuccino or caffè latte to the after-dinner *espresso* (Italians almost never drink cappuccino or other milky coffee after dinner). Freshly squeezed orange, lemon, or grapefruit juice *(una spremuta)* in season is another treat. Don't miss cooling novelties such as granita (crushed ice drenched with a coffee- or other flavored syrup) and *frappé* or *frullati* (shakes made with fresh fruit and milk or ice cream).

Closer to sundown you may want one of the classic Italian aperitifs such as Campari

soda, which often comes ready mixed. If you want the real thing ask for a Campari bitter. Nonalcoholic *aperitivi* are also common; an Italian favorite is the slightly bitter Crodino.

The choice and quality of wine are good and getting better. Chianti, Tuscany's most famous red wine, comes in many guises and has been joined by some more ambitious reds, the "super Tuscans." Brunello di Montalcino and Vino Nobile di Montepulciano are the other big names (see p. 272 for more on wine).

Local cheeses, salami, prosciutto, and bread provide an informal lunch, accompanied by red wine of the region.

After dinner, brave one of the Italian *digestifs:* Grappa is a clear (sometimes flavored) spirit distilled from the skins left after grapes have been pressed for wine. Amaro (literally "bitter") is a fortified wine full of herbs and "secret ingredients" that Italians swear is an aid to digestion; Averna is a good brand. ■

History of Florence & Tuscany

THE HISTORY OF FLORENCE AND TUSCANY GOES BACK ALMOST THREE thousand years, embracing the Etruscans, the mysterious forebears of the Romans; the rivalries of popes and emperors; the Medici—a family whose name echoes through many centuries of the region's past—and, in the Renaissance, one of the greatest periods of social, cultural, and intellectual change seen in the Western world.

THE ETRUSCANS

Tuscany's first significant inhabitants were the Etruscans, probably a mixture of indigenous peoples and settlers from Greece and Asia Minor, who inhabited much of central Italy from about the ninth century B.C. Tuscan towns with Etruscan roots include Arezzo, Cortona, and Volterra, but not Florence, whose present-day site the Etruscans overlooked in favor of Fiesole, a more easily defended redoubt in the hills nearby.

Some of Fiesole's inhabitants may have frequented a market near the Arno, probably close to the present site of the Ponte Vecchio, the river's narrowest bridging point. Others may have formed a permanent community here in the fourth century B.C.

THE ROMANS

Whatever the site's status, it remained little altered until the rise of Rome, whose empire gradually encroached on Etruscan territory. Fiesole fell to the Romans in 283 B.C. but continued to enjoy relative independence until 60 B.C., when, according to myth, a Roman force under the general Fiorino was dispatched to confront Cataline, a renegade soldier who had assumed control of the town. Fiorino decided against attacking the well-defended citadel and instead starved the town into submission from a base on the Arno—modern-day Florence. Fiorino was killed in the process, and Cataline, it is said, escaped to Pistoia before his eventual capture.

Only a sliver of this story has any grounding in fact. Cataline was a genuine figure and suffered defeat at Pistoia in 62 B.C. Fiorino was almost certainly mythical, however, as was the notion that he gave his name to the city that grew up around his camp. Equally unlikely is the idea that Rome's campaign against Fiesole was completed by Julius Caesar or that Caesar directly founded Florence—although many modern accounts record his involvement as fact.

Caesar's actual role in the birth of the city was passive. He formulated the so-called Agrarian Law of 59 B.C., which made grants of land to retired army veterans. In doing so, he created the conditions that fostered the early development of a colony on the Arno. In time this colony acquired a name—Florentia—although just how is a matter of debate. Whatever the settlement's origins, it soon prospered, the result of river trade and traffic on the Via Cassia, an important Roman road linking Rome to northern Italy.

Few memorials to the Roman colony survive, save for its original gridiron plan, whose pattern can still be seen in the streets of the modern city: Piazza della Repubblica was the old forum, Via degli Strozzi the main street, and Via de Tornabuoni and Via del Proconsolo its western and eastern limits. The major physical mementos are a handful of ancient columns appropriated by later builders for use in the baptistery and San Miniato al Monte.

POPES & EMPERORS

In about A.D. 568, after the fall of Rome, Tuscany passed under the control of the Lombards, a Germanic tribe from northern Europe. They were defeated, in turn, after 774 by the Franks, another northern European tribe, under the command of Charlemagne, one of the most celebrated rulers of the age. Charlemagne was a Christian, and he awarded

Modern festivals in medieval dress, such as Giostro del Saracino (Jousts of the Saracen) in Arezzo, often commemorate historical events.

large areas of central Italy to the papacy, thus creating the germ of the Papal States, an enclave that would provide the basis of the papacy's temporal power for more than a thousand years. In return, the papacy crowned Charlemagne Holy Roman Emperor (*R*.800–814).

These events sowed the seeds of a dispute between the papacy and the emperors that

This statue of a reclining man gives a face to the enigmatic Etruscan people.

would reverberate through Tuscan and Italian history for centuries. Henceforth popes would claim they had sanctioned imperial rule, while emperors claimed they had created papal power. In later years, supporters of the popes would become known as Guelphs; supporters of the emperors were called Ghibellines. Different towns and noble families often had different allegiances, although most were based on local rivalries rather than genuine allegiance to the empire or papacy. If your rival supported the pope, you would automatically side with the emperor. And if one or other superpower was in the ascendant, then you adapted your loyalties accordingly.

The empire and its rulers were based in northern Europe, however, and eventually allowed Tuscany to be ruled on their behalf by local Lucca-based princes known as margraves. As time went by, the physical distance between the margraves and the Holy Roman Emperors weakened links between the two. By 1077, the Margrave Matilda (1046–1115), a devout Christian, had transferred her allegiance to the pope. At her death, she went further, bequeathing all her titles to the papacy with the important exceptions of Lucca, Florence, and Siena. It was at about this time that the region was referred to as Tuscany for the first time, its name derived from the Latin *Tuscia* (used after about the third century), in turn derived from Etruria, the name given to the land of the Etruscans, or Tusci.

NEW WEALTH

As disputes between the papacy and the empire intensified, so the resulting power vacuum, coupled with an upsurge in trade, allowed for the growth of independent city-states across Tuscany. Some, such as Pisa, grew powerful on the back of maritime prowess. Others, notably Florence, owed their growth to textiles, which developed largely thanks to the water of the Arno, vital to an industry that required the washing and rinsing of both sorted and finished cloth. Innovative merchants also played their part, traveling as far afield as England in the search for wool and trawling the bazaars of the Orient for exotic dyestuffs. Dyeing would become one of Florence's major strengths, Florentine red emerging as a staple color across Europe. In the 12th century, just 100 years after the trade started in earnest, some 30,000 people—about a third of the city's population—were connected with textiles. Even in the 13th century, when trade had dropped by 90 percent from its peak, it is estimated the city was still providing the known world with a tenth of its textiles.

The relative decline of textiles proved of little consequence, for another more lucrative business had risen in its stead: banking. The business was to be of incalculable importance, and it is to Florentine bankers that we owe the pillars of modern commerce, including such fundamentals as checks, life insurance, credit, bills of exchange, and double-entry bookkeeping. The Florentines also devised the world's first major international currency—

the *fiorino*, or florin, a gold coin, whose rigorously enforced purity (and thus reliability) saw it adopted across Europe after its introduction in 1252.

On their own, such accomplishments might seem dull—if worthy—achievements. In the context of how bankers and a prosperous city might spend their profits, however, they were vital, not least because they provided the funding for many of the greatest Renaissance works of art. The city's most famous bankers were the Medici, a name that reverberated through Florentine history for centuries, but one that came relatively late to a clique of bankers that by 1250 already dominated Europe. Florence had no fewer than 24 major banking dynasties, notably the Bardi and Peruzzi, bankers to the kings of England, among others, and the Pazzi and Alberti (and later the Medici), who handled the enormous papal account. Other banking potentates are still remembered in palace and street names across the city: the Alberti, Antinori, Guardi, Strozzi, Davanzati, Tornabuoni, and many others.

Guilds

Florence's burgeoning power inevitably raised the question of who should govern the city. During the city's first stirrings of independence in the 11th century, its merchants had formed the Societas Mercatorum, a form of guild or confraternity, many of whose members served in a 100-man *comune*, or ruling council, established in 1115. In time, the Societas was replaced by the Arte di Calimala, a broad-based guild embracing most merchants. As trade diversified, this was superseded by seven powerful major guilds known as the Arti Maggiori, among whom were the lawyers (Arte dei Giudici e Notai), the bankers (Arte di Cambio), and the wool merchants (Arte della Lana). In 1289, 14 lesser guilds, the Arti Minori, were formed, embracing middle-ranking merchants—anything from bakers and innkeepers to locksmiths and leather workers. Members of these guilds, and especially those of the Arti Maggiori, would effectively rule Florence for the next 400 years.

In theory the system worked as follows: The names of selected guild members—the only people eligible for office—would be

placed in eight leather bags, or *borse*, kept in Santa Croce. Nine names were then drawn at random: six from the Arti Maggiori, two from the Arti Minori, and one to act as a standard-bearer, or Gonfaloniere. These Priori, as they were known, formed a government known as the Signoria, which served for just two months, the short tenure designed to

A 13th-century gold florin bears a fleur-de-lys, the symbol of Florence.

prevent corruption, favoritism, or the entrenchment of power.

The Signoria's authority was tempered by various committees, the number of which increased over the years. It also had to pay heed to the Podestà, an independent magistrate brought in from an outside city to act as an arbitrator in disputes. In times of greater crisis, the Signoria called a Parlemento, or assembly, which consisted of all males over the age of 14. When a quorum of two-thirds was reached, the Parlemento was asked to approve a Balia, or emergency committee, to deal with the crisis.

This was the theory. In practice, it was subverted during all but a few brief periods of Florentine history. In the first place, powerful cliques or individuals ensured that only compliant candidates were put forward for

office. Second, all the nobles and the lowly workers—the so-called Popolo Minuto— were excluded from the process. And third, controlling factions could engineer the calling of a Parlemento, often just a euphemism for the mob, if the Signoria failed to heed their wishes. It was in this way that powerful individuals or families could control Florence—and, by implication, most of Tuscany—while still paying lip service to its institutions.

THE MEDICI

The most powerful family of all was the Medici, who hailed from the Mugello, north-east of Florence. Its founding father was Giovanni di Bicci de' Medici (1360–1429), whose banking acumen laid the foundations of the family fortune. Power was consolidated by his son, Cosimo de' Medici (1389–1464), also known as Cosimo il Vecchio, or Cosimo the Elder, to distinguish him from a later Medici, Grand Duke Cosimo I (see p. 33).

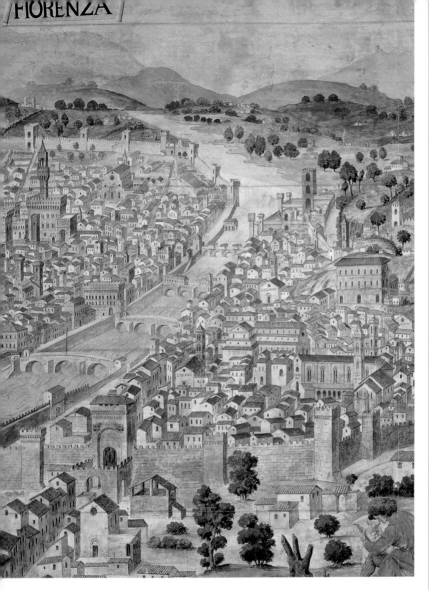

FIORENZA

Cosimo the Elder

Cosimo was a banker and politician of consummate skill, as well as an intellectual and enlightened thinker. When Cosimo first rose to prominence, however, Florence's dominant family was the Albizzi. His rise was due partly to public disenchantment with the autocratic Albizz and partly to the support for Cosimo of the disenfranchised Popolo Minuto and lesser guilds, who saw the Medici as more democratically inclined. In 1431 the authorities (with

The Pianta della Catena from the Museo di Firenze com'era shows Florence as it was during the time of Lorenzo the Magnificent.

Albizzi backing) imprisoned the rising star and then sent him into exile. He was gone just a year, invited to return after an emergency meeting of the Parlemento. In the words of Pope Pius II, he would "soon become master of the country and…King in all but name."

Benozzo Gozzoli's fresco in the Palazzo Medici-Riccardi is believed to show the young Lorenzo the Magnificent, who presided over Florence while the city was at its zenith.

In Cosimo, Renaissance Florence found the ruler—although there was never any formal title—it needed and deserved. He bought off popular discontent with donations to charity; commissioned numerous public and other buildings, including a magnificent public library; lavished patronage on artists and architects; sponsored humanist learning; founded an academy of learning based on Plato's Academy; and brought prestige to the city through the 1439 Council of Florence, a meeting of the Catholic and Eastern Orthodox churches. At the same time he was wary and discreet. "Do not appear to give advice," his father had warned him, "but put forward your views discreetly,…never display any pride,…avoid litigation and political controversy, and always stay out of the public eye."

Cosimo's skill, and the period of prosperity that accompanied it, allowed Medici hegemony to survive through the short reign of his son, Piero de' Medici (1416–1469), also known as Piero il Gottoso, or Piero the Gouty, after the disease that crippled him. It also prepared the way for the most famous of the Medici, Lorenzo de' Medici (1449–1492), better

known as Lorenzo il Magnifico, or Lorenzo the Magnificent.

Lorenzo the Magnificent

Where Cosimo had presided over the early and middle part of the Florentine Renaissance, Lorenzo ruled the city when Europe's greatest artistic flowering was at its zenith. Like his grandfather, Lorenzo was a man in tune with his times: An accomplished poet, he surrounded himself with scholars and thinkers, enjoyed the sophisticated life of the country villa, and—while commissioning surprisingly few works of art—continued to foster the atmosphere in which artistic endeavor could flourish.

But while he retained the support of the Florentine public, his power, and that of his family, inevitably aroused jealousy among other leading families. None were more roused than the Pazzi, who were responsible for the most notorious of all anti-Medici uprisings—the 1478 Pazzi Conspiracy. This attempted coup brought together several parties, led by Pope Sixtus IV, angry at having been refused a loan by the Medici to buy Imola, a town near

Installed as a puppet ruler in 1537, Cosimo de' Medici, depicted by Vasari on the ceiling of the Palazzo Vecchio, became a powerful leader and proclaimed himself Grand Duke of Tuscany.

Bologna (the Medici feared it would upset the balance of power in the region). With Sixtus was Francesco Salviati, whom the Medici had vetoed as Archbishop of Pisa, the appointment having been made in breach of an agreement between the Medici and Sixtus. Finally came Jacopo de' Pazzi, the Pazzi "godfather," and Francesco de' Pazzi, head of the Pazzi bank in Rome, desperate to usurp Medici power in Florence. A mercenary soldier, Montesecco, was recruited to provide the military muscle, along with two embittered priests, Maffei and Bagnone, and a violent sidekick called Bernardo Baroncelli.

The attack took place in Florence cathedral on April 26, 1478. Giuliano, Lorenzo the Magnificent's brother, was hacked down and stabbed 19 times by Francesco de' Pazzi. Lorenzo, however, managed to escape, sheltering behind the heavy portals of the cathedral's Sagrestia Nuova. Across the city, Salviati's attack on the Signoria failed when he became separated from his troops in the Palazzo Vecchio. Apprised of the coup, the mob gathered and dispensed summary justice. Salviati and his troops were massacred, and

Francesco was dragged from hiding and hanged next to Salviati. Maffei and Bagnone were castrated and hanged, and Montesecco was tortured and given a soldier's execution in the Bargello, as was Baroncelli. Jacopo de' Pazzi escaped, but he was captured, tortured, stripped naked, and hanged from the Palazzo Vecchio. After burial, his body was exhumed by the mob, dragged through the streets, and propped in front of the Palazzo Pitti, where his decomposing head was used as a door knocker. The rotted body was then thrown into the Arno, recovered by children, flogged, hanged again, and then hurled back into the river. Not everyone in Renaissance Florence was civilized and enlightened.

SAVONAROLA

Lorenzo's eventual—natural—death in 1492 marked the end of an era. Pope Innocent VIII, hearing of his demise, remarked: "The peace of Italy is at an end." Sure enough, there followed one of the more tumultuous periods of Florentine (and Italian) history. Lorenzo's successor, his son Piero di Lorenzo (1471–1503), proved ineffectual, being ruthless and violent

by turns; even his father had described him as foolish. Within two years, in a panic-stricken funk, he surrendered Florence to Charles VIII of France, who had entered Italy in 1494 to press his claim to the throne of Naples.

After Charles moved on, the power vacuum in Florence was filled by Girolamo Savonarola (1452–1498), one of the most extraordinary figures of the age. A monk of intense religious zeal, he was the prior of San Marco, a convent in northern Florence (see pp. 142–43), and even before Lorenzo's death had attracted immense crowds through the power of his preaching: Michelangelo would claim in old age that he could still hear the friar's speeches ringing in his ears. Savonarola saw Charles VIII as a figure of divine retribution, sent to punish the Florentines. The city's painters, he railed, made the Virgin "look like a harlot." Its prostitutes were "pieces of meat with eyes," and its "Sodomites…were to be burned alive." A torrent of decrees flowed from San Marco: Paintings were to be removed from churches; citizens would fast continually; children were to spy on their parents; and a vast bonfire of the vanities was to be built in Piazza della Signoria, piled with everything from wigs, mirrors, and false beards to books, paintings, and board games. A shell-shocked populace complied.

In Rome, the corrupt Borgia pope, Alexander VI—denounced by Savonarola as an agent of Satan—at first cajoled and then pleaded with the charismatic monk, terrified at his hold over one of Italy's most powerful cities. Excommunication followed in 1497, coinciding in Florence with poor harvests, plague, and a war with Pisa, all of which—in the absence of real control in the city—contrived to turn the fickle Florentine mob against Savonarola. The monk was arrested, tortured, and burned for heresy in Piazza della Signoria in 1498.

RETURN OF THE MEDICI

Calm of sorts returned to the city after this remarkable interregnum, aided by a period in which Florence enjoyed a brief stretch of

An unknown 15th-century artist painted Savonarola being burned for heresy in Florence's Piazza della Signoria.

genuine republican rule under Piero Soderini, the city's chancellor, and his right-hand man, the writer and diplomat Niccolò Machiavelli. In 1512, however, the republic sided with France against the combined armies of Spain and the papacy, and was duly defeated and dismembered. The papacy now held the upper hand, and the man who would shortly become pope was none other than Leo X, better known as Giovanni de' Medici (1475–1521), second son of Lorenzo the Magnificent. With his father pulling the strings, Giovanni had become a monk at 8 and Italy's youngest-ever cardinal at 16. Assuming the Holy See, the high-living Medici famously remarked: "God has given us the papacy, so let us enjoy it."

Giovanni proceeded to rule Florence in all but name, at the same time packing the papacy with cardinals (31 in all) sympathetic to the Medici. This led to the election in 1524 of Pope Clement VII, better known as Giulio de' Medici (1478–1534), illegitimate son of Giuliano de' Medici, the Medici murdered in the Pazzi Conspiracy (see p. 31). Clement's control of Florence was cut short in 1527 when Emperor Charles V of Spain and Austria (R.1516–1556) sacked Rome, rendering the papacy impotent and allowing Florence to restore a republican administration. This again proved short-lived, and when Charles and Clement made peace in 1529—a peace cemented by the marriage of Charles's daughter to Alessandro de' Medici—the Medici were returned to power in Florence.

This time, however, things were different. Neither Florence nor the Medici now had real influence. Rather, they were minor players in a game controlled by Europe's main imperial players, Austria and Spain. When Alessandro was murdered by a male lover (and distant cousin) in 1537, imperial advisers—with no direct Medici heirs—chose Cosimo de' Medici (1519–1574) from an obscure branch of the family, to act as a stooge. But Cosimo proved to be his own man and enjoyed a cunning and autocratic period in office (while being careful not to antagonize his imperial masters) that saw him take the title of Grand Duke of Tuscany in 1570. The small city-states in Tuscany that had remained free of Florentine control—Siena, in particular—now fell within the Medici and imperial orbit.

Cosimo's sons and successors, Francesco I (1541–1587) and Ferdinando I (1549–1609), were competent rulers, but they presided over a region in decline. Two ineffectual Medici followed, Ferdinando II (1610–1670) and Cosimo III (1642–1723), before the last in the family's male line, the hopeless Gian Gastone (1671–1737), bowed out without producing an heir. Some 300 years of almost continuous Medici rule ended when Gastone's sister, Anna Maria (died 1743), signed a treaty handing the Tuscan Grand Duchy to the Duke of Lorraine, later Emperor Francis I of Austria.

UNIFICATION

Tuscany then enjoyed a modest resurgence under an administration that effected various economic and social reforms. These were interrupted by the arrival of Napoleon, who overwhelmed Austria in 1799; his troops remained in Tuscany until their leader's defeat in 1815. The Austrians then returned to power until ousted by a series of nationalist uprisings in the 1850s—an independence movement known as the Risorgimento. These culminated in Tuscany's joining a united Italy in 1860. From 1865 Florence served as the capital of the new state, Rome having remained under the control of French and papal troops. Vittorio Emanuele, Italy's first king, moved into the Palazzo Pitti, and a parliament sat in the Palazzo Vecchio. In 1871, following France's defeat in the Franco-Prussian war, the capital was moved to Rome.

Foreign visitors made artistic pilgrimages to Florence and Tuscany—the 18th and 19th

be saved when every other bridge across the Arno was mined.

Since World War II, Florence and many other Tuscan towns and cities have shared in the miracle that has transformed Italy from an almost entirely agricultural country into one of the world's leading industrial nations. Rural poverty continued well into the 1950s, but

Above: Florence during the 1966 flood
Left: The Nazis destroyed all Florence's bridges except the Ponte Vecchio.

centuries were the era of the Grand Tour, a cultural round of Europe's great capitals—but neither city nor region would again feature prominently in Italy's political history, although events in Europe in the first half of the 20th century could not fail to touch them.

MODERN ERA

War memorials in every village pay testament to the lives lost in two world wars, while the modern centers of cities such as Pisa and Livorno stand as memorials to strategic bombing by the Allies as they harried a retreating Nazi army in 1944. A handful of bombs also fell on Florence, but decisions taken at the highest level on both sides largely spared the city's artistic heritage. Hitler himself, it is said, ordered the Ponte Vecchio to

even in the countryside, a revitalized wine industry and the advent of tourism have helped preserve a landscape shaped by human hand for almost 3,000 years. Nature has also brought suffering to the region, however, nowhere more dramatically than in the catastrophic floods that ravaged Florence in 1966 (see pp. 164–65). The disaster proved a brief setback and did little to interrupt the resurgence of fashion, design, and textiles as major money-spinners. In an era when many great artistic capitals are little more than fossils, Florence is an exception—a city neither living on nor overshadowed by its past glories. It may never again be, as it was during the Renaissance, Europe's artistic fulcrum, but as a living record of a time when it led the world, its future looks as assured as its past. ∎

The arts

The arts in Florence and Tuscany are dominated by one magnificent period of change and individual genius—the Renaissance—an artistic flowering that had its roots in many diverse artistic and intellectual disciplines but which came to glorious fruition in the Florence of the 15th century. The obvious changes in the painting and sculpture of the time, however, should not obscure the advances made in architecture, nor the enormous contribution that Florence and Tuscany have made across the centuries in the fields of music, literature, and—more recently—cinema.

PAINTING & SCULPTURE
Early influences

Most of Tuscany's earliest artistic creations belong to the Etruscans, whose civilization spread across much of central Italy—including Tuscany—from about the eighth century B.C. Over the centuries, the Etruscans traded extensively with Greece, adopting many Greek artistic and sculptural idioms in the process. Many of these Greek, or Hellenistic, influences can be seen in the urns and painted vases that adorn Tuscany's archaeological museums in Volterra, Cortona, and other cities and towns. At the same time, Etruscan art had its own distinctive style, often combining a vigorous and naturalistic approach with incredible delicacy, traits best seen in the exquisite jewelry in the museums of Cortona and Siena.

The artistic legacy of the Romans, whose civilization replaced that of the Etruscans, is less obvious in Tuscany than in many other parts of Italy. Here there are few of the magnificent sculptures of Rome or Naples, merely a modest scattering of busts, coins, and minor artifacts around the rather dusty archaeological museums of Florence and elsewhere. Much the same can be said of the art of the five or so centuries that followed the decline of Rome in the sixth century, for Florence and Tuscany boast little in the way of Lombard or Byzantine works of art, although the influence of such works would later infuse the region's paintings and sculptures.

Road to Renaissance

You have to move to the 12th century to find Tuscany's first autonomous Christian-era works of art: A cross painted in 1138 by Tuscan artist Guglielmo is now in Sarzana cathedral, in the neighboring region of

Liguria, and Lombard-influenced carvings adorn many of the tiny Romanesque churches of Pisa, Lucca, and Pistoia. More artists appeared a little later, about 1230, often in or around Pisa, then the richest and thus most artistically sophisticated city in Tuscany. Other minor centers included Arezzo, Siena, and Florence, where one of the most prominent early names was Coppo di Marcovaldo, an artist captured by the Sienese in battle and forced to complete paintings as part of the ransom for his return to Florence.

Pisa continued to be the motor of artistic development in Tuscany, particularly if you believe Giorgio Vasari (1511–1574), a Renaissance painter and critic whose writings have influenced art historians—some would say erroneously—almost to the present day. Vasari's premise, briefly put, was that the old artistic forms that dominated Italian art for centuries—those of the Byzantine world— first began to change in the realm of sculpture, notably in Pisa with the work of Nicola (1220– 1284) and Giovanni Pisano (active 1248–1314). Change came a little later in painting, where two key figures, Cimabue (1240–1302), whom Vasari called the father of Italian painting, and his pupil Giotto (1267–1337) pioneered a move toward greater naturalism in art. Later, this pioneering work was developed further by a favored Vasarian triumvirate: Donatello (1386–1466) in sculpture, Brunelleschi (1377–1446) in architecture, and Masaccio (1401–1428) in painting. The process culminated in the Renaissance, the 15th-century flowering of artistic endeavor that had Florence as its principal focus.

Part of "The Birth of Venus" by Sandro Botticelli, a painting epitomizing the use by Renaissance artists of classical myth

Most scholars now see this progression as too simplistic and view the long road to the Renaissance as a more complex affair, with numerous more subtle influences shaping artistic development in Italy and elsewhere. This said, Vasari's premise still makes a useful and persuasive basic model. To understand the background to events, however, and to

The central detail of Cimabue's "Madonna Enthroned," painted as an altarpiece for Santa Trìnita but now in the Uffizi

appreciate the scale of artistic change, it is necessary to grasp the state in which Italian and other European art languished in the 13th century.

Art at the time was effectively the art of Byzantium, a hybrid of classical and Asian influences introduced by Justinian, emperor of the eastern half of the Roman Empire, when he invaded parts of Italy from his capital, Constantinople (now Istanbul), in the sixth century. Its distinguishing features were abstraction, gold backgrounds, and ornamental motifs, while its main images were almost exclusively portraits of saints, painted cruci-

fixes, and the iconic figures of the Madonna and Child. It was reverential and stylized, especially in its beautiful but stilted paintings of the Madonna and Child, images conspicuously lacking in life, depth, movement, or naturalistic detail.

By the 13th century, such art had begun to seem old-fashioned, its language outmoded in the face of new and wealthy city-states, greater learning, and an increasingly sophisticated population. Some new, or reinvented, artistic language was needed to match the changes taking place in the social and economic domain. This language was first articulated in sculpture by Nicola Pisano. His work in Pisa allowed him to borrow directly from two of the richest artistic lexicons of all the Roman and Greek forms that he found woven into ancient classical sarcophagi recently brought to the city from the Holy Land.

A new artistic language

Such reworking of classical idioms was a cornerstone of later Renaissance art, and it was adopted with alacrity by Nicola's followers, Arnolfo di Cambio (1245–1302) and Giovanni Pisano, who produced astounding sculptures in Pisa, Siena, Pistoia, and other towns. Painting lagged only a short way behind, the first moves away from Byzantium's hidebound strictures coming with early fresco painters such as Pietro Cavallini (active 1273–1308) in Rome. He would come into contact with the Florentine painter Cimabue while working in the Basilica of St. Francis in Assisi, Umbria. Cimabue, in turn, taught and worked with Giotto di Bondone, perhaps in Assisi's basilica, a major melting pot of early Italian painting.

Giotto was the innovator who turned Western art on its head, laying some of the Renaissance's principal foundations in the process. Although he was not alone in effecting change, his individual genius is indisputable, as is the profound shift in artistic perception that his paintings represent. Simply put, he attempted to introduce realism and naturalism into his work, infusing his frescoes in Florence's Santa Croce and other churches with depth, detail, facial gestures, and human emotions. He also made attempts—crude to modern eyes, but attempts nonetheless—to master the notions of perspective, whose rules were still not understood, and to look to the real world for inspiration and subject.

His example was taken up not only in Florence by followers such as Maso di Banco and Agnolo di Gaddi (active 1369–1396) but also in Siena, another increasingly prosperous city. Siena's artists—most notably Duccio di Buoninsegna (1255–1318/19)—had long fused a love of Byzantine motifs with a distinctive passion for color, composition, and gold backgrounds. Front-rank artists here included Simone Martini (1285–1344) and the brothers Ambrogio (active 1319–1348) and Pietro Lorenzetti (1280–1348), who combined the lessons of Giotto with their own artistic inheritance to produce courtly and exquisitely executed paintings.

The gradual changes wrought by these and other painters dispel the notion of the Renaissance springing suddenly from thin air. Rather, this rebirth, or *rinascimento*—the Italian word for Renaissance—was a serendipitous and long-maturing mixture of social, artistic, cultural, economic, and intellectual change. In scholarship, the rediscovery and reevaluation of classical texts led to an upsurge in humanist thinking—the notion that the human and not the divine (or religious) was at the heart of existence. This freed art of its devotional obligations and reintroduced Greek and Roman ideas to intellectual debate. From there it was a short step to the reintroduction of the Greek and Roman classical ideal to art.

Art had to be paid for, however, and past commissions had come almost exclusively from the Church, whose naturally cautious and conservative approach stifled innovation and invariably demanded entirely religious statements from artists and sculptors. Genius and creativity could flourish in this environment, but they could flourish more readily in the hands of wealthy lay patrons such as the Medici, whose largesse provided the financial wherewithal for artistic exploration, free from religious constraints. Some idea of the sums involved can be gleaned from the Medici's own accounts, which for the years 1433 to 1471 show 663,755 florins spent on paintings, buildings, and charities. At that time 150 florins supported a Florentine family for a year, 1,000 florins would have bought an entire *palazzo*, and a Botticelli painting could be had for 100 florins.

Florence's golden age

That Florence should become the epicenter of the Renaissance was no surprise. During the 15th century it was one of the wealthiest cities in the known world, a cosmopolitan melting

Duke Federico da Montefeltro, disfigured by a jousting accident, was painted in left profile by Piero della Francesca.

pot whose free-thinking atmosphere provided a setting in which creativity could flourish. As its reputation rose, it attracted more artists; as more artists arrived, so the fevered atmosphere of innovation intensified.

Three artists in three disciplines are often picked out as paramount in the early years of the Renaissance, which is often described (erroneously) as beginning in 1401, the year of a competition to design Florence's baptistery doors (see pp. 66–71). They are Brunelleschi in architecture, Donatello in sculpture, and Masaccio in painting. Donatello created work the like of which has not been seen before

"Battle of San Romano" was painted by Paolo Uccello, an artist obsessed with the complexities of composition and perspective.

or since—notably in his statue of Mary Magdalene in Florence's Museo dell'Opera del Duomo (see pp. 74–77). He also reintroduced the nude, a mainstay of classical sculpture, to the mainstream of European art. Masaccio was equally groundbreaking, producing one of the first paintings to embrace the new laws of perspective— "The Trinity" in Florence's church of Santa Maria Novella—and a fresco cycle in the nearby Cappella Brancacci whose innovations staggered contemporaries and became a point of reference for many major artists of the day (see pp. 178–81).

Other hallowed names soon joined this artistic trinity, among them Fra Angelico (circa 1400–1455), a monk whose ethereal paintings, while still wedded to religious themes, combined an almost unequaled

mastery of technique and color. Far less intense but more varied paintings were produced by Angelico's pupil Benozzo Gozzoli (1420–1497), known for his lyrical frescoes in Florence's Palazzo Medici-Riccardi and the church of Sant'Agostino in San Gimignano (see pp. 134–37 and 240–41). Paolo Uccello (1397–1475), by contrast, shared Masaccio's concern for perspective, becoming obsessed with its myriad possibilities and producing challenging, almost visionary work in the process.

Something of the links engendered by Florence's hothouse atmosphere can be seen in the many master-pupil relationships and in the cross-fertilization and dissemination of ideas these links produced. Masaccio, for example, had at least two prominent followers: One was Filippo Lippi (1406–1469), a wayward friar who habitually seduced his models but also produced poetic and often innovative paintings. The other was Andrea del Castagno (1417/19–1457), whose bold frescoes can be seen in Florence's cathedral and in the church of Sant'Apollonia (see pp. 56–63 and p. 146). Similar links existed between all manner of other Florentine artists.

Florence's orbit proved so powerful that few other Tuscan centers managed to produce or hold painters in the early 15th century. Only Siena produced significant artists, and even then they tended to lag behind their Florentine rivals. Notable exceptions were painters such as Sassetta (1392–1450) and the sculptor Jacopo della Quercia (1374–1438), both innovative artists who could match their Florentine contemporaries.

Florence's hegemony began to crack as the Renaissance reached its zenith during the last quarter of the 15th century. Major painters from outside the Tuscan capital—there had always been minor ones—included Piero della Francesca (1410/20–1492), from the town of Sansepolcro, known for his precise but unsettling paintings, and his Cortona-born pupil Luca Signorelli (1441–1523), whose muscular figures would later influence the likes of Michelangelo. This said, Florence remained the hotbed of artistic activity, its annals filled with most of the great names of Renaissance art—Sandro Botticelli, Leonardo da Vinci, Domenico Ghirlandaio, Luca della Robbia, and many more. Its painters also worked beyond Tuscany, a trait that would become more pronounced when the Renaissance reached its maturity, a period from about 1500 known as the High Renaissance.

High Renaissance

Three great painters dominated this period, two of them Tuscan-born, one of them Tuscan-trained. The first was Leonardo da Vinci (1452–1519), born in a small village in the hills outside Florence, a consummate genius but one who left only three works in Florence, all of them in the Uffizi. The second was Michelangelo (1475–1564), born in eastern Tuscany, a painter, sculptor, architect, and poet who spent the early part of his career in Florence, where he completed the statue of "David" and the funerary monuments of the Cappelle Medicee (see pp. 128–31). His greatest works, however, the frescoes of the Sistine Chapel, were reserved for Rome. The third painter was Raphael (1483–1520), born in

Urbino, in the Marche region of eastern Italy. He, too, was lured to Rome, but he left many masterpieces in Florence, works now found in the Uffizi and the Palatina Gallery of the Palazzo Pitti (see pp. 170–77).

Tuscany's later artists excelled in a style Raphael had helped develop: Mannerism, a genre in which style and artifice were important and where established conventions of color, scale, and composition were ignored or deliberately subverted. Its leading exponents were Rosso Fiorentino (1494–1540), Jacopo Pontormo (1494–1556), Agnolo Bronzino (1503–1572), and—to a lesser extent—Andrea del Sarto (1486–1530) and Domenico Beccafumi (1486–1551) in Siena. Sculptors, too, embraced the style, among them Florence-based artists such as Bartolommeo Bandinelli (1488–1560), Bartolommeo Ammannati (1511–1592), French-born Giambologna (1529–1608), and the swash-buckling Benvenuto Cellini (1500–1571).

These proved some of the last Tuscan names to burn brightly in Italy's artistic firmament. Artistic primacy moved to Rome, where the ornate baroque style flourished, thanks to papal patronage and the decline of Florence as a political and economic force. In later centuries, only the so-called Macchiaioli group of painters (from the Italian *macchias*—spot or stain) rose above the humdrum, a movement whose style and outlook mirrored that of the French Impressionists. Paintings by the group's leading exponents, notably Giovanni Fattori (1825–1908), can be seen in the modern art gallery of the Palazzo Pitti. Tuscany's last well-known artist was Amedeo Modigliani (1884–1920), who was born in Livorno but spent most of his working life in Paris.

ARCHITECTURE

The appeal of Florence's and Tuscany's architecture is almost as great as that of their art. From simple Etruscan tombs and superb Romanesque churches to the surfeit of Renaissance palaces and Gothic cathedrals, the area is a treasury of fascinating and beautiful buildings whose designs span almost 3,000 years.

The Leaning Tower in Pisa, where Romanesque and then Gothic architecture first flowered in the 12th and 13th centuries

Still only partially excavated, the archaeological zone in Volterra is one of the few places in Tuscany where Roman and earlier Etruscan ruins are visible.

Etruscan & Roman

Tuscany's earliest architectural forms are the Etruscan tombs found around Sovana and Pitigliano in the south of the region. Other Etruscan architecture is almost nonexistent, largely because the Etruscans constructed many of their buildings from wood, which perished over the centuries. The region's largest Etruscan structures are tracts of defensive walls in Fiesole, most of which probably date from around the end of the fourth century B.C.

Fiesole also claims some of Tuscany's most important Roman monuments, namely a well-preserved Roman theater and the remains of a first-century Roman temple. Other similar remains survive at Volterra (see pp. 244–45), and in Lucca's Piazza dell'Anfiteatro you can still make out the shape—and occasional blocks of stone—from the city's Roman amphitheater. Elsewhere, little of Roman vintage survives, certainly not in Florence, where the only memorials are for the most part intangible—the Roman gridiron plan of the central streets, the occasional name such as Via delle Terme (the Street of the Baths), and the barely discernible outline of the old amphitheater in the streets west of Piazza Santa Croce.

Little remains, either, of the work of the Lombard (north Italian) and other masons who worked across Tuscany during the centuries following the fall of Rome, although their influence would survive in later buildings that incorporated their styles and techniques. Much the same can be said of Byzantine architecture, whose heavily decorated style, a blend of Greek, Roman, and Asian influences, was introduced to Italy from the East after the sixth century.

Romanesque & Gothic

Only in about the 11th century did Tuscan architecture begin to flourish, spurred on by the upsurge in church-building and the emergence of city-states. The new towns acquired palaces, towers, walls, piazzas, and churches, most of them built in the Romanesque manner, a style distinguished by simplicity, round arches, and—in churches—a plain basilical (rectangular) plan with a sunken crypt and raised choir (the area around the high altar). In time, the style acquired various embellishments, in particular the tiny arches, myriad columns, and inlaid marbled patterning associated with Pisan-Romanesque architecture—refinements developed in the wake of Pisa's trading links with the East.

Perhaps the supreme expression of Tuscany's early Romanesque style is found in the abbey of Sant'Antimo (see pp. 274–75), while examples of Pisan-Romanesque are scattered across the region, particularly in Pisa (Piazza del Duomo) and Lucca (San Michele in Foro). In Florence, the Romanesque is exemplified by the baptistery and San Miniato al Monte, two of the city's oldest and most beautiful buildings.

From about the 13th century, the Romanesque was enlivened and eventually replaced by Gothic architecture, a style largely introduced from France and identified by its pointed arch, vaulting, rose windows, airy interiors, and an emphasis on the vertical. Gothic designs infuse the medieval *palazzi pubblici*, civic palaces, of most Tuscan towns, whose power and wealth reached a zenith in this period, particularly those of Florence (the Palazzo Vecchio) and Siena (Palazzo Pubblico). Gothic was also uppermost in the cathedrals of Florence, Siena, and other centers, and in the great Florentine churches of Santa Croce and Santa Maria Novella.

The late Romanesque and early Gothic periods also marked the emergence of the first architects whose names have come down to us, most notably Arnolfo di Cambio, the architect responsible for Florence's cathedral, Santa Croce, and the Palazzo Vecchio. Arnolfo was followed by Giotto di Bondone, better known as one of the great painters of the age but responsible for another of Florence's most prominent landmarks, the Campanile, or cathedral bell tower.

The new wave

By the beginning of the 15th century, the forces that led to the Renaissance in painting and sculpture had also produced a revolution in architecture. Leading light of the new wave was the Florentine Filippo Brunelleschi, widely acknowledged as the first—and perhaps greatest—of all Renaissance architects. He adapted the purity and simplicity of classical Roman and early Tuscan Romanesque buildings to his own concern for the practical problems of construction and management of space. He also played a major part in mastering the laws of linear perspective, combining his many talents for the first time in Florence with designs for the church of San Lorenzo (see pp. 122–27) in about 1418 and the arched loggia of the Ospedale degli Innocenti a year later (see p. 147). His masterpiece was the construction of Florence's cathedral dome, one of the wonders of preindustrial engineering. He also created other Florentine gems, such as the Cappella dei Pazzi and the church of Santo Spirito.

Florence's other major architect of the period, Michelozzo di Bartolommeo (1396–1472), lacked Brunelleschi's genius but had the singular advantage of being a favorite of Cosimo de' Medici, one of the pillars of the Medici dynasty. He designed the Medici's first major Florentine home, the Palazzo Medici-Riccardi (see pp. 134–37), where he established a fashion for rustication—building with huge, rough-hewn blocks of stone—that can be seen across the city to this day. He also built or adapted several of the Medici's country villas, notably Careggi, as well as the tribune and sacristy of Santissima Annunziata and the cloister and library at San Marco, all projects dear to the Medici's hearts.

Santissima Annunziata's tribune was completed by the third of Florence's great architectural triumvirate, Leon Battista Alberti (1404–1472), a multitalented Renaissance man who was a playwright, painter, musician, scientist, athlete, and mathematician, as well as an architect. Alberti rarely concerned himself with the building of his works; he concentrated instead on design and theory, and in *De re aedificatoria* (1452) he produced the Renaissance's first major architectural treatise. He memorably defined beauty in architecture as "the harmony and concord of all parts achieved in such a manner that nothing could be added, or taken away, except for the worse." Alberti described decoration and ornament as "a kind of additional brightness and improvement of Beauty." He completed few buildings, but those that were finished were all masterpieces. He also worked mostly outside Tuscany, his Florentine creations amounting to the facades of Santa Maria Novella and Palazzo Rucellai, both created for the wealthy textile baron Giovanni Rucellai.

Many of Brunelleschi's and Alberti's ideas were carried forward by lesser architects, notably Il Cronaca (1457–1508) and Giuliano da Sangallo (1445–1516). They worked not only in Florence but also in places like Pienza, where Pope Pius II employed Bernardo Rossellino (1409–1464), a disciple of Alberti (he oversaw construction of Alberti's Palazzo Rucellai), to create a model Renaissance city in the place of his birth (see pp. 276–78). None of these men, however, nor other jobbing Medici architects such as Vasari, Ammanati, and Buontalenti, approached the genius of Michelangelo. The great man completed only two Florentine projects, the Sagrestia Nuova (see pp. 128–30) and Medici Library and vestibule (see p. 127), but both were masterpieces that largely transcended genre and convention.

After the Renaissance

The next great architectural style, the baroque, largely passed Florence and Tuscany by in favor of Rome, as did mannerism, appearing only briefly in the facades of Ognissanti, Santa Trìnita, and a handful of lesser churches. Although many major buildings appeared across the region during and after the 16th century—notably the Uffizi, Palazzo Pitti, and numerous villas and palaces—none would approach the stature of earlier works by Brunelleschi and his followers. Indeed, worse was in store for Florence, namely the redevelopment of the city center in the middle of the 19th century, when countless old buildings were razed to make way for the Piazza della Repubblica. More areas were cleared in the 20th century around Santa Croce and Santa Maria Novella railroad station, while swathes of the old city were also destroyed by the Nazis in 1944 to delay the advancing British and United States armies. As a result, some of the architecture in Europe's most celebrated Renaissance city is—ironically—an ugly affront to its illustrious antecedents.

LITERATURE

Tuscany's contribution to literature has been immense. Its principal role was to provide Italy with a literary language, a language that would eventually become Italian as it is spoken and written today. It also provided one of the greatest poets of any age or origin —the Florentine Dante Alighieri—and several major writers—Petrarch, Boccaccio, and Machiavelli—whose works are still widely celebrated to the present day.

Early Tuscan literature, however, was long in thrall to the literature of the classical canon, notably ancient Roman poets such as Virgil and Ovid, and writers such as Pliny, Juvenal, and Suetonius. Almost all such literature was written in Latin, which continued to be Italy's literary and scholarly language until the 13th century, when Franciscan poets such as St. Francis of Assisi, borrowing from the troubadour traditions of Provence, began to write in the everyday, or vernacular, Italian dialects of the period.

In Tuscany, the nascent literary landscape was dominated by Guittone d'Arezzo (1235–1294), whose lyrical verse adapted Provençal and Sicilian styles; the Siena-born Cecco Angiolieri (1260–1312), whose deliciously bawdy sonnets celebrated the delights of wine, women, and song; and Brunetto Latini (1220–1295), whose writing tended toward the didactic and allegorical. Latini is also remembered as the teacher of the most famous of all Tuscan and Italian writers, Dante Alighieri (1265–1321).

Dante & the new style

Dante was the first to propose, in a treatise extolling the virtues of everyday Italian (by then a long distant corruption of Latin), that Italian could be a literary language—although he presented his ideas, ironically, in a Latin text, *De vulgari eloquentia*. The importance of such literature was that it established Italian— or rather Tuscan Italian, the dialect in which Dante wrote—as a legitimate literary language. This made literature more widely disseminated: Poorly educated Italians could understand their own language, but not Latin. It also established a linguistic pattern that would eventually become the model for a standard Italian across Italy (although Italy

The staircase to the Biblioteca Medicea Laurenziana is one of only two architectural projects in Florence designed by Michelangelo.

still remains a country with a variety of strong regional dialects).

Dante wrote widely, with works on politics *(De Monarchia),* philosophy *(Il Convivio),* and love *(Vita Nuova).* His masterpiece, however, *La Divina Commedia (The Divine Comedy)* probably begun 1302, was a poem that transcended genre, and today stands in the front rank of European literature (see pp. 78–79).

Dante also formed part of a new wave of writers, a literary movement that he himself christened the *dolce stil nuovo* (the gentle new style). This not only pioneered the use of the vernacular but also moved away from poetry that dealt in spiritual and platonic ideals. The style was also embraced by Tuscan authors such as Guinizzelli (1235–1276) and Cavalcanti (circa 1250–1300). Both were accomplished writers, but both were overshadowed by two other great literary figures who continued Dante's use of the vernacular: the Arezzo-born Francesco Petrarca, or Petrarch (1304–1374), and Giovanni Boccaccio (1313–1375).

Petrarch was a traveler and diplomat, and it was while in service to the papal court at Avignon in France that he probably met Laura de Noves, the amatory inspiration for his *Canzoniere,* or *Songs,* some of the finest lyrical sonnets in the literary canon. Boccaccio is remembered for the narrative finesse of the *Decamerone,* or the *Decameron* (1348–1353), a series of 100 tales told by ten people over ten days as the Black Death raged in Florence. Petrarch and Boccaccio were not entirely wedded to the vernacular, however, and joined attempts to revive Latin and Greek as literary languages, forming part of the humanistic and classical vanguard that paved the way for the Renaissance.

Classical ideals and a more human-centered cosmology found expression in the works of humanists such as Leonardo Bruni (buried in Florence's Santa Croce) and the poet Poliziano (born in Montepulciano), a tendency encouraged by the patronage of men such as Lorenzo de' Medici, himself an occasional poet. Artists such as Leonardo da

Vinci, Michelangelo, Leon Battista Alberti, and Giorgio Vasari also wrote poetry and important artistic and architectural treatises.

Machiavelli & other greats

Florence's best-remembered writer during the early 16th century is Niccolò Machiavelli (1469–1527), a noble, a diplomat, and the

ferent kind, *Galateo* by Giovanni della Casa (1503–1556), codified everyday aristocratic etiquette and became a handbook of good behavior in royal courts across Europe. Someone who could have benefited from the work was Benvenuto Cellini, a sculptor and goldsmith whose autobiography—widely available today in translation—is not only a

Left: 14th-century writer Francesco Petrarca was among the first to write in Italian rather than Latin. Right: Niccolò Machiavelli's *The Prince* was a treatise on statecraft and politics.

chancellor of the Florentine republic. His major work was *Il Principe (The Prince)*, begun circa 1513 but only published posthumously in 1532, a masterpiece of political analysis that linked political science (the reason of state) with a penetrating study of human nature. The book explored statecraft and the idea of historical cycles, basing itself on Machiavelli's clear-eyed notion that the world has always been inhabited by human beings who have always had the same passions. Today, Machiavelli's name is synonymous with devious political machinations, something not borne out by study of his writings—*Machiavellian* was originally a French term used to denigrate not Machiavelli, but all things Italian.

Machiavelli also wrote a Florentine history *(Istorie Fiorentine*, begun circa 1520), as did another major figure of the time, Francesco Guicciardini (1483–1540). A treatise of a dif-

gripping account of a wild and often violent life but also a graphic portrait of life in 16th-century Florence.

Machiavelli also turned his hand to comedy *(Mandragola)*, a little-explored genre in Renaissance Tuscany, but was overshadowed in this area by the Arezzo-born Pietro Aretino (1492–1556), a writer of trenchant and hard-nosed satires. At the other literary extreme was the Pisan-born Galileo Galilei (1564–1642), one of the first scientists to apply modern concepts—as opposed to hidebound theological or philosophical-based approaches—to scientific research and treatises.

Later Tuscan literature produced fewer great names, a notable exception being Giosué Carducci (1835–1907), Italy's first Nobel laureate, who spent his youth in Tuscany, where he began to write the often melancholy, classically inspired poetry for which he is remembered. Literary renown of a different type was earned by Carlo Lorenzini (1826–1890), a man less well-known than the character he created: Pinocchio.

MUSIC

Composers and musicians have generally made less of an impact outside Tuscany than

French king Henry IV). Later, one of the major figures of opera's golden age, Giacomo Puccini (1858–1924), was born in Lucca and embraced a prevailing trend in opera of the time toward modern themes and *verismo* (realism) in operas such as *Tosca, Madama Butterfly,* and *La Bohème.* Today, music in performance continues to be a major part

Julian Sands and Helena Bonham Carter starred in James Ivory's *A Room with a View* in 1986, one of many movies shot or set in Florence and Tuscany.

the region's writers, artists, and architects. It was a Tuscan monk, however, Guido Monaco (995–1050), who devised the musical scale and forms of notation still used today.

The region may also have spawned Italy's greatest musical legacy—opera—whose origins many scholars trace to the *intermedii* of Florentine wedding ceremonies, entertainments that involved singing, dancing, and static performance. Members of a Florentine academy known as the Camerata, inspired by these entertainments, began to combine elements of Greek drama with musical declamation. Two of the academy's members, Jacopo Peri and Ottavio Rinucci, produced what many consider the first opera—*Dafne*—in 1597, as well as the first opera (*Euridice*) to have survived in its complete form (originally performed at Florence's Palazzo Pitti to celebrate the marriage of Maria de' Medici to the

of Tuscan life, with a large number of musical festivals and concert cycles held in towns across the region.

CINEMA

In film, Tuscany has yielded no well-known directors of the stature of Federico Fellini, but it has produced the much-loved comic actor Roberto Benigni, protagonist of the Oscar-winning *La Vita è Bella* (*Life is Beautiful,* 1998). Tuscany's sublime landscapes have also provided the settings for dozens of celebrated movies, notably Antony Minghella's *The English Patient* (1996) and James Ivory's *A Room with a View* (1986). Giorgio Galliani, location scout for almost a hundred Tuscan-shot movies, explains: "Tuscany has a great attribute—if you plant a nail in the ground and extend a string for a radius of 30 miles you find everything." ■

FLORENCE

Florence

FLORENCE (FIRENZE) IS ONE OF THE WORLD'S GREATEST ARTISTIC CITIES, home to a host of museums, galleries, churches, and sumptuous palaces filled with paintings, sculptures, frescoes, and other precious artifacts from the richest cultural flowering of the last thousand years. Hallowed names from its medieval and Renaissance past—Dante, Machiavelli, Michelangelo, Galileo, and many others—are still some of the most resonant of the modern age, a monument to a city that has had a profound effect on the course of Western culture.

The quantity of beautiful works of art in Florence may seem overwhelming, but the city itself is neither intimidating nor difficult to negotiate. Most of what you want to see lies in a well-defined area north of the Arno, the river that bisects central Florence from east to west. South of the river, across the famous Ponte Vecchio, lies the Oltrarno district (literally "over the Arno"), a self-contained enclave with a distinctive and more traditional atmosphere all of its own. North of the Arno the city hinges around two major squares: Piazza della Signoria and Piazza del Duomo.

The **Piazza del Duomo** (see pp. 53–86) is where most people begin their Florentine odyssey, drawn by three of the city's great set pieces: the Duomo, Battistero, and Campanile (the cathedral, baptistery, and bell tower), an ensemble of buildings almost without equal in Italy. Close by stands the Museo dell'Opera del Duomo, a gallery filled with precious works of art removed from these buildings over the years for safekeeping. A little farther away is the Museo Nazionale del Bargello, crammed with the city's finest Renaissance sculptures—including many works by Michelangelo.

Away from Piazza del Duomo the city divides roughly into four. The introduction to **Eastern Florence** (see pp. 87–118) is the wonderful Piazza della Signoria, Florence's second major square, from which you can visit the Galleria degli Uffizi, the world's richest collection of Renaissance paintings. To the east, the main attraction is Santa Croce, Florence's most important church, thanks to its works of art—including frescoes by Giotto—and the tombs of some of the city's most illustrious names. Around it is a district filled with interesting medieval corners, notably those in

the Sant'Ambrogio quarter and the streets between the church and Piazza della Signoria.

To the north of Piazza del Duomo, in **Northern Florence** (see pp. 119–48), lie San Lorenzo and the Cappelle Medicee, a church and series of Medici tombs with works by Michelangelo and others. Farther north are several sights with notable attractions: the Galleria dell'Accademia (Michelangelo's "David"); the Palazzo Medici-Ricardi (a fresco cycle by Benozzo Gozzoli); and the Museo di San Marco (paintings by Fra Angelico).

Western Florence (see pp. 149–66) is a little less rewarding, but it does include Santa Maria Novella, Florence's most important church after Santa Croce, thanks to its panoply of paintings and fresco cycles.

Across the river in the **Oltrarno** (see pp. 167–89) you'll discover the Palazzo Pitti, whose art gallery is second only to the Uffizi, and the Cappella Brancacci, filled with the city's most important fresco cycle. Also here is the Giardino di Boboli, the city's loveliest garden—as well as artisans' workshops, antique stores, and quiet streets and squares that are a pleasure to explore. Finally, don't miss the only sight not within walking distance of the center—the church of San Miniato al Monte. ■

Visitor information

✉ Via Cavour 1r
☎ 055 290 832 or 055 290 833
✉ Borgo Santa Croce 29r
☎ 055 234 0444 or 055 226 4524
✉ Piazza della Stazione 4
☎ 055 212 245

In Florence, business addresses are suffixed with "r," which stands for *rosso* (red). These numbers are displayed in red on the street.

Pages 50–51: Dusk falls on Florence's bridges.

Piazza del Duomo is the historic heart of Florence, home to the Duomo, the cathedral dedicated to Santa Maria del Fiore, with its awe-inspiring dome, and to the beautiful marble-clad baptistery.

Piazza del Duomo

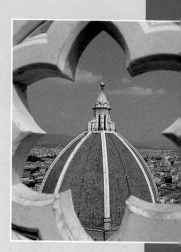

The cathedral dome

Piazza del Duomo

PIAZZA DEL DUOMO IS A STAGE FOR THE SUBLIMELY BEAUTIFUL BAPTISTERY, the soaring pinnacle of the Campanile, and the overwhelming grandeur of Florence's immense Duomo, or cathedral. This magnificent ensemble—together with the nearby cathedral museum—forms the first port of call for most visitors.

Not all of Florence's roads lead to Piazza del Duomo, yet you quickly find yourself drawn here by the looming presence of the cathedral dome, a masterpiece of medieval and Renaissance engineering that dominates the city's skyline. Up close, the dome is overshadowed by the more immediately eye-catching spectacle of the cathedral's exterior, a riot of red, green, and cream marble that makes the interior's more restrained appearance all the more surprising. Fewer artistic treasures lie concealed here than in other Florentine churches, but few works of art compare with the view that unfolds over the city from the top of the dome.

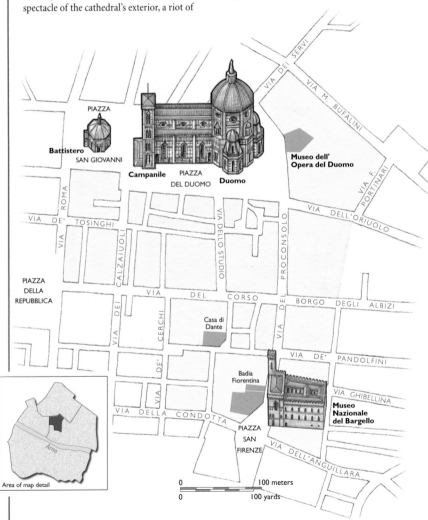

Visitors at the east doors of the Battistero in Piazza del Duomo. Michelangelo thought the doors so beautiful he is said to have described them as the "Gates of Paradise."

If you manage to resist the lure of this panorama, temptation comes your way a second time, for the vista from the nearby Campanile is just as good, perhaps even better, thanks to the fact that its bird's-eye view includes the cathedral and the distinctive octagon of Piazza del Duomo's third major component, the Battistero, or baptistery. The oldest building in Florence, the baptistery was used for centuries to baptize every Florentine child, thereby serving as a religious focus and a way of strengthening the allegiance of Florentines to the city of their birth. Unlike the cathedral, this is a building that is beautiful to look at both inside and out. The exterior's ornate marble decoration is complemented inside by a majestic mosaic ceiling, not to mention a trio of doors decorated with some of the city's finest bronze sculpture.

If the piazza has failings, then they're in the proximity of cars and buses to its great buildings, and in the school parties and tour groups crowding its cramped environs. Unusually for a major Italian square, there's next to no room for cafés from which to admire the piazza's human and architectural spectacle. You can escape some of the cars and crowds, however, by walking to the rear of the cathedral, an area that is partly set aside for pedestrians only. Here you find the Museo dell'Opera del Duomo, home to many significant works of art removed from the cathedral over the years. Most of these are statues and other carvings—including masterpieces by Donatello, Michelangelo, and Ghiberti—making this the city's most important collection of sculpture after that of the nearby Museo Nazionale del Bargello. ■

Duomo

THE DUOMO, OR CATHEDRAL, OF SANTA MARIA DEL FIORE
is one of Italy's most distinctive landmarks, a lavishly decorated poem
in stone whose magnificent dome soars in triumph above the cluster
of Florence's central streets. Views from this breathtaking vantage
point are one of the highlights of any Florentine sojourn, but the
main body of the church also contains a wealth of artistic treasures.

Duomo

- 🅰 Map p. 54
- ✉ Piazza del Duomo
- ☎ 055 230 2855
- 🕐 Closed Sun. a.m. & 1st Sat. of the month
- 🆂 Church: free. Santa Reparata & dome: $
- 🚌 Bus: 1, 6, 14, 17, 23

Santa Maria del Fiore has not
always been Florence's cathedral.
Both the baptistery and church of
San Lorenzo may once have
fulfilled the role, while the cathedral on the present site was the
cathedral of Santa Reparata,
probably founded in the seventh
century. Plans for a new Duomo
were mooted toward the end of the
13th century, when Florence's
burgeoning status as a wealthy and
important city had seen it outgrow
its former cathedral. Other Italian
cities had built or were building
splendid new churches, not least
Pisa and Siena, both major
Florentine rivals.

Grandiloquent statements in
stone were a vital part of any
medieval city's sense of worth,
hence the comment of Florence's
ruling Priorate, or council, that
Santa Reparata "was too crudely
built and too small for such a city."
In 1294 the council issued an edict
demanding a cathedral of "the most
exalted and most prodigal magnifi-
cence, in order that the industry
and power of men may never create
or undertake anything whatsoever
more vast and more beautiful." It
went on to say that the building was
to be "so magnificent that it shall
surpass anything…produced in the
times of their greatest power by the
Greeks and Romans."

For a while the Florentines had
tried to patch up and enlarge Santa
Reparata. In 1294, however, Arnolfo
di Cambio (1245–1302) was asked
to submit plans for an entirely new

structure. The architect was then
employed on a scheme designed
to provide for the city's orderly
enlargement, the fruits of which
would include Florence's last
and definitive set of city walls
(1284–1333). His plan for the new
cathedral was for a vaulted basilica—one of the simplest architectural forms—a polygonal, or
multisided, apse (the area around
the high altar), and a gargantuan
octagonal dome. How the last was
to be built—it would be the largest
dome raised since antiquity—he
neglected to say. The church's first
stone was laid on September 8,
1296, and the building was given
the name Santa Maria del Fiore, a
title that deliberately linked the
Virgin with Florence's flower *(fiore)*
emblem (see p. 27). The stubborn
citizens of Florence, however,
insisted on calling the cathedral by
its old name, Santa Reparata, until
ordered to desist by a decree of
1401. Remnants of the earlier
cathedral can still be seen below
the present building.

Work on the mammoth project
faltered after Arnolfo's death in
1302, but it received a new impetus
when the body of St. Zenobius,
Florence's first bishop, was moved
to the site in 1331 (see p. 68).
Construction was then entrusted to
Giotto, better known as one of the
most innovative artists of the age,
but he devoted himself mainly to
the Campanile, or bell tower (see
pp. 72–73). Thereafter, a series of
lesser architects labored on the

Opposite: Piazza del Duomo with the Battistero on the right and the facade and dome of the Duomo to the rear

A wealth of intricate detail embellishes the Duomo's exterior.

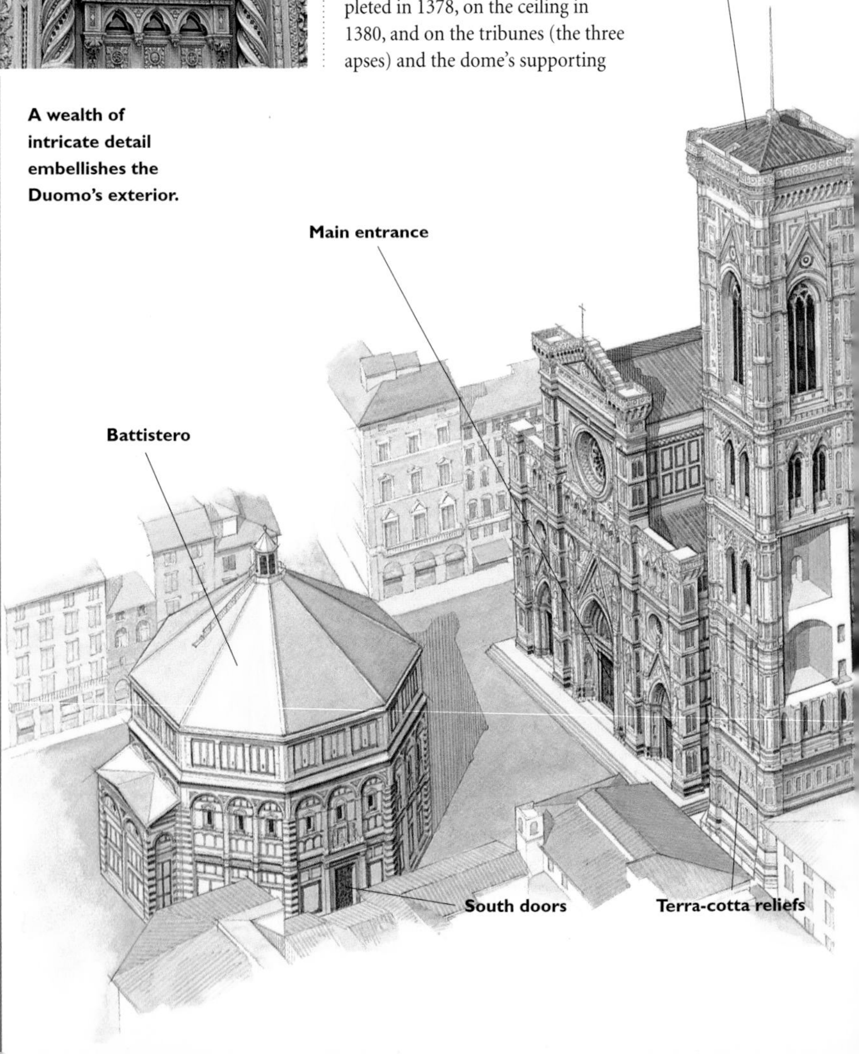

project, often working against a background of political and economic turmoil, not least the unrest caused by the Black Death, the plague that ravaged much of Europe in 1348. Financing the project was a problem at the best of times. Some 10 percent of the initial cost was met by a tax on citizens' property, and as late as 1800 money was still being deducted from every deceased Florentine's estate to pay for the building. All fines from charges of drunkenness were also set aside toward construction costs.

Work on the nave was completed in 1378, on the ceiling in 1380, and on the tribunes (the three apses) and the dome's supporting

Campanile

Main entrance

Battistero

South doors

Terra-cotta reliefs

drum in 1418. The construction of the dome, one of the greatest of all feats of medieval engineering, was a story in its own right (see pp. 64–65).

Today, the cathedral relies for its first, dazzling effect on its **facade,** which, unknown to most visitors crowded in its shadow, is a comparatively recent creation. Arnolfo's original facade was pulled down in 1587 when still only a quarter finished, the idea being to start again with a frontage more in line with the architectural taste of the late 16th century. In any event, no new facade appeared for some 300 years. The present front was built to a plan by the otherwise obscure architect Emilio de Fabris in 1887. His controversial scheme was selected after 91 other plans had been rejected. It was heavily criticized almost immediately, and even today—for all its gaudy impact—

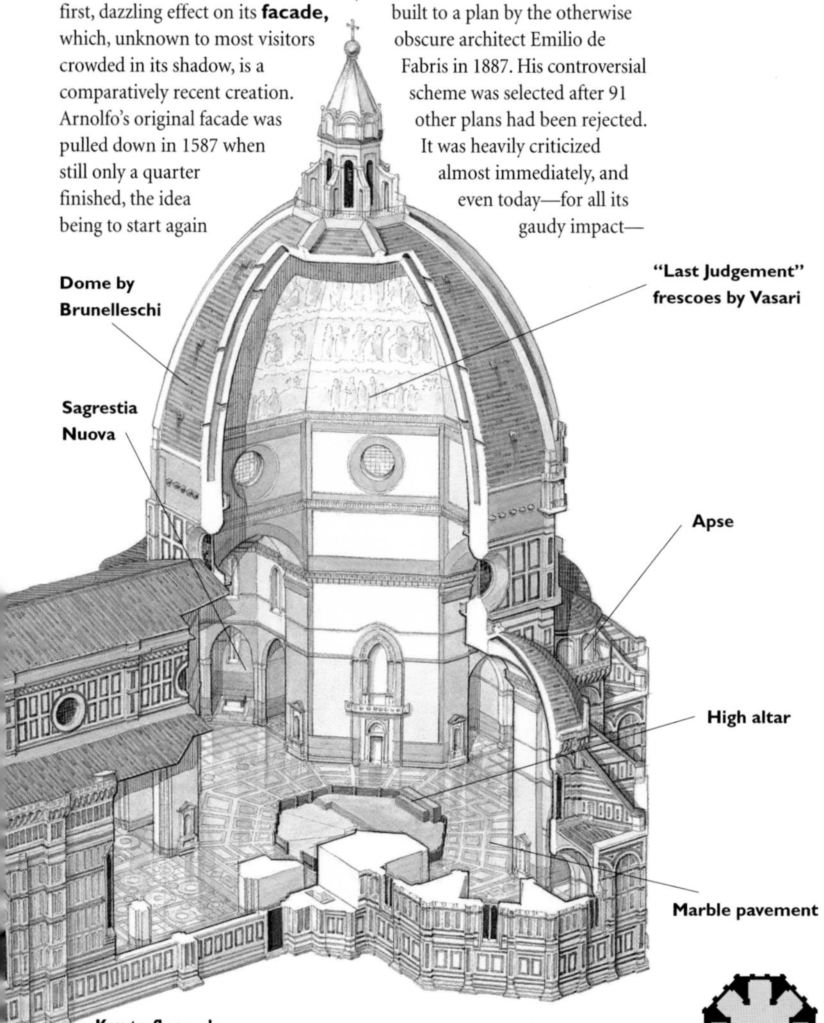

Dome by Brunelleschi

"Last Judgement" frescoes by Vasari

Sagrestia Nuova

Apse

High altar

Marble pavement

Key to floor plan

1 Paolo Uccello: clock
2 Tomb of Antonio d'Orso
3 Santa Reparata
4 Niccolò da Tolentino fresco
5 Sir John Hawkwood fresco
6 Dante and The Divine Comedy
7 Porta della Mandorla
8 Entrance to the dome
9 Sagrestia Nuova
10 Sagrestia Vecchia

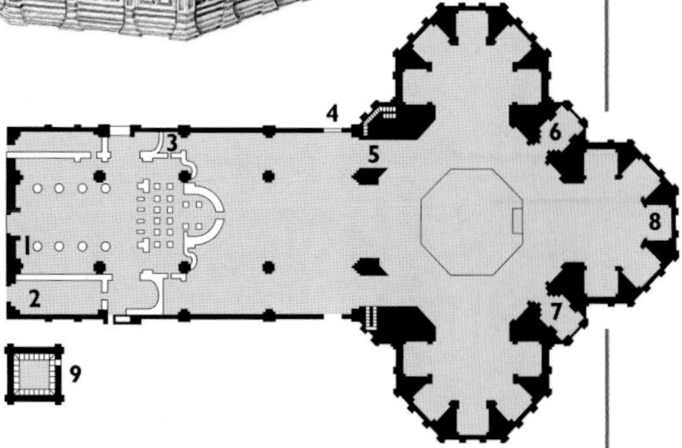

The mosaic above the main door of the Duomo, and the rest of the cathedral facade, were added between 1871 and 1887.

it is still belittled by most Florentine and other architectural purists.

Moving to the cathedral's **interior** is something of a shock. Where the exterior is all ornament and color, the interior—at least at first glance—is all space and gloomy austerity. The Priorate's demands for a "vast building" was clearly taken to heart, as size for its own sake appears to be the interior's overwhelming concern; this is Europe's fourth largest church, after Milan's cathedral, St. Paul's in London, and St. Peter's in Rome. An edifice on such a grand scale was vital, both to outdo rival cities and to provide an indoor arena—the cathedral holds some 30,000 people—that would offer a single point of focus for the city's inhabitants. For example, the cleric and

charismatic monk Girolamo Savonarola regularly preached here to full houses (see pp. 31–33), and Renaissance architect Leon Battista Alberti stressed that the cathedral dome should be "large enough to cover with its shadow all the Tuscan people" (*De re aedificatoria*, 1452).

The interior's austerity is deceptive, however, for it contains a number of artistic treasures, as well as two worthwhile side attractions. The first of these is the cathedral's **crypt,** where you can see ruins of the church of Santa Reparata; the second is the cathedral's **dome,** which offers an insight into the architectural acumen of its presiding genius, Filippo Brunelleschi. Better still, the dome offers a glorious panorama of Florence and its surrounding countryside.

Before your climb of the dome, walk around the interior to enjoy its other highlights. Start by turning to face the main facade doors through which you've just entered. Above the main door you'll see a strange **clock** set to the so-called *hora italica*, an arrangement in which the 24th hour of the day ends at sunset. This system was designed chiefly to mark the canonical or religious divisions of the day, and it remained in widespread use across Italy until the 18th century. The heads of the prophets decorating the timepiece are the work of Paolo Uccello (1397–1475), an artist whose hand you'll see again elsewhere in the cathedral. The stained-glass windows on this wall were created to designs by Lorenzo Ghiberti, the sculptor responsible for the baptistery's east doors. To the right of the central door as you face it stands the tomb of Antonio d'Orso, Bishop of Florence (1323); it is the work of Tino da Camaino.

Moving to the south (right) wall, the first statue here portrays Brunelleschi, the dome's creator, and it was carved by Andrea Cavalcanti, his pupil and adopted son, in 1446. The figure by Benedetto da Maiano (1442–1497), to its left, shows "Giotto at Work." By the nave's first right-hand pillar stands a pretty stoup, or holy water container, and the entrance to what remains of **Santa Reparata.** As far as the latter is concerned, however, it is barely worth paying the admission fee to see what amounts to little more than patchy ruins. The key point of interest is the tomb of Brunelleschi at the foot of the stairs, which you can glimpse without paying. The fact the architect was buried in the cathedral underlines the esteem in which he was held by the city.

Now walk from the nave's right-hand side to look at the cathedral's

three key paintings, all of which are on the left (north) wall opposite. From left to right, the first of these is the "Equestrian Portrait of Niccolò da Tolentino" by Andrea del Castagno (1423–1457), which shows a noted contemporary *condottiere*, or mercenary general, on horseback. The painting was clearly derived from the picture of the *condottiere* to its right, the "Equestrian Portrait of Sir John Hawkwood," painted 20 years earlier by Paolo Uccello. Notice how the latter painting's perspective is askew, the pedestal being painted as if seen from a completely different point of view to the horse and rider above. Uccello was profoundly preoccupied with perspective—see his Uffizi and Santa Maria Novella paintings for further evidence of his

A statue of Filippo Brunelleschi, the architect responsible for the cathedral's dome. Many critics thought the project could never be realized.

Light streams onto the Duomo's 16th-century marble pavement. The cathedral has more ancient stained glass than any other church in Italy.

fixation (pp. 40–41, 99, and 157). Here it seems he first painted the horse "correctly"—that is, from the point of view of an onlooker gazing at the pedestal—and as a result all that could be seen of the creature was a large portion of its belly. The cathedral authorities, understandably annoyed at the fresco's strangeness, ordered him to repaint the offending section.

The third painting lies farther along, by the side door on the north of the nave, the Porta della Mandorla, and shows "Dante and The Divine Comedy" (1465). The work of Domenico di Michelino, this picture portrays the eminent Florentine holding open a copy of *The Divine Comedy*, his most celebrated work, from which a ray of light shines on the city of Florence.

Note how Dante is shown outside the city walls, probably a symbol of his exile (see pp. 78–79). If the nearby **Porta della Mandorla** is open, incidentally, be sure to step outside to admire its sculpture. The door takes its name from the almond-shaped frame *(mandorla* means "almond") that encloses a relief of "The Assumption of the Virgin" by Nanni di Banco (1385/90–1421).

Back in the church, you pass the **entrance to the dome** (see pp. 64–65) to the right of the Porta della Mandorla. It is definitely worth paying the modest fee and climbing the 400-plus steps to enjoy the views from the top, but note that parts of the staircase are narrow and shouldn't be attempted by anyone who suffers from claustrophobia. There is no elevator.

Returning to the church, walk to the crossing, the name given to the large open area underneath the dome. The three tribunes, or apses, are arranged around it. Look up to see Giorgio Vasari's colorful but rather trite dome frescoes of "The Last Judgment" (1572–79). These showy pictures distract from the greater intrinsic merit of the **sacristies,** two enclosed areas to either side of the central apse. On the left as you face the high altar is the **Sagrestia Nuova,** or New Sacristy, decorated with exquisite 15th-century inlaid wood paneling and protected by marvelous bronze doors (1446–1467) designed by Michelozzo and Luca della Robbia. Behind these doors Lorenzo the Magnificent successfully sought refuge from would-be assassins during the Pazzi Conspiracy of 1478. His less fortunate brother, Giuliano, was hacked down on the steps of the high altar, his skull shattered and his body rent with 19 stab wounds. Small portraits

on the door handles commemorate both brothers.

Above the door of the Sagrestia Nuova is a blue-white terra-cotta lunette of "The Annunciation" (1442) that would have looked down on the carnage. The work of Luca della Robbia (1400–1482), it was the first of the glazed and colored ceramics with which his name would become synonymous. An almost identical lunette of "The Ascension" by the same artist graces the **Sagrestia Vecchia,** or Old Sacristy, on the other side of the church. Remember these sacristies when you visit the Museo dell'Opera del Duomo (see pp. 74–77), whose highlights include a pair of carved *cantorie,* or choir lofts, that once stood above each of their entrances. Finally, note the magnificent bronze

reliquary by Lorenzo Ghiberti above the altar of the central apse, crafted to contain the remains of St. Zenobius, Florence's first bishop.

On the corner of Piazza del Duomo and Via del Calzaiuoli stands the Loggia del Bigallo, an arched structure dating from around 1353. It was built for the Compagnia della Misericordia, a confraternity and hospital charity. In 1425 this charity united with the Compagnia del Bigallo, which cared for the poor, elderly, and orphans. The Compagnia used the loggia to display lost or abandoned children —with the hope they might be recognized—before the organization took responsibility for them. The Misericordia headquarters is still opposite the loggia; recognize it by the ambulances parked nearby. ■

"Dante and The Divine Comedy" (1465) by Domenico di Michelino. Notice Florence's cathedral dome and Campanile, and the towers of the Badia and Palazzo Vecchio on the right of the painting.

The dome

Planning a dome for Florence's cathedral was one thing; building it was another. Earlier medieval domes had been constructed on wooden frames, raised to hold the structures' stone in place until the mortar set. A frame the size of the cathedral's dome, however, would have required most of the wood in Tuscany. Worse still, medieval masons had no experience of a dome this size and no notion of how to contain its estimated 25,000 tons of lateral thrust.

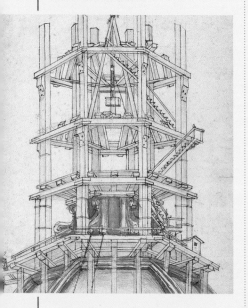

Construction of the lantern atop the dome began in 1446. A contemporary drawing shows the elaborate scaffolding.

All manner of ideas surfaced as to how the dome might be built. One suggested it could be made of pumice, a featherlight volcanic rock. Another proposed supporting the dome on a mound of earth laced with coins that would be dug away on completion by greedy Florentines. In despairing mood, the city's elders mounted a competition in 1418 to devise a solution. Its winner was Filippo Brunelleschi, who narrowly beat Lorenzo Ghiberti, the victor over Brunelleschi in the competition to design the baptistery doors in 1401 (see pp. 68–69).

Brunelleschi had been a poor loser in 1401; this time it was Ghiberti who lost with bad grace, joining the chorus of doom-mongers who ridiculed Brunelleschi's plans as unworkable. An exasperated but canny Brunelleschi eventually feigned illness as an excuse to abandon the project, upon which Ghiberti took over, only to find himself out of his depth. By 1423 Brunelleschi had been reinstated as the dome's sole "inventor and chief director."

Brunelleschi's solutions to the dome's engineering problems were ingenious. Some are still not understood today, but in essence they boiled down to the construction of two shells: A light outer covering was about 3 feet (1 m) thick, and a more robust inner shell measured around 13 feet (4 m) thick. More importantly, the inner shell used a herringbone arrangement of bricks, whose cantilevered rings were immensely strong and allowed the dome to support itself as it rose.

No detail was too small for Brunelleschi, who provided on-site kitchens for his workers to save time, created a honeycomb of corridors to speed up movement around the dome, and provided scaffolding hooks to make cleaning and repairs easier for future generations. Other innovations included lightweight materials, fast-drying mortar, and special tools, some of which can be seen in the Museo dell'Opera (see pp. 74–77).

Completion of the dome in 1436 allowed for the cathedral's consecration on March 25 of the same year. The present lantern, however—the very top of the cupola—was still not built, mainly because many critics believed the dome would collapse if subjected to any further weight. Brunelleschi was again forced to suffer the indignity of a competition—which he won—and work on the missing lantern began a few months before his death in 1446. Only the exposed brickwork of a proposed gallery now remains unfinished, abandoned after criticism of the plan by one of the dome's most fervent admirers—Michelangelo. ∎

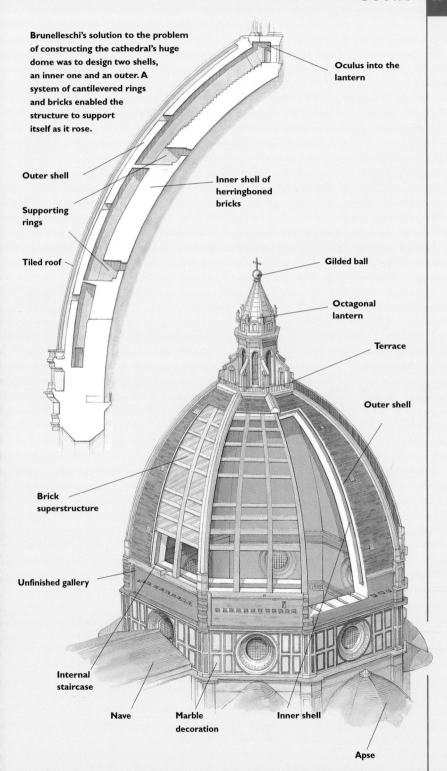

Brunelleschi's solution to the problem of constructing the cathedral's huge dome was to design two shells, an inner one and an outer. A system of cantilevered rings and bricks enabled the structure to support itself as it rose.

Oculus into the lantern

Outer shell

Inner shell of herringboned bricks

Supporting rings

Tiled roof

Gilded ball

Octagonal lantern

Terrace

Outer shell

Brick superstructure

Unfinished gallery

Internal staircase

Nave

Marble decoration

Inner shell

Apse

Battistero

THE BATTISTERO DI SAN GIOVANNI, OR BAPTISTERY, IS probably Florence's oldest building. For centuries, every Florentine child was baptized here, lending it a symbolic significance that made it more precious to the city than the cathedral. Its octagonal interior is swathed with some of Europe's finest mosaics, but even these are eclipsed by the splendor of its three celebrated bronze doors.

Battistero

⬛ Map p. 54

✉ Piazza San Giovanni-Piazza del Duomo

☎ 055 230 2885

🕐 Closed Sun. p.m. & Mon.–Sat. a.m.

💲 $$

🚌 Bus: 1, 6, 14, 17, 23

Opposite: The Battistero, or baptistery, seen from the Campanile. The dome in the background belongs to the church of San Lorenzo.

In today's world of record-keeping and documentation, it's hard to believe that for much of the Middle Ages the Florentines forgot the origins of their baptistery. For many years they thought it was a structure of Roman origin, a pagan temple to Mars, god of war, built to commemorate Florence's defeat of Fiesole and the creation of Florence in the first century A.D. (see p. 24). It became a Christian building— or so they believed—in the fourth century, during the reign of the Emperor Constantine, the first Christian emperor.

Today this theory is discounted, although scholars are still unsure of the baptistery's precise genesis. It is generally accepted that the present building occupies the site of a first-century Roman edifice—probably a grand *domus,* or house—although many of the interior's immense granite columns probably came from the Roman-era Capitol building in Florence, parts of which also found their way into San Miniato al Monte (see pp. 184–87).

The first documentary reference to a building here comes in 897, when it is mentioned as the city's cathedral. Much of the classically inspired decoration dates from about 1059 to 1128, perhaps later, a period of remodeling that saw the addition of the exterior's geometric medley of pillars, cornices, and colored marble friezes. This style of decoration would influence Tuscan architects and the appear-

ance of Romanesque churches across the region for centuries.

The decoration's splendor was no accident. It was commissioned and paid for by the Merchants' Guild, the Arte di Calimala (or Arte di Mercanto), the most powerful of the city's guilds and the body entrusted with the baptistery's upkeep. In caring for one of the city's most important buildings, it found itself in competition with a rival guild, the almost equally wealthy Arte della Lana (Wool Guild), which was responsible for the cathedral.

Some idea of the baptistery's standing among Florentines can be gleaned from the fact that it was invariably the baptistery, not the cathedral—at least early on—that received the most lavish works of art. Nowhere is this more obvious than in the baptistery's three sets of doors, its most significant artistic features. The earliest of these are the **south doors**, designed by Andrea Pisano (1290–1348), a Pisan sculptor chosen partly because Pisa's recently completed cathedral was already celebrated for its magnificent bronze doors (see pp. 247–48). Pisano completed working wax models for the doors in just three months, their casting being entrusted to the Venetian Leonardo d'Avanzo; the Venetians at the time were acknowledged as Europe's finest bronzesmiths. Casting took an incredible six years, and the doors were only installed in

Ghiberti's 28-panel north doors for the Battistero retain the Gothic quatrefoils surrounding the reliefs.

A.D. M.CCC.XXX"—which records that Andrea Pisano *"me fecit"* (made me) in 1330.

Walk from the doors toward the apse, the area protruding from the building on the side away from the cathedral. Low down you'll see a panel with a relief of a naval battle, probably part of a fourth- or fifth-century **sarcophagus.** On the apse itself are two lions about to devour human heads, symbols of the castigation of sinners and common motifs on 12th- and 13th-century Romanesque churches. Continuing around the building you see the **Colonna di San Zanobi** (1384), a freestanding pillar that marks the spot where a miracle is supposed to have occurred as the body of St. Zenobius, Florence's first bishop, was being moved from San Lorenzo to Santa Reparata (then the cathedral) on January 26, 429. Richard Lassels, an early visitor to Florence, describes the miracle in *The Voyage of Italy,* (1603). He tells his readers "to take notice of a little round pillar with the figure of a tree in iron nayled to it, and old words engraven upon it, importing, that in this very place, stood anciently an Elm tree, which being touched by the hearse of St. Zenobious [sic] budded forth with green leaves though in the month of January."

The baptistery's second set of doors, the **north doors,** are now on your right, commissioned as a votive offering to spare Florence the ravages of another plague similar to the Black Death of 1348. This time the choice of sculptor was less clear-cut than with the south doors, and a competition to select a suitable candidate was arranged in 1401, a date often seen as marking the "beginning" of the Italian Renaissance. The judges were ultimately unable to decide between two panels—both representing

1336, when they were placed at the baptistery's main entrance (facing the cathedral). They were moved to their present position in 1452 to make way for Lorenzo Ghiberti's east doors (see below).

The 20 upper reliefs of the doors' 28 panels portray episodes from the life of St. John the Baptist, Florence's patron and the saint to whom the baptistery is dedicated (Giovanni is Italian for John). The eight lower reliefs represent "Humility" and the "Cardinal and Theological Virtues." The doors' bronze frame is by Vittorio Ghiberti, son of Lorenzo Ghiberti, and was created when the doors were moved in 1452. Note the inscription at the top of the doors—"ANDREAS UGOLINI NINI DE PISIS ME FECIT

"The Sacrifice of Isaac"—submitted by two young goldsmiths, Lorenzo Ghiberti and Filippo Brunelleschi. As a result, it seems both were asked to work together on the doors, at which point Brunelleschi appears to have stated that if he was not the outright winner, he was not interested in the commission. He then left Florence for Rome to study architecture, but he would later return to design, among other things, Florence's cathedral dome, the churches of San Lorenzo and Santo Spirito, and the Cappella dei Pazzi alongside Santa Croce. Significantly, however, he rarely turned again to sculpture.

The victorious Ghiberti devoted much of the next 20 years to the north doors. The finished project was mostly traditional in outlook and retained the Gothic quatrefoil—the square that framed the reliefs—and 28-panel scheme of Pisano's earlier doors. At the same time, Ghiberti's reliefs are far more vivid and realistic than Pisano's. They also demonstrate the maturing of his style over 20 years, from the simple narrative of the early reliefs to the far more detailed and crowded scenes of later panels. The upper 20 reliefs describe "Stories from the New Testament," the eight lower panels the "Four Evangelists" and "Four Doctors of the Church."

So pleased were the Arte di Calimala with Ghiberti's doors that they commissioned a second set in 1425. The **east doors** would be the artist's masterpiece and one of the supreme works of the Florentine Renaissance. Michelangelo is said to have declared them so beautiful they might serve as the gates of Paradise, hence their alternative name, the Porta del Paradiso. Ghiberti worked on them for 27 years with, as he put it, "the greatest diligence and greatest love."

The doors on the baptistery today are copies—the originals are in the Museo dell'Opera del Duomo (see pp. 74–77)—but they still convey both Ghiberti's brilliance and the marked departure from what had gone before. He replaced the previous doors' 28-panel schemes, for example, with just ten reliefs; the traditional diamond quatrefoil was abandoned in favor of simple squared panels; several scenes in a story were often condensed into a single panel; the only recently understood notions and rules of perspective were skillfully employed; and the subtlety of expression, realism, narrative power, and compositional sophistication expressed all the newly emerged attributes of Renaissance artistic endeavor.

Bronze reliefs on the bapistery's east doors portray episodes from the Old Testament.

The tomb of the antipope John XXIII (R.1410–1419) was created by Donatello and Michelozzo, two of the finest sculptors of their day.

Opposite: The mosaics on the Battistero's ceiling were completed in the 13th century.

the Florentines to guard their city, rewarding them on their return with two porphyry columns plundered from Mallorca. The columns' polished surfaces were said to have magical powers, being able to predict acts of treason. The Pisans therefore deliberately ruined the surfaces of the pillars by baking them in embers before handing them over. On arrival, they proved too weak for structural use and were relegated to the baptistery's exterior, where they have remained ever since.

Your first impression of the interior is of a bland shell. A glance upward, however, reveals a majestic **mosaic-covered ceiling,** a mostly 13th-century work begun by Venetian craftsmen using plans by local artists, the Florentines having had little or no grounding in mosaic technique. Its immensely complex narrative embraces episodes from the lives of Christ, Joseph, the Virgin, and John the Baptist. To the right of the *scarsella,* or apse, stands Donatello and Michelozzo's tomb of the antipope John XXIII, an adviser and friend of the Medici, who died in the city in 1419. Also worthy of note are the interior's band of granite columns, probably removed from the old Roman Capitol, and the intricately tessellated marble pavement, where the outline of the original octagonal font can still be seen. ∎

Before entering the baptistery, take in the two **columns** on either side of the east doors. They come with a little tale attached. In 1117, so the story goes, the Pisans set off on a voyage of conquest to Mallorca, an island off the Spanish coast. Fearful of an attack from Lucca in their absence, they asked

Baptisms

Baptism was important in medieval Tuscany, but not merely for religious reasons. In Siena, children were baptized in the church of their *contrada,* or parish, while in Florence all children born in a single year were baptized communally in the Battistero on March 25, the Feast of the Annunciation. In both cities the idea was to pledge the child to its respective parish and city, as well as to God. In Florence, additionally, a black bean was dropped into an urn for a boy baby, a white one for a girl, allowing the birthrate to be calculated. During the 14th century there were roughly 6,000 births a year in a city with a population of around 90,000. ∎

Campanile

THE CAMPANILE IS THE CATHEDRAL'S BELFRY. ONE OF Italy's most beautiful medieval towers, it was designed by Giotto, the period's most accomplished painter, and adorned with reliefs and statues by Donatello, Luca della Robbia, and other leading Renaissance sculptors. Perhaps surpassing its artistic appeal are its breathtaking views of the cathedral and over Florence's rooftops to the hazy Tuscan hills beyond.

A downward view reveals the Campanile's interior.

distinctive windows, the latter a motif borrowed from Sienese bell towers, from 1348 to 1359. When you look at the Campanile, the different work of the three architects is patently clear, suggesting that any plans by Giotto for a unified scheme were quietly overlooked.

The completed Campanile's 275-foot (84.7 m) height was considerably in excess of a law promulgated in 1324 and designed to restrict the height of privately built towers. Such laws were common—Italy's most notable towered village, San Gimignano, had one (see pp. 232–41)—towers being an obvious means by which leading families could make their wealth and power conspicuous.

The tower's present decorative sculptures are copies. The age-darkened originals—well worth studying in detail—now reside in the Museo dell'Opera del Duomo (see pp. 74–77). The sculpture's arrangement and themes were carefully chosen, showing humanity's transition from a state of original sin (at the base of the tower) to a position of divine grace at the top. Christian and other philosophical thought of the day believed this transition was achieved through manual labor, the arts, and the sacraments and was guided by the influence of the planets and the cardinal and theological virtues.

The apparently disparate sculptural reliefs can therefore be seen as a coherent philosophical whole.

Campanile

- Map p. 54
- Piazza del Duomo
- 055 230 2885
- $$
- Bus: 1, 6, 14, 17, 23

The tower was begun in 1334 under the guidance of Giotto, then employed as the city's *capo maestro*, or "master of works." He completed only the first of the tower's five stories before his death in 1337, but he probably left plans for the remaining levels that mirrored the multicolored decorative scheme devised by Arnolfo di Cambio for the exterior of the nearby cathedral (then also in the first stages of its construction).

Work subsequently proceeded in two phases, the first under Andrea Pisano, designer of the baptistery's north doors (see pp. 66–71). He built the second story up to the level of the first pair of twin windows (1337–1342), and then Francesco Talenti completed the remaining three stories and their

Opposite: The Campanile as seen from the cathedral's dome

Thus the lowest register in hexagonal frames by Andrea Pisano and his pupils illustrates the "Creation, Art, and Works of Man." The upper register's diamond-shaped panels are allegories of the "Seven Planets" (whose movement was believed to influence human lives), the "Seven Sacraments" (which sanctify human life), and the "Seven Virtues" (which shape human behavior). About a century after these reliefs were made, Luca della Robbia added the "Five Liberal Arts" on the side of the tower facing the cathedral. These arts—Grammar, Music, Arithmetic, Philosophy, and Astrology—were believed to nourish and shape the human spirit. Other works by Pisano in the second-story niches were later replaced by statues of the "Prophets, Sibyls, Patriarchs, and Kings" (1415–1436) by Donatello and Nanni di Bartolo. The originals of these works are also in the Museo dell'Opera del Duomo.

A climb to the top of the tower —there is no elevator—is rewarded with sensational views of the city: The bird's-eye view of the baptistery and cathedral dome are especially memorable. Don't undertake the climb lightly, however. There are 414 steps and a rather ominous first-aid post near the top. In a letter of 1861, English novelist George Eliot recorded her climb up "Giotto's tower, with its delicate pinkish marble, its delicate windows,…twisted columns, and its tall lightness." It was, she wrote, "a very sublime getting upstairs indeed— and our muscles were much astonished at the unusual exercise."

As you climb, you gain an insight into how the tower was built and how the bells were rung in such a tall structure. Notice, for example, the pulleys and central stays used to keep the bell ropes in place. ■

Museo dell'Opera del Duomo

Opposite: Donatello's "Mary Magdalene"

The entrance courtyard of the museum

THE MUSEO DELL'OPERA DEL DUOMO CONTAINS MANY works of art removed for safekeeping from the Duomo, Battistero, and Campanile. It opened in 1891 in a building that since 1291 had been occupied by the Opera del Duomo, a body created to care for the fabric of the cathedral. Today it has one of the city's finest collections of sculpture—only that of the Bargello is more compelling—and a wealth of paintings, silverware, ceramics, and manuscripts.

Museo dell'Opera del Duomo

- Map p. 54
- Piazza del Duomo 9
- 055 230 2885
- Closed Sun. p.m.
- $$
- Bus: 14, 23

RESTORATION

The museum opened again in March 2000 after restoration; at the time of writing the arrangement of some exhibits had yet to be finalized.

Pause for a moment in the glass-covered entrance courtyard of the museum, for it was here that Michelangelo sculptured much of his "David" before it was moved to Piazza della Signoria. After the modern ticket hall you pass a couple of minor rooms filled with sculpture removed from the cathedral's facade. Note the line near the entrance that marks the water level in the building following the flood of 1966 (see pp.164–65).

The museum's first major room is the **Sala dell'Antica Facciata del Duomo,** or Room of the Ancient Facade of the Cathedral. Here you're confronted by a host of statues, most of them rescued from Arnolfo di Cambio's quarter-finished cathedral facade, which

was pulled down on the orders of Grand Duke Ferdinand I de' Medici in 1587. The most eye-catching works are both by Arnolfo di Cambio: The "Madonna of the Glass Eyes," famous for its otherworldly gaze, and a statue of a seated "Boniface VIII," a vicious medieval pope easily identified here by his distinctive hat. Arnolfo was also responsible for a fine "Madonna and Child," a "Madonna of the Nativity" with a relief of animals and shepherds above, and a statue of "Santa Reparata," one of Florence's patron saints. This last work was so accomplished it was long believed to be of Greek or Roman origin. Also notice the three statues of the Evangelists: "St. Luke" by Nanni di Banco, Donatello's "St. John," and Bernardo Ciuffagni's "St.

Matthew." All three were carved between 1408 and 1415, reputedly as part of a competition to see who would have the honor of creating a statue of St. Mark, the fourth Evangelist. Apparently Ciuffagni was accused of cheating by copying Donatello's "St. John," by far the most distinguished of the three statues. As a result, the contest was declared void and the job of carving Mark given to another sculptor entirely, Niccolò Lamberti (1370–1451).

Other parts of this floor contain paintings, sculptures, illustrated manuscripts, and choral chants—the latter used in the cathedral until as recently as 1930. Also here is the **Ottagono delle Oreficerie** (1954), a modern octagonal chapel that features several precious reliquaries, ornate vessels used to house saintly and other relics (which here include the jaw of St. Jerome and a finger belonging to St. John the Baptist). Overshadowing these, however, is a lovely altarpiece painting of "St. Catherine and St. Zenobius" (1334) attributed to Bernardo Daddi.

MICHELANGELO'S "PIETÀ"

As you go upstairs, you pass Michelangelo's "Pietà" (1550–53), a late and unfinished work moved from the cathedral in 1981 and probably intended for the sculptor's own tomb; the figure of Nicodemus may well be a self-portrait. Michelangelo became disillusioned by the sculpture and the quality of the marble, and in frustration he smashed its left arm and leg. The damage was later repaired by a pupil, but signs of Michelangelo's frenzy and the obvious discrepancy in styles are still clearly evident. By any standards, however, this remains a remarkable work, of note particularly for the extraordinary, limp body of Christ and what—

without the small figure of Mary Magdalene on the left, added later by a pupil—would have been a curiously (but deliberately) lopsided and "unfilled" composition.

UPPER FLOOR

The first room on this floor contains two stunning and contrasting *cantorie,* or **choir lofts,** one by Donatello, the other by Luca della Robbia. Both were removed in 1688 from the entrances to the cathedral's two sacristies on the occasion of the marriage of Grand Duke Cosimo III de' Medici (1642–1723) to Violante Beatrice of Bavaria. Both lofts are filled with depictions of dancing children playing instruments, but there the similarities end. Whereas Luca della Robbia's children are blithe, innocent creatures, those of Donatello have more the air of rowdy, free-spirited urchins. Donatello was also responsible for the room's bald-headed Old Testament prophet "Abacuc," or Habbakuk (1423–25), one of 16 figures removed from the Campanile. The figure is a favorite of the

Florentines, who have nicknamed him *lo zuccone*, or "marrow head," after the shape of his bald pate.

Also on this floor, in a room devoted to items from the baptistery, is Donatello's celebrated wooden baptistery statue of "Mary Magdalene" (1453–55), a work that underlines this sculptor's virtuosity and variety of style. Indeed, it is said Donatello had so many different approaches to his work that he lacked any distinctive or recognizable style. Here his mood is one of disturbing realism: Mary, with her pitted, sunken face and matted hair, appears strikingly contemporary to modern eyes. Nothing else in the Renaissance remotely resembles this sculpture, save for a similar work by the same artist in Venice.

The enormous altar here, a masterpiece of 14th-century Florentine gold and silver work, originally stood in the baptistery. Begun in 1366, it was not completed until 1480, but it extravagantly fulfilled the demands of the Arte del Calimala, the baptistery's custodians and the altar's commissioning agents, that "no other similar work should be its equal." Its decoration embraced the detailed labors of such artists as Michelozzo (the central statuette of "St. John the Baptist"), Andrea del Verrocchio (the "Decapitation" on the right), and Antonio Pollaiuolo (the enameled predella below, and the "Birth of Jesus" statue on the left).

Also look out here for Giovanni di Bondo's extraordinary triptych of "St. Sebastian" (few pictures of this saint can contain quite so many arrows); an exquisite little Byzantine mosaic; statuettes of "Christ in the Act of Blessing" and "Santa Reparata" by Andrea Pisano; a marble bust of an unknown woman by Tino da Camaino; and 12 gold and silk altar panels (1466–87) from the baptistery, whose nar-

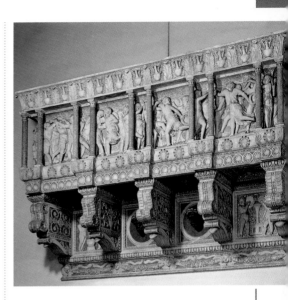

rative panels depict episodes from the life of St. John the Baptist. Another room on this floor features more refugees from the belltower, this time the allegorical reliefs full of intricate detail by Andrea Pisano, Luca della Robbia, and their pupils that were removed from the tower's first story between 1965 and 1967. Despite their age-darkened appearance, the reliefs are still full of intricate detail and fascinating narrative.

A ramp to the newer area of the museum passes exhibits devoted to **Filippo Brunelleschi** and the cathedral dome's construction. Among the objects are ropes, pulleys, and other pieces of equipment used on the dome, some specially invented by Brunelleschi, as well as a death mask of the sculptor and a wooden model of the lantern. Rooms off the corridor contain a miscellany of exhibits; one that contains drawings has stairs leading down to a courtyard designed to display Ghiberti's restored panels from the **east doors** of the baptistery in a facsimilie of their original setting (see p. 69). ■

Donatello's *cantoria* is one of two sculptured choir lofts removed from the cathedral and now in the Museo dell'Opera del Duomo.

Opposite: The damage inflicted by Michelangelo on his "Pietà" clearly shows on Christ's left arm.

Dante Alighieri

Dante Alighieri was one of the greatest poets of any age. His most celebrated work—*La Divina Commedia, or The Divine Comedy*—is a masterpiece that stands in the front rank of literary works. He also served Florence as a diplomat and politician, but he was poorly treated by the city of his birth and spent his final years in bitter exile.

Dante was born in 1265 into a minor and impoverished aristocratic family. At the age of nine he met Beatrice Portinari, the girl who would blight much of his romantic life but inspire many of his literary endeavors. Then aged just eight, Beatrice was, in the words of fellow writer Giovanni Boccaccio (1313–1375), "so delicate and beautifully formed, and full, besides mere beauty, of so much candid loveliness that many thought her almost an angel" *(Life of Dante, 1321)*. Dante, for his part, said that "she appeared to be born not of mortal man but of God."

Dante would never marry or even become close to Beatrice, however, for she had been promised by her family to Simone de' Bardi, whom she married at the age of 17. Such dynastic marriages were common. Dante himself was pledged to Gemma Donati at the age of 12. It may well be significant, however, that he married much later than Beatrice, at the age of 30. Beatrice's place in Dante's heart was cemented by her early death at the age of 24.

Dante's early career was neither romantically nor poetically inclined; it leaned instead toward politics. He fought against the cities of Arezzo and Pisa, then enemies of Florence, and served on a number of civic committees after joining the Apothecaries' Guild. In 1300, in his most notable diplomatic enterprise, he was sent to San Gimignano to talk the town into an alliance against Pope Boniface VIII, who was gathering his strength for an assault on Tuscany.

In the same year he attempted to heal the widening breach between the two factions of Florence's ruling Guelph party. One side, the Black Guelphs, were ranged against the imperial powers of the old Holy Roman Empire, while the Whites—to whom Dante belonged—were more conciliatory. The Blacks contained leading papal bankers —families such as Pazzi, Bardi, and Donati—while the Whites included many imperial bankers (Cerchi, Mozzi, Davanzati, and Frescobaldi).

As the dispute intensified, Boniface VIII sided, predictably, with the Blacks, who eventually emerged triumphant. Dante's White sympathies condemned him, and he was exiled from Florence on trumped-up charges for two years. While many of his fellow exiles later returned home, an embittered Dante forsook forever his city of "self-made men and fast-got gain." For years thereafter he wandered between Verona, Padua, Venice, and elsewhere, probably writing much of *The Divine Comedy* as he went.

This great epic takes as its narrative theme the passage of Dante in the guise of a pilgrim through Hell and Purgatory to God and Paradise. In doing so, it traces the redemption of both Dante and humanity, beginning in a dark wood, a symbol of the poet's state of moral and spiritual darkness following the death of Beatrice. Woven into the poem are countless references—many of them critical and vitriolic—to contemporary and historical figures and events. The work was completed about 1321, just before Dante's death in Ravenna, where he is buried. Florence still sends a gift of oil to light the lamps on his tomb each September 14, the anniversary of his death. ∎

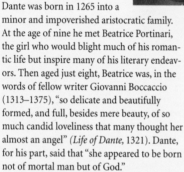

Opposite top: A 16th-century painting of Dante by the Tuscan artist Luca Signorelli Below: Part of a 1313 manuscript copy of Dante's *The Divine Comedy*. In the illustration, from Canto XXIII, Dante and Virgil witness the crucifixion of Caiaphas.

The Bargello's *cortile*, one of the finest medieval courtyards in Italy, was once a place of execution.

Museo Nazionale del Bargello

THE MEDIEVAL BUILDING OF THE MUSEO NAZIONALE DEL Bargello has had a long and often troubled history. It began life as the Palazzo del Podestà in 1255, when it served as the headquarters of the Podestà, Florence's chief magistrate. It acquired its present name in 1574 when the Medici abolished the position of Podestà and gave the palace to the Bargello, or chief of police. Today it is home to Italy's greatest collection of Gothic and Renaissance sculpture.

The museum was created in 1865, when it became Italy's first national museum (Museo Nazionale) outside the Vatican. Today, it is visited mainly for its half-dozen or so rooms of sculpture, containing most of the finest works of the Tuscan Renaissance, including masterpieces from Michelangelo, Donatello, and many others. At the same time, it is important to stress that the museum's many other rooms—often overlooked—contain a collection of ceramics, textiles, carpets, ivories, tapestries, silverware, and other beautifully crafted

works by Michelangelo. The most obvious is a lurching and very clearly drunk "Bacchus," carved when the sculptor was just 22. Rarely can inebriation have been portrayed so convincingly. This was the first major work in which Michelangelo was inspired by the sculpture of the classical world. It predated by about a year the work that secured his reputation—the more celebrated "Pietà" in St. Peter's in Rome. The famous statue of "David" was begun some five years later, in 1501. Compare Michelangelo's "Bacchus" with the nearby statue of the same figure by Jacopo Sansovino (1486–1570)—a work that shows its subject rather steadier on his feet.

The second Michelangelo in the room, chronologically speaking, shows the sculptor in a subtler light: The unfinished "Pitti Tondo," or "Madonna and Child" (1504), is a beautifully delicate shallow relief that exemplifies a technique known as *sciacciato*. This stresses the subtlety of line above the depth of a sculpture, testing a sculptor's ability to create space and contrast in a shallow working area. Note the skill with which Michelangelo has carved the figure of a young St. John the Baptist behind the Virgin's shoulder, a figure so insubstantial at first glance as to be almost invisible. Once seen, however, it lends the work an extraordinary impression of depth.

The room's third Michelangelo, a figure of "David-Apollo" (1530–32), skips some 30 years of the sculptor's life and artistic development, during which time, among other things, he had painted the ceiling of the Vatican's Sistine Chapel. Scholars are unsure of the work's precise theme. Renaissance painter and art critic Giorgio Vasari claimed it represented Apollo drawing an arrow from his quiver;

Giambologna's iconic statue of Mercury

artifacts that could easily take up as much of your time as the famous sculptures themselves.

You enter the palace in the shadow of the **Torre Volognana,** a medieval tower that predated the palace and was incorporated into the first phase of its building (1255–1261). Traditionally its mighty bell is rung once every hundred years, at the turn of each century. From here you walk into the ticket office and then turn right into the first room, formerly the Bargello's armory, the core of the earliest palace.

MICHELANGELO'S WORKS
In barely the blink of an eye you're confronted with the cream of Italy's greatest late Renaissance sculpture. Most people make straight for four

Museo Nazionale del Bargello
- Map p. 54
- Via del Proconsolo 4
- 055 238 8606
- Closed Mon., & Tues.—Sun. p.m., but open a.m. 1st, 3rd, & 5th Mon. of the month
- $$
- Bus: A, 14, 23

It was reportedly commissioned by an anti-Medici city council to celebrate the assassination of Alessandro de' Medici in 1537. Alessandro was probably the bastard son of Pope Clement VII, otherwise known as Giulio de' Medici, and proved to be one of the least appealing of all the many Medici (see p. 33). He is said to have been murdered by his lover and distant cousin, Lorenzaccio, whom Vasari claimed was the model for Michelangelo's statue.

Scattered around the room are sculptures by Michelangelo's contemporaries. Chief of these are pieces by Benvenuto Cellini, a flamboyant character responsible here, among other things, for a "Bust of Cosimo I," his first foray into bronze, and several preparatory bronzes for his great statue of "Perseus" in the Loggia della Signoria (see p. 93). French-born Giambologna is represented by his famous winged "Mercury," an image that has become the standard representation of the god. In any other company the works of Bandinelli, Ammannati, and the other sculptors displayed would shine: Here they can't help but appear second rate.

Cross the Bargello's courtyard, formerly the scene of executions, to take in the less arresting Gothic works by Arnolfino di Cambrio

Filippo Brunelleschi created the bronze panel of "The Sacrifice of Isaac" for the 1401 competition to design the baptistery doors.

others think the figure is the Biblical hero David and suggest the object beneath the statue's feet is the head of Goliath.

No doubt surrounds the Bargello's fourth Michelangelo, a proud-faced head of "Brutus," the only bust completed by the artist.

Still lives

Paintings of condemned criminals were commissioned from some of Florence's leading artists to decorate the Bargello's walls and courtyard. Andrea del Castagno painted the members of the Albizzi family, hanged for subversion, producing a work described by one critic as a "perfect wonder," with the corpses portrayed in "the strangest attitudes...infinitely varied and perfectly fine." Botticelli (1445–1510) painted men executed following the Pazzi Conspiracy (at 40 florins a cadaver), as did Leonardo da Vinci, who carefully made a note of one corpse's "turquoise blue jacket" and black satin vest as the body dangled from one of the Bargello's windows. ∎

Opposite: Michelangelo carved the statue of the drunken "Bacchus" when he was just 22. It was the sculptor's first major work.

and others in the ground floor's remaining two rooms. The crests around the courtyard walls belong to the various Podestà (magistrates) who occupied the palace through the centuries.

Elsewhere sculpture dots the courtyard, notably an ancient Roman sarcophagus adapted for use as a fountain (notice the dolphins), a 16th-century figure of Cosimo I de' Medici in the guise of a Roman emperor, and a group of late 15th-century figures by Benedetto da Maiano representing six musicians.

DONATELLO & CONTEMPORARIES

Climb the courtyard's external stairs to the second floor, where you're greeted by a wonderfully eccentric menagerie of bronze animals by Giambologna. Turn right and you come to the gallery's second major room, the **Salone del Consiglio Generale.**

The works here are generally earlier than those on the lower floor and represent the pinnacle of Renaissance sculptural achievement. Michelangelo's preeminent role downstairs is here taken by Donatello, whose most famous sculpture is the androgynous "David" (1430–1440), a work described by the American writer Mary McCarthy in *The Stones of Florence* (1959) as a "transvestite's and fetishist's dream of alluring ambiguity." Contrast the figure's raffish hat and sinuous lines with the sculptor's earlier marble "David" (1408–1409) nearby, a far more traditional treatment of a common theme. Compare it, too, with Donatello's heroic and more artistically adventurous "St. George," removed for safekeeping from its niche on the exterior of Orsanmichele (see p. 105). It was commissioned by the Arte dei Corazzai e Spadai, or Armorers'

depicting "The Sacrifice of Isaac" by Lorenzo Ghiberti and Filippo Brunelleschi. These were the joint winning entries of the famous competition held in 1401 to choose a sculptor for the baptistery doors (see pp. 68–69). Also noteworthy are the distinctive polychrome (multi-colored) glazed terra-cottas of Luca della Robbia, as well as works by Michelozzo, Vecchietta (1412– 1480), Agostino di Duccio (1418– 1481), Desiderio da Settignano, and other great names of Renaissance sculpture.

DECORATIVE ARTS

Most of the rest of the Bargello is given over to a ravishing collection of the decorative arts. Particular highlights on the second floor include the carpets and Islamic art in the **Sala Islamica** (Islamic Room), which follows soon after the Salone del Consiglio Generale, and the varied carpets, textiles, ceramics, and other treasures of the **Sala Carrand,** a room that houses a private collection bequeathed to Florence by the French antiquary Louis Carrand in 1888.

Just beyond the latter rooms lies the beautifully decorated **Cappella di Santa Maria di Maddalena.** This contains frescoes (1340) by the School of Giotto, discovered in 1840 when the chapel was being converted from a prison cell. The painting of "Paradiso" on the end wall features a depiction of Dante (in maroon in the right-hand group of the saved, fifth from the right). Many Renaissance critics believed the figure was painted by Giotto himself. The chapel's lovely pulpit, lectern, and stalls (all 1483– 88) were originally carved for the church of San Miniato al Monte (see pp. 184–87). A little beyond the chapel lies the **Sala degli Avori,** or Room of the Ivories, home to

The Bargello has an outstanding collection of Moorish and other Islamic artifacts, including this work in ceramic and enamel.

Guild, which took St. George as its patron saint and protector.

Other works in the room by Donatello attest to the sculptor's virtuosity and flexibility. The "Marzocco," Florence's heraldic lion, represents a simple piece of civic sculpture (a copy of this work sits in Piazza della Signoria), while the "Bust of Niccolò da Uzzano," a mercenary soldier, or *condottiere,* is a triumph of naturalistic portraiture. "Crucifixion" shows the sculptor working in a conventional Christian context, while the strange figure of the "Amor-Atys"—a prancing Cupid-like figure—shows he is also more than at home in the pagan world. Another work with Donatello's stamp is the bronze of "San Giovannino" (the young St. John the Baptist), long attributed to the artist but now credited to a pupil of Donatello, Desiderio da Settignano (circa 1428–1464), an artist who adopted many of the low reliefs and portraiture techniques pioneered by his master.

Two other works of historical and artistic significance worth seeking out are a pair of reliefs

hundreds of intricately worked artifacts, some dating back as far as the fifth century.

On the third floor, watch for the enameled terra-cottas of the della Robbia family (Andrea, Luca, and Giovanni); bronzes and other sculptures by Antonio del Pollaiuolo and the Sienese artist Vecchietta; the Medagliere Mediceo, a collection of medals begun by Lorenzo de' Medici; the **Sala delle Armi,** a display of arms and armor; and the **Salone del Camino,** home to Italy's finest collection of miniature bronzes. The last has works by all the country's leading bronzesmiths, including many artists whose work on a larger scale you have already seen, notably Giambologna and Benvenuto Cellini.

Retracing your steps, don't miss the so-called **Sala del Verrocchio,** given over in part to works by Verrocchio, an artist, sculptor, and head of a workshop that included the Umbrian master Perugino and Leonardo da Vinci among its pupils. Here he is responsible for another statue of

"David," a bronze commissioned by the Medici in 1470 that makes an interesting comparison with Donatello's earlier statues of the same figure. Also compelling is his bust of "Dama col Mazzolino," or "Noblewoman with a Nosegay," remarkable for the incredible delicacy of the figure's hands and layers of clothing.

The bust is one of many in the room. Such busts would once have been common in the homes of Florentine nobles, and the examples here toward the final rooms of the museum are often overlooked. This is a shame, for anywhere but Florence they would be accounted the pride of most collections. Works worthy of note include Verrocchio's bust of "Piero di Lorenzo de Medici," a "Young Warrior" by Antonio Pollaiuolo, the bust of "Battista Sforza" by Francesco Laurana, and a number of works by other famous Tuscan names, such as Mino da Fiesole, Antonio Rossellino, and Benedetto da Maiano. ∎

This Portuguese tablecloth is part of the Bargello's large collection of tapestries and other decorated fabric.

Matteo de' Pasti designed this small medallion in the 15th century.

More places to visit near Piazza del Duomo

BADIA FIORENTINA

The Badia Fiorentina, or Florentine Abbey, lies opposite the Museo Nazionale del Bargello, its presence marked by a distinctive hexagonal bell tower (built 1310–1330), one of the more prominent features of the Florentine skyline. Founded in 978, the Badia was the creation of Willa, the widow of one of the margraves of Tuscany, erstwhile rulers of the region who had their headquarters in Lucca. In time it was further endowed by her son, Ugo, and became one of Florence's most important buildings.

In 1031 a hospital was opened in the complex, the city's first. The abbey bells tolled the divisions of the Florentine working day. During the 1280s it was rebuilt, probably by Arnolfo di Cambio, architect of the Duomo and Palazzo Vecchio. In 1307, however, part of the new building was demolished on the orders of the city, a punishment for the resi-

The Casa di Dante is now a small museum. The poet's real Florentine house and birthplace are unknown.

dent monks for the nonpayment of tax. It was altered again in 1627, this time acquiring a heavy baroque gloss, though most of the interior's works of art escaped destruction. Opening times for the church are variable, but its dark interior is definitely worth a few minutes if you're lucky enough to find it open.

The main lure is Filippino Lippi's "Apparition of the Virgin to St. Bernard" (1485), the painting on the left just after you enter the main body of the church. Note the figure at the bottom of the painting, Piero del Pugliese, the man who commissioned the work from Lippi. On the wall behind, to the right as you face the painting, is a tomb monument (1469–1481) to Willa's son, Ugo, the work of Mino da Fiesole. The same sculptor was responsible for the altar frontal of the "Madonna and Child with St. Leonard and St. Lawrence" (on the wall opposite the Lippi painting) and—around the corner to the left as you face the frontal—the tomb of Bernardo Giugni (1464–1470). The latter is accompanied by figures representing Justice and Faith, added because Giugni was a lawyer and diplomat. Don't leave without taking the door and stairs to the right of the high altar as you face it. They lead to the **Chiostro degli Aranci** (1432–38), Cloister of the Oranges, named after the fruit trees that once grew here. Two sides of the cloister are covered in an anonymous fresco cycle (1436–39) depicting scenes from the life of St. Benedict.

▲ Map p. 54 ✉ Via Dante Alighieri-Via del Proconsolo ☎ No phone ⏱ Generally open Mon. p.m. only 🚌 Bus: A, 14, 23

CASA DI DANTE

Don't be fooled by the Casa di Dante, or House of Dante. The eponymous poet wasn't born here and never lived here. How could he, when the house, for all its persuasive old-fashioned appearance, is actually a medieval pastiche built in 1910? This said, the building is right at the heart of a district with many Dantesque associations (see pp. 78–79), and it's likely the poet was born close by, probably somewhere on the street that bears his name. The Casa di Dante serves as a modest museum devoted to the poet, its chief exhibits being different editions of his major work, *The Divine Comedy*. Note the church of San Martino opposite the house, the Alighieri family's place of worship.

▲ Map p. 54 ✉ Via Santa Margherita 1-Via Dante Alighieri ☎ 055 219 416 ⏱ Closed Tues. 💲 $ 🚌 Bus: A ∎

Piazza della Signoria, the second of the city's great squares, is the gateway to eastern Florence. A few steps away lie the Uffizi, Europe's finest art gallery, and a tangle of medieval streets that leads to the magnificent church of Santa Croce.

Eastern Florence

Battista Sforza by Piero della Francesca

Eastern Florence

PIAZZA DELLA SIGNORIA IS SOMEWHERE YOU'LL RETURN TO AGAIN AND again, testimony to the role for which it was designed—to provide Florence with a meeting place and a setting for its civic (as opposed to religious) seat of power. To its east lies Santa Croce, one of Italy's most exalted churches, housing glorious works of art and the tombs of some of Florence's most illustrious individuals.

The Palazzo Vecchio, an early 14th-century building, provides the piazza's centerpiece, a castlelike monolith that served as the headquarters of the city's ruling bodies and many of its despots over the centuries. Inside, you can wander through a number of its beautifully decorated rooms, within which you encounter several artistic treasures, including sculptural masterpieces by Donatello and Michelangelo.

Many visitors hurry past the Palazzo, however, bewitched by the more tempting artistic allure of the adjacent Galleria degli Uffizi, home to the world's finest collection of Renaissance paintings. This is probably the one sight you should see in Florence and Tuscany if you see no other, but it's one that is also besieged by hundreds of visitors virtually every day of the year. If you don't want to join the lines, call the special telephone number to reserve a place in advance (see p. 101).

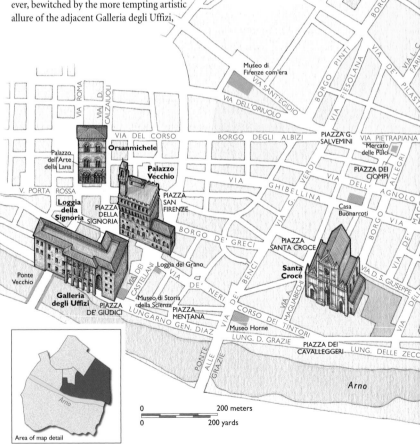

Having sated yourself with paintings, turn back to Piazza della Signoria and give it the time it deserves. Ranged across its eastern flank is a row of eye-catching statues from a variety of eras. Opposite the Palazzo Vecchio is Rivoire, one of the more famous (and expensive) of the city's cafés and a good place to indulge in a drink while you take in the square and its buzz of activity.

This activity is no accident, for the piazza has long been a natural meeting place. Political rallies and festivals were held here from earliest times—the city's Roman theater was close by—and in times of crisis the mob

The Piazza degli Uffizi looking toward the Palazzo Vecchio. The Uffizi Gallery occupies the buildings on the left and right.

would be summoned to its precincts by the tolling of the Palazzo Vecchio's huge bell. The Loggia della Signoria, or Loggia dei Lanzi, on the Piazza della Signoria's southern side, is an open-air gallery of sculpture.

From the square you should walk briefly back toward Piazza del Duomo to see Orsanmichele, an easily missed church known for its exterior statues and peaceful medieval interior, the latter home to a magnificent 14th-century tabernacle. From here you should walk eastward, winding through some of central Florence's oldest and most fascinating streets to Santa Croce and its eponymous quarter, which—with the Sant'Ambrogio district to its north—contains some of the city's most interesting little stores, markets, bars, and restaurants. ■

Piazza della Signoria

PIAZZA DELLA SIGNORIA IS HOME TO THE PALAZZO Vecchio, the seat of Florence's government for seven centuries. It houses several notable pieces of public sculpture and is also a meeting place for visitors and Florentines alike. Close by lies the entrance to the most exalted of all Florence's museums, the Uffizi.

Piazza della Signoria

Map p. 88

Bus: B or 23

Originally the area had been close to the ancient heart of the Roman city: An old theater and *terme* (bath complex) were nearby, and on the piazza's southern (riverside) flank stood a *fullonica*, a colossal Roman building used to dye and manufacture textiles. All three structures, plus a church—San Romoloa—a loggia, and a huge fifth-century early Christian basilica, were lost, buried, or pilfered for stone over the centuries.

The origins of the piazza itself are encrusted with myth. The area is said to have belonged to the Uberti family, the leading lights of one of Florence's many opposing Guelph and Ghibelline factions (see p. 26). When the family was humbled in 1268, its land was confiscated and its property razed. In time, much of the area was also paved, reputedly to prevent the Uberti from ever building on their former domain. This land was then

concentrated on the Palazzo dei Priori and Loggia della Signoria. Contemporary reports spoke of the area as little more than a rubble-filled building site, and it was 1385 before the square received its first proper layer of protective paving. The piazza suffered further alterations after 1560, when Cosimo I made extravagant changes to the Uffizi, and again in 1871, when the medieval Loggia dei Pisani was demolished to open up the square to the west. Its indignities continued as late as the 1980s, when controversial archaeological excavations led to the removal of the original medieval paving stones. Many of the stones subsequently "disappeared," probably having been sold illegally to pave the drives of various villas in the Tuscan countryside.

THE STATUES

The square's most eye-catching features today—the Palazzo Vecchio aside—are its statues and the Loggia della Signoria. From left to right as you face the Palazzo Vecchio, the statues stand ranged across the piazza's eastern flank. The work on the extreme left is an equestrian monument (1594–98) to the Medici duke Cosimo I by Giambologna. It was designed to recall the famous first century A.D. Roman equestrian statue of the Emperor Marcus Aurelius in Rome. In doing so, it drew parallels between Cosimo and the emperor, and aimed to link the glory of ancient Rome with that of 16th-century Florence. The three reliefs at the statue's base commemorate key events in Cosimo's career: the Florentine senate's granting him the Florentine dukedom (in 1537); his entering the conquered city of Siena (1555); and the acquisition of the title of Grand Duke of Tuscany from Pope Pius V (1569).

This copy of Michelangelo's "David" replaces the original statue (now in the Galleria dell' Accademia), which stood in the Piazza della Signoria for over 350 years until moved in 1873.

considered tainted—one reason, supposedly, why it remained undeveloped and why the piazza today has such an unusual and asymmetrical shape.

In truth, the piazza's shape is probably a result of the piecemeal manner in which it evolved. Work on the square proper began in 1307, when the city set aside a small area for the Palazzo dei Priori, a civic council chamber that in time grew into the present Palazzo Vecchio. The choice of site—close to, and on a line with, Piazza del Duomo—was deliberate. Today, this original square corresponds to the open tract immediately north of the Palazzo Vecchio.

Work on the square was largely abandoned later in the 14th century, when the city's efforts were

Giambologna's "Rape of the Sabine Women" in the Loggia della Signoria. Despite its title, the work was originally intended as a study of old age, male strength, and female beauty.

Cosimo appears again as the figure of Neptune in the next statue, the "Fontana del Nettuno," or "Neptune Fountain" (1563–1575). The work of Bartolommeo Ammannati and assistants (including Giambologna), it was ridiculed by Michelangelo, who wrote: *"Ammannato [sic], Ammannato, che bel marmo hai rovinato"* (Ammannato, Ammannato, what a beautiful piece of marble you have ruined). Florentines refer to the work as "Il Biancone," or "The White Giant," and claim it wanders around the piazza when struck by the light of a full moon. Look for the stone inscription on the ground in front of the statue, the spot where Girolamo Savonarola and two fellow Dominican monks were burned for heresy on May 23, 1498 (see p. 33).

Next comes Donatello's statue of the "Marzocco" (1418–1420), a copy of the one now in the Bargello (see p. 84). The Marzocco, or lion, was Florence's traditional heraldic symbol and can be seen in many Tuscan towns conquered by the city after the 13th century. Captured prisoners were traditionally obliged to kiss its posterior. Its form may be based on a battered equestrian statue of Mars *(Martocus)* that stood by the Ponte Vecchio until a flood in 1333. Alternatively, it may derive from the lions kept in the dungeons behind the Palazzo Vecchio, whose behavior was watched for auguries in times of crisis (the street behind the palace is still called Via dei Leoni, or Street of the Lions). Donatello's statue was originally carved for a papal apartment in the church of Santa Maria Novella and moved to the piazza in 1812.

Beside the "Marzocco," to the right, stands Donatello's electrifying "Judith and Holofernes," another copy of an original statue now in the Palazzo Vecchio's Sala dei Gigli (see p. 95). It was uprooted from the Palazzo Medici-Riccardi in 1495, after the Medici's temporary removal from power, and later erected in the piazza as a monument to the overthrow of tyranny. To its right rises "David," a copy of Michelangelo's sculpture in the Galleria dell' Accademia (see pp. 138–40). It stands on the spot occupied by the original statue until 1873.

Nearby are the figures of "Hercules and Cacus," carved by Baccio Bandinelli (1488–1560) as a companion piece for the "David." While the "David" was commissioned by Florence's republican council to celebrate the (brief) defeat of the Medici, among others, Bandinelli's statue was commissioned by the Medici to celebrate the defeat of their enemies; it was also a riposte to Michelangelo's "republican" masterpiece. For once the Medici were outclassed, for Bandinelli's work was ridiculed from the moment it was unveiled. One fellow sculptor, Benvenuto Cellini, described the muscle-bound figures as resembling "a sackful of melons." What is more tantalizing, the piece of marble had originally been offered to Michelangelo.

LOGGIA DELLA SIGNORIA

You should now ignore the Palazzo Vecchio and Uffizi—at least for the time being—and stroll around the Loggia della Signoria on Piazza della Signoria's eastern side. The triple-arched space was begun in 1376, possibly with a design by the artist Jacopo di Cione (active 1365–1398), to protect city officials from the weather during Florence's numerous public ceremonies. Craftsmen were called away from their work on the city's cathedral to build the loggia, hence the similarity between its arched interior and the cathedral's soaring vaults. In time the loggia was also used to greet visiting foreign dignitaries and as a shelter for the Swiss lancers *(lanzi)* of Cosimo I's guard; its alternative name is the Loggia dei Lanzi. Today it is a small outdoor museum for two major and several minor pieces of sculpture.

The most famous work is Benvenuto Cellini's "Perseus," one of Europe's most distinguished bronze statues. It shows the mythical Greek hero, the son of Zeus and Danae, holding the severed and snake-covered head of Medusa, whose gaze was said to turn humans to stone. The statue took almost ten years to complete (1545–1553), the size and difficulty of casting so huge a figure having resulted in countless false starts. Cellini, a larger-than-life figure,

described in his *Autobiography* of 1554 how the furnaces melting the bronze for the statue became so hot they set fire to his house. As the inferno raged, Cellini and his assistants hurled all available metal in the house into the melt—including the cutlery and family pewter. When the bronze cooled, the statue was revealed as complete—a feat many had said was impossible—save for three toes on the right foot, which were added later.

To Perseus's right stands Giambologna's "Rape of the Sabine Women" (1583), a virtuoso work carved from a single piece of flawed marble—the largest piece of stone ever brought to Florence. Despite the statue's title, it was originally intended as a study of old age, male strength, and female beauty. ■

Donatello executed "Marzocco," Florence's traditional heraldic symbol, in stone. This copy stands outside the Palazzo Vecchio.

Palazzo Vecchio

Palazzo Vecchio

- ▲ Map p. 88
- ✉ Piazza della Signoria
- ☎ 055 276 8465
- ⏰ Closed Sun. p.m. & all Thurs.
- $ $$

The central fountain of the Palazzo Vecchio's courtyard, dating from 1565, replaced a well that provided the palace with water.

THE PALAZZO VECCHIO HAS DOMINATED PIAZZA DELLA Signoria for centuries, work having started on the building in 1299, probably to a design by the cathedral's architect, Arnolfo di Cambio. Initially it housed the Priori, or Signoria, the city's ruling council, but in 1540 it became home to Cosimo I. Cosimo remained in residence just nine years before moving to the Palazzo Pitti, the point at which his "old" *(vecchio)* palace acquired its present name.

Today the palazzo once again houses the city's council, although much of its interior is also open to the public. You enter the complex via an inner **courtyard**, designed by Michelozzo in 1453 and delightfully decorated by Giorgio Vasari on the occasion of the marriage of Francesco de' Medici (first-born son of Cosimo I) to Johanna of Austria in 1565. The bride's country of origin accounts for the paintings, which portray a series of towns and cities controlled by the Austro-Habsburg empire. The central **fountain** was added at the same time and features a *putto* (cherub)

and dolphin by Andrea del Verrocchio, the teacher of Leonardo da Vinci. It was removed from the garden of the Medici villa at Careggi outside Florence. The present works are copies; the originals are inside the palace on the Terrazza di Giunone.

The precise route for visitors to reach the upper floors varies, but in an ideal world you should try to climb Vasari's magnificent main staircase to the **Salone dei Cinquecento,** or Room of the Five Hundred. This vast hall is the palace's centerpiece and was designed to accommodate the members of the Consiglio Maggiore, the republic's ruling assembly. Vasari was responsible for its 39 ceiling paintings, which depict the "Apotheosis of Cosimo I," and for the bombastic wall paintings, which illustrate various Florentine military triumphs.

Of greater artistic interest is Michelangelo's statue of "Victory" (1533–34) on the wall almost opposite the room's entrance. Originally conceived as a female figure, it depicts the figure of Genius slaying Reason. The sculptor's nephew gave it to the Medici, who had Vasari install it here in 1565 to commemorate Cosimo I's victory over Siena a decade earlier. On the opposite (entrance door) wall stands a model for Giambologna's "Virtue Overcoming Vice," commissioned as a companion piece for the "Victory." The room's other statues

depict the "Labors of Hercules" and are masterpieces by an otherwise obscure sculptor, Vincenzo de' Rossi (1525–1587). Before leaving the Salone don't miss the tiny **Studiolo di Francesco I**, a study created for Cosimo I's son and adorned with the decorative efforts of more than 30 artists. With your back to the Salone's entrance door, it lies off the end of the room to your right.

Climb the stairs from the other side of the Salone and turn left and you come to a suite of rooms, the Quartiere degli Elementi, which leads to the Terrazzo del Saturno, a belvedere, for some charming city views. Turn right on the same staircase and you can look down on the Salone before coming to the Quartiere di Eleonora, the apartments of Cosimo I's wife. The highlight of these rooms is the tiny **Cappella di Eleonora**, a sumptuously decorated chapel by the mannerist artist Agnolo Bronzino (1503–1572).

Among the following rooms, the **Sala dell'Udienza** has good views over the Piazza della Signoria and a glorious ceiling by Giuliano da Maiano (1432–1490), who was also responsible, with his brother, for the carved doorway into the neighboring **Sala dei Gigli.** Named after its decorative lilies (*gigli*), this room features another fine Maiano ceiling, a fresco sequence depicting "Saints Zenobius, Stephen and Lawrence" by Domenico Ghirlandaio (1448–1494), and the original of Donatello's powerful statue of "Judith and Holofernes" (see p. 92) from Piazza della Signoria. The next-door Cancelleria room was once Machiavelli's office, and the Sala delle Carte next door, now filled with lovely 16th-century maps, once housed Cosimo I's state costumes. ■

Galleria degli Uffizi

THE GALLERIA DEGLI UFFIZI—MORE COMMONLY KNOWN as the Uffizi—is one of the world's greatest art galleries, home to a collection of Renaissance and other paintings that contains the most hallowed names in Italian and European art of the last eight hundred years. Its collection of Renaissance masterpieces is unequaled, but the huge gallery also features paintings from Italy's medieval, mannerist, and baroque heydays, as well as outstanding works of art from famous artists of Holland, Spain, and Germany.

The Uffizi draws huge numbers of visitors. You can beat the lines by telephoning to prebook your entry time.

treasures can only touch on its highlights. Around 2,000 works can be admired at any one time, with another 1,800 kept in storage. Given the scale of the gallery, it can be a good idea to consider making two visits: One to take in the first 15 rooms, which contain the masterpieces of the Florentine Renaissance, and another to revel in the works of other Italian and foreign artists arranged in the remaining 30 rooms. Steel yourself for the possibility you will have to wait in line at almost any time of the day and in any season, though note that tickets guaranteeing entry at an allotted time can generally be arranged in advance (see p. 101).

A medley of sculptures and frescoes of "Famous Men" (1450) by Andrea del Castagno make up the Uffizi's prelude: Only with three paintings of the "Maestà," or "Madonna Enthroned," in the **second major room** does the gallery get into its stride. Italy's three most eminent 13th-century artists—Giotto, Cimabue, and Duccio—were responsible for this trio of seminal paintings. Each artist orchestrated moves toward more realism in paintings and away from the stylization of Byzantine art, which had dominated Italian and other art for centuries.

This sense of transition can be seen in the manner in which the saints in Cimabue's painting of about 1275-1280 are ranged around

Galleria degli Uffizi

- Map p. 88
- Loggiata degli Uffizi 6, off Piazza della Signoria
- 055 238 8651
- Closed Mon.
- $$$
- Bus: B, 23

Opposite: Part of "La Primavera" by Sandro Botticelli, one of the most famous of the Uffizi's countless Renaissance masterpieces

Florence can thank the Medici for the Uffizi. The austere palace that contains the collection was built in 1560 as a rambling collection of offices *(uffizi)* for Grand Duke Cosimo I. The collection itself, gathered together by the family over the centuries, was left to the city—on condition that it was never moved from Florence—by Anna Maria Luisa, sister of the last Grand Duke, Gian Gastone Medici. Sculpture from the collection was later moved to the Bargello, while Etruscan and other antique art went to the Museo Archeologico. The paintings—which in their day were considered less important than the sculpture—passed to the Uffizi and Palazzo Pitti.

The gallery has more than 45 rooms, and any brief account of its

shade are used to suggest the falling drapery. Duccio's painting also has a softer line and gentler and more realistic coloring.

But where Cimabue and Duccio struggled with half-realized innovation, Giotto's advances were marked and decisive. His "Maestà" —painted in 1310 for the church of Ognissanti (see p. 166)—retained some of the conventions of the Byzantine Madonna and Child. These included the gold background, Christ's hand raised in blessing, and the manner in which the Virgin points to the Child with her right hand. Giotto subtly subverted conventions, however, so that in the Virgin's gesture, for example, the pointed hand is turned into a hand resting on the Child's knee, a gesture of genuine human emotion missing from most earlier representations. In the same vein, the Virgin is portrayed for almost the first time as a real woman. There is, for example, the suggestion of breasts beneath her robes. Giotto's innovations also extend to the onlookers, who gaze with genuine eye-contact and expression at the Holy Family. They also wear robes—as do the Madonna and Child—that are painted with a more realistic folding and use of light and shade.

The painting's iconoclasm and realism also extend to its composition: The Madonna and her throne have solidity and depth; the surrounding saints and angels are standing on solid ground in a real three-dimensional space; and the pointed throne and three-point axis of angels and Madonna create a powerful pyramidal effect. This triangular compositional model would be emulated by other painters for centuries.

That Giotto's lessons were not universally heeded is clear from the paintings of Italy's Gothic masters

the Virgin's throne. Cimabue's saints and angels stand in fixed and more realistic positions, while those of Duccio (painted about 1285), a painter more wedded to Byzantine tradition, seem to float haphazardly. And where Byzantine paintings were invariably "flat," Cimabue introduces hints of perspective to create a sense of space and depth.

At the same time, Cimabue's statuelike Virgin is still the aloof, detached Virgin of the Byzantine icon, while his Christ sports the harsh and unrealistic garb of a Roman general. Cimabue also uses gold to pick out the folds of the Virgin's cloak—very much a Byzantine device. Duccio's Virgin is equally aloof, but her throne is more realistically painted, as are the folds of her cloak, where light and in **Rooms 3** to **6,** beginning with works from Siena, where painters continued to borrow heavily from the fading conventions of Byzantine art. Finest of all are Simone Martini's (circa 1285–1344) exquisite "Annunciation" and the works by Pietro and Ambrogio Lorenzetti (active 1319–1348), two brothers who both probably died during the plague epidemic that swept Italy in 1348. Almost as beautiful are the exponents of the so-called International Gothic, a detailed and courtly style exemplified by the rapturous "Adoration of the Magi" by Gentile da Fabriano (1370–1427) and the lyrical "Coronation of the Virgin" by Lorenzo Monaco (active 1388–1422). These paintings have the detail of tapestry and also the escapist and ethereal beauty of fairy tale, with little of the realism that would be associated with Renaissance art.

The first flowering of this style is seen in **Room 7,** which presents works by early Renaissance iconoclasts such as Masaccio, Masolino (1383–circa 1447), and Fra Angelico (circa 1400–1455). One of the most eye-catching works is Paolo Uccello's "Battle of San Romano" (1435 or 1456) (see pp. 40-41), painted to recall the Florentines' victory over the combined armies of Milan and Siena in 1432. Uccello was concerned with the newly discovered rules of perspective to the point of obsession, a trait seen here in the almost surreal labyrinth of lances and horses disappearing to a single, central vanishing point. The painting adorned the bedroom of Lorenzo the Magnificent, along with two sister panels now in the Louvre in Paris and London's National Gallery.

Room 7 also features a painting of the "Sacra Conversazione"

(1445), or "Sacred Conversation," by one of the rarest of Italian painters, Venice-born Domenico Veneziano (died 1461), an artist with only 12 confidently attributed paintings to his name. Nearby hang two well-known works by one of Veneziano's pupils, Piero della Francesca (1410/20–1492)—portraits of Federico da Montefeltro, Duke of Urbino, and his wife, Battista Sforza. Federico was always portrayed in left profile, as here, after a jousting accident disfigured the right side of his face. Battista was depicted against a background that includes the town of Gubbio in Umbria, where she died after giving birth to her ninth child and first son. The portrait was completed two years after her death. Both pictures show the Renaissance in full

The "Maestà," or "Madonna Enthroned," by the Sienese artist Duccio is one of three similar works that open the Uffizi's magnificent collection of paintings.

and "La Nascita di Venere," or "The Birth of Venus" (1485), both by Botticelli (1445–1510). The latter, the "girl in a half shell," was the first pagan nude of the Renaissance and, like "La Primavera," drew heavily on classical myth and contemporary humanist scholarship. Significantly, neither of these paintings contains the religious content that had infused Western art for about a thousand years. According to the myth on which Botticelli drew, Venus was conceived by the ocean following the castration of Uranus and then rose from the sea, the tale suggesting beauty (Venus) was the result of a union between the physical and spiritual (Uranus). In the myth—and in the painting—the nymph Chloris and Zephyr, the god of wind, blow the risen Venus to the shore, where she is cloaked by the figure of Hora.

The theme of "La Primavera" is more uncertain. The name was actually chosen arbitrarily years later by the critic and painter Giorgio Vasari. Some critics suggest the work is an allegory of spring or all four seasons, others say it represents the Triumph of Venus, the attendant figures of the Graces in the painting representing her beauty, Flora her fecundity. What is certain is that the central figure is again Venus, goddess of spring and love, with her son, Cupid, depicted above her head. To the left, Mercury wards off the clouds of winter with his staff, while on the right you see the transformation of Chloris, after her rape by Zephyr, into the goddess Flora (shown scattering flowers). Other scholars have suggested the painting embodies the philosophy of the time as it related to love and beauty: Spring becomes the spur to awakening human emotions and desires, and Zephyr drives away the clouds of melancholy so that these desires may evolve unim-

The "Madonna and Child with Two Angels" was painted by Filippo Lippi, whose work influenced artists such as Botticelli and Leonardo da Vinci.

flower, as becomes clear when you compare Piero's careful attention here to perspective, landscape, and detail—the jewelry, the wrinkles on the skin—with the paintings you've seen in earlier rooms. Battista's high, shaved forehead was a fashionable affectation of the time; in **Room 8,** it is shown on the Virgin in the painting by Filippo Lippi (1406–1469) of the "Madonna and Child with Two Angels." Lippi was the teacher of Sandro Botticelli (see below). He was also a monk by upbringing but something of a wanton by nature: Seduced nuns were among his models.

Rooms 10 to **14** are likely to be the Uffizi's most crowded, for these are the rooms given over to the gallery's most famous paintings: "La Primavera," or "Spring" (1478),

peded. Zephyr, Chloris, and Flora may also symbolize the trinity of lust, chastity, and beauty.

Whatever the paintings' precise meaning, the classical myth of their inspiration and their human-centered nature are unmistakable. As such, they contrast strongly with another famous painting in the room, the "Portinari Triptych" (1475–1480), commissioned by Tommaso Portinari, a manager of the Medici bank in Bruges (in today's Belgium), painted by the Flemish artist Hugo van der Goes (active 1467–1482). It created a

In "The Birth of Venus" by Sandro Botticelli, the male figure on the left is Zephyr, god of the west wind. The figure on the right portrays Hora, the daughter and attendant of Aurora, goddess of dawn.

Advance tickets

Lines for many museums in Florence are horrendously long most of the year and at almost any time of the day. To reserve tickets for the state museums and skip the lines, telephone 055 294 883 between 8:30 a.m. and 6:30 p.m. Monday to Friday (Saturday 8:30 a.m.–12:30 p.m.). Most staff speak English, but telephone lines are frequently busy for long periods. If spaces are available, you will receive a reservation number for the day and time of your visit. Tickets are held at meeting points for each museum. Pick them up at the allotted time and then enter the gallery directly. A small reservation fee ($) is charged over and above the cost of normal admittance. ■

The "Madonna and Child with Angels" by Parmigianino is remarkable for the deliberately lengthened figure of Christ and the elongated neck and fingers of the Virgin.

Opposite: The "Medici Venus," a 1st-century copy of a Greek original, is considered one of the most erotic statues of the ancient world.

sensation when it arrived in Florence, where its use of light and background detail proved hugely influential. Although completed just before Botticelli's paintings, it was still almost entirely religious in inspiration and content. A nude along the lines of the Venus on the half shell would then have been unthinkable in a northern European context, a measure of the advances being made in Florentine art of the time.

The speed and development of these advances is borne out in the following rooms. **Room 15** contains two of only a handful of paintings existing in Florence attributed to Leonardo da Vinci: "Annunciation," painted when the artist was just 20, and the "Adoration of the Magi." Note how

Leonardo omits many of the traditional elements of the "Adoration" theme—the stable, Joseph, and the Three Kings—in order to focus attention on the Madonna and Child. As an 18-year-old, Leonardo also painted the angel on the left of Verrocchio's nearby "Baptism of Christ" (about 1475). Verrocchio, who was Leonardo's teacher, confessed he could never paint anything as beautiful. Looking at his own inferior angel—with its bony head and short hair—you can understand his lament. Leonardo's paintings also overshadow pictures elsewhere in the room, notably those of Luca Signorelli (1441–1523) from Tuscany and Perugino (1445/50–1523), the greatest of Umbria's Renaissance artists.

The octagonal **Tribune** (Room 18) marks a point of transition between the largely Italian pre-Renaissance and Renaissance painting you have already seen and the later and more widely sourced art that follows. The room was specially built by the Medici to house their most precious works of art, among which the "Medici Venus," a Roman statue, figured large. Widely celebrated as Europe's most erotic statue—the English poet Lord Byron stood before it "dazzled and drunk with beauty"—the figure was the only Florentine statue removed to France by Napoleon after his invasion of Italy. This room is also the only one in the gallery to retain the arrangement originally devised for all the Uffizi's rooms, which was to contrast the art of the ancient world—represented by Roman and Greek statues from the Medici collection (now mostly removed to the Bargello)—by placing it alongside the "modern" art of painting, as exemplified by the masterpieces of Renaissance Italy.

The outstanding work in the six rooms devoted to Florentine, Venetian, German, and Flemish canvases is the "Sacred Allegory" in **Room 21** by Giovanni Bellini (1430/40–1516), arguably the finest of all Venetian painters. In **Room 25,** well over halfway around the gallery, you come to the Uffizi's only painting by Michelangelo: the "Holy Family" or "Doni Tondo" (1504), painted on the occasion of the marriage of local aristocrats, Angelo Doni and Maddalena Strozzi (or possibly on the birth of their first child). It was painted around the time the artist was working on his statue of "David," a project with which he was far more enamored. Easel painting, as opposed to fresco or sculpture, he considered a chore, and this is the only such painting he brought close to completion. Little of the content is understood, but the pagan nudes to the rear of the painting and the wall—a symbol of exclusion—may be intended to suggest the exclusion of the pagan world from Christian salvation. Notice the unorthodox and original way Joseph is shown handing the Christ Child to the Virgin. The complex over-the-shoulder maneuver, among other things, allowed Michelangelo to indulge in twisted compositions and almost sculptural contortions that challenged his virtuosity.

The painting's deliberately obscure meaning, contorted com-position, and often bright coloring profoundly influenced a style of painting known as mannerism, a genre whose leading lights are represented in the next four rooms. Look in particular for "Supper at Emmaus" by Jacopo Pontormo (1494–1557) in **Room 27** and "Madonna and Child with Angels" by Parmigianino (1503–1540), the latter famous for the Virgin's pecu-liarly elongated neck **(Room 29).**

Another late Renaissance painter who significantly influenced the mannerists was Raphael, the cream of whose Uffizi paintings are found in **Room 26.** The most notable are the "Madonna of the Goldfinch" and unflinching portraits of the Medici pope, Leo X, and cardinals Giulio de' Medici and Luigi de' Rossi. Raphael also influenced Titian (1487–1576), whose infamous "Venus of Urbino" (1538), one of the most explicit nudes in Western art, was described by Mark Twain as "the foulest, the vilest, the obscenest picture the world possesses."

Rooms 30 to **35** deal largely in paintings by artists from areas of northern Italy, notably Venice and Emilia-Romagna, though it might be as well to hurry past these and save some energy for the exceptional works in the gallery's final rooms. **Room 41** is dominated by Van Dyck (1599–1641) and Rubens (1577–1640), and in particular the paintings commissioned from Rubens following the marriage of King Henry IV of France (R.1589–1610) to Maria de' Medici (1573–1642). Caravaggio (1573–1610) flies the flag for Italy in **Room 43,** his bold drama in marked contrast to two introspective self-portraits by Rembrandt (1606–1669) in the next room. ■

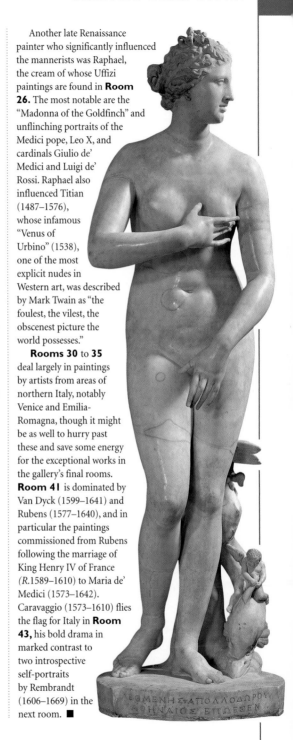

Orsanmichele

A detail from the tabernacle by Andrea Orcagna in Orsanmichele. The relief depicts the "Assumption of the Virgin."

ORSANMICHELE, A GAUNT AND FORTRESS-LIKE MEDIEVAL church, stands incongruously amid the hurly-burly of Via dei Calzaiuoli. Its name comes from a corruption of San Michele ad Hortum, an oratory that once stood in the garden—Latin *hortum* or Italian *orto*—of a Benedictine abbey. Today, the church is celebrated for its tabernacle and remarkable collection of exterior sculptures.

Orsanmichele
- Map p. 88
- Via dell'Arte della Lana
- 055 284 944
- Church: closed Sun. a.m. & daily L for 3–4 hours. Museum: open for once-hourly guided tours a.m. except 1st & last Mon. of the month
- Bus: A or services to Piazza del Duomo

A market for selling grain replaced the original abbey oratory here around 1290. Despite the building's secular use, remnants of the site's religious past clung to it thanks to a revered image of the Virgin painted on one of its pillars, a picture believed to possess miraculous powers. Over the next hundred years the building was reshaped several times. By 1380 its lower half was once again a church—more or less the building you see today—while its upper portions were used as a granary.

The city's guilds were entrusted with adorning the building in 1339. Each of its exterior niches was in the care of a particular guild, which in turn was responsible for commissioning artists to create a statue of the guild's patron saint for individual niches. The guilds cannot have been keen, for only one statue proved forthcoming—a figure of the Arte della Lana's "St. Stephen."

With hindsight, it's easy to see how the 70-year hiatus worked to posterity's advantage. Instead of being produced at a time when Florentine sculpture was in a period of relative decline, the statues were actually created on the cusp of the Renaissance. As a result, some of the most distinguished artists of the period labored on the project, among them Donatello, Verrocchio, Michelozzo, and Ghiberti.

There are 14 statues in all, although some of the present works are copies, the originals having been moved for safety to the Bargello, Museo dell'Opera del

Duomo, and elsewhere. Starting on Via dei Calzaiuoli, where there are three statues, the key works are those on the left and in the center as you face the church: The former portrays "John the Baptist" (1412–1416) and was produced by Lorenzo Ghiberti for the Arte di Calimala (Textile Guild). The guild was convinced so large a bronze could not be cast and made Lorenzo responsible for the huge cost of the materials should he fail. He didn't—only one toe was missing when the casting was revealed. To the right stands Verrocchio's "St. Thomas" (1473–1483), created for the Mercatanzia (Merchant's Tribunal). Its niche is the work of Donatello and Michelozzo. Donatello was also responsible for the figure of "St. George" (1416–17) on the Via Orsanmichele flank of the church. The present statue is a copy, but the original is one of the stars of the Bargello (see pp. 83–84).

Inside, the church provides a restful retreat from the crowds on Via dei Calzaiuoli. Patches of frescoes appear around the walls as your eyes become accustomed to the gloom, most of them images of the guilds' patron saints, pictorial equivalents of the statues outside. To the rear stands a magnificent **tabernacle** by Andrea Orcagna (1308–1368), built partly to house a painting of the "Madonna and Child" (1347) by Bernardo Daddi, a work said to have inherited the miraculous powers of the Virgin on the pillar, which had been destroyed in a fire. The greatest work of its kind in Italy, the tabernacle was financed by votive offerings prompted by the Black Death of 1348. So great was the income from these offerings that it exceeded the city's annual tax revenues. Orcagna, for his part, has few surviving works, although he was perhaps the most important artist, sculptor, and

architect to work in the period following Giotto's death.

The church's upper levels house rooms reached by a small bridge from the neighboring **Palazzo dell'Arte della Lana,** whose museum contains some of the original statues from the exterior of Orsanmichele. ∎

Donatello's "St. George" is one of the statues made for the exterior of Orsanmichele. The original is now in the Bargello.

A walk from Piazza della Signoria to Sant'Ambrogio

This route provides an opportunity to see the many faces of Florence, from the grandeur of the medieval city to the sights and sounds of the markets and cafés around Sant'Ambrogio.

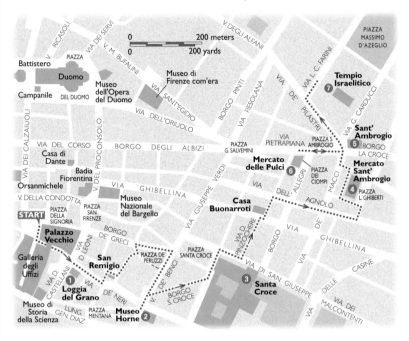

As you face the Palazzo Vecchio, take Via della Ninna to its right. At the end of the street you come to Via dei Leoni, named after the lions *(leoni)* that were once kept in dungeons at the rear of the Palazzo Vecchio. Continue on to Via de' Neri. Immediately on your right is the **Loggia del Grano ❶**, commissioned by Cosimo II in 1619 and the last of a series of loggias designed to be used as markets; the others were the Loggia del Mercato and Loggia del Pesce (see p. 107).

Via de' Neri takes you into one of Florence's best-preserved medieval quarters. Several houses and palaces here date from at least the 14th century, notably Palazzo Bagnesi (No. 25), Palazzo Grifoni (No. 6), and Palazzo Nori (No. 4). At the junction with Via della Mosca, turn left and you come to a square containing the 11th-century church of **San**

▲ Also see area map, pp. 88–89
▶ Piazza della Signoria
⟳ 1.75 miles (2.8 km)
⊕ 2 hours
▶ Piazza Sant'Ambrogio. Walk or take bus A from Borgo La Croce back to the center of Florence.

NOT TO BE MISSED
- Santa Croce
- Sant'Ambrogio

Remigio, whose interior is tinged with traces of 14th-century frescoes. Then walk to the left of the church, turn left on Via de' Rustici, and bear left along Via dei Bentacordi to Borgo de' Greci. Turn right to Via de' Benci and walk

Florentine superstition claims that the central figures of the Fontana di Nettuno in Piazza della Signoria prowl the square when struck by the light of the full moon.

south to Borgo Santa Croce, perhaps first visiting the nearby **Museo Horne** ❷ (see p. 117). Midway along Borgo Santa Croce you pass three notable buildings on the right: The late 15th-century **Palazzo Antinori Corsini** (No. 6), which belonged to two powerful noble families; the **Casa di Giorgio Vasari**, home of the 16th-century painter and art historian (No. 8); and **Palazzo Spinelli** (No. 10), built in 1460 and notable for the painted "graffito" decoration of its facade and courtyard. Similar decoration adorns the **Palazzo Morelli** at No. 19.

At the end of Borgo Santa Croce you come to Piazza Santa Croce and the church of **Santa Croce** ❸ (see pp. 108–115). Note **Palazzo dell'Antella** halfway down the piazza on the south side (Nos. 20–22), notable for its exterior frescoes (1619) of the "Virtues and Divinities," completed by 12 artists in just 20 days. Follow Largo Piero Bargellini to the left of Santa Croce and take the first left, Via delle Pinzochere. From here you enter one of Florence's traditional blue-collar districts, whose character is best enjoyed in the **Mercato Sant'Ambrogio** ❹ (Closed Mon.–Sat. p.m. & all Sun.), a food market reached by turning right off Via M. Buonarroti

(the northern continuation of Via delle Pinzochere) onto Via dell' Agnolo. You may like to visit the **Casa Buonarroti** (see p. 116) on Via Ghibellina.

On the northwest edge of the market square, at the corner of Via de' Macci, is the Cibreo restaurant and café (see p. 309). Turn right (north) on Via de' Macci and you will reach the church of **Sant'Ambrogio** ❺ (see p. 118) at the junction of Borgo La Croce and Via Pietrapiana. Turn left on Via Pietrapiana and you quickly come to Piazza dei Ciompi, site of the Loggia del Pesce (old fish market) and the **Mercato delle Pulci** ❻, Florence's flea market (Open Tues.–Sat. & 1st Sun. of the month).

Return to Sant'Ambrogio and turn left on Via de' Pilastri in front of the church, and then take the second right on Via L. C. Farini. Here you'll find the **Tempio Israelitico** ❼, or Jewish Synagogue (Via L. C. Farini 4, tel 055 245 252, closed Fri. p.m., & all Sat. Oct.–March), a Spanish-Moorish style building constructed in 1882 after the old Jewish quarter of the city was redeveloped in the 1860s to make way for Piazza della Repubblica. Its small museum has ritual and other artifacts (Closed Fri. p.m., & all Sat.). ■

Santa Croce

SANTA CROCE IS FLORENCE'S MOST MAJESTIC CHURCH. Its importance stems not only from its art—it contains sublime fresco cycles by Giotto and other medieval masters—but also from its status as the burial place of Galileo, Michelangelo, Machiavelli, and around 270 of the city's eminent citizens. In the Cappella dei Pazzi, it has one of the most perfect early Renaissance buildings.

Santa Croce
- Map p. 88
- Piazza Santa Croce
- ☎ 055 244 619
- Closed Sun. a.m. & 2 hours daily L Nov.–March
- Bus: 23

Museo dell'Opera di Santa Croce & Cappella dei Pazzi
- Piazza Santa Croce 16
- ☎ 055 244 619
- Closed Wed.
- $ $
- Bus: 23

**Opposite:
Michelangelo was laid to rest in this tomb in Florence despite spending most of the last 25 years of his life in Rome.**

Santa Croce was built for the Franciscans. Its design has been attributed to Arnolfo di Cambio, the architect also largely responsible for Florence's cathedral and Palazzo Vecchio. It was started around 1294, partly to overshadow Santa Maria Novella—then being built across the city—the mother church of the city's Dominicans. Work was completed in 1385 but the church was only consecrated in 1443. Do not be fooled by the facade; it is not original but was added in mock-Gothic style between 1853 and 1863. Its architect claimed to have discovered long-lost plans for an earlier medieval facade. In truth, he simply adapted his design from the great tabernacle in Orsanmichele (see pp. 104–105).

The Francisans and others spent colossal sums on the church, despite the order's supposed vows of poverty. Much of the funding came from prosperous Florentines, many of whom considered it an act of humility to associate themselves with, and be interred among, the humble Franciscans. Wealthy bankers also viewed sponsorship of churches as a means by which they might be freed from the stigma associated with usury, or lending money with interest, then still considered a sin.

The riches lavished on Santa Croce explain the considerable majesty of its countless chapels, most of which were named after the men that paid for their adornment. They also account for the splendor

of its numerous tombs, the first of which—Giorgio Vasari's monument to Michelangelo—you find almost immediately on entering the church's soaring interior (opposite the first pillar on the south, or right, wall), placed close to the church's entrance at Michelangelo's personal request. The reason for its location, so the story goes, is that the artist wished to see the dome of Florence's cathedral as his first waking sight on rising from his tomb on the Day of Judgment.

From here, the most satisfactory way of seeing the church is to follow the right (south) wall, look at the frescoed chapels at the top right of the church, cross in front of the high altar, and then work back down the left side of the nave. Start by walking to the first pillar close to Michelangelo's tomb to admire the lovely relief by Antonio Rossellino (1427–1479) of the "Madonna del Latte," or "Madonna of the Milk." To the left of Michelangelo's tomb stands a **Cenotaph to Dante.** This is not a tomb, as the poet is buried in Ravenna on Italy's east coast, where he died in exile in 1321 (see p. 78). Beyond this comes a noteworthy pulpit (1472–76) by Benedetto da Maiano (third pillar of the nave), and then Antonio Canova's (1757–1822) "Monument to Alfieri," an 18th-century Italian poet known as much for his romantic liaisons as his literary achievements. To the left is the **tomb of Machiavelli**, crafted in 1787, some two centuries after the

writer's death. It is unremarkable save for its famous inscription: *"Tanto nomini nullum par elogium"* (No praise can be high enough for so great a name.)

Beyond these tombs, and past a recessed and gilded stone relief of the "Annunciation" (1435) by Donatello, lie the tombs of the opera composer Gioacchino Rossini (1792–1868) and—to its right—that of the 15th-century humanist scholar Leonardo Bruni (1370–1444). This tomb was the work of Bernardo Rossellino (1409–1464), and it became one of the most influential of all early Renaissance funerary monuments, mainly because it was the first time a non-religious figure—as

opposed to the Madonna and Child—had dominated on a secular tomb. Among the works it influenced was the church's other great secular tomb, the 1453 monument by Desiderio da Settignano to Carlo Marsuppini (1399–1453), another humanist scholar. It lies across the nave almost opposite the Bruni tomb (see p. 114).

Opposite: The facade of Santa Croce was added to the church in the mid-1800s.

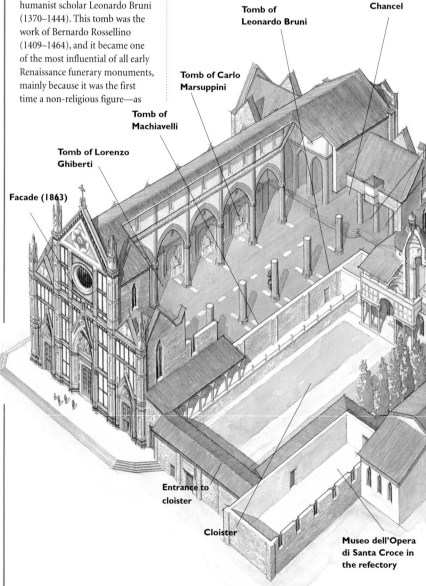

Tomb of Leonardo Bruni

Chancel

Tomb of Carlo Marsuppini

Tomb of Machiavelli

Tomb of Lorenzo Ghiberti

Facade (1863)

Entrance to cloister

Cloister

Museo dell'Opera di Santa Croce in the refectory

Patches of faded fresco adorn many of Santa Croce's walls, sharpening the appetite for the church's pictorial highlights, most of which are contained in the chapels ranged across the apse and chancel, the area at the "top" of the church around the high altar. The first chapel, on the right beyond Rossini's tomb, is the **Cappella**

Neo-gothic Campanile (1842)

Giotto frescoes

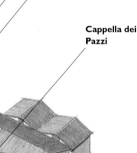

Cappella dei Pazzi

Key to floor plan

1 Tomb of Michelangelo
2 Cenotaph to Dante
3 Tomb of Machiavelli
4 Donatello "Annunciation"
5 Tomb of Leonardo Bruni
6 Tomb of Rossini
7 Cappella Castellani
8 Capella Baroncelli
9 Sacristy

10 Cappella Rinuccini
11 Capella Peruzzi
12 Capella Bardi
13 Chancel
14 Tomb of Galileo
15 Museo dell'Opera
16 Capella dei Pazzi

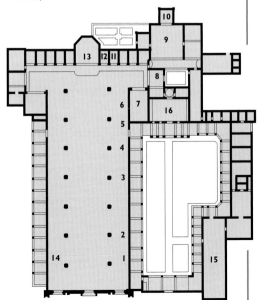

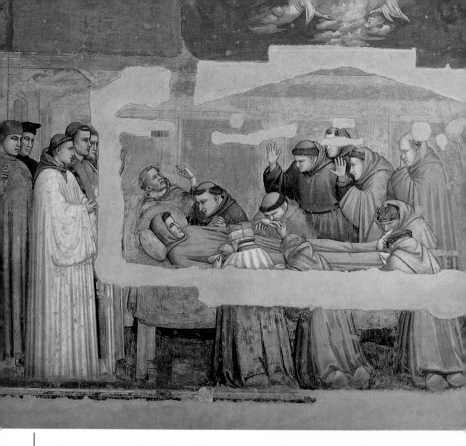

"The Death of St. Francis" is part of a fresco cycle by Giotto in the Cappella Bardi of Santa Croce.

Castellani, with paintings by Agnolo Gaddi (1333–1396) and assistants. The right wall as you face the chapel contains scenes from the lives of St. John the Baptist and St. Nicholas of Bari. Nicholas is, among other things, the patron saint of children and is the original Santa Claus. Here he is shown reviving three murdered boys and preventing girls without marriage dowries from falling into prostitution. On the left wall are scenes from the life of St. Antony Abbot, a theme often explored in Franciscan churches, as Antony gave away much of his wealth, making him particularly popular with the poverty-conscious Franciscans.

The adjoining chapel, the **Cappella Baroncelli,** was painted by Agnolo's father, Taddeo

(1300–1366), whose chosen theme was the "Life of the Virgin." Taddeo was a longtime pupil and assistant of Giotto, who was probably responsible for the chapel's altarpiece, the "Coronation of the Virgin." The corridor here leads to the **Cappella Medici** (usually closed) and a door that opens into the **sacristy,** a lovely room with a fine "Crucifixion" by Taddeo Gaddi and the small **Cappella Rinuccini** (behind a 1371 grille). The latter is smothered in frescoes on the life of the Virgin (on the left) and the life of St. Mary Magdalene (on the right) by Giovanni da Milano, an accomplished disciple of Giotto.

Giotto himself was responsible for the greatest of all Santa Croce's works of art: the **Cappella Bardi**

unable to believe the veracity of the saint's stigmata (the wounds of Christ, which Francis miraculously manifested). Michelangelo and Masaccio were just two of the later Renaissance artists who made a careful study of these frescoes.

Fresco cycles by artists influenced or taught by Giotto fill several nearby chapels. To the left of the Cappella Bardi, for example, the **chancel** area around the high altar is frescoed with the "Legend of the True Cross" (1380) by Agnolo Gaddi. The theme of the frescoes in this most important of positions (by the high altar) was determined by the name of the church—Santa

Monuments and tombs for some of Florence's most illustrious figures line the walls and chapels of Santa Croce's nave.

and **Cappella Peruzzi** (both 1320–25), two chapels in the main body of the church to the right of the high altar. In them, he frescoed scenes from the life of St. John the Baptist and the life of St. John the Evangelist (in the Peruzzi Chapel) and episodes from the life of St. Francis (in the Bardi Chapel). Notice, in particular, the extraordinary composition of the "Funeral of St. Francis" in the latter, celebrated for its remarkable horizontal emphasis; virtually all the figures are prostrate, mirroring the stretched body of the saint and a deliberate echo of the lamentation over the body of Christ. Further parallels with the story of Christ are underlined by the Doubting Thomas figure, who pokes a finger into the wound in Francis's side,

Lucca della Robbia designed the four tondi, or round reliefs, on the ceiling of the Cappella dei Pazzi. They portray the four Evangelists.

Croce, or Holy Cross. The story they tell is the same one as Piero della Francesca's better known cycle in Arezzo (see p. 285).

The **Cappella Bardi di Vernio,** the fifth chapel to the left of the high altar, has scenes from the life of St. Sylvester (1340) by Maso di Banco, one of Giotto's more innovative followers. Another Cappella Bardi to its left contains a wooden "Crucifix" (1412) by Donatello, a work reputedly dismissed by Brunelleschi as resembling "a peasant on the Cross."

From here, turn your back on the high altar and walk toward the church's entrance. The first major monument on your right (to the right of the side door) is the tomb of Carlo Marsuppini (1453) by Desiderio da Settignano, a major work heavily influenced by the Bruni tomb opposite (see p. 110). Farther down, on the wall almost opposite the nave's fourth pillar, is a "Pietà" (1560) by Agnolo Bronzino (1503–1572), a leading mannerist painter. To its left lies a pavement slab marking the tomb of Lorenzo Ghiberti, the sculptor responsible

for, among other things, the baptistery's hallowed east doors (see pp. 66–70). Way down near the entrance, opposite the nave's first left-hand pillar, is the tomb of the noted scientist, Galileo Galilei (1564–1642).

CAPPELLA DEI PAZZI

To the right of Santa Croce as you face the facade is the entrance to the church's cloister, now home to a small museum, the **Museo dell'Opera di Santa Croce.** Its highlights are Cimabue's celebrated late 13th-century "Crucifix," one of the principal artistic casualties of the 1966 flood; Donatello's gilded statue of "St. Louis of Toulouse" (1424), created for the church of Orsanmichele; a detached mid-15th century fresco of "St. John the Baptist and St. Francis" by Domenico Veneziano; and Taddeo Gaddi's huge composite fresco of the "Last Supper," "Tree of Life" (1333), and other scenes.

The museum ticket also grants you entry to the **Cappella dei Pazzi** at the top of the cloister, commissioned from Brunelleschi in 1429 as a chapter house and family mausoleum by Andrea de' Pazzi, a leading light of the banking dynasty that famously tried to topple the Medici in the abortive Pazzi Conspiracy of 1478 (see pp. 30–31). Brunelleschi labored on and off on the chapel until his death in 1446, but financial shortfalls meant the work was only completed in the 1470s. Completion coincided with the family's downfall, and none of the de' Pazzi's was ever interred in their chapel.

To the modern eye the chapel can appear austere, but to earlier sensibilities it represented one of the pinnacles of early Renaissance architecture. In particular, it is admired for the manner in which its decoration complements its

simple geometrical form. The decoration begins with a frieze of medallions and angels' heads above the porch, the work of Desiderio da Settignano. Luca della Robbia was responsible for the tondo of "St. Andrew," above the beautiful main door by Giuliano da Maiano (active 1350–1369), and for the colored lining of the portico's dome and the garland of fruit clasped around the Pazzi coat of arms.

If you have seen Brunelleschi's Sagrestia Vecchia in San Lorenzo (see pp. 122–27), you will recognize similarities with his work here. There are, for example, four similar tondi in the cupola, which represent the Evangelists, the work of Luca della Robbia and his workshop, possibly to designs by Donatello and Brunelleschi. Luca also produced the 12 tondi of the Apostles around the walls. ∎

The Cappella dei Pazzi appears simple, but it hides a complex architectural and decorative scheme.

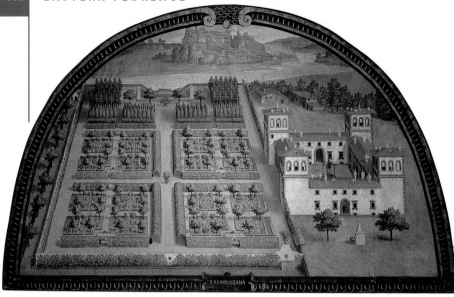

The house and garden of the Villa Ambrogiana, one of a series of frescoes in the Museo di Firenze com'era by Flemish artist Justus Utens that portrays villas owned by the Medici

More places to visit in eastern Florence

CASA BUONARROTI

The Casa Buonarroti stands on the site of a property once owned by Michelangelo Buonarroti, the full name of the artist more commonly known simply as Michelangelo. Today it houses a sleek, modern museum with a handful of minor works by Michelangelo, as well as a wide range of artifacts connected with, or created in honor of, the great man. A variety of beautifully furnished and decorated rooms provides the setting for the exhibits.

Admission to the museum is relatively expensive for what you can see. The two most important sculptures are in a room on the upper floor: The "Madonna della Scala" (1490–92) is Michelangelo's earliest known work, probably carved when he was little more than 16 years old. The accompanying "Battle of the Centaurs" was created a short time later, when the artist was apprenticed to the Medici household. In an adjacent room is a wooden model (1517) for Michelangelo's never-completed facade of San Lorenzo (see pp. 122–27). Nearby is a strange-looking wax-and-wood torso of a "River God" (1524), probably the model for a sculpture destined

for San Lorenzo's Medici chapels (see pp. 128–131). Another room features a small crucifix by Michelangelo from the church of Santo Spirito in the Oltrarno. A well-documented work, it was only found in 1963, having long been feared lost.

⚿ Map p. 88 ✉ Via Ghibellina 70 ☎ 055 241 752 🕐 Closed p.m. & all Tues. 💲 $$$ 🚍 Bus: 14 to Via Ghibellina

MUSEO DI FIRENZE COM'ERA

The Museum of Florence As It Was is one of the city's most charming small galleries, partly because of its contents and partly because of its setting in a pretty, garden-fronted former convent. Its wide-ranging exhibits—pictures, prints, engravings, maps, photographs, and topographical paintings—trace the festivals, history, and everyday life of Florence from about the 15th century.

One of the museum's most striking paintings comes in virtually its first room—the so-called "Pianta della Catena," or "Chain Map," a vast 1887 copy of an original 1470 bird's-eye view of 15th-century Florence (the original is in Berlin). The artist is unknown, but he may have left a self-portrait in the red-cloaked figure in the picture's right-hand foreground. Look for some of the city's familiar landmarks, and note which of today's monuments have yet to be built: The Uffizi and Cappelle Medicee, for example, are conspicuous by their absence, and the Medici and Pitti palaces are a fraction of their present size.

The gallery's most popular pictures—you'll probably have seen reproductions of them as posters and cards for sale across the city—are 12 gorgeous lunette paintings by the Flemish artist Justus Utens. Dating from 1599, they show the Medici family's country villas and estates. Elsewhere, the museum contains a collection of architectural engravings of Florence's major buildings, displays devoted to the Roman and the 18th-century city, and a graphic picture by Telemaco Signorini (1835–1901) of the execution of Savonarola in Piazza della Signoria.

Map p. 88   Via dell'Oriuolo 24   055 261 6545   Closed until 2001 for restoration, telephone for details $ Bus: A to Borgo degli Albizzi or A, 14, or 23 to Via del Proconsolo

MUSEO HORNE

The art collection in this modest gallery may pale alongside most others in the city, but you still can't help but be envious of its former owner, Herbert Percy Horne (1864–1916), an English art historian who lived and worked in Florence. Today, he is best known for his biography of Sandro Botticelli, a book that rescued the artist—today one of the most popular of all Italian painters—from almost complete obscurity. In his own time, Horne dabbled in the art market, accumulating a collection of paintings, sculptures, ceramics, and objets d'art, and some exceptional furniture. Eventually he purchased the museum's present home, the **Palazzo Corsi-Alberti,** as a suitable setting for his collection. He left both the building and his collection to the city on his death.

The palace, built by the Corsi family in 1489, is just as interesting as the exhibits. It represents a typical textile merchant's house of the period, complete with an open gallery for drying finished cloth and roomy cellars in which material would have been dyed. The

One man's collection of paintings, objets d'art, sculptures, and furniture fills the Museo Horne in the Palazzo Corsi-Alberti.

collection itself has few genuine masterpieces, but it is both eclectic and interesting. It includes the occasional big name, notably Masaccio (a tiny panel of "St. Julian"); Giotto (a panel showing "St. Stephen," part of a larger painting); Benozzo Gozzoli ("Deposition," his last documented work); and Filippino Lippi (a small and time-worn "Crucifixion").

Map p. 88   Via de Benci 6   055 244 661   Closed p.m. & all Sun. $$ Bus: B, 13, or 23 to Via de' Benci

MUSEO DI STORIA DELLA SCIENZA

The Museum of the History of Science is a fantastic museum for anyone with a passion for science or the beauty of old scientific and other instruments. Its sheer range and the intrinsic interest of its exhibits should also appeal to the nonspecialist, as well as to children. As a further recommendation, it's a modern and well-presented museum—not always the case in Florence.

The artifacts here help to underline Tuscany's considerable contribution to scientific endeavor, an intellectual discipline often overshadowed by the region's better-documented achievements in the fields of painting and sculpture. One of the greatest of all scientists, Galileo, lived and worked in Florence, and in 1657 Grand Duke Ferdinando de' Medici and his brother Leopoldo founded one of the world's first scientific academies at the Palazzo Pitti, the Accademia del Cimento, or Academy of Experiment (motto: "Try and try again").

Individual rooms around the museum are devoted to a different branch of science or technology. Each is filled with the most beautiful old objects: Astrolabes, armillary spheres, telescopes, ancient quadrants, fabulous antique globes and maps, beautiful clocks and timepieces, pneumatic pumps, prisms, and a host of other exquisitely fashioned scientific instruments.

Some of the most fascinating rooms lie at the end of the two-floor gallery, namely the medical section, which features some quite terrifying medical instruments and

This astrolabe, in the **Museo di Storia della Scienza,** was used for plotting charts of the heavens.

gruesomely detailed anatomical wax models. Another interesting exhibit is the room that has been transformed into a medieval pharmacy, where some of the potions displayed are of dubious scientific efficacy. One wonders, for example, what ailments might have been cured by *Sangue del Drago*

(Dragon's Blood) and *Confetti di Seme Santo* (Confections of Blessed Seed).
🅜 Map p. 88 ✉ Piazza de Giudici 1 ☎ 055 239 8876 🕐 Closed Tues., Thurs., & Sat. p.m. & all Sun. 💲 $$ 🚍 Bus: B or 23 to Piazza de' Giudici

SANT'AMBROGIO

Sant'Ambrogio is one of Florence's more outlying churches, but it can easily be combined with a visit to the Sant'Ambrogio market (see pp. 106–107)—one of the city's most authentic general markets—and the pretty Cibreo café. One of the city's older foundations, the church is mentioned in a document of 988, although restoration has left the present building a shadow of its former self.

Most of the church's treasures remain, however, most notably the **Cappella del Miracolo,** or Chapel of the Miracle, to the left of the high altar. This is dominated by a tabernacle by Mino da Fiesole (1430–1484), an accomplished sculptor born in nearby Fiesole. He is buried in the church and commemorated by a pavement slab at the entrance to the chapel. Another artist, Andrea del Verrocchio (died 1488), the teacher of Leonardo da Vinci and Perugino, among others, is buried in the fourth chapel.

Alongside Mino's tabernacle is a fresco by Cosimo Rosselli (1439–1507), whose lovely narrative describes the miracle that gave the chapel its name. The story in question revolves around the discovery in 1230 of a chalice full of blood. This became precious to the Florentines, who believed it saved them from a virulent outbreak of plague in 1340 (although not, sadly, from the Black Death eight years later). The original chalice is enclosed within the tabernacle.

Other paintings worth hunting out around the church include a triptych attributed to Bicci di Lorenzo (in the chapel to the right of the high altar) and "The Madonna Enthroned with St. John the Baptist and St. Bartholomew," attributed to Andrea Orcagna or the school of Orcagna (second altar on the right).
🅜 Map p. 89 ✉ Piazza Sant'Ambrogio ☎ No phone 🕐 Closed Sun. a.m. 🚍 Bus: A to Borgo La Croce ■

Northern Florence is best known for Michelangelo's "David," but it also contains the Medici family's tombs, Florence's most colorful market, and a museum devoted to the sublime paintings of Fra Angelico.

Northern Florence

The emblem of Florence

Northern Florence

NORTHERN FLORENCE LAY OUTSIDE THE OLD ROMAN CITY, WHOSE LIMIT was marked by the present-day Piazza del Duomo. This didn't stop the district's early development, which took place along the line of Via San Gallo, a northerly continuation of the *cardo maximus,* the name given to one of the main streets in a Roman colony.

During the Middle Ages, the area was known as the Quartiere di San Giovanni, or Quarter of St. John, one of four large parishes into which the medieval city was divided. Much of it comprised a closely packed—but now largely vanished—maze of residential streets. This labyrinth was particularly rich in convents, hospitals, and pilgrims' lodgings, the descendants of which survive in the area to this day.

Change, when it came, was largely the result of Medici meddling. It was Florence's most powerful family, for example, who enlarged the old cathedral church of San Lorenzo, one of the district's pivotal points, now visited for a pair of pulpits by Donatello, the Medici library, and Brunelleschi's Old Sacristy. It was also the Medici who added the Cappelle Medicee to the rear of the church, later graced with several outstanding sculptures by Michelangelo. They also patronized the San Marco convent to the north now the Museo di San Marco, a museum given over to the works of Frà Angelico, one of the most exalted of all Renaissance painters. And it was the Medici who built the Palazzo Medici-Riccardi near the cathedral, an enormous palace that remained the family's headquarters for about a hundred years. Its most enchanting sight is a fresco cycle by Benozzo Gozzoli, one of the most lyrical of all Italian painting cycles.

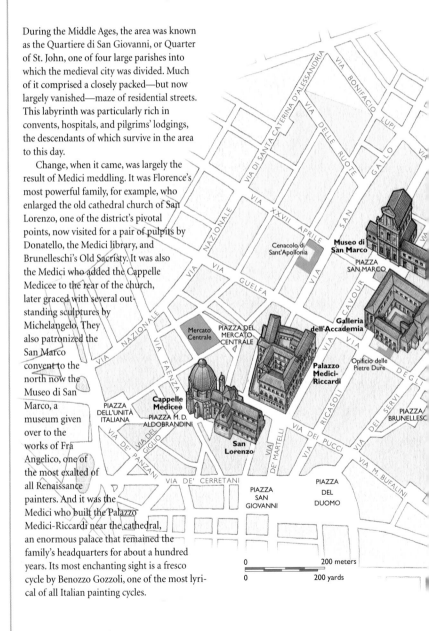

On the map:

PIER ANTONIO MICHELI

GIARDINO DEI SEMPLICI

Santissima Annunziata

VIA GINO CAPPONI

VIA GIUSEPPE GIUSTI

GIARDINO DELLA GHERARDESCA

PIAZZA DELLA SANTISSIMA ANNUNZIATA

Museo Archeologico

Ospedale degli Innocenti

ALFANI

BORGO PINTI

PINTI

BORGO PINTI

SANTEGIDIO

Arno

Area of map detail

Art is everywhere in Florence, even on T-shirts for sale at one of the clothing stalls in the San Lorenzo market.

Strangely, the Medici had no hand in the district's most famous sight, Michelangelo's "David," which is housed in the Accademia, an art academy between the cathedral and San Marco. Michelangelo's statue is so compelling that visitors often overlook the Accademia's other exhibits, including several lesser sculptures by the same artist and a range of Italian Renaissance and other paintings that would shine elsewhere. There are often long lines here, so consider reserving a preestablished admittance time by telephone (see p. 101).

No such measures are necessary for northern Florence's less prominent sights. Don't miss the San Lorenzo market, a busy labyrinth of stall-filled streets around the San Lorenzo church, nor the Mercato Centrale, Europe's largest covered food market. The latter is a cornucopia of sights, smells, and mouthwatering cheeses, hams, vegetables, fruit, and other gastronomic treats.

Finally, among the lesser sights, leave time for Piazza Santissima Annunziata near the Museo di San Marco, a planned Renaissance square that provides a setting for the church of Santissima Annunziata and Europe's first orphans' hospital. ■

San Lorenzo

San Lorenzo

⚐ Map p. 120

✉ Piazza San Lorenzo

☎ 055 216 634

⊕ Closed L & Sun.
   during services

🚌 Bus: 1, 6, or 17 to
   Via Cavour

SAN LORENZO IS PROBABLY FLORENCE'S OLDEST CHURCH. For many years it served as the city's cathedral, and it was also the Medici's preferred place of worship. Several vast grants from the family helped transform the old church on the site into the present-day building, a restrained Renaissance masterpiece designed by Filippo Brunelleschi and scattered with works of art by Michelangelo, Donatello, and Filippino Lippi (1457–1504).

The Biblioteca Medicea Laurenziana rises beyond the cloisters of San Lorenzo.

Opposite: This bronze panel is from a pulpit by Donatello in San Lorenzo. The relief portrays Christ brought before Pontius Pilate.

There is more to San Lorenzo than first meets the eye. The church itself contains a variety of treasures, and annexed to the complex are two further architectural masterpieces —the Ricetto (Vestibule) and the Biblioteca Medicea Laurenziana (Medici Library)—both of which were wholly or partly designed by Michelangelo. Also part of the church, but with a separate entrance, are the Cappelle Medicee, or Medici Chapels, the burial place of many of the Medici's principal figures (see pp. 128–131). Other prominent members of the family are buried in the main body of the church, and four of them were interred in the Sagrestia Vecchia, or Old Sacristy, San Lorenzo's architectural and decorative tour de force (see p. 125).

The original church here was reputedly founded in 393 and consecrated by St. Ambrose, the bishop and patron saint of Milan. At that time it stood outside the city's walls. The date of its consecration was significant, for it came only a few years after Christianity had been proclaimed the official religion of the Roman Empire. The church was dedicated to the martyred St. Lawrence (Lorenzo) and St. Zenobius, Florence's first bishop, who was buried here. It then served as the city's cathedral until the seventh century, when Zenobius's body was moved to the new Santa Reparata cathedral, later replaced by the present cathedral.

In 1059, the first San Lorenzo was rebuilt as a Romanesque church. This structure survived until 1418, when nine wealthy parishioners, among them Giovanni di Bicci de' Medici (1360–1429), founding father of the Medici fortune, offered to finance a new church. Giovanni's motives were not entirely philanthropic, for his intention, among others, was that the new building would become a Medici mausoleum, thus further enhancing the family's already considerable standing. Three years later, the commission for the new church was awarded to Filippo Brunelleschi, then also busy working on the cathedral.

Construction of the church's Sagrestia Vecchia was completed before the death of Giovanni in 1429, but further progress was hampered by political and other upheavals, not least the death of Brunelleschi in 1446. Impetus was only regained in the wake of a 40,000-florin grant from Giovanni's son, Cosimo de' Medici, better known as Cosimo il Vecchio, or Cosimo the Elder (1389–1464). Some idea of the scale of Cosimo's generosity can be gauged from the fact that at the time 150 florins would support the average Florentine family for a year. The architect Antonio Manetti made full use of the Medici largesse, utilizing the funds in the years between 1447 and 1460 to bring the building to completion.

"The Martyrdom of St. Lawrence" by Bronzino depicts St. Lawrence, or San Lorenzo in Italian, martyred on a gridiron over a fire.

Biblioteca Medicea Laurenziana

✉ San Lorenzo, Piazza San Lorenzo 9

☎ 055 210 760 or 055 211 590

🕐 Closed p.m.

Or not quite to completion, for the church's bare brick **facade** remains unfinished to this day. Pope Leo X (1475–1521), son of Lorenzo de' Medici or Lorenzo the Magnificent (1449–1492), called upon Michelangelo to provide a suitably grand frontage in 1518. The artist's working models for the project can be seen in the Casa Buonarroti (see p. 116). Leo wanted stone for the church to be quarried from Pietrasanta on the Tuscan coast. The habitually difficult Michelangelo preferred the superior marble of Carrara in the Apuan mountains, to the north. After arguments as to where the marble was to be mined, work petered out, never to be resumed.

Inside, the church's simple, almost bland, **interior** marks a deliberate attempt by Brunelleschi to draw on his studies of the great classical buildings of Rome. The result was one of Italy's earliest Renaissance church interiors, and its harmonic proportions, lovely marble pavement, coffered ceiling, Corinthian pillars, and broad arches all profoundly influenced subsequent buildings in Florence and elsewhere. Its decorative coloring, for example, is something you'll see time and again around the city—a system of so-called *creste e vele* (waves and sails), with "sails" of creamy-colored walls and gray *pietra serena* stone.

The first artistic highlight is Rosso Fiorentino's (1494–1540) painting of the "Marriage of the Virgin" in the second chapel on the south wall. The locally born Fiorentino—one of Italy's finest mannerist painters—would eventually despair of what he saw as the poor rewards of working in his native land. Within a few years of completing this painting he quit Florence for France "to raise himself…out of the wretchedness and poverty, which is the common lot of those who work in Tuscany." He may have had a point, for he achieved considerable renown in his adopted country, and among French critics Fiorentino is now considered one of the most influential artists of his day.

In the middle of the nave stand two raised **pulpits** whose superb bronze reliefs were among the last works of Donatello with the help of his assistants. The renowned sculptor is buried in the church; his memorial is on the right wall of a chapel in the left (north) transept. The raised pulpits make their sculptures rather difficult to decipher, but the episodes portrayed on the panels are the events before and after Christ's Crucifixion. Savonarola once thundered his ser-mons from the pulpits, but today their use—in honor of the Holy Week theme of their reliefs—is traditionally restricted to Easter.

To the pulpits' right as you face the high altar lies a tabernacle, the "Pala del Sacramento" by Desiderio da Settignano, while beneath the church's main dome an inscription on the floor—"Pater Patriae" (Father of the Fatherland)—and three small grilles mark the tomb of Cosimo de' Medici (Cosimo the Elder), Donatello's chief patron and the church's main benefactor.

Further Medici tombs lie in the **Sagrestia Vecchia** (1421–26), entered through doors to the left of the high altar. This tiny but exquisite space was commissioned as a private chapel by Cosimo the Elder's father, Giovanni Bicci de' Medici. Its dedication was to St. John the Evangelist, Giovanni's namesake and patron saint. The sacristy was the only one of Brunelleschi's many architectural projects completed in his lifetime. Its apparently simple design—a combination of cube and hemispherical dome—disguises a masterpiece of spatial subtlety and decorative innovation.

On the left as you enter the sacristy stands an easily missed **tomb** (1472), the work of Verrocchio and the burial place of Giovanni and Piero de' Medici, the grandsons of Giovanni di Bicci de' Medici. Don't

be fooled by its plainness: The people of Florence admiring the monument would have been aware that it was made from three of the most precious materials of antiquity—bronze, marble, and porphyry. Giovanni di Bicci de' Medici himself is entombed with his wife, Piccarda Bueri, beneath the larger

In Donatello's "St. Stephen and St. Lawrence," located in Sagrestia Vecchia, St. Lawrence holds the grill on which he was martyred.

The Medici saints

San Lorenzo's sponsor, Giovanni di Bicci de' Medici, chose St. John the Evangelist as his patron saint, but the patron saints of the Medici family in general were Saints Cosmas and Damian, or Cosma and Damiano in Italian. This was partly because they were doctors and the Medici were originally apothecaries, and partly because of a play on the word *medici,* which means "doctors" in Italian. The saints are particularly associated with works commissioned by Cosimo de' Medici, who, by remarkable coincidence, was reputedly born on September 27, the saints' feast day. ∎

but far plainer, marble slab (1434) in the middle of the room.

Decoration in the sacristy was provided by Donatello between 1434 and 1443, some 20 years before his work on the pulpits in the main nave of the church. He crafted the eight colored tondi, or round reliefs, which depict the four Evangelists and four episodes from the life of John the Evangelist. He was also responsible for the frieze of cherubim (in blue) and seraphim (in red), as well as the two large reliefs above the doors on the end wall, one of which (on the right) depicts Saints Cosmas and Damian (see sidebar p. 125), the other the Saints Stephen and Lawrence, twin protectors of Florence (on the left). The bust of St. Lawrence, nearby, also long attributed to Donatello, is now thought to be the work of Desiderio da Settignano.

Donatello is still credited with the **bronze doors** on the opposite end wall, their reliefs portraying several Christian martyrs on the left and the Apostles, John the Baptist, and the Fathers of the Church on the right. The left door opens onto a pretty marble lavabo, or wash basin, attributed to Verrocchio. Notice its various motifs; the falcon and lamb, for example, are heraldic symbols of Piero de' Medici, or Piero the Gouty (1416–1469), the man who commissioned the work. Finally, look up to the ceiling and its lovely fresco of the constellations and path of the sun. Scholars are unsure whether it represents the position of the heavens on July 4, 1442; July 16, 1416, the birthday of Piero de' Medici; or July 6, 1439, the date on which the union of the Eastern and Western churches was celebrated in Florence.

Leave the church at the top of the north aisle, pausing to admire Filippino Lippi's altarpiece of the

"Annunciation" (1450) and Bronzino's fresco of the "Martyrdom of St. Lawrence." Lawrence was martyred by being roasted to death on a gridiron, and he is reputed to have told his tormentors at one point that he was "done" on one side and could be turned over.

From the church a corridor leads to the cloisters. A door to the right leads to the **Ricetto** (1559–1571), a small but bizarrely original vestibule designed by Michelangelo. The work has many odd touches, all doubtless intended to be deliberately provocative—pillars that carry no weight, columns sunk into walls, and brackets that support nothing but air. None, though, are as strange as the huge black staircase and rough rendering of the walls. This

is one of the most unusual small architectural creations in the city, and it would influence later mannerist architects.

The staircase from the Ricetto leads to the main reading room of the **Biblioteca Medicea Laurenziana** (begun 1524), or Medici Library, commissioned by Pope Clement VII, formerly Giulio de' Medici (1478–1534), nephew of Lorenzo the Magnificent. Its purpose was to house the Medici's 100-year-old collection of 15,000 precious books and manuscripts. The Medici were not always cultured souls—an inventory of Giovanni di Bicci de' Medici's possessions in 1418 listed just three books. It was left to Cosimo de' Medici and his son and grandson, Piero de' Medici and Lorenzo de'

Medici, to scour Europe in the quest to create the family library. The Medici also founded notable libraries in the convent of San Marco (see p. 143) and the Badia Fiorentina (see p. 86).

Everything in the reading room, which was opened to the public in 1571, was designed by Michelangelo, even the desks. While it is not as eccentric as the Ricetto below, it has some interesting touches. Note, for example, the Medici crest incorporated into every window and the fact that all you can see of the room from the Ricetto is an entirely blank wall. The books and manuscripts from the collection on show vary, but the oldest work held, a fifth-century copy of works by Virgil, the Roman poet, is rarely brought out of safekeeping. ∎

The ceiling of the Sagrestia Vecchia bears a striking resemblance to that of the Cappella dei Pazzi (see p. 114). Brunelleschi designed both buildings.

Cappelle Medicee

THE CAPPELLE MEDICEE, OR MEDICI CHAPELS, ARE CELE-
brated for three major groups of sculpture by Michelangelo in the
Sagrestia Nuova, one of three components of the rambling private
mausoleum built for the Medici. The crypt contains many minor
members of the dynasty, while the Cappella dei Principi is the last
resting place of six Medici Grand Dukes.

Cappelle Medicee
- 🅰 Map p. 120
- ✉ Piazza Madonna degli Aldobrandini 6
- ☎ 055 238 8602
- 🕐 Closed 1st, 2nd, & 5th Mon. & 2nd & 4th Sun. of every month
- 💲 $$
- 🚌 Bus: 1, 6, 17 to Via Cavour

You walk from the chapels' ticket office straight into the gloom of the **crypt,** home to the entombed bodies of 49 less notable Medici scions. Grand Duke Ferdinand III de' Medici placed many of them here in 1791, though according to one contemporary account the unfortunate corpses were thrown "together pell-mell…caring scarcely to distinguish one from the other." The bodies were exhumed in 1857—though only after much wrangling—and left in their present arrangement.

From the crypt steps you enter the cavernous **Cappella dei Principi,** or Chapel of the Princes, the costliest single project the Medici ever commissioned. It was still a drain on the family's coffers in 1743 when the Medici line died out, almost 140 years after work on the chapel began. The immense interior contains the tombs of the six Medici Grand Dukes, Cosimo I having adopted the title "Grand Duke" in 1570. All six tombs are in highly questionable taste, matched in their gaudiness only by the vividly colored marbles gilding the walls. The most appealing things here are the stone coats of arms inlaid around the walls, which represent the 16 major Tuscan towns that came within the Medici orbit.

SAGRESTIA NUOVA

A corridor from the Cappella leads to the Sagrestia Nuova, or New Sacristy, so-called to distinguish it from Brunelleschi's Sagrestia

Vecchia (Old Sacristy) in the nearby San Lorenzo (see pp. 122–27). The term *sacristy* is slightly misleading, for the Medici Pope Leo X and his cousin, Cardinal Giulio de' Medici, commissioned the chapel in 1520 from Michelangelo to act as a mausoleum for two earlier Medici scions: Lorenzo the Magnificent and his brother Giuliano, the latter murdered during the infamous Pazzi Conspiracy of 1478.

The project was Michelangelo's first major architectural undertaking and, like most projects with which the artist was involved, was hampered by mishaps and false starts. Things went well until 1527 and the attack on Florence by the forces of Emperor Charles V (R.1519–1556), when Michelangelo was called away to assist with the siege defenses around San Miniato al Monte. After the restoration of the Medici to power in 1530, the artist worked half-heartedly on this and other projects before leaving Florence for Rome in 1534.

The result was a chapel based on the simple cube and half-sphere arrangement of Brunelleschi's Sagrestia Vecchia (Michelangelo probably inherited an existing floor plan). Here, however, in a striking departure from conventional practice, Michelangelo decided not to place the tombs and funerary statues at the center of the room, as was customary, but around the walls. Most of the statuary was completed when the sculptor abandoned the project, but its definitive

Opposite: In the Cappella dei Principi in the Cappelle Medicee, the large sarcophagi contain the remains of Grand Dukes Cosimo I and Ferdinand I.

arrangement was decided later (1554–55) by the Medici Duke Cosimo I and the artists Giorgio Vasari and Bartolommeo Ammannati.

MICHELANGELO'S SCULPTURES

With your back to the door after entering, the tomb on your left belongs to Lorenzo de' Medici, Duke of Urbino (1492–1519), the grandson of Lorenzo the Magnificent; the tomb on the right is that of Giuliano de' Medici, Duke of Nemours (1478–1516), Lorenzo the Magnificent's third and youngest son. It is one of the chapel's enduring ironies that its grandest tombs belong to two of the Medici's most wretched offspring, whereas the tombs of the more deserving family members for whom it was designed—Lorenzo the Magnificent and his brother—

Michelangelo's "Madonna and Child" remained unfinished at the sculptor's death.

remained unfinished. The Duke of Urbino combined arrogance with feeblemindedness and died young from a combination of tuberculosis and syphilis. The Duke of Nemours was more easygoing, but equally ineffectual, and ruled Florence after 1512 in name only, spending much of his short life in thrall to his elder brother, Giovanni de' Medici, better known as Pope Leo X.

Here, therefore, it is a case of admiring the sculpture and forgetting the man within. The **tomb of Lorenzo de' Medici** aimed to represent its protagonist as a man of thought; hence, the main figure is seated with head on hand and the two allegorical statues below symbolize "Dawn" and "Dusk," the times deemed most appealing to the contemplative mind. "Dusk" is a male figure, portrayed exhausted and heavy with impending sleep; "Dawn" is the more animated female figure, sprightly with the vigor of a new day. The figures may also represent the imbalance of Lorenzo's mind. Michelangelo was not unaware of the true character of his protagonists, and critics have suggested that Lorenzo's rather absurd hat may also be a hint from the sculptor as to his subject's feeblemindedness.

The Medici emblem

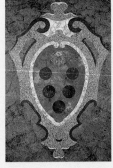

The Medici's principal emblem—a group of balls—is seen across Tuscany. According to myth, the Medici descended from an eighth-century knight in Charlemagne's army, whose shield received six dents while he was fighting a giant. As a reward for the knight's bravery, Charlemagne allowed him to represent these marks on his coat of arms. Others say the balls represent medicinal pills, tokens of the Medici's origins as apothe-

caries or doctors, or that they are the traditional ball or coin symbol of pawnbrokers. Others claim they are *bezants* (Byzantine coins) connected to the arms of the Arte del Cambio, or money changers' guild, of which the Medici were prominent early members. Although the emblem usually has six balls, in the 13th century there were twelve; San Lorenzo's Old Sacristy has eight, and Cosimo I's Cappella dei Principi tomb has five. ■

The **tomb of Giuliano de' Medici** depicts Giuliano as a man of action—a Roman general, no less, complete with commander's baton. Below him recline the allegorical figures of "Day"—the rough, unfinished male figure on the right—and "Night," the female form on the left, the latter portrayed with the moon, stars, and symbols of sleep: the poppy, owl, and "mask of dreams."

Neither of the main tomb figures was taken from life. Michelangelo aimed to transcend simple portraiture and create timeless statues, hence his own preferred names for the two principal statues: "La Vigilanza" ("Vigilance") and "Il Pensiero" ("Thought"). When criticized for failing to create accurate portraits, the sculptor replied that in a thousand years no one would know—or care—what Lorenzo and Giuliano actually looked like. He was right.

The chapel's third group of statues centers on an unfinished "Madonna and Child," flanked by "St. Cosmas" and "St. Damian," the Medici's patron saints (see sidebar p. 125). Only the Madonna is by Michelangelo, the saints having been completed by assistants to their master's original plan. Both saints gaze toward the Madonna, as do the figures of Lorenzo and Giuliano, imposing a subtle unity on the chapel, a device used here for the first time. The Madonna looks at the main altar wall opposite, the altar serving as a symbol of Christ's death and Resurrection—and thus eternal life.

The notion of Resurrection should have been reinforced by a Michelangelo fresco of the subject on the sacristy's ceiling. Similarly, the tombs of Lorenzo the Magnificent and his brother should have faced one another in the same way as those of their feckless

descendants (the pair are actually buried in a simple tomb near the "Madonna and Child"). Also missing are statues representing Heaven and Earth, intended for the niches either side of the Duke of Nemours, as well as statues of river gods representing the Tiber and Arno, symbols of Lazio and Tuscany, the regions ruled by the duke. These were all part of Michelangelo's original grand design for the chapel. His intention was to unite painting, architecture, and sculpture in an artistic and philosophical study of the progression from the material and temporal world (represented by the river gods) through humankind (the figures of Giuliano and Lorenzo) to the eternal life represented by the Resurrection. ■

On the tomb of Giuliano de' Medici by Michelangelo, the lower statues are allegories of "Day" and "Night."

The art of fresco

The wall paintings known as frescoes formed the most common mode of large-scale artistic expression in Italian art after the 14th century, when they largely superseded mosaics. They take their name from *fresco*, or fresh, because they were painted on wet (or fresh) plaster, a procedure that resulted in the medium's particular strengths and weaknesses.

A sinopia by Antonio Pisanello shows a fragment of a battle scene.

A fresco's main strength was its durability, a feature guaranteed by the chemical reaction that lay at its heart. Add paint to dry plaster, and any moisture or physical deterioration in a wall eventually lifts the paint off. But put paint on wet plaster—a mixture of lime, water, and fine sand—and, as the plaster dries, the lime (calcium hydroxide) combines with carbon dioxide in the air to create calcium carbonate. This then crystallizes around the sand particles, cementing them to the wall. If pigments are applied at the same time, then the process also fixes their particles, leaving them resistant to further action by moisture.

Much preparation was required, however, before an artist could proceed to the pigment stage. Base layers of plaster, known as the *arrichio*, were first applied to the wall. An artist or assistant would then scratch this with the painting's main outlines. A more detailed sketch was then drawn in red ocher—a study known as the *sinopia* for the red pigment used. This sketch often was made away from the painting's proposed site. Sinopie are often brought to light and preserved in Florence and elsewhere, notably in Sant'Apollonia (see p. 146). Preliminary sketches, or cartoons, were created as pictures became more complex, and chalk was dusted onto the wall through pinpricked outlines in the drawing.

Once a painting was under way, an artist could only work on an area small enough to be completed before the plaster dried. Assistants therefore divided the arrichio into *giornate*, or days, and then applied a thin layer of preparatory white finishing plaster, or *intonaco*. Yet another sketch—this time in a mixture of lime and black pigment *(verdacchio)*—then had to be drawn over the obscured portion of arrichio.

Even then, an artist's problems were only just beginning. Painting was a race against the drying plaster. Once a wall was dry, a mistake could only be rectified by stripping off the dry plaster, creating another layer of arrichio, and starting all over again. The range of suitable pigments, and thus colors, was also limited, and the pigments were difficult to mix to create more depth of tone or more delicate shades. Skill, technique, and the use of subtle base layers of color were an artist's only recourse.

By contrast, painting on wood or canvas using tempera, a technique in which egg yolk was used to fix pigment, produced glorious colors, as many Sienese and other paintings testify. The introduction of oil-based paints toward the end of the 15th century also allowed for new subtlety of color. Neither, though, was suitable for large-scale frescoes, and when artists of the caliber of Leonardo da Vinci rebelled against the limitations of wet plaster, their paintings were doomed. Leonardo's "Last Supper" in Milan—painted on dry plaster using innovative pigments—is a case in point. Glorious when unveiled, the fresco was soon ravaged when the thin layer of paint sitting on the wall's surface began to flake off. ■

The making of Piero della Francesca 's fresco "Madonna del Parto" (1455)

Coarse plaster: Base layers of plaster were applied to walls. An assistant then scratched or sketched the painting's main outline.

Bare wall: The bare walls of churches or palaces had to be prepared with plaster (*arricio*) before an artist could paint.

Final fresco: Artists had to work quickly and with a limited choice of color.

Fresh coat of *intonaco*, or fine plaster. Frescoes can only be applied to wet plaster. Any unpainted dried plaster was hacked off and relaid the next day.

Artist's sketch: With complex compositions a "cartoon," or rough sketch, of the intended fresco was incised or drawn in chalk on the plaster.

Palazzo Medici-Riccardi

THE PALAZZO MEDICI-RICCARDI WAS HOME TO THE Medici for almost a century, being their principal seat in the city from 1462—when it was completed for Cosimo de' Medici the Elder—to 1540, when Cosimo I moved the Medici court to the Palazzo Vecchio. Today, it is visited for one surviving jewel from the period, the Cappella dei Magi, a tiny chapel decorated with a three-panel fresco cycle (1460) by Benozzo Gozzoli.

Palazzo Medici-Riccardi

🅰 Map p. 120
✉ Via Cavour 1
☎ 055 276 0340
🕐 Closed Wed.
💲 $$
🚌 Bus: 1, 6, 17 to Via Cavour

Little else remains to suggest the palace's former splendor, restructuring over the years having turned the building into a rather brooding bureaucratic labyrinth. Nothing, though, detracts from the appeal of Gozzoli's paintings, which are some of the most charming in Florence, thanks largely to their colorful narrative and the minutely observed beauty of their decorative detail. This also makes them some of the most popular pictures in the city, so be prepared for lines.

The paintings' declared subject is the "Journey of the Magi," with one panel given over to each of the three kings from the story of the Nativity. Gozzoli, however, probably included aspects of the annual procession of the Compagnia dei Magi, the most important of Florence's medieval confraternities (semireligious and charitable organizations). Several Medici belonged to the organization, among them Piero de' Medici, who may have commissioned the frescoes. Gozzoli may also have been inspired—and have included elements from—two other historical episodes, namely the council of bishops in Florence in 1439, which briefly led to the union of the Roman and Greek churches, and the visit to the city in 1459 (the year Gozzoli began work on the frescoes) by Aeneas Silvius Piccolomini, better known as the Sienese Pope Pius II (1405–1464).

The Medici already knew of Gozzoli, having seen his work in the Convent of San Marco, where he painted a fresco in the monastic cell reserved for Cosimo de' Medici (see p. 143). This fresco also portrayed the Magi, underlining the Medici's special affinity with the three kings and the feast of the Epiphany. The American art critic Diane Cole Ahl suggests this was because "as temporal kings and the first Gentile witnesses to Christ, the magi were exemplars of worldly power humbled by faith. The portrayal of the Medici and their partisans in the magi's guise at once conveyed their authority and piety."

That the Medici had a chapel for Gozzoli to paint was testament to the family's standing. Only two other palaces in the city had chapels within their walls, a special dispensation having been issued personally in 1422 by Pope Martin V allowing Cosimo de' Medici and his wife the privilege of a portable altar for their devotions. Such dispensations were rare; this one was also granted in perpetuity, which allowed the altar to be transferred to the palace, thus facilitating the creation of the chapel.

No expense was spared on the frescoes. The gold leaf needed for cycle alone ran to 1,500 sheets and had to be specially imported through the rival city of Genoa. The frescoes' splendor was not merely a matter of simple ostentation, for the chapel was intended as a reception chamber as well as a place of worship. Visiting dignitaries would

Opposite: Lorenzo the Magnificent may be the king portrayed in Benozzo Gozzoli's fresco cycle in the Palazzo Medici-Riccardi.

await an audience with the Medici here, doubtless reflecting on the obvious wealth of their hosts as they did so.

Given the Medici's intimate involvement with the chapel, it comes as little surprise to find that many of the family feature as protagonists in the paintings. Nor was it an accident that they appear in the most splendid of the panels, which—not surprisingly—was placed on the east wall, an allusion to the magi's origins in the Orient.

Putting definitive names to faces, however, has proved difficult. The obvious cloaked figure leading the procession on a white horse is often said to be a young Lorenzo the Magnificent, son of Piero de' Medici, the frescoes' probable sponsor. However, the figure's features and pictorial clues here are not specific, unlike the mounted riders just behind, where the nearer red-hatted figure in blue astride the light brown mule—a symbol of humility—is Cosimo de' Medici, while the red-hatted figure on his

Above: Prominent Medici are shown in the main panel of Benozzo Gozzoli's fresco cycle.

Left: The frescoes depict the "Journey of the Magi." Each panel portrays a king from the biblical story.

Opposite: The red hats worn by the frescoes' figures were popular with contemporary Florentine scholars.

turned to one another, are probably Piero's sons, Giuliano (on the right), who would be murdered in the Pazzi Conspiracy, and Lorenzo the Magnificent (in half profile on the left with the distinctive up-turned nose). The two young men on horseback in the far left foreground below are Galeazzo Maria Sforza and Sigismondo Malatesta. Both appear for political reasons: They were the sons of two of Cosimo's principal allies. Gozzoli's self-satisfaction is further underlined by the fact that he painted himself in another fresco, namely the picture on the west wall with the white-bearded king. He stands on the right making a "V" with his fingers above the dismounting man. The sign is a visual pun, in that it mirrors the horses' ears just below, suggests a farewell as he turns to join the procession, indicates his artistic dexterity (the hand, deliberately, is the right, or *dexter)*, and stresses he has fulfilled his contractual obligation to paint the work by his own hand. ■

left in green and gold velvet is Piero de' Medici. Note the gold-embossed crimson livery on his white horse, which bears the Medici symbols of seven balls and three feathers. The word *semper,* meaning "always," is a reference to the supposedly eternal nature of the family's reign.

Gozzoli has also included a self-portrait in the crowd behind the riders: He stands on the left, a couple of rows from the rear with the words *Opus Benotii*—the Work of Benozzo—picked out in gold on his red cap. The word *Benotii* was a deliberate pun, as *ben noti* means "well known" and *noti beni* means "take good note"; both meanings were designed to underline Gozzoli's achievement.

The two young boys just below him in the east wall fresco, half-

Galleria dell'Accademia

Opposite:
Michelangelo
enlarged the head
and hands of
"David" to create
an added illusion
of size.

IT WOULD BE HARD TO VISIT FLORENCE WITHOUT SEEING Michelangelo's "David," the most celebrated—and arguably most overexposed—Renaissance image in Western art. Having stood for years in the Piazza della Signoria, the statue was moved to its present home in the 19th century, occupying pride of place in an academy created in 1784 by Grand Duke Pietro Leopoldo (1747–1792) to house a collection of Florentine paintings and sculpture.

Michelangelo's "David" dwarfs visitors to the Accademia. The statue is over 13 feet (4 m) tall.

Galleria dell'Accademia

- 🅰 Map p. 120
- ✉ Via Ricasoli 60
- ☎ 055 238 8609
- 🕐 Closed Mon.
- 💲 $$$
- 🚌 Bus: 1, 6, 17 to Via Cavour

On entering the Galleria you find yourself in a hallway. Beyond this stretches the so-called **Galleria del David,** where Michelangelo's looming statue is framed in its own domed space, the neoclassic Tribuna del David (1882). Walking along the Galleria you pass other works by Michelangelo, but you'll probably want to see the "David" first and return to these later. Several rooms off the Galleria and Tribuna can also wait, as can a quartet of salons on the first floor, which contains the Accademia's other paintings and sculptures.

MICHELANGELO'S "DAVID"

Michelangelo's celebrated statue was commissioned in 1501 by the Opera del Duomo, the body respon-sible for the care of the cathedral's fabric. At the time Michelangelo was just 26. The statue's subject—David, the Israelite shepherd boy, the slayer of Goliath—was chosen because of parallels with Florence's recent history, in particular the city's (short-lived) liberation from Medici rule and its ability to withstand more powerful Italian and foreign foes. Once completed, it became a republican symbol of the city and of its passion for independence. It also firmly cemented Michelangelo's reputation, already heightened by his statue of the "Pietà" created for St. Peter's in Rome six years earlier.

The image of the boy warrior, at once alert and ready for battle, but also calm with the certainty of victory, is so familiar that it is easy to ignore its greatness. Michelangelo's achievement becomes still more remarkable when you learn that the statue was carved from a single block of marble over 13 feet (4 m) high. Not only that, but the marble in question—an almost impossibly thin and fault-riddled block—was widely considered too damaged for artistic use. Several prominent artists, Leonardo da Vinci and Agostino di Duccio among them, had already failed to make anything of the stone. Indeed, until Michel-angelo's arrival, the slab had lain unworked since being quarried from the Tuscan hills some 40 years earlier. Michelangelo confounded the doubters, completing the work in just three years.

Where to put the statue then immediately became a subject of controversy. During its gestation, the assumption had been that it would join a collection of statues outside the cathedral. This notion was quickly challenged. No fewer than 30 leading artists were asked to arbitrate in the ensuing dispute, some continuing to argue for the area in front of the Duomo, others—including such notables as Botticelli and Leonardo da Vinci—favoring the Loggia della Signoria in Piazza della Signoria. After a lengthy debate, it was decided to place the statue in front of the Palazzo Vecchio, then known as

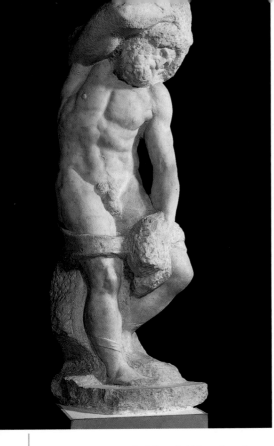

Michelangelo probably meant for his "Prisoner" or "Bearded Slave" to be rough-hewn and unfinished in appearance.

statue on its plinth. Matters weren't helped by the fact the statue had to be protected night and day from stone-throwing supporters of the Medici. The family at the time had been removed from power, but it still had defenders. Ructions in 1527, again caused by the Medici's temporary absence, saw the statue's left arm smashed—the resulting scars are still clearly visible. Echoes of this act of vandalism sounded in 1991, when an onlooker smashed one of the statue's toes.

"David" remained in the square until 1873, where its long exposure to the elements resulted in the loss of the gold-coloring that once tinted its hair and chest. Also now vanished is the original skirt of copper leaves designed to placate Florence's more prudish citizens.

Away from the "David," the Galleria del David contains a variety of pleasing paintings and other works by Michelangelo, notably a statue of "St. Matthew" (1505–06) and four "Slaves" or "Prisoners" (1521–23 or circa 1530). The last were originally intended to form part of a colossal tomb for Pope Julius II (1443–1513) in Rome. But the tomb never materialized, and in 1564 Leonardo Buonarroti, Michelangelo's nephew, gave the unfinished statues to Cosimo I, the Medici Grand Duke. He in turn had them installed in Buontalenti's grotto near the entrance to the Boboli Garden (see pp. 176–77), where they remained until 1909, when they were moved to the Accademia. Two further "Slaves" from the group found their way to the Louvre in Paris.

The statues' rough and deliberately unfinished appearance exemplified Michelangelo's notion that sculpture was the liberation of an existing form "imprisoned" within unworked stone. The figure of "St. Matthew," by contrast, was

the Palazzo Pubblico, whose function as the seat of Florence's ruling council made it the obvious symbol and guardian of the city's civic and political freedoms.

Choosing the piazza was one thing; moving the statue there was another. One contemporary chronicler, Luca Landucci, recorded the transfer from the Opera del Duomo, where Michelangelo had worked on the statue, in his *Diario Fiorentino* (1504): "They had to break down the wall above the Opera door to allow it through," he wrote, adding that it was "moved along by 40 men" and that "beneath it were 14 greased beams, which were changed from hand to hand…it took four days to reach the piazza." Another three weeks were then required to raise the one of 12 figures of the Apostles commissioned in 1503 for the exterior of the Duomo. The only one of the group even started, it languished in the Opera del Duomo's workshop until 1831, when it was moved to its present home.

Two doors lead off right from the Galleria into the **Salone del Colosso** and the three-roomed Sale Fiorentine. At the heart of the first of these is a plaster model (1582) for Giambologna's "Rape of the Sabine Women" in the Loggia della Signoria (see pp. 92–93). Also here are a variety of paintings, among which the highlight is "Deposition," begun by Filippino Lippi and completed after his death in 1504 by the Umbrian master Perugino, possibly with the help of Raphael, who was then his pupil. The picture was originally intended to form part of a massive four-picture altarpiece in the church of SS Annunziata (see p. 148). Another painting worthy of note is Fra Bartolommeo's (1472–1517) "Mystical Marriage of St. Catherine," originally painted for the church of San Marco.

The chief treasure in the first of the **Sale Fiorentine** is the Cassone Adimari, a 15th-century chest probably painted by Giovanni di Ser Giovanni, or Lo Scheggia, the half-brother of Masaccio, who frescoed much of the Brancacci Chapel (see pp. 178–81). The paintings include a charming partial view of Florence as it appeared during a medieval festival.

Moving on, notice the tiny "Visitation" (1470), one of the first works completed by Perugino after his move to Florence from Umbria, and the large "Trinity with St. Benedict and St. Giovanni Gualberto," removed from the church of Santa Trìnita (see pp. 58–59 for more on Gualberto and Santa Trìnita). In the same room is

a curious study known as "Tebaide," or "Solitude." The picture has been called one of Italy's most problematic 15th-century paintings, as neither its theme nor its artist are known—it is currently attributed to Paolo Uccello.

The last room features an accomplished painting of "Three Saints" by Benozzo Gozzoli and a "Madonna and Child with St. Giovannino and Two Angels" by Botticelli. Other rooms leading off the left side of the Tribuna del David contain sculptures and busts, plus a variety of Byzantine and other paintings, among them some 22 small panels by Taddeo Gaddi removed from the church of Santa Croce. The upstairs rooms feature lesser works from the 14th and 15th centuries. ∎

The "Madonna del Mare," or "Madonna of the Sea," takes its name from the landscape in the background. It was long attributed to Botticelli but is likely the work of the young Filippino Lippi.

Museo di San Marco

THE MUSEO DI SAN MARCO MAKES A FITTING HOME FOR
the paintings of Fra Angelico, one of the most sublime of all
Renaissance painters. The artist was both a monk and a prior of San
Marco, the Dominican convent now given over to the world's finest
collection of Angelico's work. The convent was also patronized by
Cosimo de' Medici (the Elder), who helped create a library within its
walls and paid for its enlargement in 1437.

The first area you come to is the
Chiostro di Sant'Antonino, a
cloister designed before 1440 by
Michelozzo, an architect who was
much favored by the Medici. It
takes its name from Antonino
Pierozzi (1389–1459), Archbishop
of Florence, the convent's first prior
and Fra Angelico's religious mentor.
Admire the weather-faded frescoes
in the cloister's four corners, all
painted by Fra Angelico, then move
to the **Ospizio dei Pellegrini** to
see more majestic paintings by the
same artist. The Ospizio was originally used to offer hospitality to pilgrims; it lies off the cloister on the
right as you stand with your back to
the museum entrance. The many

paintings here—which have been
collected from churches and palaces
around Florence—include two of
the artist's greatest works: The
"Madonna dei Linaiuoli" (1433)
and the "San Marco Altarpiece"
(1440), the latter commissioned by
the Medici for San Marco, a church
that you can visit immediately to
the west of the convent. Among
other things, the altarpiece features
Saints Cosmas and Damian, who
were almost certainly included by
the artist because they were the
Medici's patron saints (the pair
were doctors, or *medici* in Italian).

A door off the top right-hand
corner of the cloister opens into the
Sala del Lavabo, which takes its

name from *lavare*, meaning to wash; this was where the monks washed before eating. The entrance walls contain more frescoes by Angelico, while off to the right the large refectory—the name given to the rooms where monks gathered to eat—is dominated by a painting of the "Last Supper," the work of the 16th-century artist Giovanni Sogliani. Depictions of the Last Supper, or "Cenacolo" in Italian, are often found in monastic refectories, and there are several versions in buildings around Florence, among them the version painted in 1480 by Domenico Ghirlandaio in San Marco's **Refettorio Piccolo** (Small Refectory). The painting is interesting for its symbols: Peacocks symbolize the Resurrection; ducks represent the heavens; oranges are symbols of fruits of heaven; and the cat represents evil—the reason it is painted close to the figure of Judas, the disciple who betrayed Christ.

The **Chapter House** by the convent bell retains a fresco of the "Crucifixion" (1441) by Fra Angelico. Beyond the refectory a passage leads to the Foresteria, the convent's former guest rooms. Today, it is full of archaeological fragments and has good views of the Cloister of San Domenico.

Florence has many artistic surprises, but none as wonderful as the sudden sight of Fra Angelico's "Annunciation," an intensely moving painting at the top of the stairs leading to San Marco's upper floor. Note the work's inscription, which reminded monks to say a Hail Mary as they passed the image. The next thing to catch the eye is a magnificent wooden ceiling, followed by a pair of corridors containing 44 **dormitory cells.** Most of the latter are painted with simple, pious frescoes by Fra Angelico and his assistants, each designed as an aid to devotion for the monk who

occupied the cell. Cell numbers 1 to 11 of the corridor ahead of you on the left contain the frescoes in which Angelico's hand is most evident. Of these, numbers 1, 3, 6, and 9 are worthy of special attention and depict "Noli mi Tangere," (meaning "do not touch me"), "Annunciation," "Transfiguration," and "Coronation of the Virgin" respectively. Also look at Cell 7, whose strange fresco illustrates "The Mockery of Christ" by isolating individual body parts of Christ's tormentors—a face spitting, a hand holding a scourge, and another hand holding a vinegar-soaked sponge.

Turn right at the end of this corridor and you come to a trio of rooms once occupied by Girolamo Savonarola (see pp. 31–33). Turn right by the "Annunciation" along the nearer corridor and you come to the convent's Michelozzo-designed and Medici-donated **library** (1441–44). Beyond the library, the last two cells on the right, both larger than their neighbors, were reserved for the use of Cosimo de' Medici. ■

The "Madonna dei Linaiuoli" takes its name from the Linaiuoli, or Linen Weavers Guild, which commissioned the work from Fra Angelico.

A walk from Santissima Annunziata to Santa Trìnita

On this walk around the streets and squares of Florence, from Piazza della Santissima Annunziata, south to the Arno, across into the Oltrarno and back again to Santa Trìnita, you'll discover a captivating array of the city's architecture and works of art.

Piazza della Santissima Annunziata
❶ is a stately square laid out in 1420 by Brunelleschi and dominated by Giambologna's statue of "Grand Duke Ferdinand I" (1608) and the church of **Santissima Annunziata** (see p. 148), completed in 1481.

On the square's eastern flank stands the **Ospedale degli Innocenti** (see p. 147). Created as an orphanage in 1445, it's known for Brunelleschi's delightful facade (1419–1426) and two interior courtyards, and for a modest museum of Renaissance paintings and sculptures. Just north of the Ospedale, the Palazzo della Crocetta completes the eastern side of the square. It contains the **Museo Archeologico,** an outstanding collection of Etruscan antiquities, many from the Medici collection, and Greek, Roman, and ancient Egyptian treasures. The museum was badly damaged in the 1966 floods, and restoration work is still continuing.

Walk south from the piazza on Via dei Servi, turn left on Via M. Bufalini, right on Via F. Portinari, and then left on Via dell'Oriuolo to arrive at the **Museo di Firenze com'era** ❷ (see p. 116), an intimate museum whose beguiling collection of topographical prints and paintings presents the city *com'era* (as it was). Flemish artist Justus Utens' 12 lunette pictures of the Medici villas are especially charming (see p. 117). Walk west to Piazza del Duomo (see pp. 53–86) and then south (left) on Via dello Studio midway down the piazza's southern side. The poet Dante Alighieri was born somewhere in the tangle of streets here, but not in the so-called **Casa di Dante,** a modest museum devoted to the poet (see p. 86). Two nearby churches have Dantesque associations: Santa Margherita de' Cerchi was the parish church of the Portinari, the family name of Dante's beloved Beatrice, and San Martino del Vescovo, opposite the Casa di Dante, was the Alighieri family church.

Walk east on Via Dante Alighieri, then right down Via dell Proconsolo, and you will pass the **Badia Fiorentina** ❸ on your right (see p. 86), a tenth-century abbey church where Dante is first said to have glimpsed Beatrice. Its highlights are Filippino Lippi's painting of the "Apparition of the Virgin to St. Bernard" and the Chiostro degli Aranci (Cloister of the Oranges), a cloister with an anonymous 15th-century fresco cycle depicting the life of St. Benedict.

Turn east past the **Bargello** museum (see pp. 80–85) on Via della Vigna Vecchia to the church of **Santa Croce** ❹ (see pp. 108–115), perhaps with a detour en route to Vivoli, makers of Florence's best ice cream on Via Isola delle Stinche (*No. 7r*). Devotees of Michelangelo could detour north of the church to the **Casa Buonarroti,** a well-presented museum with a handful of minor works by the sculptor (see p. 116).

Otherwise, walk south from Santa Croce on Via de' Benci past the **Museo Horne** (see p. 117), a small but high-quality art collection amassed by the English art historian Herbert Percy Horne. Then cross the river on Ponte alle Grazie and walk straight to the **Museo Bardini** ❺ (see p. 188), an eclectic collection put together by Sergio Bardini (1836–1922), the greatest international art dealer of his day.

> ► Piazza della Santissima Annunziata
> ↔ 2 miles (3.2 km)
> ⊕ Allow a morning
> ► Piazza di Santa Trìnita
>
> **NOT TO BE MISSED**
> • Museo di Firenze com'era
> • Santa Croce
> • Museo Bardini
> • Santa Felicità
> • Santa Trìnita

Walk west from the museum on Via de' Bardi to the Ponte Vecchio (see pp. 162-63), where a left turn brings you to the church of **Santa Felicità** ⑥ (see p. 189), worth a visit for the Cappella Capponi (just past the entrance on the right), known for Pontormo's strange painting of the "Deposition." Return to the Ponte Vecchio, cross the river, and walk up Via por Santa Maria.

Bear west on Via Porta Rossa past the Mercato Nuovo. Midway down the street on

the left is one of the city's most charming museums, the **Palazzo Davanzati,** whose interior perfectly preserves the decor and appearance of a medieval Florentine house (see pp. 160–61). The piazza at the end of the street contains the interesting church of **Santa Trìnita** ⑦, renowned for Domenico Ghirlandaio's fresco cycle (1483–86) on the life of St. Francis and the altarpiece in the Cappella Sassetti to the right of the high altar (see pp. 158–59). ∎

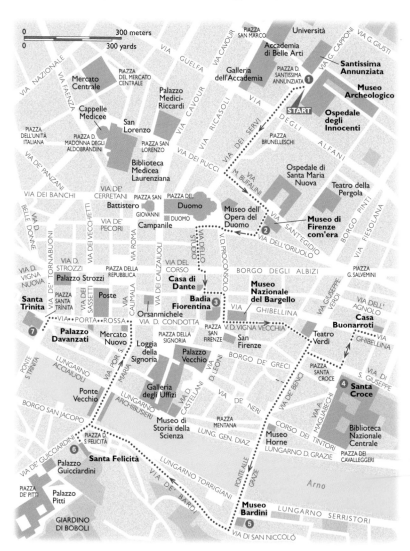

A stallholder shows off a piece of parmigiano (parmesan) cheese in the Mercato Centrale, Florence's central covered market.

More places to visit in Northern Florence

CENACOLO DI SANT'APOLLONIA

Cenacolo means "Last Supper" in Italian and refers to a painting often placed—for obvious reasons—in the refectories, or eating halls, of medieval convents and monasteries. Florence has several such paintings; you can see another version, for example, in the refectory of the nearby Dominican convent of San Marco, better known these days as the Museo di San Marco (see pp. 142–43).

The "Cenacolo di Sant'Apollonia" (1450) is only a few minutes' walk away from San Marco, so aim to see it after visiting the Museo di San Marco. The painting is the work of Andrea del Castagno, an influential early Renaissance painter, and is perhaps the most arresting and disturbing of all the Florentine "Last Suppers." It is housed in a former Benedictine convent, most of which has now been turned into private apartments. The painting's predominant color is blood red, and a sinister, black-bearded Judas—not Christ—is its principal character. Note how Judas is placed on the viewer's side of the table, a traditional 14th-century arrangement in paintings of this subject that was abandoned

by Leonardo da Vinci and other, later painters in favor of a seating plan that placed all the disciples with Christ. Notice, too, the *sinopie*, or sketches, for this and other frescoes around the walls (see pp. 132–33 for more on sinopie). ⓜ Map p. 120 ✉ Via XXVII Aprile ☎ 055 238 8607 🕐 Closed p.m., 1st & 3rd Mon., & 2nd & 4th Sun. of the month 🚌 Bus: 1, 6, or 17 to Piazza San Marco or 7, 10, & 11 to Via XXVII Aprile

MERCATO CENTRALE

You'd have to be hard-hearted not to warm to the Mercato Centrale, Florence's main central food market, whose fantastic cornucopia of stalls sells mouthwatering cheeses, fruit, fish, pasta, vegetables, meats, hams, olive oil, and countless other gastronomic treats from Tuscany and beyond. Even if you have no intention of buying anything—and this is a good place for picnic provisions or treats to take home—then there's still plenty in the way of sights, smells, and sounds to satisfy the senses. One of the busiest little stalls is **Ottavino,** a small traditional bar for authentic Florentine snacks that's popular

Markets are good places to buy cold meats and cheeses for a picnic, and stallholders are usually knowledgeable and helpful.

with both shoppers and market workers *(Open daily until 1:30 p.m. & Sat. p.m. in winter).* Don't confuse the Mercato, Europe's largest covered food hall, with the San Lorenzo market of clothes and general goods that fills many of the surrounding streets. This market is good for inexpensive leather goods and woolens.
🅜 Map p. 120 ✉ Piazza del Mercato Centrale ☎ No phone 🕑 Closed Sun. year-round & p.m. daily except Sat. in winter
🚍 Bus: 1, 6, 7 to Via Cavour & all services to Piazza del Duomo & Via de Cerretani

OPIFICIO DELLE PIETRE DURE
Pietre dure means "hard stones" and refers to the craft of cutting and inlaying precious and semiprecious stones in mosaics and other works of art. The possibilities of stone as a decorative medium can be seen all over Florence, most notably in the Cappella dei Principi in the Cappelle Medicee (see pp. 128–131), the building for which this Opificio, or workshop, was first established by Grand Duke Ferdinando de' Medici (1549–1609) in 1588. Since the 1966 flood, the Opificio has achieved an international reputation as a school and center of restoration. It's occasion-

ally possible to see restoration in progress, but generally all that's on view are the stones and imitation painted marbles in the small adjoining museum.
🅜 Map p. 120 ✉ Via degli Alfani 78 ☎ 055 265 111 or 055 287 123 🕑 Closed p.m. & Sun.; unscheduled variations possible 💲 $
🚍 Bus: 6, 31, or 32 to Piazza Santissima Annunziata or 1, 6, or 17 to the junction of Via Cavour & Via degli Alfani

OSPEDALE DEGLI INNOCENTI
The Ospedale (or Spedale) degli Innocenti was Europe's first foundling hospital, or orphanage, a function most of the elegant Renaissance building on the eastern flank of Piazza Santissima Annunziata (see p. 148) fulfills to this day. Commissioned in 1419 as a charitable work by the Arte della Seta, or Silk Weavers Guild, it was designed mainly by Brunelleschi, who was also responsible for much of the piazza, hence the architectural harmony of both the square and Ospedale.

The building's exterior **loggia,** the first in Florence to be extended across the width of a building, was one of the city's first purely Renaissance creations. Notice its clever proportions: The width of the arches is the same as both the height of the columns and the depth of the portico behind. The loggia also artfully advertised the building's function using lovely glazed terra-cotta medallions of babies by Andrea della Robbia (1435–1525). Unwanted infants destined for the hospital would once have been left in a *rota*, or rotating door, the remains of which can still be seen at the left-hand side of the loggia as you face it. The device was abandoned only in 1875. Inside the Ospedale, you have to pay to see two unexceptional adjoining cloisters: the main **Choistro degli Uomini** (Men's Cloister) and narrower **Chiostro delle Donne** (Women's Cloister) to the right. You can also visit a small art gallery up the stairs in the near left-hand corner of the main cloister. This is a minor affair by Florentine standards, but it does boast one significant painting: Domenico Ghirlandaio's "Coronation of the Virgin" (1488).

🅼 Map p. 121 ✉ Piazza della Santissima Annunziata 12 ☎ 055 249 1708 🕐 Closed p.m. & all Wed. 💲 $ 🚌 Bus: 6, 31, & 32 to Piazza della Santissima Annunziata

PIAZZA DELLA SANTISSIMA ANNUNZIATA

This piazza just to the east of the Accademia and Museo di San Marco is called one of the most beautiful in Florence, a claim rather undermined by its somewhat dilapidated appearance. It was laid out in the 1420s by Brunelleschi, taking its name from the Annunziata, or Annunciation—the moment the angel Gabriel appeared to the Virgin Mary. It was at this moment, too, that the Incarnation of Christ took place, for which reason the Feast of the Annunciation is celebrated on March 25, nine months before the Nativity. The feast has a special importance across the Christian world, but is of particular significance to Florence, whose old calendar began on this day.

The square contains two significant monuments—the church of **Santissima Annunziata** (see below) and the **Ospedale degli Innocenti** (see pp. 147-48). At its heart is a statue of Grand Duke Ferdinand I on horseback (1608), the last work of French sculptor Giambologna. The statue was finished by one of Giambologna's pupils, Pietro Tacca

(1577–1640), who cast the piece using metal from cannon captured from the Turks in the Battle of Lepanto in 1571. Tacca added the statue's water monkeys, bizarre additions that dribble water over two whiskered sea slugs.

🅼 Map p. 121 🚌 Bus: 6, 31, & 32 to Piazza della Santissima Annunziata

SANTISSIMA ANNUNZIATA

The church of Santissima Annunziata (often written SS Annunziata) dominates the northern flank of Piazza della Santissima Annunziata. It is the mother (main) church of the Servites, or Servi di Maria (Servants of Mary), a religious order founded in 1234 by Filippo Benizzi, a Florentine nobleman. The church and its order grew in stature after 1252, the year a painting begun by a Servite monk was miraculously completed by an angel. Pilgrims flocked to venerate the image, and in 1444 a new Medici-financed church was commissioned from Michelozzo. The architect and theorist Leon Battista Alberti completed the project in 1481, laying out the present-day Via dei Servi at the same time, a link designed to unite SS Annunziata and the cathedral, then the city's two most important churches devoted to the Virgin Mary.

The church's covered entrance porch, or **Chiostrino dei Voti**, features an important fresco cycle commissioned in 1516 to celebrate the canonization of Filippo Benizzi. Three leading painters of the day were involved— Andrea del Sarto, Jacopo Pontormo, and Rosso Fiorentino—and although time has not been kind to some of the panels, the cycle's effect remains dazzling. Two walls are devoted to scenes from the life of the Virgin, two to episodes from the life of St. Filippo Benizzi.

Pride of place in the main body of the church goes to a **tabernacle** immediately on your left as you enter, commissioned from Michelozzo by the Medici to house the church's original miraculous painting (now heavily overpainted and concealed). The many lamps and candles here are votive offerings. It's also a tradition among newly married Florentine brides to leave their bridal bouquets at the shrine.

🅼 Map p. 121 ✉ Piazza della Santissima Annunziata ☎ 055 239 8034 🕐 Closed L 🚌 Bus: 6, 31, & 32 ■

Western Florence boasts one of the city's two greatest churches: Santa Maria Novella, and one of the area's more modest, fresco-filled gems, Santa Trìnita. Also here is one of its single most famous sights—the Ponte Vecchio.

Western Florence

Ornamental detail in the Farmacia di Santa Maria

Western Florence

AT FIRST GLANCE WESTERN FLORENCE IS NOT THE CITY'S PRETTIEST NOR ITS most coherent quarter. Most people give it short shrift, preferring the sights around Piazza del Duomo and Piazza della Signoria, or the more immediately enticing districts of Santa Croce and the Oltrarno. The area, however, has one of Florence's most important religious monuments in Santa Maria Novella, and there's a medley of other, unsung, churches and medieval corners to be discovered.

One reason for the area's unfocused character is the fact that for centuries it lay outside the city limits. The western edge of the old Roman colony was marked by modern-day Via de' Tornabuoni, a border that remained unchanged when the city walls were built in 1078. Only with the second set of walls, raised in 1173, did the expanding city embrace some of the district's major sights—notably the church of Santa Trinita and the Ponte Vecchio. The church of Santa Maria Novella, begun in 1246, was only enclosed by the city's third set of walls, built between 1284 and 1333.

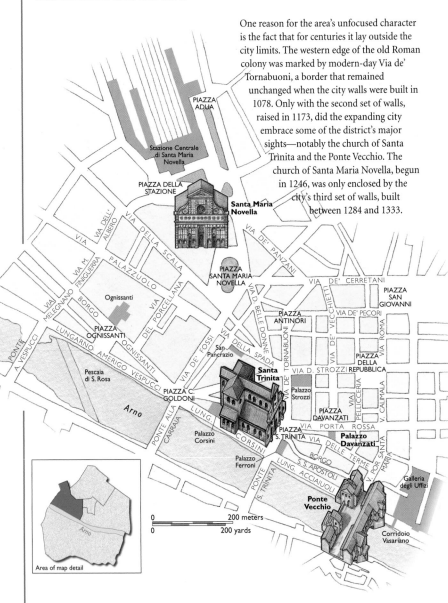

PIAZZA ADUA

Stazione Centrale di Santa Maria Novella

PIAZZA DELLA STAZIONE

Santa Maria Novella

PIAZZA SANTA MARIA NOVELLA

VIA DELL' ALBERO

VIA DELLA SCALA

VIA DE' PANZANI

VIA DE' CERRETANI

PIAZZA SAN GIOVANNI

VIA M. FINIGUERRA

PALAZZUOLO

VIA DEL PORCELLANA

VIA D. BELLE DONNE

PIAZZA ANTINORI

VIA DE' PECORI

VIA DE' VECCHIETTI

Ognissanti

VIA J. MELEGNANO

BORGO OGNISSANTI

VIA DE' FOSSI

VIA DELLA SPADA

PIAZZA ROMA

VIA DE' TORNABUONI

PIAZZA DELLA REPUBBLICA

PONTE A. VESPUCCI

PIAZZA OGNISSANTI

LUNGARNO AMERIGO VESPUCCI

San Pancrazio

VIA D. STROZZI

VIA PELLICCERIA

V. CALIMALA

Pescaia di S. Rosa

Santa Trinita

Palazzo Strozzi

Arno

PIAZZA C. GOLDONI

PONTE ALLA CARRAIA

LUNG. CORSINI

Palazzo Davanzati

PIAZZA PORTA ROSSA

Palazzo Corsini

PIAZZA S. TRINITA

VIA DELLE TERME

VIA POR SANTA MARIA

Palazzo Ferroni

PONTE S. TRINITA

LUNG. ACCIAIUOLI

BORGO S.S. APOSTOLI

Galleria degli Uffizi

Ponte Vecchio

Corridoio Vasariano

0   200 meters
0   200 yards

Arno

Area of map detail

Young love blossoms against the background of the Ponte Vecchio. Italians are rarely shy about showing their emotions, especially in matters of the heart.

Santa Maria is the key to the district, despite being near the unappealing area by the main railroad station. One of the most important Gothic buildings in Florence, it was built by the Dominicans on the site of an 11th-century church. Just as the Franciscan church of Santa Croce dominates eastern Florence, so Santa Maria dominates the city's western fringes. Behind the church's glorious facade lie several outstanding fresco cycles, one of the greatest of all early Renaissance paintings, and a little-visited museum dominated by an array of huge wall paintings.

The church of Santa Trìnita is far more modest but worth a visit for its fresco cycles, sculptures, and fascinating assortment of architectural styles. It also lies close to some of the area's best shopping streets. To the north, Via de' Tornabuoni and Via della Vigna Nuova and the streets between them are the home of the city's big designer stores, not to mention the church of San Pancrazio and many of the Renaissance palaces—Palazzo Strozzi, Palazzo Rucellai, Palazzo Corsini, and Palazzo Ferroni.

Streets to the east, by contrast, offer fewer shopping opportunities but lots of interesting churches and secret corners. Here the best streets to stroll are Via Porta Rossa, Via delle Terme, and Borgo SS Apostoli, along with the countless *chiassi*, tiny alleys, that run between them. Follow any of these to the waterfront and you come to the Ponte Vecchio, gateway to the Oltrarno district across the river. Streets to the west are less rewarding, but persevere with Borgo Ognissanti to see Ognissanti, a church that has links with Botticelli and Amerigo Vespucci (1454–1512), the Medici employee who gave his name to two continents. ■

Santa Maria Novella

THE MOTHER CHURCH OF FLORENCE'S DOMINICAN
order was begun in 1246. In time it would become the city's second
most important church after Santa Croce. Both the facade and
interior are exceptional, the latter housing a trio of captivating fresco
cycles and one of the Renaissance's most influential paintings.
Alongside the church lies Santa Maria's museum, visited chiefly for its
painted cloister and a gloriously frescoed chapel.

**Santa Maria
Novella**

🅼 Map p. 150

✉ Piazza Santa
Maria Novella

☎ 055 210 113

🚌 Bus: 1, 14, 17, 22,
23

**Opposite:
Vasari altered
the Gothic
interior of Santa
Maria Novella in
1565, removing
the screen and
friars' stalls.**

Before entering the church, take a
look around Piazza Santa Maria
Novella, not the loveliest of
Florentine squares but of passing
interest for its two large obelisks.
Both are supported by amusing
bronze turtles (1608), the work of
sculptor Giambologna, and were
raised in imitation of an ancient
Roman *circo*, or circus, a chariot
racetrack that used similar posts to
mark the starting and finishing
points of races. Cosimo I introduced his own chariot race to
Florence in 1563, the Palio dei
Cocchi, an event held annually in
the piazza on June 23, the eve of
the Feast of St. John, until the
middle of the 19th century.

Having looked at the piazza,
turn your attention to Santa Maria's
facade. While the church's interior

was largely completed by 1360, its
Romanesque front remained half-
finished until 1456, when Giovanni
Rucellai, a local textile merchant,
commissioned the architect Leon
Battisti Alberti to complete the
facade in a more modern and classically influenced style. Rucellai's
name in a latinized version—
Iohanes Oricellarius—is stamped
across the facade near the top,
together with the year of the
facade's dedication (MCCCCLXX,
1470). Also present are Rucellai's
personal emblem, the billowing sail
of Fortune, the Rucellai family
emblem (feathers in a ring), and—
in the topmost triangular pediment
—a huge shining sun, the symbol
of the Dominicans.

Inside, the church's overriding
impressions are of size and sobriety.
Note the trompe l'oeil effect that
makes the church seem even larger
than it is: The columns of the aisles
become progressively closer, a trick
designed to confuse your sense of
perspective. Another triumph of
perspective lies midway down the
nave on the left as you face the high
altar—Masaccio's groundbreaking
fresco of the "The Trinity" (1427),
one of the first Renaissance works
in which the new ideas of mathe-
matical proportion were employed.
Florentines queued for days to
share in the miracle of a picture
that apparently created a three-
dimensional space in a solid wall.
Records suggest the painting took
Masaccio a total of 24 days to

complete. Note the kneeling figures at the painting's base—representing the judge and his wife who paid for the picture—and the skeleton with its chilling epigram: "I was that which you are, you will be that which I am." The painting's theme was suggested by the fact that the Dominicans' religious calendar began with the Feast of the Trinity.

Turn to your left as you face the painting, and alongside the second pillar in the nave is a **pulpit** (1443) paid for by Giovanni Rucellai, the

Nuns gather in the cloister of Santa Maria Novella, outside the Spanish Chapel.

Key to floor plan

1 Pulpit
2 Masaccio's "The Trinity"
3 Cappella di F. Strozzi
4 Chancel
5 Cappella Gondi
6 Cappella Strozzi
7 Sacristy
8 Chiostro Verde
9 Ucello's "The Flood"
10 Cappellone degli Spagnoli

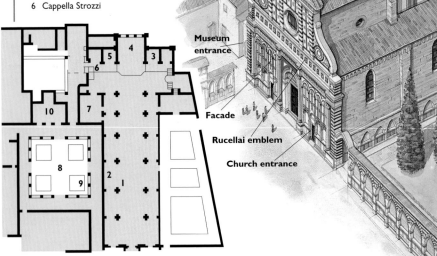

Cappellone degli Spagnoli

"The Trinity" by Masaccio

Chiostro Verde

Dominican sun emblem

Museum entrance

Facade

Rucellai emblem

Church entrance

Museo di Santa Maria Novella

✉ Piazza Santa Maria Novella

☎ 055 282 187

🕐 Closed p.m. daily & Fri.

💲 $

sponsor of the church's facade, designed by Brunelleschi, and executed by Andrea Cavalcanti, Brunelleschi's adopted son. It was from this pulpit, incidentally, that the Dominicans first denounced Galileo for espousing the Copernican view of the heavens—the idea that the Earth circled the sun, not vice versa. The

Dominicans also ran the city's Inquisition, and the denouncement led eventually to the scientist's arrest and trial.

Santa Maria is known less for its historical associations, however, then for its fresco cycles. The first of these lies in the **Cappella di Filippo Strozzi,** the chapel immediately to the right of the chancel, the area around the high altar. Sponsored by the banker Filippo Strozzi, the paintings (1489–1502) are the work of Filippino Lippi and deal with episodes from the life of Strozzi's namesake, St. Philip (San Filippo in Italian) the Apostle. At the rear of the chapel stands the banker's tomb (1491–95), an accomplished work by Benedetto da Maiano.

Long before the frescoes appeared, this chapel's predecessor was the fictional setting for the opening of *Il Decamerone,* or *The Decameron,* one of the foremost works of medieval literature. Written by Giovanni Boccaccio in the wake of the 1348 Black Death, this 100-tale epic is told by ten people over the course of ten days (see box, p. 156). For most scholars it marks the beginning of Italian prose, and it influenced many subsequent writers, among them Chaucer, Rabelais, and Shakespeare. Boccaccio reveled in a world turned upside down by the plague, a world where for a short while the normal moral, religious, and social constraints of life were suspended. Bawdy tales, courtly love, sexual high jinks, and high culture are mixed in a zestful and realistic narrative that starts when "seven ladies young and fair" meet in Santa Maria after Mass and decide to flee the pestilence-ridden city for the countryside.

Chancel

High altar

Cappella Gondi

Cappella di F. Strozzi

Old cemetery

"Avelli," or grave niches

Moving on, the church's second and most important cycle, a work by Domenico Ghirlandaio, is ranged around the **chancel,** or **Cappella Tornabuoni,** to the left. It, too, was commissioned by a banker, Giovanni Tornabuoni. Here the themes are the life of St. John the Baptist (right wall) and the life of the Virgin. The cycle is crammed with numerous contemporary portraits—including members of the Tornabuoni family—and a wealth of fascinating insights into the daily life of 15th-century Florence. The chancel's previous fresco cycle, by Orcagna, was reputedly destroyed a century earlier after being struck by a bolt of lightning.

The chapel to the left of the chancel as you face the altar is the **Cappella Gondi,** known for Brunelleschi's wooden "Crucifix," the only such work by a man who scarcely returned to sculpture after failing to secure the commission for the baptistery doors in 1401 (see pp. 66–71). Legend has it Brunelleschi executed the work because he was horrified by the uncouth nature of Donatello's similar "Crucifix" in the church of Santa Croce (see pp. 108–115). The story goes that Donatello was so struck on seeing his rival's work that he dropped a basket of eggs.

Boccaccio

Giovanni Boccaccio (1313–1375) was probably born in Paris, the illegitimate son of an Italian merchant. He grew up in Florence but fell in love with Naples in his 20s, having traveled there on business. He studied the classics and became part of the city's courtly circle before returning to Florence in 1340.

In Florence he met fellow writer Petrarch (1304–1375), with whom he shared an interest in reviving Latin and Greek as literary languages. He also wrote his first major work, *Fiammetta* (1343), a romance based on a love affair at the Neapolitan court. He wrote his most famous work, the *Decamerone,* or *Decameron,* following the Black Death in 1348. He is also remembered for a life of Dante, *Vita di Dante,* written about 1360, and the *Teseide,* or Knight's Tale. ■

Santa Maria's third fresco cycle lies in the **Cappella Strozzi,** the raised chapel in the north transept. Its paintings (1350–57) were paid for by Tommaso Strozzi, a banking ancestor of Filippo Strozzi, and were commissioned to help expiate the sin of usury (lending money with interest), a practice then considered a sin by the Church. They are the work of Nardo di Cione (died 1366), brother of the more celebrated Orcagna (Andrea di Cione), who was responsible for the chapel's main altarpiece. The principal frescoes depict "Paradiso" (on the left wall as you face the altar) and a pictorial version of Dante's "Inferno" (right wall). Dante has been painted as one of the saved in the "Last Judgment" fresco behind the chapel's altar; he is the figure third from the left, second row from the top. Tommaso is also present, shown being led to Paradise with his wife by St. Michael.

Moving back down to the main level of the church, you turn right through the transept door into the **sacristy,** whose highlights are a pretty glazed terra-cotta marble basin (1498) by Giovanni della Robbia and a huge painted "Crucifix with the Madonna and St. John the Evangelist," an early work by Giotto (before 1312).

Outside the church, go into the **Museo di Santa Maria di Novella** through a door on the left of the facade. Inside lies the 14th-century **Chiostro Verde,** or Green Cloister, named after the predominant green *terra* pigment of its frescoes. The frescoes in question were painted in 1425–1430 by Paolo Uccello and depict faded stories from Genesis, of which the most famous panel is "The Flood" on the right (east) wall, with its twin images of Noah's ark before and after the deluge.

Leading off the cloister is the **Cappellone degli Spagnoli,** or Spanish Chapel, so-called because it was used by Eleonora of Toledo, the Spanish wife of Cosimo I. Most of its interior is adorned with magnificent frescoes, some of the most extensive in Florence, by the little-known painter Andrea da Firenze (active 1343–1377). Those on the left wall depict "The Triumph of Divine Wisdom," those on the right wall "The Mission, Work and Triumph of the Dominican Order" with intricate symbolism. ■

This detail from the "Birth of St. John the Baptist" is part of Ghirlandaio's fresco cycle.

Opposite: "The Trinity" by Masaccio shows a mastery of perspective.

Santa Trìnita

THE CHURCH OF SANTA TRÌNITA IS A FASCINATING HYBRID of styles. Founded in 1092, it was rebuilt between 1300 and 1330, lending the interior a largely Gothic appearance that contrasts with the mannerist style of the replaced Gothic facade (1593) and fragments from the original 11th-century church. The building's main glory is artistic rather than architectural, however—a lovely Renaissance fresco cycle by Domenico Ghirlandaio.

Santa Trìnita
- Map p. 150
- Piazza Santa Trinita
- 055 216 912
- Closed L & early p.m.
- A, B, 6, 11, 36, 37

Above: Detail of two shepherds from "The Adoration of the Shepherds" (opposite)

The church was founded by the Vallombrosans, a religious order established by Giovanni Gualberto, a nobleman turned Benedictine monk. One Good Friday, so the story goes, Gualberto was scouring Florence seeking to avenge the murder of his brother. On finding the murderer, however, he spared his life—in honor of the holy day—and proceeded to the church of San Miniato al Monte to pray. There a crucifix miraculously bowed its head at Gualberto's act of mercy, a crucifix eventually installed in Santa Trìnita. A series of frescoes in the church portrays episodes from Gualberto's life (see p. 159).

The best way to visit the church is to work around the side chapels beginning on the south (right) wall. The fourth chapel is the **Cappella**

Bartolini-Salimbeni. It contains a fresco cycle by Lorenzo Monaco (1370–1425) of scenes from the life of the Virgin. These precede the church's chief pictorial highlight, a fresco cycle by Domenico Ghirlandaio of episodes from the life of St. Francis (1483–86) in the **Cappella Sassetti** (the second chapel to the right of the high altar). The paintings were commissioned by Francesco Sassetti, a manager of the Medici bank and friend of Lorenzo the Magnificent, partly to outdo the frescoes of Sassetti's rival, Giovanni Tornabuoni, in Santa Maria Novella, also by Ghirlandaio (see p. 156).

As in Santa Maria, Ghirlandaio uses a religious theme as a partial excuse to portray the world of 15th-century Florence. The panel in which St. Francis heals a sick child, for example, is set in Piazza Santa Trìnita; note the old Santa Trìnita bridge and the Santa Trìnita church still with its original Gothic facade (see above). "St. Francis Receiving the Franciscan Rule" (in the lunette) is set in Florence's Piazza della Signoria, complete with the Loggia della Signoria and a portrait of Sassetti between his son, Federigo, and Lorenzo the Magnificent (in the right foreground). Below Lorenzo stands the humanist scholar and teacher Angelo Poliziano (1454–1494) and three of his charges—Lorenzo's sons. The figure standing with his hand on his hip is Ghirlandaio.

Ghirlandaio also painted the chapel's altarpiece, "The Adoration of the Shepherds," a painting with a striking Renaissance fusion of Christian and classical iconography. Thus, Christ's manger is an old Roman sarcophagus, Mary and the shepherds are portrayed amid classical columns, and the background features a triumphal arch borrowed from Rome's ancient forum. The chapel's donors, or sponsors, Francesco Sassetti and his wife, Nera Corsi, are portrayed to either side of the painting (their bodies reside in the dark tombs on either side of the chapel).

In the next chapel to the left is the miraculous crucifix that bowed to Gualberto (see p. 158). Moving past the high altar, once home to Cimabue's majestic "Maestà," one of the paintings that opens the Uffizi gallery (see pp. 96–103), the second chapel on the left contains the church's other main treasure, Luca della Robbia's tomb of Benozzo Federighi, Bishop of Fiesole (1454–56). Moving down the church's north wall toward the entrance, the first chapel contains a statue of Mary Magdalene (1455) by Desiderio da Settignano, a work influenced by Donatello's similar statue in the Museo dell'Opera (see pp. 74–77). The next chapel, the Cappella Compagni, has frescoes by Lorenzo di Bicci on the life of St. Giovanni Gualberto—note the scene in which Gualberto pardons his brother's murderer—and Nero di Bicci's painting (1455) of the same saint with members of the Vallombrosan order. ■

Domenico Ghirlandaio's painting of "The Adoration of the Shepherds" forms the altarpiece of the Cappella Sassetti in the church of Santa Trinita.

Palazzo Davanzati

Palazzo Davanzati
- Map p. 150
- Via Porta Rossa 13
- 055 238 8610
- Re-opening in 2001 after restoration. Phone for details
- Bus: A to Via Pelliceria

The courtyard of the Palazzo Davanzati could be sealed against attackers in time of danger.

POSTERITY HAS DONE AWAY WITH MUCH OF MEDIEVAL Florence, building over its streets and houses, redesigning its churches and palaces, and consigning its paintings and sculptures to museums. This makes the Palazzo Davanzati all the more precious, for its beautiful interiors—complete with furniture and other period decoration—still perfectly capture the look and spirit of a Florentine medieval home.

The palace was built about 1330 by the Davizzi, a family of wealthy wool merchants. In 1578 it passed to the Davanzati—whose coat of arms still adorns the facade—and remained with the family until 1838, when its last owner committed suicide by jumping from an upper story window. It was then converted into apartments, before being restored in 1906 to something approaching its original state. Since 1956, it's been maintained as the Museo della Casa Fiorentina Antica, or the Museum of the Old Florentine House.

Before entering the house, look up at its facade. It is crowned by a loggia and dotted with hooks and rails once used for tying up animals, drying wool or clothes, or hanging banners during festivities. The courtyard provides a graphic glimpse of the realities of medieval life, where defense and survival in the event of attack were paramount. The huge doors were designed to be siege-resistant, the store rooms could accommodate provisions for a year, and the well—a luxury at a time when much of Florence still relied on public fountains—ensured a constant water supply. Note the majestic wooden staircase, the only one of its kind to have survived in Florence. Have a look, too, at the courtyard's rear right-hand pillar, whose carvings are said to include portraits of the Davizzi family.

The emphasis on defense is maintained on the first floor, where in the main Sala Grande, or **Sala Madornale**, a room used for family gatherings, you can still make out four *piombatoi di difesa* (wooden hatches) used to pour molten lead onto attackers below. This sala's ornate ceiling and lovely

decoration set the tone for many of the beautiful rooms that follow. Off to the left, for example, lies the Sala dei Pappagalli, named after the *pappagalli* (parrot) motifs of its frescoes. Such paintings would once have been common. Today these are some of the last in the city.

The most beautiful room of all is the nearby **Sala dei Pavoni,** or Camera Nuziale (Wedding Room), where another sublime ceiling is complemented by a wall frieze of trees, peacocks *(pavoni)*, and the coats of arms of the families related to the Davizzi. Note the en suite bathroom, an almost unheard of luxury at the time. The more usual Florentine arrangement—as described in Giovanni Boccaccio's *Decameron* (see p. 156)—was a plank placed over a large communal pit. Drains in Florence were introduced at about the time the palace was built, and it was only in 1325 that a law had been passed forbidding the tipping of sewage onto the streets. Before that, the law required only that you utter three warning shouts before emptying a chamber pot from your window.

As you explore the palace's many rooms and move up through its four stories, you come across all manner of decorative touches and pieces of period furniture, not to mention numerous incidental antiques, tapestries, sculptures, ceramics, and textiles. One of the most fascinating rooms, however, is also one of the most austere—the medieval **kitchen.** This room, as in most old palaces, was on the top floor as a precaution against fire. The palace's women and servants would have spent most of their time here; in winter it would have been the warmest as well as the busiest part of the house. Many of the kitchen utensils on display are fascinating, notably the unwieldy *girapolenta,* used for stirring polenta, and the *impastatori,* used for mixing pasta and bread dough.

Take a look at the views from the kitchen windows, but don't be fooled by the present leaded windows. For much of the Middle Ages, the best windows most people could hope for were rags soaked in turpentine (for waterproofing) and stretched across rickety frames. ■

The Sala dei Pavoni takes its name from the 14th-century frieze of peacocks *(pavoni* in Italian) around the upper walls.

Ponte Vecchio

THE PONTE VECCHIO IS AMONG FLORENCE'S MOST famous sights, but the fact that it has survived for almost seven centuries is something of a miracle. It easily could have been destroyed in one of the many floods to have ravaged the city or have fallen victim to the Nazis in 1944: It was the only bridge spared—apparently on Hitler's orders—as Field Marshal Kesseling attempted to slow the advance of the United States Fifth Army.

The arched spaces near the center of the Ponte Vecchio were originally designed to allow garbage to be tipped directly into the Arno.

Ponte Vecchio

Map p. 150

A bridge has probably existed on the site of the Ponte Vecchio—raised at the Arno's narrowest point—since the Etruscans were here. During Roman times it carried the Via Cassia, a vital highway that linked Rome to northern Italy, although some historians suggest the Roman-era bridge was located farther upstream. For centuries the crossing remained the city's only trans-Arno link, but its wooden superstructure was replaced on several occasions, usually in the wake of floods.

The reorganization of Florence's defenses in 1172 brought large areas south of the river within the city's orbit, a move that made the crossing still more important as a pivotal point in the urban fabric. When floods swept away the

wooden bridge in 1117, the city fathers commissioned what was probably the first stone bridge on the site, albeit one that still had a wooden roadbed. When floods destroyed this structure in 1333, the city decided enough was enough and commissioned the present stone bridge in 1345.

At this point the crossing took its present name—which means the "old bridge"—coined by the Florentines to distinguish it from the Ponte alla Carraia (1218) upstream, then known as the Ponte Nuovo, new bridge. At the same time the bridge was made the fulcrum of the city's riverside defenses. All adjoining facades on the Arno deemed a threat in the event of attack were altered so as to be "blind," or without windows.

The Ponte Vecchio's famous shops had actually appeared on previous incarnations of the bridge during the 13th century. Most belonged to butchers and fishmongers, who were attracted to the river because it made a convenient dumping ground for their waste. Next came the tanners, who used the river to soak their hides before tanning them in horse's urine.

The bridge received a major facelift in 1565, when Grand Duke Cosimo I built the **Corridoio Vasariano,** a covered passageway from the Uffizi, then the Medici's offices, to the Palazzo Pitti, a newly acquired Medici palace across the river. The passageway was built to

celebrate the marriage of Cosimo's son, Francesco (1541–1587), to Joanna of Austria. Construction was trusted to Giorgio Vasari, a painter and writer best known for his biographies of great Italian painters. Vasari made much of the fact the project took only five months to complete, boasting that it would have taken any other man five years. He also cited some illustrious antecedents, claiming to have been inspired by the passageway that linked the palaces of Priam and Hector in ancient Troy.

Today, the corridor runs in an obvious but rather bland line across the top of the bridge's shops. Once across the Arno it skirts above Santa Felicita, passing over the church's main portico in order—so it's said—that Cosimo could attend services without having to mix with the congregation. Inside, the corridor is lined with self-portraits but is only intermittently open (by way of the Uffizi). Contact the Uffizi or visitor centers for current details.

A future Medici Grand Duke, Ferdinando I, found himself disturbed by the noxious smells and noises emanating from the bridge's shops. In 1593 he banished the practitioners of what he called these "vile arts." In their place—at double the rent—he installed some 50 jewelers and goldsmiths, many of whose descendants still trade from the pretty *madielle,* or hatches, of their wooden-shuttered shops. A bust (1900) of one of Florence's most famous goldsmiths, Benvenuto Cellini, stands at the middle of the bridge. ■

This view along the Ponte Vecchio looks toward the cathedral dome. Many shops on the bridge are more than 400 years old.

Floods

Of all the episodes in Florence's recent history, none has captured attention as forcibly as the events of a November dawn in 1966 when a flood of staggering intensity hit the still slumbering city. Many people were killed and innumerable works of art either lost or damaged beyond repair. And yet the castatrophe was not without precedent, for this was simply the latest episode in a history of flooding.

Visit Florence in summer and gaze down at the benign, slowly flowing waters of the Arno, and you may wonder how such an innocuous-looking river could ever threaten the city. Mark Twain, writing of the river in *Innocents Abroad* in 1869, was unimpressed: "This great historical creek," he wrote, "with four feet in the channel…would be a very plausible river if they would pump some water into it." Compare this with the account of K. K. Taylor, another American writer, who described a very different scene in her 1966 *Diary of Florence in Flood:* "A tumultuous mass of water stretches from bank to bank," she wrote, "a snarling brown torrent of terrific velocity, spiraling in whirlpools and countercurrents …this tremendous water carries mats of debris: straw, twigs, leafy branches, rags, a litter that the river sucks down and spews up again in a swelling turbulence."

Florentine chronicles over the years tend more to Taylor's view than Twain's. "A great part of the city became a lake," lamented one writer in 1269, when floods carried away the Carraia and Trinita bridges. In 1333 a four-day storm unleashed floods so violent that church bells were tolled to drive out the devils blamed for the watery disaster.

But why is Florence prey to such disasters? The main culprits are the surging meltwaters of the Apennine mountains and Florence's own position—ringed by hills and just downstream of the Sieve, a major tributary of the Arno. In 1966 the potential for disaster had been magnified by almost 40 days of rain. The final straw came on the night of November 4, when sluice gates above Florence were opened to prevent the collapse of a dam.

Meticulous work has restored many of the paintings and books damaged by water and slurry when the Arno flooded in 1966.

Almost the only people made aware of the dangers were the Ponte Vecchio jewelers, summoned by a night watchman as the bridge began to shake. At dawn, water crashed through the city, moving with such ferocity that commuters in the railroad station subway were drowned where they stood. Thirty-five Florentines perished in all, and many hundreds were made homeless. Great damage was done to the city's buildings and works of art. In places water reached 20 feet (6 m) above street level. Damage was exacerbated by heating oil, recently delivered for the winter and flushed out of basements by the water. Such was the power of the torrent that five of Lorenzo Ghiberti's bronze panels were torn from the Baptistery doors and dumped over a mile away. Slurry slopped around paintings in the Uffizi's cellars and damaged books and manuscripts in the Biblioteca Nazionale.

Donations and volunteers flowed into the city to help with the cleanup. Many advances were made in restoration techniques, but even today only about 70 percent of the stricken paintings are on show; two laboratories—one for sculptures, one for paintings—still operate to repair the damage of a single night. ■

Above: Cars and debris were tossed like corks as floodwater coursed through Florence.

Water in the baptistery rose almost hip-height on Donatello's Mary Magdalene.

More places to visit in Western Florence

CENACOLO DI GHIRLANDAIO

This painting of the Cenacolo, or "Last Supper," is one of several across Florence (see p. 146); it was painted in 1480 by Domenico Ghirlandaio for the refectory (eating place) of the convent next to the church of Ognissanti (see below). Like many paintings by this artist, notably the frescoes in the churches of Santa Trìnita and Santa Maria Novella, the work is placid and lyrical in tone, and overflowing with narrative detail.

◪ Ognissanti: Map p. 150 ✉ Borgo Ognissanti 42 ☎ 055 239 6802 🕓 Closed p.m., & all Wed.–Fri., & Sun. 🚌 Bus: B

OGNISSANTI

For much of Florence's medieval history, the core of its thriving textile industry was located in a western district of the city close to the river, a useful source of water for the various

Giotto painted the "Maestà," now in the Uffizi, for the church of Ognissanti.

processes involved in preparing and treating wool. At this area's heart lay the church of Ognissanti, or All Saints, founded around 1251 by the Umiliati, a religious order from Lombardy in northern Italy renowned for expertise in weaving woolen cloth. Some idea of the order's wealth can be gleaned from the fact that it commissioned Giotto's "Maestà."

Inside the church, on the second altar on the south (right) wall, is a painting of the "Madonna della Misericordia" (1473) by Domenico Ghirlandaio (the lower of two paintings here). Look for the face squeezed between the Madonna and the dark-cloaked figure. It belongs to Amerigo Vespucci, a Medici agent in Seville, Spain, whose voyages to the New World in 1499 and 1501 would see the Americas named in his honor.

The reason he is here is that the altar was paid for by his family, a prominent local family of silk merchants. Other family members feature in the painting, not least Simonetta Vespucci (at the Virgin's left hand), considered the most alluring woman of her day. She was the mistress of Giulio de' Medici, as well as the model for Venus in Botticelli's famous painting now in the Uffizi (see pp. 100-101). Botticelli's involvement with the Vespucci was no accident, for he came from a family—the Filipepi—who lived locally and were on friendly terms with the Vespucci. The artist is buried in the church beneath a round tomb marker in the south (right) transept. He also painted "St. Augustine's Vision of St. Jerome" (1480) between the third and fourth altars on the wall opposite Ghirlandaio's "Madonna."

◪ Map p. 150 ✉ Borgo Ognissanti ☎ 055 239 6802 🕓 Closed L & all Sun. 🚌 Bus: B

SAN PANCRAZIO

San Pancrazio's long life as a church—it is one of Florence's oldest—came to an end when it was deconsecrated in 1808. Today, it houses the **Museo Marino Marini,** devoted to the works of the noted Pistoia-born painter and sculptor Marino Marini (1901–1980). Also worth seeing here is the **Cappella Rucellai,** formerly part of the church but now entered from Via della Spada. Although remodeled for Giovanni Rucellai (see p. 152), it preserves its original design and the classically inspired Tempietto del Santo Sepolcro (1467), a copy of Jerusalem's Holy Sepulcher. Both the design and the temple were the work of the artist and architectural theorist Leon Battista Alberti.

◪ Map p. 150 ✉ Piazza San Pancrazio ☎ 055 219 432 🕓 Closed Sun. p.m., all Tues., & Aug. 💲 $$ 🚌 Bus: B ■

The River Arno divides Florence. In the past this division was more marked and led to the development of a district on the river's southern bank with its own name and its own identity—the Oltrarno, or beyond the Arno.

Oltrarno

Detail from a Cappella Brancacci fresco

Oltrarno

THE OLTRARNO IS THE SOUTHERN PART OF FLORENCE. THE CITY'S ORIGINAL
Roman colony developed on the Arno's northern bank at the narrowest bridging point
across the river. But while there was a bridge to the southern shore, not to mention an
important Roman road that traversed the area to the south, Florence remained a city confined to its northern bank for many centuries after its foundation.

This state of affairs continued until at least
1218, the year a second bridge was forced
across the river—the Ponte alla Carraia.
The new link was prompted in part by the
Oltrarno's growing importance as a commercial center, and in particular as one of the
city's main areas of textile production. Textile
businesses were attracted primarily by the
river, whose water was vital for washing,
dyeing, and other processes involved in the
manufacture of wool and other cloth.

The area maintained a reputation as a
blue-collar district for centuries afterward,

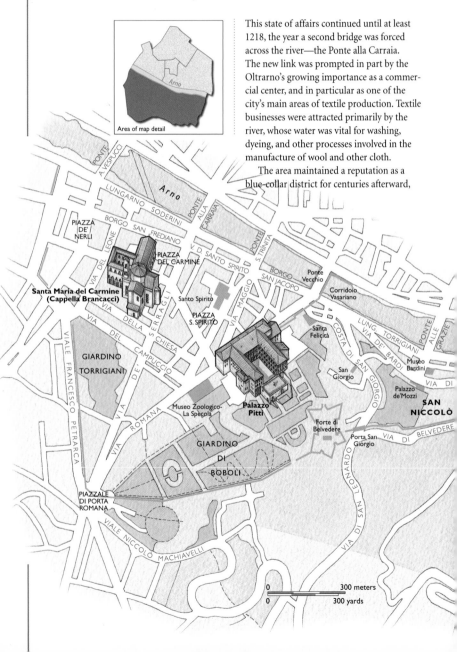

Area of map detail

and although this has changed a little in recent years, one of the Oltrarno's charms is still the large number of artisans' workshops, the existence of villagelike neighborhoods, and the earthier and more traditional atmosphere of its streets and squares.

Further impetus to the district's growth came in the 13th century with the building of two major churches—Santo Spirito and Santa Maria del Carmine. So marked was Santo Spirito's effect that, when the city was divided into four areas in the 14th century, the whole Oltrarno area was given its name. Another strong spur to the area's development came in the 15th century with the construction of the Palazzo Pitti, a vast palace that became the Medici's principal home and court.

The palace is one of the Oltrarno's key sights, one whose colossal and rambling structure dominates—and seems out of place in—what is otherwise a modest and intimate district. Today, the palace serves as a vast museum complex, although only two or three of its museums are of interest to most visitors. The main one is the Galleria Palatina, whose beautiful salons provide a splendid setting for part of the Medici's extensive collection of

The 16th-century bronze statue of "Neptune" by Stoldi Lornzi cuts a chill figure on a fall day in the Boboli Garden.

paintings. With numerous works of art by Raphael, Titian, and others, this gallery is second only to the Uffizi in terms of the quality and quantity of its paintings.

Despite the importance of the Palazzo Pitti, the Oltrarno continued to be somewhat marginalized, and there is a a relative shortage of major monuments compared to the area north of the river. This said, those that do exist are some of the most exquisite in the city. The fresco cycle in the Cappella Brancacci is one of the most important in Western art; the hilltop church of San Miniato al Monte is among Tuscany's most beautiful Romanesque buildings; and the Giardino di Boboli, or Boboli Garden, behind the Palazzo Pitti, is the loveliest open space in the city. Last, but not least, the *coste*, or old lanes, leading to San Miniato, provide walks through an almost rural city enclave, with views to the Tuscan hills. ■

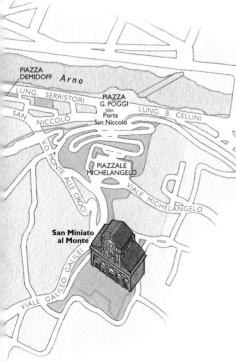

Palazzo Pitti

THE PALAZZO PITTI MAY NOT BEAR THE MEDICI NAME, BUT members of Florence's first family were the owners of this monolithic palace for many centuries. Its countless rambling rooms house several museums, the most important of which is the Galleria Palatina, whose beautiful salons are filled from floor to ceiling with paintings from the Medici's private collection.

Palazzo Pitti

Map p. 168

Piazza de' Pitti

Bus: D

The palace was begun about 1458 by Luca Pitti, a merchant and banker. Part of his intention in conceiving so grandiose a building was to challenge the Medici, his despised business rivals. The original design may have been the work of Brunelleschi, who is said to have taken the plan to Pitti after Cosimo de' Medici (the Elder) rejected it as too ostentatious. Cosimo's taste was notoriously sober, as is clear from the plain-faced Palazzo Medici-Riccardi, begun for him by Michelozzo 14 years earlier (see pp. 134–37). The wily Medici godfather was not necessarily modest, however; he simply realized that too conspicuous a show of wealth and power would alienate many everyday Florentines.

The project rejected by Cosimo eventually crippled the Pitti financially, forcing them—ironically—to sell out to the Medici in 1549. The palace was bought by Duke Cosimo I, partly on the prompting of his Spanish wife, Eleonora di Toledo, who had little time for Cosimo's previous lodging, the Palazzo Vecchio. Eleonora immediately set about expanding the palace, which at the time was only a single room deep, being hemmed in by the hills of the Boboli Garden to the rear. Cosimo, for his part, linked his new home with the old Medici offices, or Uffizi, now the gallery of the same name. To do so, he commissioned the artist and critic Giorgio Vasari to construct the Corridoio Vasariano, a raised and enclosed

passageway that still runs across the top of the Ponte Vecchio (see pp. 162–63).

The palace remained the seat of the Medici court and that of the family's successors, the Lorraine dynasty, for some three centuries. Following Italian Unification in 1860, it was also used as the seat of the Savoy kings during Florence's brief spell as the Italian capital between 1865 and 1870. (Rome at the time was still occupied by French and papal troops.) By this time it had expanded to its present enormous size, the facade alone being three times the width planned for the Pitti some four centuries earlier.

The spacious palace interior and parts of the Boboli Garden to the rear are given over to a series of museums that, at first sight, present an intimidating sightseeing prospect. In fact, only two of the galleries are essential viewing—the **Galleria Palatina,** which holds much of the Medici's private art collection, and the **Museo degli Argenti,** a collection of the family's silver, antiques, and other precious objets d'art.

Whether you see the other galleries will depend on time and your tastes. The **Appartamentali Reali** are a suite of richly decorated royal apartments; the **Galleria delle Porcellane** is a collection of Medici and Lorraine porcelain housed in the Casino del Cavaliere in the Boboli Garden (Closed p.m., & 1st, 3rd, & 5th Mon.

Opposite: The Sala di Marte, or Hall of Mars, in the Galleria Palatina of the Palazzo Pitti

with the idea that the works on display are second-rate leftovers. The collection has no fewer than 11 works by Raphael and 14 by Titian, plus paintings by all the other great names of the Florentine canon, many works by Venetian masters, and paintings by Caravaggio, Pieter Paul Rubens, Antonie Van Dyck, and others.

The Galleria, like the palace, can be disorientating. Having bought your ticket, walk to the rear right-hand corner of the immense inner courtyard, and climb the imposing staircase to the Palatina's entrance. You then pass under a magnificent chandelier—all of the palace is gloriously decorated—and walk through two rooms with lovely views over the Boboli Garden. In the third room you come to the start of the gallery's set itinerary, a route that takes you through seven art-filled rooms and then back through five similar but still more spectacular rooms, with several masterpieces by Raphael.

A glorious "Madonna and Child" (1450) by Filippo Lippi dominates the first major room, the **Sala di Prometeo** (Hall of Prometheus), off which opens a warren of rooms to the right crammed with minor paintings. Then comes the **Sala di Ulisse** (Hall of Ulysses), which contains Raphael's "Madonna dell' Impannata" (1514) and a work by the young Filippino Lippi—the son of Filippo Lippi—the "Death of Lucretia," painted when the artist was still studying in the workshop of Botticelli. Moving on, you come to the **Bagno di Napoleone,**

Raphael painted the "Madonna della Seggiola" about 1514 for Pope Leo X, a Medici.

& 2nd & 4th Sun. of the month); the **Museo delle Carrozze** is a collection of Medici and Lorraine state carriages (currently closed); the **Galleria delle Costume** features an array of sumptuous 18th- and 19th-century clothing (housed in the Palazzina della Meridiana, entered from the Boboli Garden). The **Galleria d'Arte Moderna** is a 30-room collection of mostly uninspiring paintings and sculptures from the early 18th century onward.

Whichever of these you decide to see, make sure that your first visit is to the Galleria Palatina, laid out in its present guise toward the end of the 18th century. It houses the parts of the Medici's immense art collection that couldn't be fitted into the Uffizi. But, don't come here

Galleria Palatina

- ✉ Palazzo Pitti, Piazza de' Pitti
- ☎ 055 238 8710
- 🕐 Closed Mon., & Sun p.m. Nov.–Feb.
- 💲 $$$

converted in 1813 into a bathroom for Napoleon, and then to the beautifully tiled **Sala della Stufa,** or Room of the Stove, so-called because it provided the heating for the palace's other principal rooms.

From here you enter the **Sala dell'Educazione di Giove,** the last of the gallery's first line of principal parallel rooms. Its star turn is Caravaggio's "Sleeping Cupid" (1608), painted in Malta for a Florentine nobleman. The room also contains Cristofano Allori's (1577–1621) "Judith and Holofernes," one of 17th-century Florence's most popular paintings. It is a curiously bloodless picture, given the theme—Judith is shown clutching Holofernes's recently severed head—and is notable for the fact that the models for the main figures were the artist, his mother, and his mistress.

Raphael is the star of the **Sala dell'Iliade** (Hall of the Iliad), the first of the six rooms on the return side of the palace, with "La Gravida" (1506), or the "Expectant Mother," an unusual theme for the time. In the next room, the **Sala di Saturno** (Hall of Saturn), you can trace Raphael's development in a series of paintings that span almost his whole career. One of the earliest is the "Madonna del Granduca" (1506), which shows the soft-toned influence of Leonardo da Vinci and Raphael's teacher, Perugino. Its name comes from the fact that its owner, Grand Duke (Granduca) Ferdinand III of Lorraine, is said to have taken the painting with him wherever he went. A year or so later Raphael painted "Agnolo and Maddalena Doni" (1506–1507), portraits whose style would influence portraiture for years. Maddalena's pose, you may notice, deliberately copies that of Leonardo's famous "Mona Lisa." The pictures were painted to

"Judith and Holofernes" by Cristofano Allori. The model for the main female figure was the artist's mistress.

celebrate the couple's marriage, an event also commemorated by Michelangelo's "Doni Tondo," the Uffizi's only painting by the artist (see p. 103).

Also here are the "Madonna del Baldacchino," left unfinished when Raphael went to Rome in 1508, a "Portrait of Tommaso Inghirami" (1510), and perhaps the gallery's finest work, the "Madonna della Seggiola" (1513–14), whose tondo, the round panel on which it is painted, is said to have come from the bottom of a wine barrel. Tondo paintings were common in Florence, and Raphael was keen to excel in the discipline their particular form imposed. He succeeded, and for centuries this was the most popular image of the Madonna in Italian art.

A 16th-century silver and crystal casket by the Renaissance artist Valero Belli is on view in the Museo degli Argenti.

The **Sala di Giove** (Hall of Jove) was once the palace's main throne room. Today, it contains some of Florence's most precious paintings, including the "Three Ages of Man" (1500), attributed to Giorgione, a painter whose known works are one signed painting and a fresco, though others are attributed to him, and several of a total of 17 works by Andrea del Sarto in the gallery. Andrea was perhaps the major artist working in Florence from about 1510 onward, when his most notable contemporaries, Raphael and Michelangelo, were dominant in Rome. Ironically, the works of the first of these, Raphael, provide the cornerstone of both this room, much as they have in the preceeding rooms. Here you can see his "Donna Velata" (1516), or

"Veiled Woman," an idealized portrait of a Roman baker's daughter-turned-model who was reputedly the painter's mistress.

The next room, the **Sala di Marte** (Hall of Mars), is dominated by an immense painting by Rubens called the "The Consequences of War" (1638), an allegory of the Thirty Years' War, a conflict that ravaged much of Europe between 1618 and 1648. Describing the painting, the artist explained that the central figure of a "grief-stricken woman is the unfortunate Europe, who, for so many years now, has suffered plunder, outrage and misery." Don't miss the Medici's six-ball symbol emblazoned across the ceiling (see p. 130), nor the room's trio of fine portraits: Van Dyck's "Cardinal Bentivoglio," a Bolognese prelate who was papal ambassador to the Low Countries (present-day Luxembourg, the Netherlands, and Belgium); the almost modern-looking "Portrait of a Man" by the Venice-based painter Veronese (1528–1588); and Titian's "Ippolito de Medici," a Medici scion made a cardinal at 18 and poisoned at 24. Here he is shown setting off to lead an expedition against the Turks in defense of Vienna.

Titian also features in the next room, the **Sala di Apollo** (Hall of Apollo), most notably with a sensuous "Mary Magdalene," and "A Portrait of an Englishman," one of his best known and most penetrating portraits (the sitter's identity is unknown). The room's most eye-catching picture is an altarpiece of the "Madonna and Saints" (1522) by Rosso Fiorentino, a disillusioned mannerist artist who eventually left Florence for France. Also interesting is a double portrait of King Charles I of England (R.1625–1649) and his wife, Henrietta Maria (1609–1669), a picture long attributed to the Flemish master Van Dyck. Its date and actual artist are unknown, but Henrietta was a scion of the Medici family, who at one time tried to assemble a portrait collection of all the crowned heads of Europe. This project explains why you will find a rather out of place portrait of Queen Elizabeth I of England (R.1558–1603) in the Sala dell'Iliade.

The beautiful **Sala di Venere** (Hall of Venus) is as fine as the previous rooms. Its ceiling—like those of the preceeding four rooms—is covered in frescoes by Pietro da Cortona (1596–1669), a program of mostly mythological scenes intended to glorify the Medici by associating them with the legends of the classical world. Below, the walls are smothered in painting, their apparently haphazard arrangement the one preferred by the Medici. Here, as elsewhere, you can only pick out the absolute highlights, so wander until you find something that catches your eye.

The Sala di Venere takes its name from the "Venere Italica," or "Italian Venus," by Antonio Canova, a statue commissioned in 1812 to replace the famous "Medici Venus" removed to Paris from the Uffizi by Napoleon. Canova's work was moved here when the stolen statue was returned to the Uffizi after Napoleon's defeat (see p. 102). The key paintings are all by the Venetian artist Titian, or Tiziano (1485/89–1575), and include the "Portrait of Pietro Aretino," a lecherous poet and friend of the artist; "Portrait of Pope Julius II," copied from a portrait by Raphael now in London's National Gallery; and "The Concert," an early work purchased by Leopoldo de' Medici in 1564 in the mistaken belief he was buying a picture by the equally celebrated Venetian artist Giorgione (1478–1510). Don't miss two fine marine paintings in this room by the Neapolitan painter Salvator Rosa (1615–1673) and two gargantuan landscapes by Pieter Paul Rubens.

MUSEO DEGLI ARGENTI

Elsewhere in the Palazzo Pitti, be sure to visit the Museo degli Argenti, which you enter from the palace's main courtyard. Its beautifully decorated rooms are attractions in their own right, almost overshadowing the exhibits, which consist of precious artifacts from the Medici's private collection. These include glorious pieces of goldware and silverware (*argento* is Italian for "silver"), stunning *pietre dure* (inlaid stone) vases, precious stones, caskets, fabrics, carpets, furniture, and a host of other extravagant (and sometimes gaudy) precious objects.

Museo degli Argenti

✉ Palazzo Pitti, Piazza de' Pitti

☎ 055 238 8709

🕐 Closed p.m., also 2nd & 4th Sun., & 1st, 3rd, & 5th Mon. of month

💲 $

GIARDINO DI BOBOLI

The Giardino di Boboli, or Boboli Garden, Florence's principal park, lies behind the Palazzo Pitti. One of Italy's largest gardens, it was begun by Duke Cosimo I in 1549 and opened to the public in 1766. In high summer, parts can be dust-dry and a little dog-eared, but during the rest of the year this makes a a good place to stroll and take a break from city sightseeing.

Moving from west to east, the garden's main sights are the **Forte di Belvedere** on the hill above (see p. 188) and one of three grot-

Amphitheater

Neptune fountain

Ancient cypresses and 17th- and 18th-century statues flank the long avenue of the Viottolone.

Forte di Belvedere

Kaffeehaus

La Grotta di Buontalenti

Bacchus fountain

Giardino di Boboli

✉ Entrances: From Pitti Palace courtyard; Via Romana; Porta Romana

☎ 055 265 1816

🕐 Closed first & last Mon. of month

💲 $

toes in the garden, **La Grotta di Buontalenti,** a folly that contains casts of Michelangelo's "Slaves" (see p. 140) and lascivious 16th-century statues of "Venus Bathing" and "Paris Abducting Helen of Troy" by Giambologna and Vincenzo de' Rossi.

You can buy refreshments in summer at the 1776 roccoco-style **Kaffeehaus,** or Coffee House. One of the garden's most bizarre sights is the **Bacchus fountain,** a copy of a 1560 statue of Cosimo I's court dwarf, shown naked in the guise of Bacchus astride a tortoise.

Above: Statues dot the Isolotto, a small lake and island.

Viottolone

Piazzale dell' Isolotto

Perseus

Prato delle Colonne

Palazzo Pitti

The **Neptune Fountain** stands in a small lake amidst terracing dotted with Roman statues.

South of the fountain lies the **Amphitheater,** a quarry for stone used to build the Palazzo Pitti that was later landscaped and used for musical performances. East is the **Viottolone,** a walkway lined by cypress trees and statues. It ends at the **Piazzale dell' Isolotto,** a late mannerist mix of lake, island, garden, and sculpture begun in 1618. Cross the **Prato delle Colonne,** a grassy area named for its columns *(colonne),* to a 16th-century statue of **Perseus.** ∎

Cappella Brancacci

FLORENCE HAS MANY MAJESTIC AND IMPORTANT WORKS of art, but few are held in such high esteem by art historians as the frescoes by Masaccio, Filippino Lippi, and Masolino da Panicale in the Cappella Brancacci, a chapel adjoining the church of Santa Maria del Carmine. Begun when the Renaissance was close to its peak, the innovation and invention of the paintings would influence Florentine and other painters for generations to come.

The chapel and its paintings were paid for by Filippo Brancacci, a silk merchant and diplomat, who commissioned them in 1423 on his return from a posting to Egypt as the Florentine ambassador. Work on the frescoes probably began a year later and was initially undertaken by Masolino (1383–1447) and his promising young assistant, Tommaso di Ser Giovanni di Mone Cassai (1401–28), better known as Masaccio, a nickname that meant "Mad Tom." Masaccio's talents were given room to blossom in 1426 when Masolino, who held the post of official painter to the Hungarian court, was called to Budapest. When he returned to Florence in 1427 he found himself in the shadow of his former assistant.

The pair's frescoes embraced a new sense of realism, dramatic narrative, and handling of perspective that surpassed anything seen in Italy, dazzling other artists of the time. In the words of Giorgio Vasari, the 16th-century artist and art historian, "the most celebrated sculptors and painters…became excellent and illustrious in studying their art." The pictures, he added, were nothing less than a *scuola del mondo,* or a "school for the whole world." Even Michelangelo came here to sketch Masaccio's paintings.

Masaccio died when he was just 28, and in 1428 Masolino was called to Rome, never to return. Work on the chapel ceased completely in 1436 when Brancacci was exiled by

"The Expulsion of Adam and Eve from Paradise" by Masaccio. Clothes added to conceal the pair's nudity in 1652 were removed during 1990s restoration.

Opposite: In Masaccio's "St. Peter Healing the Sick," the figure in the red hat is a portrait of Masolino, the artist who worked with Masaccio on the Cappella Brancacci.

the Medici, his crime having been to marry the daughter of Palla Strozzi, leader of the city's defeated anti-Medici faction. The cycle was completed some 50 years later by Filippino Lippi, whose copying skills proved so consummate that his part in the chapel was only recognized as recently as 1838.

That the paintings have survived is something of a miracle. When Brancacci was exiled, for example, the Carmelite monks in charge of the chapel, anxious to placate the Medici, removed all portraits of their disgraced patron. And by 1680, when artistic tastes had changed, the chapel's new sponsor, one Francesco Ferroni, argued that "these ridiculous men in their cassocks and old-fashioned outfits" should be scrubbed out. In 1771 a fire ruined the pictures' frames and added to the wear and tear caused by centuries of candle grease and varnish. Proper restoration took place between 1983 and 1990.

Masaccio was responsible for the cycle's most famous image, the stark, emotionally charged panel portraying "The Expulsion of Adam and Eve from Paradise" (upper register, far left, on the entrance arch as you look at the frescoes). Compare Eve's open-mouthed cry of pain and Adam's head-in-hands despair with Masolino's more anodyne rendering of "Adam and Eve" in the fresco in the same position on the opposite wall. No other scene better

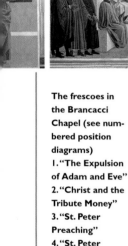

The frescoes in the Brancacci Chapel (see numbered position diagrams)

1. "The Expulsion of Adam and Eve"
2. "Christ and the Tribute Money"
3. "St. Peter Preaching"
4. "St. Peter Visited by Paul"
5. "Raising of Theophilus's Son"; "St. Peter Enthroned"
6. "St. Peter Healing the Sick"

1	2	3
4	5	6

Cappella Brancacci

🅰 Map p. 168

✉ Santa Maria del Carmine, Piazza del Carmine. The entrance is to the right as you face the church.

illustrates the psychological depth and emotional intensity Masaccio brought to Florentine painting.

All other panels in the cycle deal with episodes from the life of St. Peter, who is picked out in every scene by his orange cloak. The most striking panels, all by Masaccio, are "Christ and the Tribute Money," "St. Peter Healing the Sick," and the combined "Raising of Theophilus's Son" and "St. Peter Enthroned." The first is one of the most complicated and accomplished compositions of the early Renaissance, its single panel embracing no fewer than three separate episodes. At the center, Masaccio paints Christ at the gates of Capernaum being asked to pay a tribute owed to the city (the figure at the extreme right of the

group may be a self-portrait of the artist). On the left, St. Peter picks coins from the mouth of fish to pay the tribute (Christ can be seen in the central scene clearly indicating where the money will be found), and in the right-hand scene St. Peter hands over the tribute money to an official.

In "St. Peter Healing the Sick" (lower register, left of the altar), the sick are shown being healed as the saint's shadow passes over them; depicting beggars and the infirm with such graphic realism was revolutionary at the time. The fresco on the same lower level to the right of the altar shows Saints Peter and Paul giving alms, a reference to the customs of the early church, where part of one's wealth was given in charity. Also shown is the fate of Ananias, who withheld some of his wealth with the knowledge of his wife, Sapphira, and died with her after being castigated by Peter.

In the "Raising of Theophilus's Son" and "St. Peter Enthroned"

7	8	9
10	11	12

(completed by Lippi), Masaccio depicts the episode in which St. Peter raises the dead son of the Prefect of Antioch. In return, the grateful citizens build a throne from which the saint can preach, a scene portrayed to the right. The figures in the doorway to the right of the throne are thought to be Masaccio, Brunelleschi, and Renaissance architectural theorist Leon Battista Alberti. Masaccio originally painted himself touching Peter's cloak, a reference to the statue of the saint in St. Peter's, Rome, which pilgrims touch for good luck. When he completed the panel, Lippi thought the contact inappropriate and painted out the arm. Look closely: Signs of the alteration are still clearly visible.

There are more portraits in the fresco on the facing (right) wall (11), which combines the episodes of St. Peter's crucifixion (left) and Peter being sentenced to death by the Emperor Nero. The figure looking out at the spectator in the group to the left of the cross is Botticelli, Filippino Lippi's teacher, and the figure in a beret at the right of the Nero scene is a self-portrait of Lippi.

It is thought that Masaccio was responsible for panels 1, 2, 6, 7, and 10 (see plan), while Masolino da Panicale worked on panels 3 and 9. Filippino Lippi was responsible for panels 11 and 12. It is interesting to note the panels on which two artists worked. Masaccio began work on panel 5 but it was completed by Lippi. The other clear collaboration is panel 8, where Masaccio worked on the left-hand section and Masolino on the right. Masolino, in general, had a more decorative style than Masaccio's simpler and more realistic approach. ∎

7. "St. Peter Baptizing the Converts"
8. "St. Peter Healing the Cripple"; "Raising Tabitha"
9. "Temptation of Adam and Eve"
10. "St. Peter and St. John Giving Alms"
11. "St. Peter's Crucifixion"; "Before the Proconsul"
12. "The Release of St. Peter"

☎ 055 238 2195 or 055 294 883 (reservations)

🕐 Closed Sun. a.m. & all Tues. Groups of 30 admitted for a maximum of 15 min.

💲 $

🚌 Bus: D

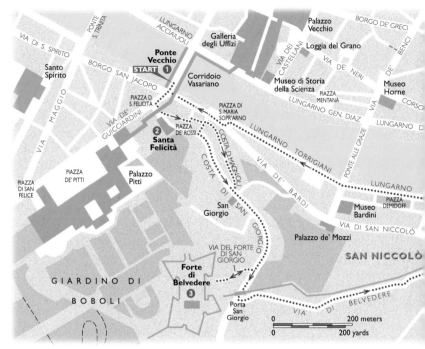

A walk through the Oltrarno to San Miniato al Monte

This pretty walk takes you from the Ponte Vecchio to the hilly slopes above the Arno and the glorious Romanesque church of San Miniato al Monte.

It's often said that Florence's main failing is its shortage of gardens and open space. This walk corrects that notion, taking you quickly into an almost rural part of the city just minutes away from its visitor-filled center. It's not a long walk, but it is uphill, so you may want to take a bus to San Miniato and follow the itinerary in reverse (downhill). Alternatively, take the bus on the return. Be sure to time your walk so as to see inside San Miniato; the church is usually closed daily from noon for a couple of hours.

Start on the southern side of the **Ponte Vecchio** ❶ (see pp. 162–63) and walk across Borgo San Jacopo, the street running along the river to your right as you face away from the bridge. You step almost immediately into Piazza di Santa Felicità, where you should stop to see the church of **Santa Felicità** ❷ and

its strange mannerist paintings (see p. 189). Then take the small lane to the left of the church, which brings you to Piazza de' Rossi, from whose eastern edge you can proceed up either Costa de' Magnoli or Costa di San Giorgio.

Ultimately you want to follow the picturesque Costa di San Giorgio—Costa de' Magnoli meets it after a short time—for its entire length to the Porta San Giorgio. This is a steep climb, so pause for breath occasionally, notably at No. 19, once home to the scientist Galileo Galilei, and again at the church of San Giorgio, whose plain facade contrasts with its richly decorated interior. Near the top of the street watch for Via del Forte di San Giorgio, where you should turn right if you want to make a short detour to the **Forte di Belvedere** ❸ (see p. 188).

Overhanging houses and workshops on the Ponte Vecchio. The older workshops are supported by timber struts called *sporti*.

you have gained, leaving you to climb once more when you reach the first major turning on the right, Via del Monte alle Croci. Turn right here and then left on the lane ahead lined with trees and crosses. This emerges at Viale Galileo Galilei, where a left turn brings you quickly to **Piazzale Michelangelo ④**, a busy and often visitor-choked area (it's one of the city's most famous viewpoints). Return to Viale Galileo Galilei and this time turn right; then climb the steps leading off the left side of the road to **San Miniato al Monte ⑤** (see pp. 184–87).

If you want to walk back via a different route, follow the steps and road back to Piazzale Michelangelo. Then take the lane-path leading off the extreme left side of the piazza, and bear right to follow a series of winding paths and steps steeply down to Porta San Niccolò. From here you can walk west on Lungarno Serristori along the river to Ponte alle Grazie or the Ponte Vecchio. ∎

- 🗺 Also see area map, pp. 168-69
- ▶ Ponte Vecchio
- ⟳ 1.5 miles (2.4 km)
- ⏱ Allow half a day
- ▶ San Miniato al Monte
- 🚌 Bus: 12 or 13 to/from Piazzale Michelangelo

NOT TO BE MISSED

- Ponte Vecchio
- Santa Felicità
- View from Piazzale Michelangelo
- San Miniato al Monte

Otherwise continue to Porta San Giorgio, a gateway that still contains a fresco of the "Madonna Enthroned with St. Leonard and St. George" (1430) by Bicci di Lorenzo.

Through the Porta turn left on Via di Belvedere (the street of the beautiful view), which follows the line of the old city walls and, as its name suggests, has a fine panorama over olive groves and pastoral countryside to the south. The street loses much of the height

San Miniato al Monte

The facade of San Miniato al Monte has the typical white and green marble decoration of Tuscan Romanesque churches.

TUSCANY'S MOST BEAUTIFUL ROMANESQUE CHURCH CAN be seen from across the city atop its hill on the Oltrarno's leafy fringes. It sits over the site of an earlier chapel dedicated to San Miniato, a saint martyred and buried on the spot in A.D. 250. Initially run by the Benedictines, the church passed in 1373 to the Olivetans, a minor Benedictine order, which lives there to this day.

San Miniato al Monte

- 🗺 Map p. 169
- ✉ Via del Monte alle Croci–Viale Galileo Galilei
- ☎ 055 234 2731
- 🚌 Bus: 12 or 13 from city center to Piazzale Michelangelo, a couple of minutes' walk from the church

Opposite: The Byzantine-style mosaic of San Miniato's front contrasts with its classically inspired pillars.

St. Minias, or San Miniato, was probably Florence's first martyr. Whether he was a Greek merchant or Armenian prince, no one is sure, but he originally came to Italy on a pilgrimage to Rome and settled in Florence about A.D. 250. He was martyred during the Christian persecutions by the Emperor Decius (R. A.D. 249–251). It is said that after being beheaded near the present-day Piazza della Signoria, he picked up his severed head and carried it across the Arno and up the hill to the site of San Miniato al Monte. The saint had already lived nearby as a hermit, and the hill—then known as Mon Fiorentius—was scattered with pagan temples.

Documentary evidence records the presence here of a chapel to the saint in the eighth century. Construction of the present church began in 1018 on the orders of Bishop Ildebrando, who in turn was acting on the instructions of Henry II, the Holy Roman Emperor (R.1002–1024), who endowed the church, according to one chronicler, "for the good of his soul." Building progressed in several phases and was only completed in 1207, a date you can see inscribed on the marble pavement inside.

Before entering the church, admire the sweeping panorama over the city, and then turn your attention to the church's magnificent exterior. Among Florentine Romanesque buildings, only the baptistery, on which San Miniato's

appearance was modeled, comes close to matching the beautiful **facade.** It is perhaps no coincidence both structures were mistaken during the Middle Ages as buildings of Roman origin. No similar facade would be built in the city until that of Santa Maria Novella, completed in the 15th century—and even that copied San Miniato.

The frontage was probably built in several stages, the simple five-arched lower register dating from the 11th century, the upper order being added a century later. From 1288, the church's upkeep was the responsibility of the Arte di Calimala, or Cloth Merchants Guild, which is why its emblem crowns the facade's summit—an eagle clutching a *torsello,* or 12 lengths of cloth. The mosaic below portrays "Christ Between the Virgin and St. Minias" (1260). It is noteworthy, among other things, for Christ's unusual blue Oriental bolster. The unfinished bell tower (begun 1523) replaced the original, which toppled in 1499; it was in turn threatened with destruction in 1530 during the siege of Florence by the troops of Emperor Charles V. During the conflict the tower was used as an artillery post, and thus it attracted the attention of enemy gunners. Michelangelo, enlisted to advise on the city's defenses, wrapped the tower in mattresses to protect it from cannon balls.

If the exterior dazzles, then the interior is beyond compare. The beautiful **pavement** dates from

of the Crucifix, created to house a miraculous crucifix that bowed its head to St. Giovanni Gualberto; the shape made for the now missing cross is still clear. (Turn to pages 158–59 for a description of Santa Trìnita and the story of Gualberto and the crucifix's fate after 1671.) The space left by the cross is bordered by painted panels (1394–96) attributed to Agnolo Gaddi and depicting the "Annunciation," stories of the Passion, and scenes from the lives of Saints Gualberto and Miniato.

The chapel was commissioned by Piero de' Medici, or Piero il Gottoso (Piero the Gouty), the father of Lorenzo the Magnificent. It was one of only a handful of commissions he made during his brief period as head of the Medici clan. Parts of the frieze and the marble medallion to the rear are adorned with Piero's personal symbols and motifs, namely the eagle with three feathers, an uncut diamond, and the motto *semper*, meaning "always." The last two motifs are references to the toughness and durability of Medici power. Note, also, the two eagles, symbols of the Arte di Calimala. They are designed to remind onlookers that while Piero de' Medici may have commissioned the chapel, the guild was responsible for organizing its actual creation. The glazed terra-cotta in the Cappella is the work of Luca della Robbia.

Steps to the side of the chapel lead down to the **crypt,** the oldest part of the church, housing the tomb of San Miniato and 36 ancient and mismatched columns. Bishop Ildebrando confirmed the bones interred here in the 11th century as those of Miniato, conveniently overlooking a well-documented account of how the "real" bones had earlier been

The simple floor plan of San Miniato al Monte was copied from the design of old Roman basilicas.

1207 and is covered in symbolic and other figures, although no one is quite sure what they mean. Some obviously depict the zodiac, but others may be taken from precious Sicilian fabrics or derive from Byzantine models introduced to Italy either through trade or during the crusades. Much of the interior, of course, has been restored and added to, but it still appears much as it must have almost a thousand years ago. Its three distinct levels—the nave, sunken crypt, and raised presbytery (the area by the high altar)—are unchanged, as are most of the pillars and capitals, many of which were salvaged from Roman and Byzantine buildings.

The center of the nave is dominated by Michelozzo's **Cappella del Crocefisso** (1448), or Chapel

removed to Metz in Germany.

Back in the main body of the church, steps lead up to the raised choir, where you're greeted by a superlative Romanesque **pulpit, screen,** and glittering apse **mosaic** of 1297. The last—as on the facade—portrays Christ between the Virgin and San Miniato. It's believed the same artist may have been responsible for both works. The crucifix above the high altar is attributed to Luca della Robbia, while the fine panel (1320) to the right of the altar, adorned with episodes from the life of San Miniato, is by an obscure Tuscan artist, Jacopo del Casentino. The corresponding panels (1354) left of the altar contain scenes from the life of St. Giovanni Gualberto. The artist is not known. Off to the right of the raised presbytery stands the sacristy, whose walls are covered in a memorable fresco cycle by Spinello Aretino (active 1373–1410) portraying episodes from the life of St. Benedict (1387).

In the lower part of the church, off the north aisle, is the **Cappella del Cardinale del Portogallo** (1473), which features the tomb of Iacopo di Lusitania, a young Portuguese scholar, cleric, and diplomat who died in Florence in 1459. Iacopo was the nephew of King Alfonso V of Portugal (*R.*1438–1481) and had been sent to Perugia, in central Italy, to study law. Later he became Archbishop of Lincoln, a cardinal, and ultimately ambassador to Florence. On his death in the city, his aunt and humanist friends in Florence united to pay for the chapel, making the cardinal the only person, San Miniato aside, buried in the church. This is an extraordinarily low number of tombs for a Florentine church; Santa Croce, by comparison, has well over 250. The chapel is one of Italy's great

Renaissance ensembles, a carefully unified composite of sculptures and paintings by Antonio Rossellino, Alesso Baldovinetti (1426–1499), and Luca della Robbia. The whole effect is superb. Della Robbia's ceiling and the four glazed terra-cotta sculptures of the

"Cardinal Virtues" (1461) are especially fine, but many of the individual details are also worthy of special attention. Notice, for example, the grille behind the cardinal's effigy, a metaphor for the Gates of Paradise, and the empty judge's throne, an allusion to the Last Judgment. The angel holding the Virgin's crown symbolizes the cardinal's chastity, as do the unicorns, a reference to the traditional belief that the mythical single-horned horse could only be captured by a virgin.

The chapel's main altarpiece painting is a copy of a work by Antonio and Piero Pollaiuolo now in the Uffizi. Among other figures it includes a depiction of St. James, featured because he was the young cardinal's patron saint. ∎

"Temperance," a glazed terra-cotta roundel by Luca della Robbia, is from the Cappella del Cardinale del Portogallo.

The view from the ramparts of the Forte di Belvedere overlooks the Tuscan hills. The fortress takes its name—*bel vedere*, or beautiful view—from its panoramic location.

More places to visit in the Oltrarno

FORTE DI BELVEDERE

The Forte di Belvedere is the large fortress looms over the Boboli Garden (see p. 176–77). Its main attractions are its ramparts, with broad views of the city, the Arno Valley, and the distant silhouettes of the Tuscan hills. The fortress was commissioned by Grand Duke Ferdinando I to defend the city and discourage insurrection. Architect Bernardo Buontalenti sank its foundations in 1590, burying with them 20 bronze portraits of Ferdinando and a picture of how he hoped the fort would look on completion. Most of the building was finished the following year. The castle's bastions are grouped around the **Palazzina di Belvedere,** an earlier building now used for temporary exhibitions.

Map p. 168 Access from Via di Belvedere and Costa di San Giorgio Closed until 2002 Free except during exhibitions

MUSEO BARDINI

The Museo Bardini takes its name from Sergio Bardini (1836–1922), the foremost art dealer of his day. Bardini sold major Italian works to many of the great galleries of Western Europe and North America. He also collected on his own behalf and built the museum for his hugely eclectic collection, which was bequeathed to Florence on his death. Bardini's methods were often questionable. An old church on the site was pulled down on his wishes, and much of the gallery's interior detailing was "salvaged" from medieval buildings around Tuscany.

The museum contains a wealth of beautiful objects—paintings, ceramics, musical instruments, swords, armor, carpets, and much more. Many of the artifacts packed into its 20 or more rooms are unlabeled and randomly displayed, allowing you to wander and admire works that catch your eye.

Map p. 168 Piazza de Mozzi 1 055 234 2427 Closed until 2002. Phone for details Bus: D, 13, 23

MUSEO ZOOLOGICO–LA SPECOLA

The Zoological Museum, which forms part of the natural history museum of the University of Florence, was founded by Grand Duke

Pietro Leopoldo in 1775. It occupies the third floor of a former astronomical observatory *(la specola* means "telescope," hence the museum's colloquial name). Most people come here not for the mounted animals but for its remarkable and often ghoulish collection of medical and other waxworks. They include about 1,400 beautifully crafted models of arms, legs, organs, and other body parts, an eye-opening obstetrics section, and a series of entire corpses in which every muscle, sinew, vein, and capillary has been splayed and displayed in loving detail. The collection was created as a teaching aid between 1775 and 1814.

Tucked away in one of the museum's side rooms, the four-piece wax tableau by a Sicilian cleric, Zumbo, shows vignettes of Florence during the plague. The tiny three-dimensional scenes show piles of variously rotted corpses, along with such details as rats gnawing on spilling intestines and mushrooms growing from putrefying flesh.

🅰 Map p. 168 ✉ Via Romana 17 ☎ 055 228 8251 🕐 Museo Zoologico closed p.m. & all Wed. Waxworks open Tues. & Sat. a.m. only; closed Aug. 💲 $ 🚌 Bus: D, 11, 36, 37

SANTA FELICITÀ

Santa Felicità is one of the oldest churches in Florence. It was probably founded on the site of an early Christian cemetery and fourth-century basilica dedicated to Felicità, an early Christian martyr beheaded or thrown into boiling oil for refusing to renounce her faith. Archaeological evidence suggests the church lay close to the Via Cassia, an important Roman road to the south, and may have been the work of Greek and Syrian merchants responsible for introducing Christianity to the city. Rebuilding over the centuries culminated in the creation of the present church in 1739, and nothing remains to suggest the site's antiquity. The church contains one of Florence's strangest paintings, Jacopo Pontormo's "Deposition" (1525–28), which lies behind railings in the Brunelleschi-designed Cappella Capponi, or Cappella Barbardori, immediately on your right as you enter. Normally a painting on this theme—Christ being taken from the Cross—would contain the Cross itself, Roman soldiers, and the thieves crucified with Christ. Here all you

see are an ethereal background cloud and an unrelated and vaguely androgynous group of figures (the brown-cloaked figure on the group's extreme right is believed to be a self-portrait of the artist). Many of the figures owe something to the sculptural forms of Michelangelo, but their extraordinary range of colors was unique at the time. Only Christ is painted with any attempt at verisimilitude; the rest of the painting is a bizarre palate of acid pink, electric blue, and puce green.

Pontormo's more restrained two-part "Annunciation" hangs on opposite sides of the window on the right-hand wall as you look at the chapel. Three of the four ceiling tondi (round paintings) of "The Evangelists" are also by Pontormo. The fourth, of St. Mark, is a copy of a work by Agnolo Bronzino, a painter who shared many of Pontormo's strange mannerist concerns.

🅰 Map p. 168 ✉ Piazza di Santa Felicità ☎ 055 213 018 🕐 Closed L 🚌 Bus: D

SANTO SPIRITO

In its day, Santo Spirito was the most important church in the Oltrarno, giving its name to a quarter of the city. Architectural purists revel in the building, which is considered one of Filippo Brunelleschi's masterpieces; its interior, however, may seem rather too gloomy for modern tastes. Brunelleschi designed the church in 1434, but construction only started in 1444, two years before his death, by which time barely a single column of the nave had been raised. Work was more or less completed in 1487, obliterating virtually all traces of the 13th-century Augustinian church on the site.

Amid the welter of chapels and works of art, just two paintings stand out. The first is Filippo Lippi's "Madonna and Child with Saints" (1493–94) in the south, or right, transept—second chapel from the left of the four chapels on its south, or back, wall. The other, in the left transept opposite, is the strange and unmistakable "St. Monica and Augustinian Nuns," attributed to the little-known artist Francesco Botticini (1446–1497)—second chapel on the right wall as you stand with your back to the main body of the church.

🅰 Map p. 168 ✉ Piazza Santo Spirito ☎ 055 210 030 🕐 Closed 4 hours L & Wed. p.m. 🚌 Bus: D ■

TUSCANY

Tuscany

TUSCANY IS A REGION THAT IS OUTSTANDING IN EVERY REGARD, EVEN BY Italy's exalted standards. Not content with Florence, the country's premier artistic center, it also boasts two of Europe's most perfect medieval towns—Siena and San Gimignano— as well as historical gems such as Lucca, Pisa, and Pienza of which any country would be proud. If these were not enough, the region is also renowned for its food and wine, its beaches, its islands, and for some of the world's most beautiful and varied landscapes.

Most people leave Florence for the gracious medieval town of Siena. The best way to travel here is on a slow road through Chianti, a pastoral region of wooded hills and vineyards that is synonymous with Italy's most famous red wine. Siena is well worth a couple of days to do justice to its cathedral and main square, the Campo, Italy's finest piazza, and an outstanding medley of churches, galleries, pretty streets, and hidden medieval corners.

Outside Siena, Tuscany is a region of almost unimaginable artistic and cultural richness. You'll need a car to explore it properly. You'll also need to be selective: Remember that while traveling between the highlights you'll stumble on many an unexpected treasure, so leave time to admire far-reaching views, wander hilltop villages, or explore some unsung Romanesque church.

We've divided the region broadly into north and south, suggesting a rough itinerary that allows you to travel from Siena to the north and west of the region before heading south into the Tuscan heartlands. First stop should probably be San Gimignano, always busy with tourists, but it is the Tuscan town that you should see if you see none other. Conveniently located just north of Siena, it's best known as the "medieval Manhattan" after its crop of ancient towers.

Moving west, you'll probably wish to visit Pisa—its Leaning Tower is among Italy's most familiar sights—although the rest of the mostly modern city fails to live up to its celebrated centerpiece. Nearby Lucca is less well known but far more appealing, an urbane little town full of cobbled streets, tiny churches, and interesting galleries protected by some of the region's most perfectly preserved old walls.

Pages 190–91: Dusk falls over Monte Amiata in southern Tuscany.

Foremost among the villages south of Siena is tiny Pienza, planned as a model Renaissance city in the 15th century but now little more than a sleepy backwater. Nearby Montalcino is another charming place, renowned for two prized red wines, Brunello and Rosso di Montalcino. Slightly farther afield lies Montepulciano, an archetypal Tuscan hill town also known for its wine, Vino Nobile di Montepulciano. Dotting the pastoral countryside roundabout are lonely abbeys such as Sant'Antimo and Monte Oliveto Maggiore, both essential diversions. Heading back toward Florence, don't miss Arezzo, ugly on its outskirts, delightful at its medieval heart—and home to one of the region's most important fresco cycles—nor Cortona, one of the highest and most ancient of all Tuscan towns.

If time is short you won't be disappointed by the landscapes of southern Tuscany and Chianti, both filled with cypress-topped hills, fields of wheat and summer poppies, rustic stone farmhouses, refined Renaissance villas, bucolic vineyards, and age-old olive groves. If you have more time, however, then explore the Garfagnana, a little-visited region north of Lucca that embraces the high mountain scenery of the Orecchiella and Alpi Apuane. Or follow the country roads from Arezzo through the Casentino and Pratomagno, self-contained enclaves as scenic as Chianti but with the difference that they're virtually unknown to outsiders.

Tuscany has a long coastline, with plenty of places to swim, sail, and sunbathe. Viareggio and Forte dei Marmi are two of the most popular resorts in the north, while Castiglione della Pescaia, Talamone, and exclusive Porto Ercole and Porto Santo Stefano are the best in the south. The region boasts several offshore islands, one of which, Elba, might occupy a fortnight's vacation on its own. ∎

Siena is Europe's most perfect medieval city, a supremely urbane little place whose calm and myriad medieval charms make it the ideal antidote to Florence's crowds and Renaissance finery.

Siena

Flags of the Siena *contrade*

Siena

SIENA IS A MEDIEVAL JEWEL. INTIMATE AND MANAGEABLE, THE CITY IS AN immediately likeable place, crammed with art, culture, and outstanding churches and museums, and laced with countless quiet streets and hidden corners.

Myth claims that Siena was founded by Senius and Acius, sons of Remus—hence the statues around the city of the she-wolf who suckled Rome's mythical founders, Romulus and Remus. In fact, Siena—like Florence—began as an Etruscan settlement, evolving into a Roman colony, Saena Julia, at the beginning of the first century A.D. Flourishing banking and textile concerns in the Middle Ages then made it one of Europe's most important medieval cities. Its stature inevitably drew it into conflict with Florence, with first one, then the other city achieving dominance. Siena's greatest triumph over its rival came in 1260 at the Battle of Montaperti, a contest fought a few miles east of the city. In 1348 the scales tipped the other way, when the Black Death wiped out 70,000 of Siena's 100,000-strong population (today's population is 56,000). Mortally wounded, the city struggled to retain its independence until 1554, when Montalcino, the last bastion of the Sienese Republic, surrendered to Florence and the Medici Grand Duke Cosimo I. Thereafter, Florence deliberately suppressed the city, whose decline was one of the reasons for its remarkably unsullied appearance today.

Nowhere is this unspoiled appearance more striking than in the Campo, or Piazza del Campo, an enthralling medieval square. The stage for Siena's twice-yearly horse race, the Campo is enjoyable year-round for the Palazzo Pubblico, with its museum and panoramic tower, and the pleasure of watching the world go by from one of its sidewalk cafés.

After the Campo, the next natural target is another piazza, Piazza del Duomo. This is the setting for the city's ravishingly decorated cathedral and the Museo dell'Opera (or cathe-

Visitor information

- 🇦 195 D3
- ✉ Piazza del Campo 56
- ☎ 0577 280 551
- 🕐 Closed Sun.

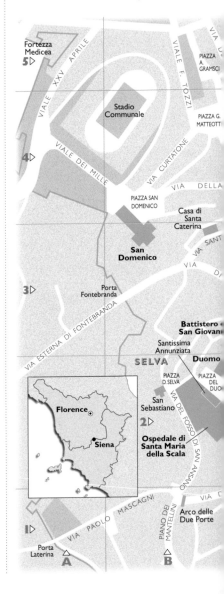

dral museum), which in Duccio's painting of the "Maestà" has one of Europe's medieval masterpieces. More pictures await in the Pinacoteca Nazionale, a leading art gallery and the best place to see the style of painting produced by Sienese artists over five centuries.

These superb sights are only the start. While you could rush through Siena in a day, the city really needs two or three days. Then you'll have time to visit its major churches—San Domenico, San Francesco, and Santa Maria dei Servi—and to duck into smaller galleries such as the archaeological museum. Finally, you'll have the chance to explore the city's old streets and alleys and their tempting nooks and crannies. If you're staying in Siena, aim to be in the city center and book hotels well in advance during most of the year. ■

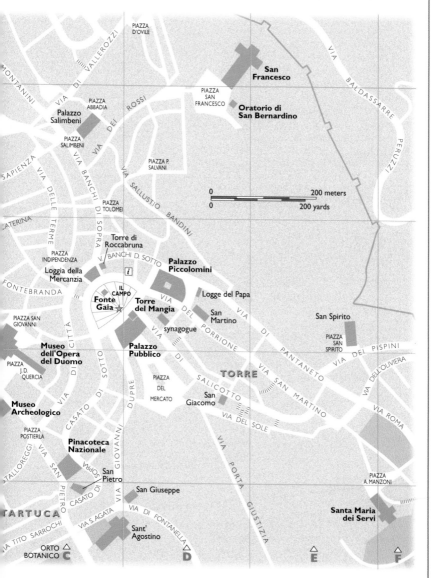

Il Campo

THE CAMPO IS A MAGNIFICENT SCALLOP-SHAPED SQUARE at the heart of Siena, a sweeping piazza ringed by soaring towers, huge palaces, and countless other medieval buildings. As well as being a natural meeting place, it is also the seat of the Palazzo Pubblico, housing one of Tuscany's foremost art galleries, and the setting for the city's famous twice-yearly Palio horse race.

Il Campo
🗺 195 C3 & D3

Torre del Mangia
✉ Piazza del Campo
☎ 0577 292 263
💲 $$

Museo Civico
✉ Piazza del Campo
☎ 0577 292 263
💲 $$

Few Tuscan experiences are as memorable as the moment you first see the Campo. The huge, sloping space of its broad arena comes as a wonderful surprise after the city's narrow medieval streets. Today, the piazza's site appears naturally ordained, for it sits at the convergence of the city's three hilly spurs, at the meeting point of its three *terzi*, or traditional districts (literally "thirds"). In truth, its emergence as the city's natural focus was a result of circumstance. When Siena's 13th-century ruling body, the Council of Nine, began acquiring land in 1294 to create the square, this was the only central area that belonged to none of the terzi or *contrade* (parishes) and thus remained free of the rivalries that divide the city to this day.

The square was paved in brick and marble between 1327 and 1349, when the fan-shaped area of paving was divided into nine distinct portions, an arrangement that becomes clearer when seen from the vantage point of the Torre del Mangia, the piazza's colossal tower (see p. 201). The layout was designed both to recall the Council of Nine and to suggest the layers of the Madonna's cloak symbolically sheltering the city beneath its protective embrace. In this it evoked a type of medieval painting known as the "Madonna della Misericordia," a genre in which the Madonna is shown holding her open cloak over the members of a religious order or a town's inhabitants.

The Campo is incomparable as a general ensemble but lacks specific sights. The best thing to do is to enjoy its spectacle from one of the square's many cafés; be prepared for high prices. As you sip your drink, notice the **Fonte Gaia,** the fountain near the square's highest point, a 19th-century copy of a work by Jacopo della Quercia (1374/5–1438), one of Siena's greatest Renaissance sculptors (the original is in the Palazzo Pubblico's Museo Civico). Take in the largely Gothic **Cappella di Piazza,** the distinctive arched structure that juts from the foot of the Torre del Mangia. This was begun by the city's council in 1352 to mark the passing of the Black Death four years earlier. The upper level was added over a century later, between 1463 and 1468, hence its distinctly different appearance.

PALAZZO PUBBLICO
A door to the right of the Cappella ushers you into the courtyard of the Palazzo Pubblico, the huge building beneath the **Torre del Mangia**, where you have a choice of climbing the Torre (entrance on your left) or seeing the **Museo Civico,** which occupies the palace's upper floors (the ticket office is to your right). Climbing the tower's 503 steps might not leave you in the mood for art, so it makes sense to see the museum first.

This starts in rather disappointing fashion with a lackluster five-room gallery of undistinguished

Opposite: The Palazzo Pubblico and Torre del Mangia dominate the Piazza del Campo.

paintings. Then comes the **Sala del Risorgimento,** a room decorated in the 19th century with pictures celebrating the exploits of Italy's first king, Vittorio Emanuele (*R.*1861–1878), and his part in the Risorgimento, the 19th-century unification of Italy. With the next

room, however, the **Sala di Balia** (or Sala dei Priori), the gallery quickly finds its feet. The Sala's walls are covered in paintings by Spinello Aretino (1345–1410) and his son, Parri, of the life of Alexander III, a pope born in Siena. Many of the pictures portray episodes from Alexander's long-running conflict with Frederick Barbarossa, the Holy Roman Emperor. Note, in particular, the scene of the naval battle, which shows the Venetians—then allies of the pope—capturing the emperor's son and the efforts of the imperial forces to rescue him.

The next room is the **Anti-camera del Concistoro,** or Sala dei Cardinali, noted chiefly for Ambrogio Lorenzetti's 14th-century detached fresco of "Three

Saints and Donor" (by the entrance door). A donor was the person who commissioned a painting and was often depicted kneeling at the feet of the Virgin. The missing Madonna suggests this was once part of a larger painting.

From here you move to the **Sala del Concistoro,** passing through a beautifully ornate marble doorway designed by Bernardo Rossellino (1409–1464), an artist whose work you will see again if you visit the southern Tuscan town of Pienza (see pp. 276–78). The room's ceiling frescoes are the work of Domenico Beccafumi (circa 1485–1551), Siena's most accomplished mannerist painter. The paintings portray episodes from Greek and Roman myth and history, but they were actually intended to symbolize or evoke parallels with the history and triumphs of Siena—as were virtually all the other works of art commissioned for the palace.

Turn back into the Anticamera and take the first door on your right into the **Vestibolo** to see, among other things, a gilded bronze statue by an unknown artist of the "She-Wolf Suckling the Twins Romulus and Remus" (1429). You'll see several similar statues around Siena, as ancient chroniclers believed Siena was founded by Senius and Acius, sons of Remus. The small room to the left of the Vestibolo is the **Anticappella,** which is adorned with frescoes by Taddeo di Bartolo (1362–1422) depicting "St. Christopher" and further scenes intended to glorify Siena by association with episodes from the past. Beyond the Anticappella lies the **Cappella del Consiglio,** with more frescoes by Taddeo—on the life of the Virgin—a fine set of inlaid wooden choir stalls, and a redoubtable wrought-iron screen,

Left: Café tables in the Piazza del Campo make a perfect place to take a break from sightseeing.

probably forged to a design by Jacopo della Quercia, both from the 15th century.

From either the Vestibolo or Anticamera you walk into the **Sala del Mappamondo,** the museum's centerpiece, where you find two of the greatest—and most controversial—of all Sienese paintings. On the left wall as you enter the room is Simone Martini's sensational "Maestà" (1315), or "Madonna Enthroned," the first major work commissioned for the Palazzo and the first major work by a painter who would become—with Duccio—Siena's most renowned artist. The work firmly links Siena with Christ and the Madonna: The Christ Child is shown holding a parchment that records the city's motto of Justice, and the steps

below the Virgin's throne are emblazoned with two stanzas from Dante reminding onlookers that the Virgin will not protect those who betray her or oppress the poor.

The opposite (right) wall contains the equestrian portrait of "Guidoriccio da Fogliano." For centuries this painting was also attributed to Martini, but in recent years it has become the subject of one of the bitterest disputes in Italian art history circles. The pro-Martini camp includes most of Siena and many Italian scholars. The anti-Martini group numbers several prominent foreign scholars, most notably American Gordon Moran, who for a time was banned from the Palazzo and accused of being in the pay of the C.I.A. The intricacies of the debate are complicated, but

The views across the medieval rooftops of Siena toward the Tuscan hills barely have changed in more than 500 years.

The "Madonna Enthroned" by Simone Martini dominates the Palazzo Pubblico's Sala del Mappamundo. This subject—known as the "Maestà"—was much favored by Sienese artists.

in essence boil down to a question of timing: The picture was probably painted about 1328, which begs the question of why it is painted over (not under) a fresco to the right by Lippo Vanni, executed in 1364. The controversy is still not settled, despite the arbitration of independent experts, but you'll probably find the debate irrelevant. The painting is a compelling work, whatever its authorship. It offers a strange but striking image of medieval chivalric endeavor, with Guidoriccio, a mercenary leader, portrayed setting forth to lay siege to a small walled village (probably present-day Montemassa, southwest of Siena).

Other paintings in the room are less contentious, beginning with a pair of saints (1529) below the fresco by Giovanni Antonio Bazzi, or Sodoma (1477–1549), and two large scenes by Lippo Vanni and Cristofori Ghini, painted in 1364 and 1480 respectively, depicting Sienese military triumphs in the Val di Chiana and Poggio Imperiale (both in Tuscany). On the pillars below the latter are paintings by a

trio of notable artists. From left to right these are Sodoma's "Blessed Tolomei," a portrait of the founder of the abbey at Monte Oliveto Maggiore (see pp. 268–69), "St. Bernardino" by Sano di Pietro (1406–1481), and "St. Catherine of Siena" by Vecchietta (1412–1480).

Most palace-museums would be content with the two masterpieces of the Sala del Mappamondo: Not the Palazzo Pubblico, whose last major room, the **Sala della Pace,** features one of Europe's great secular (nonreligious) fresco cycles— Ambrogio Lorenzetti's "Allegories of Good and Bad Government" (1338). The two large frescoes show the effects of good and bad civic rule on a city clearly intended to represent Siena, graphically illustrating these effects with fascinating contemporary details and activities—dancing, farming, building, and many more. The paintings work wonderfully well on the level of simple narrative; note, for example, the executed bandits in the countryside, hanged by Good Government. But they also contain more complicated meanings, which

would have been clearly understood by Siena's more educated citizens. In the fresco of Good Government, for example, the throned figure represents Siena's Comune, or council, and is garbed in the city's colors to make the point more strongly. The Virtues are portrayed as figures to his side and include the reclining white-robed figure of Peace (*pace* in Italian), from whom the room takes its name; Faith, Hope, and Charity circle the throned figure's head. To the left, you see the seated figure of Justice (with Wisdom shown above) dispensing punishment and reward; Harmony is portrayed below, advising politicians of their civic responsibilities. In Bad Government, by contrast, the central figure is Fear (or the devil) surrounded by the Vices, the effects of his reign made abundantly clear in the painting's ravaged crops, scenes of robbery, garbage-strewn streets, and tumbledown buildings.

One more room remains beyond the Sala della Pace, the **Sala dei Pilastri** (or Sala delle Colonne), where the highlights are "Massacre of the Innocents" by Matteo di Giovanni (1435–1490), a graphic and violent depiction of the slaughter of the first-born ordered by Herod; Guido da Siena's "Maestà" (probably 1261), in which the face of the Madonna is said to have been painted by Duccio; and Neroccio di Bartolomeo's (1447–1500) "St. Bernardino Preaching in the Campo," interesting for the detail that shows Bernardino's listeners chastely separated by a sheet into groups of men and women.

Back in the Palazzo's courtyard you can climb the 503 steps of the 330-foot (102 m) **Torre del Mangia** (1338–1348), designed by a leading Sienese painter, Lippo Memmi (active 1317–1347). The bell tower was reputedly named after its first watchman and bell-ringer, Giovanni da Balduccio, a notable *mangiaguadagni*, literally an "eater of profits," or profligate. The views are magnificent. The tower's sonorous bell was originally used to mark the end of the working day, as well as the opening and closing of the city gates in the morning and the evening. ■

This equestrian fresco in the Sala del Mappamondo portrays the medieval mercenary soldier Guidoriccio da Fogliano. The identity of the artist responsible is more controversial.

Palio

The twice-yearly Palio is Italy's most dramatic pageant. A spectacular bareback horse race, it involves just three laps of the Campo, but the excitement, processions, drumming, flag-waving, and colorful spectacle associated with the event can go on for months. This makes it far more than an exhibition created for the sake of visitors, for the race is a living embodiment of rivalries and traditions that have been played out for over 700 years.

The Palio has been run in some shape or form since the 13th century. In its infancy it was run around the city streets; the three-lap circuit of the Campo was only instigated in 1656. The prize, though, has always been the same: the embroidered banner, or *pallium*, from which the race takes its name. The dedication, which is to the Virgin, has also remained inviolate and this is why the races are run on July 2 and August 16, feast days devoted to the Madonna. Occasionally, races are held for another reason, notably those to commemorate the end of World War II and the first lunar landing.

The race is a vivid expression of the rivalries between Siena's *contrade*, the parishlike districts into which the city has long been divided. Today there are 17 contrade, fewer than in times past, when Siena has had as many as 42. Each contrada has its own church, social club, heraldic device, museum, flag, and symbolic animal that often lends the contrada its name. Allegiance to a contrade is absolute: Baptism of a contrada baby, for example, is held in the contrada church and is followed by baptism in the child's contrada fountain. Each contrada also holds its own yearly procession and supports a band of drummers *(tamborini)* and flag-throwers *(alfieri)*; you'll often see drummers going through their drills on the streets.

The ten contrade that can take part in the Palio are drawn by lot. Riders from the other contrade have the consolation of accompanying the Carroccio, or chariot, that parades the pallium in the prerace procession. This procession is just one area in which the skulduggery associated with the race can bear fruit. All

Riders make three circuits of the Campo in the Siena Palio. The race lasts just 90 seconds, but preparations take months.

the contrade are fiercely independent, but each also has its own special rival, and as much planning goes into ensuring a rival's humiliation as securing one's own victory. Alliances are forged and bribes arranged. Horses may be doped, and it's even been known for men and animals to be kidnapped. Riders and animals are therefore watched day and night. Religion also plays its part, namely in the blessing of horses and riders in the contrada churches: "Va' e torna vincitore" intones the priest—"Go, and return the winner."

If you can be in Siena on race day you're in for a feast of pageantry, whether or not you're

Right: Victory for the Chiocciola (Snail) contrada. Celebrations in the winning parish may go on for many weeks.

in the Campo for the race itself (Italian TV shows the race if you can't be there). Horses gather for the 90-second dash at around 7 p.m., when all but one of the riders are gathered together. The race begins when the lone rider charges his rivals. From this point almost anything goes. The only rule is that jockeys can't interfere with another rider's reins. The race is hectic, fast, violent, and dangerous, both for riders and horses: Sand and mattresses are laid out to help prevent serious injury. Defeat is acrimonious, and rumors and memories of dark doings can fester for years among the beaten contrade and their members. ■

Duomo

SIENA'S DUOMO IS ONE OF ITALY'S MOST BEAUTIFUL cathedrals. Superior to that of Florence in all respects—artistic and architectural—save for Brunelleschi's dome, it contains statues by Michelangelo, a sublime pulpit, gorgeous frescoes, and countless other outstanding paintings and sculptures.

Duomo

- 194 B2
- Piazza del Duomo
- 0577 283 048
- Closed L Nov.–March

Above: "Madonna and Child" tondo, almost certainly by Donatello, above the door into the south transept. Opposite: Much of Siena's cathedral is built in the Gothic style, but the marble-striped bell tower is typical of Tuscan Romanesque architecture.

The building rises at one of the city's highest points, the site's exalted position having long made it a place of special significance. One of the city's most important Roman shrines, a temple to Minerva, was probably built here, and a Christian church existed nearby in the ninth century, possibly earlier. The present cathedral is traditionally said to have been consecrated in 1179 by the Siena-born pope, Alexander III, although the bulk of the construction work was completed in 1215. The cupola was added between 1259 and 1264, and the lower part of the extraordinary **facade** was created by the eminent Pisan sculptor Giovanni Pisano (1245/8–1318) in the years up to 1296. Many of Pisano's statues and other sculptures have been replaced with copies, the originals having been moved to the nearby Museo dell'Opera (see pp. 213–15).

Save for the odd additional flourish, 1296 might have marked the end of the building's history. By 1339, however, the growth in Siena's population and wealth, and the desire to emulate the cathedral of the city's hated Florentine rivals, prompted the start of the so-called Duomo Nuovo, or New Cathedral. If realized, this would have been the largest church of its day.

But the scheme was defeated by political upheavals and the chaotic and impoverished aftermath of the Black Death of 1348. A hint of what might have been can be seen to the right of the cathedral as you look at it: The outline and partly finished stone frame of the proposed nave are still visible.

Thwarted in their ambitions, the Sienese decided to make do with the original building, adding finishing touches to the apse (the area behind the high altar) and completing the upper part of the facade (1376) in the ornate style of the cathedral in Orvieto, a town a few miles away in the neighboring region of Umbria. The three upper mosaics were added in the 19th century by Venetian mosaicists.

Unlike Florence's cathedral, whose interior is relatively unadorned, Siena's cathedral dazzles with its wealth of interior works of art. Almost the first thing you notice are the countless sculptured heads around the upper walls. These are 15th- and 16th-century works that represent 172 different popes and—at intervals below—36 assorted Holy Roman Emperors. Less immediately eye-catching, but infinitely more precious, is the cathedral's **pavement,** or floor, which is covered in a series of 56 *graffito* (incised) marble panels. Many—sadly—are kept covered to

In the 13th century the Sienese planned to enlarge the Duomo to make it Italy's largest church. The scheme was later abandoned.

Libreria Piccolomini

✉ Piazza del Duomo

☎ 0577 283 048

🕐 Closed L Nov.–March

$ \$. Combined ticket (Biglietto Cumulativo) with Battistero di San Giovanni & Museo dell'Opera: \$\$

protect them from wear and tear. The first were created about 1369 and feature simple geometric patterns. The last one, dated 1547, is far more ornate. In all, some 40 artists, including most of the leading Sienese painters of their day, provided designs for the panels' complex biblical, allegorical, and secular narratives.

Several key works stand out among the plethora of other paintings and sculptures around the walls. The first is the staggering **pulpit** toward the end of the nave on the left, with its celebrated bas-reliefs of the life of Christ. It was the work of Nicola Pisano (circa 1215–1278), father of Giovanni Pisano, the sculptor responsible for much of the facade. Giovanni assisted his father on the project,

along with Arnolfo di Cambio, the architect of Florence cathedral, and in doing so helped to create one of the supreme masterpieces of Italian medieval sculpture.

The second notable work of art is another piece of sculpture, the so-called **Piccolomini Altarpiece,** on the north (left) side of the church to the left of the entrance to the Libreria Piccolomini (see p. 207). Much of its elegant sculpture is by Andrea Bregno (1421–1506), an accomplished, if second-rank, sculptor. What lends the piece a special importance is the fact that four of the statues in the lower niches —Saints Gregory and Paul on the right, Peter and Pius on the left— are the work of the young Michelangelo.

The interior's third and most lavish work of art is the **Libreria Piccolomini,** or Piccolomini Library, which is decorated with a fresco cycle by the Umbrian artist Pinturicchio (1454–1513). The area was originally set aside in 1495 by Cardinal Francesco Piccolomini, later Pope Pius III (whose reign lasted just ten days), to house the library of his Tuscan-born uncle, Enea Silvio Piccolomini, better known as Pope Pius II.

The frescoes, which are remarkably well preserved, retaining their vibrant colors, depict ten episodes from the life of Pope Pius II and may owe something to the hand of Raphael, who is believed to have assisted Pinturicchio with their initial design. Raphael lived and worked in neighboring Umbria for

several years, where he was the pupil of Pinturricchio's fellow Umbrian master, Perugino.

The paintings trace Pius's secular and religious careers and are typical of Pinturicchio's delightful narrative style, being full of detail, color, and incident. The cycle starts to the right of the window with Pius's diplomatic career, beginning in panel 1 with his attendance at the Council of Basle as secretary to an Italian bishop; the storm scene here is one of the first in Western art. Panel 2 depicts Pius presenting himself as an envoy to King James II of Scotland (R.1437–1460); panel 3, his coronation as a poet laureate in 1442 by the Holy Roman Emperor, Frederick III (R.1440–1493); and panel 4, his representing Frederick on a mission to Pope Eugenius IV (R. 1431–37).

Panel 5 shows Pius—by now Bishop of Siena—at a meeting between Frederick III and his prospective bride, Eleanora of Portugal, held by Siena's Porta Camollia. Panels 6 and 7 detail Pius's promotion to cardinal in 1456 and pope in 1458, followed in panel 8 by his proclamation in 1459 in the northern Italian city of Mantua of an ultimately unsuccessful crusade to retake Constantinople (now Istanbul) from the Turks. Panel 9 shows his canonization of St. Catherine of Siena in 1461, and panel 10 his arrival and death in Ancona on Italy's eastern coast, a town he visited to encourage the troops about to depart for his crusade. His death in 1464, it is said, may have been brought on by poison administered by soldiers disenchanted with their mission.

At the center of the room stands a famous statue of the "Three Graces," a Roman copy of a Greek original that inspired artists such as Raphael and the 19th-century

Nicola Pisano created the cathedral pulpit. The upper bas-reliefs portray scenes from the life of Christ.

Pinturicchio's "The Coronation of Pope Pius II" in the Libreria Piccolomini

neoclassic sculptor Antonio Canova, who sculptured his own version of the Three Graces, now in London's Victoria and Albert Museum. Also exhibited in the room are several illustrated 15th-century miniatures and choir books from the Duomo and Ospedale.

The Libreria is far from the last of the cathedral's highlights. Turn left out of the library and move down the north (left) wall and you turn into the left transept, where the circular chapel in the corner, the **Cappella di San Giovanni**, contains more frescoes (1504) by Pinturicchio, a lovely 15th-century font, and a statue of St. John the Baptist by Donatello. Donatello was also responsible for a bronze pavement tomb of Bishop Giovanni Pecci, positioned just past the

transept in the angle on the right beyond Pisano's pulpit. On the wall above is Tino di Camaino's (1285–1337) tomb of Cardinal Riccardo Petroni, a work that had a great influence on funerary sculpture during much of the 14th century.

Next walk across the church to the high altar, which is topped by a large bronze altarpiece (1476) by Vecchietta, one of the finest of Siena's Renaissance artists and sculptors. The work was originally housed in the nearby Ospedale di Santa Maria della Scala (see pp. 210–12) but was brought to the cathedral in 1506, when it replaced Duccio's celebrated "Maestà" as the altar's centerpiece.

Continue to the right transept to see the circular **Cappella della**

Madonna del Voto, or Cappella Chigi, a highly ornate work designed by the Roman baroque master Gian Lorenzo Bernini (1598–1680). Bernini also created the gilded bronze angels and the figures of St. Giralomo and Mary Magdalene by the chapel entrance. *Voto* means "votive," hence the many votive offerings—thanks or pleas for intercession by the Virgin—that cover the walls.

Outside the cathedral, but part of its structure, lies the **Battistero di San Giovanni,** the baptistery of St. John. Unlike Florence, Siena did not build a separate baptistery. It was included within the cathedral and can be reached by walking along the right side of the building as you face the facade and down the steps straight ahead of you. The

baptistery entrance lies on your left in Piazza San Giovanni at the foot of the steps.

The small admission charge is well worth paying, for inside stands an unexpected artistic bonus: the 15th-century baptistery font, with bronze reliefs by three of the leading sculptors of their day—Sienese Jacopo della Quercia ("The Announcement of the Baptist's Birth"), Florentine Lorenzo Ghiberti ("The Baptism of Christ" and "St. John in Prison"), and Donatello (the panel of "Herod's Feast" and the tabernacle's sculptured angels). Also well worth the price of admission are the many 15th-century frescoes including the Apostles and an "Assumption" around the walls, most of which are by the Sienese artist Vecchietta. ■

"The Baptism of Christ" by Lorenzo Ghiberti, a bronze panel from the font in the Battistero di San Giovanni

Battistero di San Giovanni

✉ Piazza San Giovanni

☎ $. Combined ticket (Biglietto Cumulativo) with Libreria Piccolomini & Museo dell'Opera: $$

Ospedale di Santa Maria della Scala

UNTIL THE 1990s, THE OSPEDALE DI SANTA MARIA DELLA Scala had served as Siena's principal hospital for almost a thousand years. Today, it is being converted into the city's main art and cultural center, providing a home for exhibitions and a unique setting for some of the superb works of art—notably an outstanding fresco cycle—commissioned for the hospital over the centuries.

Legend claims Santa Maria was founded by Beato Sorere, a ninth-century cobbler and monk renowned for his work among orphans and abandoned children. Sorere was actually a mythical figure, his name probably a corruption of the Italian word *suore* (nuns), a reference to the members of religious orders who tended the sick and orphaned as part of their religious vocation. The first written reference to the institution comes in 1090, when its development was prompted by the huge numbers of pilgrims traveling the Via Francigena, a major medieval pilgrimage route between Rome and northern Europe. The road ran beneath Siena's walls, its presence one reason for the city's early growth. All manner of inns and resting places *(ospedali)* grew up along the route to provide "hospitality" to pilgrims, with 40 in Sienese territory alone. Hospital work in the modern sense—caring for the sick—came later.

Bequests of money to the Ospedale turned it into one of the city's wealthiest and most important institutions. Part of its income was diverted to artistic and other ends, including the purchase of saints' relics—of which the Ospedale has a bewildering collection—and the construction of the long stone bench outside the building, which was used to provide shade for the hospital's dignitaries

during long civic and other ceremonies. More significant commissions included the major paintings inside the hospital, the main reason for a visit today.

The first of these comes in the tiny vestibule, or **Cappella del Manto,** beyond the ticket office, which contains a lovely fresco of "St. Anne and St. Joachim" (1512), the parents of the Virgin Mary, by the Sienese mannerist artist Domenico Beccafumi. The pair are shown kissing, a moment that symbolizes the Immaculate Conception of the Virgin. Turning left you come to a vast open hall once used as a ward. Turn left again and you enter another similar ward, the **Sala del Pellegrinaio,** covered in an outstanding fresco cycle (1440–43) by Domenico Bartolo and other artists.

Each of the cycle's eight major panels portrays aspects of the hospital's history and work. The secular content is extraordinary for a painting of this period—at the height of the Renaissance—a time when most works of art had a predominantly religious slant. Beginning at the far wall on the left, the first panel—the work of the Sienese artist Vecchietta—describes "The Dream of the Mother of Beato Sorere." This depicts the vision in which Sorere's mother sees her son's future work with the Ospedale's abandoned children, who are shown climbing a ladder

Ospedale di Santa Maria della Scala

- 194 B2
- Piazza del Duomo 2
- 0577 224 811
- $$

(scala) to Paradise and the arms of the Madonna. A ladder, or step, provided the hospital with its name and symbol, perhaps for the proximity of the cathedral's steps or because a three-rung ladder, seen as a symbol of the Trinity (Father, Son, and Holy Ghost), was found during its construction. Stages of this construction are shown in the ward's second fresco. The third fresco depicts the "Investiture of the Hospital Rector," while the fourth shows Pope Celestine III (pope 1191–98) awarding Santa Maria the right to elect this rector, a vital point in the hospital's history, for it transferred control of the institution from the city's religious guardians to its lay authorities. The paintings on the end wall are later 16th-century works, but they portray a fascinating aspect of the hospital's work, the employment of large numbers of "wet" nurses to suckle the huge numbers of orphans cared for by the hospital. The nurses are being paid in cash on the right and grain on the left.

Moving to the ward's other long wall, you come to the cycle's fifth and most celebrated panel, "The Tending of the Sick"; notice the monk on the right hearing the confession of a patient before surgery. To the right of this panel, the sixth fresco shows "The Distribution of Charity"—bread being given to the poor—and the next panel illustrates how the hospital provided for the reception of young girls from an early age, along with their subsequent education and marriage. You can see wet nurses in action on the

The fresco entitled "The Education and Marriage of Orphan Children," by Domenico di Bartolo, adorns the Sala del Pellegrinaio.

The center of Vecchietta's "The Dream of the Mother of Beato Sorore" shows orphan children ascending to heaven.

left, along with other scenes to suggest weaning, learning, and play. The eighth and final painting shows the feeding of the poor and elderly, but it is less convincing than other scenes, largely because of the unfortunately sited window. It's said this was built by a lazy 19th-century supervisor so he could watch over his patients without going down to the ward.

Just beyond the Sala on the left is the **Sagrestia Vecchia,** or Old Sacristy, which contains a fresco cycle by Vecchietta illustrating the "Articles of the Creed." This is less immediately impressive than the cycle you've just seen and rather more difficult to understand without a sound biblical knowledge. Suffice it to say that each panel shows an Apostle holding one of

the Articles, while the accompanying fresco contains a story from the Old Testament that illustrates the text. Domenico Bartolo's fine altarpiece here of the "Madonna della Misericordia" (1444) shows the Virgin casting a protective cloak over Siena's citizens.

Vecchietta features again in the hospital's church, Santissima Annunziata, where he was responsible for the high altar's bronze statue of the "Risen Christ" (1476). Down in the depths of the building, be sure to see the **Oratorio di Santa Caterina della Notte,** a gloomy but atmospheric oratory whose highlight is Taddeo di Bartolo's glorious triptych (three-paneled painting) of the "Madonna and Child with St. Andrew and St. John the Baptist" (1400). ■

Museo dell'Opera del Duomo

THE MUSEO DELL'OPERA HOUSES WORKS OF ART REMOVED for safekeeping from Siena's cathedral over the centuries. Among these are a wide variety of sculptures, some lovely pictures, and one of the greatest of all early European medieval paintings, Duccio's "Maestà." The gallery also offers magnificent views over the city.

The museo, to the right and rear of the cathedral as you face it, is housed in a building that occupies what would have been part of the nave of the 14th-century Duomo Nuovo (see p. 204). The first room you come to on the ground floor is the **Sala delle Statue,** or Hall of the Statues. At its center, ahead of you, are two sculptural masterpieces. The first is a delicate honey-colored relief of the "Madonna and Child" by the Florentine sculptor Donatello (removed from one of the cathedral's doorways); the second is a relief of the "Madonna and Child with St. Giralmo" by Jacopo della Quercia, Siena's leading Renaissance sculptor. Around the walls stand sculptured prophets and other figures (1284–1296) by Giovanni Pisano; removed from the cathedral facade, the group ranks among Europe's most significant Gothic sculptural ensembles. If the figures seem oddly distorted, remember they were designed to be viewed from below and at a distance—hence the irregularities. Similar considerations accounted for the physical distortions in Michelangelo's "David" in Florence.

Stairs from the gallery's lower level then lead you to the **Sala di Duccio,** whose low, almost reverential light is designed to protect one of Italy's most marvelous paintings, the "Maestà" by Duccio di Buoninsegna (1255–1319). Painted on two sides, and with no fewer than 45 accompanying

panels, this was, as far as scholars can tell, the most expensive painting ever commissioned at the time. Duccio was an unruly character, if his many fines for various misdemeanors are anything to go by, and it took him some four years to finish the work. On completion, it was accounted a masterpiece and paraded around the Campo en route for the cathedral, where it was inaugurated with a special Mass.

The painting's main subject is the "Madonna Enthroned," or "Maestà" ("majesty" in Italian), a form of painting in which the Virgin is depicted as the Queen of Heaven surrounded by a heavenly court of saints and angels. The genre was a Sienese invention. You can see similar paintings—to name but two examples—by Simone Martini in Siena's Palazzo Pubblico (see pp. 196–201) and the Museo Civico in San Gimignano, a village that once formed part of Sienese territory (see pp. 232–41). The preoccupation with the Virgin was no accident, for she had been declared the patroness and protector of the city on the eve of a famous Sienese victory over the Florentines at Montaperti in 1260.

Every Italian town and village had a patron. Some covered themselves by appointing several protectors, hence Siena's quartet of "secondary" patrons—Saints Ansano, Savino, Crescenzio, and Vittore—who stand in the front

The statue of "Simon," by Giovanni Pisano, was removed for safe-keeping from the facade of the cathedral and is now in the Museo dell'Opera del Duomo.

Museo dell'Opera del Duomo
🅰 195 C2
✉ Piazza del Duomo 8
☎ 0577 283 048
🕐 Closed p.m. Nov.–March
💲 $$

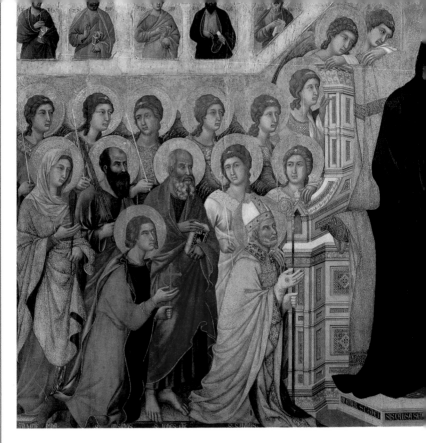

This "Maestà" or "Madonna Enthroned," painted by Duccio in the 13th-century, served as the high altarpiece of the cathedral until 1505.

rank of characters before Duccio's Virgin. The picture's abundance of detached panels, each a tiny masterpiece of narrative and detail, describe 19 episodes from the lives of Christ and the Virgin, and 26 scenes from the Passion, the events leading up to Christ's Crucifixion. Unfortunately, the entire painting was dismembered in 1771 and its panels dispersed before the picture was moved to the gallery in 1887. Most have since been recovered, with only a handful still in foreign hands. These overseas owners—to understandable Sienese indignation—refuse to release them to restore one of the world's masterpieces. The guilty parties include London's National Gallery (three panels), the National Gallery of Art in Washington, D.C. (two),

and the Frick and Rockefeller collections in New York (three).

The "Maestà" rather overshadows the room's other highlights, which include a "Madonna and Child," an early work by Duccio, the "Nativity of the Virgin," a late endeavor by Pietro Lorenzetti, and a series of sculptures in side rooms that feature works by Jacopo della Quercia (two gilded figures of the Madonna and Child, four saints, and St. John the Baptist). Another room has some interesting 19th-century drawings of the designs on the pavement of the cathedral.

Steps then lead you to the **Sala del Tesoro,** where the most captivating works are the 13th-century "Reliquary of San Galgano," one of many religious artifacts here, and

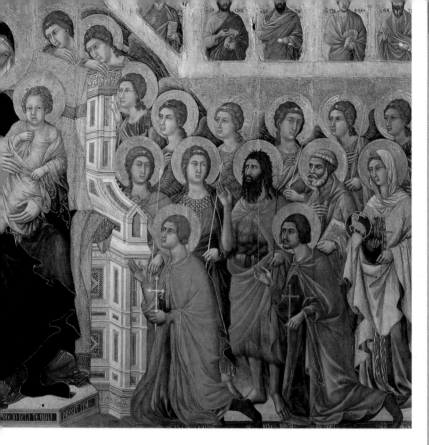

Giovanni's tiny wooden statue of the "Crucifixion" (1280). The latter shows Christ on a strange Y-shaped tree growing from the skull of Adam. This alludes to the Tree of Life, or Tree of Knowledge, which in the apocryphal biblical story grew from a shoot planted in the dead Adam's mouth and was eventually used to make the cross of Christ's Crucifixion. The story is the same one told in Piero della Francesca's famous fresco cycle in Arezzo (see pp. 285–91).

Moving on, you enter the **Sala della Madonna dagli Occhi Grossi,** or Hall of the Madonna of the Large Eyes, named after a striking work here by an unknown 13th-century painter; it occupied the cathedral's high altar before being ousted by Duccio's "Maestà."

Before the Battle of Montaperti in 1260, Siena's entire population came to pray before this painting, pledging themselves to the Virgin.

Don't miss other paintings in the same room, notably several works by Sano di Pietro (1406–1481): These include "St. Bernardino of Siena Preaching in the Campo" and "St. Bernardino Preaching in Piazza San Francesco"—both interesting for their contemporary views of Siena—and a "Madonna and Child with St. Apollonia," the patron saint of dentists. Rooms beyond this Sala contain paintings from later periods, among which the works of Domenico Beccafumi stand out. The gallery's grand finale is provided by the magnificent views from its exterior ramparts; follow signs for the Panorama. ■

Pinacoteca Nazionale

Pinacoteca Nazionale
- 195 C2
- Via San Pietro 29
- 0577 281 161
- Closed Mon. p.m. & Sun p.m.
- $$

Below: "Madonna and Child" by Simone Martini Opposite: "Prophet" by Sassetta

SIENA'S ARTISTS DEVELOPED A DISTINCTIVE STYLE, OR school, of painting in the centuries before the Renaissance. Examples of their art are scattered across Tuscany and beyond, but the best single place to study both the range and the development of their work is the city's Pinacoteca Nazionale, or art gallery.

The gallery has been housed in the impressive 14th-century Palazzo Buonsignori since 1932. Be warned, however, that the arrangement of paintings is often altered, and over the next few years various exhibits may be moved to as yet unfinalized locations elsewhere in the city— probably to the Ospedale di Santa Maria della Scala (see pp. 210–12).

Whatever the collection's final destination, its basic chronological order and its main highlights will remain the same.

The lower of the gallery's two principal floors is often used for temporary exhibitions. The main upper floor, by contrast, traces the roots of Sienese art. It begins with its origins in Byzantine art, whose stylized appearance, austere and formal beauty, and fondness for gold backgrounds continued to infuse the city's paintings long after such attributes had been abandoned by Florence's more forward-thinking artists. Highlights of this early period include a "Crucifix" from the end of the 12th century, removed from the church of San Pietro in Villore, and three scenes from the life of Christ (1280) by Guido da Siena. The latter picture is one of the earliest known works painted on canvas as opposed to wood. Despite this hint of innovation, Guido's work still looked for inspiration to Byzantine art, as its jewel-studded surface—a Byzantine device—makes clear.

DUCCIO & MARTINI

Successive rooms move on to the work of Duccio, who, with Simone Martini, was the most eminent of Siena's plethora of artists. He is also widely considered by art historians as the last of the great medieval painters before the more naturalistic work of pioneers such as Giotto. As a painter he was much respected in his own time, but if the heavy fines imposed on him by the city

are anything to go by, he led a far from blameless life. His greatest masterpiece, the "Maestà," is elsewhere in the city (see p. 213), but **Rooms 3** and **4** feature several other preeminent works, including the tiny but lauded "Madonna dei Francesani" and a polyptych, or multipaneled painting, of the "Madonna and Child with St. Agnes, St. John, St. John the Baptist, and Mary Magdalene."

Hard on the heels of these paintings come two diverting pictures by Duccio's pupil, Simone Martini, an artist whose lyrical and courtly style produced some of the most beautiful of all 14th-century Italian paintings. According to the Renaissance critic Giorgio Vasari, the Sienese themselves considered him the finest of all their painters. Look for his "Madonna and Child," removed from the parish church of Lucignano d'Arbia, a village just south of Siena, and the picture depicting "The Miracles of Beato Agostino," removed from the church of Sant'Agostino in Siena. Look for works by Lippo Memmi, Simone Martini's brother-in-law, a leading painter in his own right—although the two often worked in partnership on the same painting.

THE LORENZETTI BROTHERS

The next major artists represented —and note numerous lesser names are interspersed with these highlights—are Pietro and Ambrogio Lorenzetti, brothers who probably perished in the 1348 Black Death. Like Martini, the pair established a reputation far beyond the walls of their native city; both, however, showed greater concern with naturalistic forms than the more lyrical Martini. Pietro's single greatest work is the "Allegories of Good and Bad Government" in the Palazzo Pubblico (see pp. 200–201), but his

"Two Saints" by Sassetta, one of the most influential 15th-century Sienese artists

to enter one of its most fertile phases. Henceforth the major names come one after the other, among them Bartolo di Fredi (1353–1410), best known for his paintings in San Gimignano (see pp. 232–241); his pupil, Taddeo di Bartolo; and Sassetta (active 1423–1450). The last was Siena's leading 15th-century painter and one of the first of the city's artists to take on board such Florentine advances as the use of perspective. His principal paintings include "St. Antony Beaten by Devils," "Last Supper," and two lovely fragments of landscape—"A Town by the Sea" and "A Castle on the Lake Shore."

While Sassetta and others forged ahead, numerous highly accomplished Sienese painters of the 15th century were happy to plow a more traditional furrow. These included Sano di Pietro, Giovanni di Paolo, and Matteo di Giovanni, whose hidebound paintings, while beautiful, were executed at the same time as more radical pictures were becoming commonplace just a few miles to the north in Florence.

Although Siena reached its artistic zenith in the 14th and 15th centuries, it was not entirely without hallowed names in its 16th-century dotage. Two of the leading artists in this later period were Tuscan-born Domenico Beccafumi and Giovanni Antonio Bazzi. The latter, from the town of Vercelli in northern Italy, is better known by his nickname Sodoma, probably after an exaggerated account of his life by the Renaissance critic Giorgio Vasari—who hated him. Vasari claimed he was "always surrounded by young men, in whose company he took great pleasure." Paintings by both artists can be seen in the final rooms of the gallery's main upper floor.

Beccafumi spent part of his apprenticeship in Rome, where he came into contact with the

outstanding painting here is the "Carmine Altarpiece" (1329), parts of which, like Duccio's "Maestà," have been lost to overseas museums. What remains is still captivating, especially the five little *predella* paintings (small panels below the main painting) describing episodes from the founding of the Carmelite religious order. Ambrogio's most compelling works are the "Piccolo Maestà" and "Annunciation," the latter poignantly dated 1348, the year of his premature death.

ZENITH OF SIENESE PAINTING

The Black Death also partly accounts for the lull in Sienese painting in the second half of the 14th century. Late in this same century, however, Sienese art recovered

late works of Raphael and Michelangelo, both of whom produced paintings that looked forward to a style of painting that would become known as mannerism. On his return to Siena in 1513, Beccafumi began to paint in the same style, employing strong, or exaggerated, perspective; portraying intense displays of emotion; using occasionally lurid colors; and often painting dramatic and unnatural effects of light. Strange perspective provides the dominant note in his painting of "St. Catherine Receiving the Stigmata," while his mastery of light can be seen to good effect in the "Nativity of the Virgin." Don't miss the cartoons, or preparatory sketches, that Beccafumi made for his pavement panels in the cathedral (see p. 204-206).

Interspersed with the paintings by Beccafumi and others are works by Sodoma, a hint of whose character can be gleaned from the tax return he filed in 1531. In it he wrote: "I have an ape, a talking raven …and three beastly she-animals, which are women, and I have also 30 grown up children, which is a real encumbrance…and as 12 children exempt a man from taxation I recommend myself to you. Farewell." Sodoma's masterwork is the fresco cycle on the life of St. Benedict at the abbey of Monte Oliveto Maggiore (see pp. 268–69), but he is also well represented in the Pinacoteca Nazionale—watch for his painting of "The Scourging of Christ" (1511–14)—and elsewhere in the city, notably in the church of San Domenico. ∎

Beccafumi's painting "The Mystical Marriage of St. Catherine"

A loop walk from the Campo

This short circular walk enables you to visit some of Siena's most impressive churches and monuments, from the cluster of palaces around the Campo to the half-hidden churches in the south and west of the city.

Standing in the **Campo** ❶ (see pp. 196–201) facing the Fonte Gaia and away from the Palazzo Pubblico, take the alley just ahead of you—Vicolo di San Pietro. This leads you to the junction of Via di Città, Via Banchi di Sopra, and Via Banchi di Sotto, an intersection marked by the **Torre di Roccabruna**—one of the city's highest towers until it was truncated in the 16th century—and the **Loggia della Mercanzia** (1428–1444) ❷, a three-arched loggia built in Gothic-Renaissance style. Two of its pillar tabernacle statues, St. Peter and St. Paul (1460–62), are by Vecchietta.

Turn right on Via Banchi di Sotto, passing the **Palazzo Piccolomini** ❸ on the right (see p. 223). Immediately past the palazzo you see the **Logge del Papa** ❹ (1462), raised on the orders of the Tuscan-born Pope Pius II (Enea Silvio Piccolomini). Bear right here and you come to the baroque church of San Martino and **Via del Porrione,** one of the city's most ancient streets. It takes its name from the Latin *emporium,* meaning "place of the market," recalling the Roman markets that once stood nearby. If you have time, it's well worth following Via del Porrione and its con-

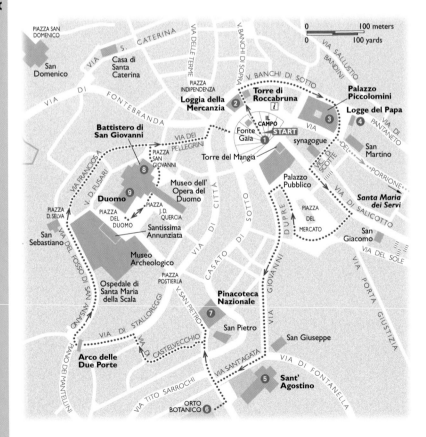

The paving of the Piazza del Campo is divided into nine sections to symbolize the cloak of the Madonna and the Council of Nine, Siena's medieval rulers.

tinuations (Via San Martino and Via San Girolamo) for some good city views and the interesting church of **Santa Maria dei Servi** (see p. 224).

Otherwise, cross Via del Porrione immediately and continue down Vicolo delle Scotte, passing Siena's synagogue on the right. This district was the heart of the city's Jewish ghetto, which was created in 1571 on the orders of Grand Duke Cosimo I de' Medici. Turn left on Via di Salicotto, take the first right, and you come to the large Piazza del Mercato. Cross the square and bear right to pick up Via del Mercato. Then turn left almost immediately to follow Via Giovanni Dupre, named after the 19th-century sculptor who was born on this street at No. 35. At the church of San Giuseppe on your left take Via

---

Also see area map, pp. 194–95
► Il Campo
1.75 miles (2.8 km) without diversion to Santa Maria dei Servi
Allow a morning, depending on sights visited
► Il Campo

NOT TO BE MISSED
- Il Campo
- Palazzo Piccolomini
- Pinacoteca Nazionale
- Battistero
- Duomo

Sant'Agata straight on to an open grassy area on your left that fronts the 13th-century church of **Sant'Agostino** ⑤, whose interior ($) contains notable paintings by Sodoma ("Epiphany") and Ambrogio Lorenzetti (a fresco of the "Maestà"). At the junction of Via Sant'Agata and Via San Pietro, a left turn takes you to the city's **Orto Botanico** ⑥, or Botanical Garden (*Via Pier Andrea Mattioli 4, closed Sat. p.m. & Sun.*). Turn right on Via San Pietro, by contrast, and you come to the church of San Pietro (on your right) and the **Pinacoteca Nazionale** ⑦ beyond (see pp. 216–19). Just before the church, turn left on Via di Castelvecchio and follow it as it bears right to Via di Stalloreggi. If time is short, a right turn on Via di Stalloreggi will take you back to the city center. Alternatively, turn left to the **Arco delle Due Porte,** an arch that formed part of the city's 11th-century walls. En route, you pass the house at Nos. 91–93 where Duccio painted his famous "Maestà" (see p. 213).

Turn right after the arch and follow Via del Fosso di San Ansano as it dips into a quiet corner of the city. At Piazza della Selva notice the *contrada* church of San Sebastiano (see p. 222), and take any of the three alleys leading to the right off the piazza. Via Franciosa or either of its two companions will take you to Piazza San Giovanni, home to the **Battistero** ⑧, with the **Duomo** ⑨ and **Museo dell' Opera del Duomo** up the steps to your left (see pp. 213–15). Via dei Pellegrini leads from the Piazza San Giovanni to Via di Città and thus back to the Campo. ■

The weekly market in Siena is held each Wednesday morning in La Lizza, near the church of San Domenico.

More places to visit in Siena

CONTRADA CHURCHES

Each of Siena's 17 *contrade*, or parishes, has its own church, social club, heraldic device, fountain, piazza, and museum. Visits to the museums usually have to be arranged by appointment at least a week in advance, making them beyond the scope of most casual visitors. The visitor center *(Piazza del campo 56, Siena, 0577 280 551)*, however, carries lists of contact numbers. The contrada churches and fountains are much easier to see, and you often find yourself stumbling across them by accident as you wander the streets.

All but two of the contrade are named after birds and other animals—the exceptions are the two largest, the **Torre** (Tower) and **Selva** (Forest). The creatures in question invariably feature as figures in the relevant fountains. The Torre's territory lies just east of the Campo, with a museum at Via Salicotto 76 *(Tel 0577 222 181 or 0577 222 555)* and a church nearby in the shape of the 16th-century Oratorio di San Giacomo. The Selva domain lies on and around Via dei Fusari just northwest of the cathedral, where a little alley called Vicolo San Giralmo, leads to contrada's spiritual home, the early 16th-century church of San Sebastiano in Valle Piatta. Its museum is in Piazzetta della Selva *(Tel 0577 45 093).*

MUSEO ARCHEOLOGICO

You could easily miss Siena's archaeological museum, a small but sprightly collection of mainly Etruscan artifacts tucked away in

Piazza del Duomo's southern corner. A spruce, frescoed entrance hall sets the tone for the well-presented displays, most of which are arranged according to provenance. There are finds from Pienza, Casole d'Elsa, and Siena itself, small centers some way from the mainstream of Etruscan life in central Italy. The jewelry and goldware in Rooms 8 and 9, removed from a tomb near Monteriggioni, are especially appealing.

🗺 195 C2 ✉ Piazza del Duomo ☎ 0577 49 153 🕓 Closed p.m. 💲 $

PALAZZO PICCOLOMINI

Only a tiny proportion of Siena's visitors bother to step inside the Palazzo Piccolomini, just off the Campo, one of three palaces in the city commissioned by Pope Pius II (Enea Silvio Piccolomini). Much of the building is given over to council offices, but its upper floors also house the extraordinary **Archivio di Stato,** or Sienese State Archives. Some visitors may simply be ignorant of this hidden gem, while others are perhaps put off by the notion that you have to see the archives in the company of a city employee. In practice, however, visiting this unmissable minor sight could hardly be easier. Enter the palace courtyard and take the stairs to your left. These bring you to a reception area where someone will accompany you to the archives.

The walk is memorable in its own right, as you pass through corridors and rooms lined with enormous bundles of ancient papers and manuscripts—a total of some 60,000 documents pertaining to each town and village in the old Sienese Republic. Each bundle of these invaluable historical records is labeled in ornate medieval script, and each is dated with the year—1387, 1389, 1390, and so on down through the centuries. You may also be able to steal a glance through windows overlooking the Campo, catching a unique and little-seen view of the square.

Eventually, your guide leaves you alone to admire the archive's artistic highlights—the Tavolette di Biccherna (the city's account books), the Gabelle (its tax records), and a series of selected manuscripts and documents dating back to earliest days (the first is from the year A.D. 736). Among the documents are ninth-century papal bulls and letters of artistic

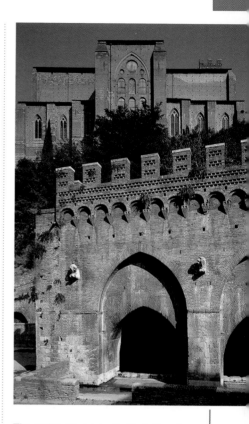

The medieval fountain, the Fonte Branda, stands below the 13th-century red-brick church of San Domenico.

commission for such famous works as Duccio's "Maestà" and Nicola Pisano's cathedral pulpit. More immediately impressive, however, are the Tavolette di Biccherna, which take their name from Blacherne, the name of the imperial treasury in the Byzantine capital of Constantinople (modern-day Istanbul). The Tavolette are painted wooden panels, and they were commissioned by magistrates and officials in the city's tax and account departments at the end of their six-month terms of office to act as covers for their documents. What lends them significance is that in the period they were created—between 1258 and 1682—they were commissioned from some of the leading artists of their day (Pietro and Ambrogio Lorenzetti, Sano di Pietro, Vecchietta, Domenico Beccafumi, and many others). Initially the scenes were religious but quickly moved to symbolic and secular subjects, providing a fascinating documentary record of daily life in Siena over some four centuries.

🖼 195 D3   ✉ Banchi di Sotto 52   ☎ 0577 247 145   🕓 Closed p.m. & all Sun.

SAN DOMENICO

San Domenico's gaunt Gothic outline dominates northern Siena. Begun in 1226, the austere, brick-built church is closely associated with St. Catherine of Siena, patron saint of both Siena and—with St. Francis—of Italy. It was here that she performed several miracles, became a Dominican nun, and received the stigmata (the wounds of Christ). Her links with the church are commemorated in the **Cappella delle Volte**—which contains her portrait—and in the **Cappella di Santa Caterina** (midway down the south aisle), whose 15th-century marble tabernacle contains part of her skull. The latter chapel also

The view from the campanile of Santa Maria dei Servi takes in Siena's red rooftops.

has two frescoes by Sodoma of episodes from her life. Chapels on either side of the high altar feature several Sienese paintings, and the high altar itself is adorned with a tabernacle and angels (1465) by Benedetto da Maiano.

🖼 194 B3   ✉ Piazza San Domenico   ☎ 0577 280 893   🕓 Closed Sun. a.m.

SAN FRANCESCO

Fire and heavy-handed restoration have battered San Francesco over the years, leaving its gloomy interior almost bereft of character and works of art. Its best remaining artifacts are the 14th-century tombs of the Tolomei at the end of the south aisle, burial places of several members of one of the city's leading medieval families. Also worth searching out are frescoes by Sassetta (right of the main door) and Pietro and Ambrogio Lorenzetti (first and third chapels left of the high altar). More remarkable still is the **Oratorio di San Bernardino** to the south of the church, whose lovely wood-paneled salon upstairs contains frescoes (1496–1518) on the life of the Virgin by the painters Sodoma, Beccafumi, and Giralmo del Pacchia.

🖼 195 D5   ✉ Piazza San Francesco   ☎ 0577 289 081; Oratorio: 0577 42 020   🕓 Closed Sun. a.m.; Oratorio: closed Nov.–mid-March

SANTA MARIA DEI SERVI

Santa Maria dei Servi lies about ten minutes' walk southeast from the center of Siena (take Via di Salcotto from the Campo, then Via S. Girolamo to Via dei Servi), but the walk is worth the effort, both for the church itself and for the magnificent city-wide views from its tree-lined piazza.

The oldest of its paintings (first altar of the south aisle) is the "Madonna di Bordone" by Coppo da Marcovaldo (born 1225), a Florentine artist captured in battle by the Sienese and forced to paint this picture as part of his ransom.

At the end of the same aisle is Matteo di Giovanni's harrowing "Massacre of the Innocents" (1491). A similarly violent depiction of the same event by Pietro Lorenzetti graces the right wall of the second chapel to the right of the high altar. Lorenzetti also painted in the second chapel left of the altar, along with one of his followers, Taddeo di Bartolo, whose "Adoration of the Shepherds" (1404) also hangs here. Taddeo's pupil, Giovanni di Paolo, painted the glowing "Madonna della Misericordia" in the nearby north transept (the painting is occasionally removed).

🖼 195 F1   ✉ Via dei Servi   ☎ 0577 222 633 🕓 Closed L ■

Northern Tuscany embraces the region's most famous village—San Gimignano; its loveliest city after Florence and Siena—Lucca; and the vineyards and wooded hills of its most celebrated rural enclave—Chianti.

Northern Tuscany

The Leaning Tower of Pisa

Northern Tuscany

TUSCANY IS A LARGE AREA, AND TO SEE EVEN ITS HIGHLIGHTS REQUIRES careful planning. Most visitors head south to Siena after Florence, but to get the most out of the rest of the region it makes sense first to head north and west from the Tuscan capital. Some places you can see as day trips from Florence, notably Fiesole, Prato, or Pistoia, but these are minor attractions by Tuscan standards.

The city that really deserves your time is Lucca, the loveliest of the region's cities after Florence and Siena. This, too, you could see in a day from Florence—direct trains take a little over an hour—but its pretty streets, superb churches, and many other monuments merit an overnight stay. If you have a car, Lucca provides a starting point for exploring some of Tuscany's most spectacular and little-known landscapes, notably the Alpi Apuane and Orecchiella to the north, whose high mountain scenery is at odds with Tuscany's prevailing pastoral image. This is touring or hiking country, however, as there are few towns of interest. Nor should you expect too much of the coastline here: Viareggio is the best of the area's generally mediocre resorts. Lucca is also close to Pisa, whose overall charms are less tempting than the fame of its notorious Leaning Tower might suggest. Much of the city was rebuilt after devastating World War II bombing, and its surviving historic buildings—beautiful as they are—should occupy you only for a morning.

Far more time is required for the towns, villages, and countryside south of Florence. Chianti has the best known countryside, a surprisingly wild region of high wooded hills interspersed with villas, farmhouses, isolated villages, and large vineyards. This is a pretty and relaxing area to stay in if you are renting a house or villa, but it offers little to see or do if you are merely driving through. One option is to take the specially designated Chiantigiana road, which threads through the best of the region between Florence and Siena, perhaps stopping off on the way to visit one or two of the vineyards responsible for some of Tuscany's top wines; there are plenty to choose from.

Alternatively, you could take the fast *superstrada* four-lane highway between the two cities, turning off close to Siena for San Gimignano, one of the most celebrated of all Italian villages, and on your way see Monteriggioni and Colle di Val d'Elsa, both interesting little medieval centers.

Although best known for its crop of medieval towers, San Gimignano also boasts a good little museum, several exceptional fresco cycles, and plenty of medieval corners to explore. In high season, however, it can become extremely busy, so try to stay overnight to enjoy the streets and piazzas without the day-trippers.

From San Gimignano you could then travel west to see the last of northern Tuscany's major towns, Volterra, stranded in lonely, little-visited countryside on the road to Pisa and the coast. ■

Fiesole

FIESOLE IS A SMALL TOWN SET IN THE CYPRESS-SCATTERED hills above Florence. A popular excursion from the city, it is a place that can trace its history back to Etruscan times—about 600 B.C. It predates the Tuscan capital by several centuries but in 1150 surrendered its independence to its larger rival. Its leafy surroundings make it a favored place in which to escape Florence's summer heat.

There's plenty to see here during a day trip, and some pretty walks, but be warned that in summer the streets can become crowded. If your trip's confined to Florence, then by all means come here. If you're headed into Tuscany, then your time can be better spent elsewhere. The best way to reach the town, which is 5 miles (8 km) from central Florence, is to take a No. 7 bus from the line of bus stops immediately outside the Santa Maria Novella railroad station (on its eastern side). The city transit's standard 60-minute flat-fare ticket is valid for the trip (one-way). Journey time is about 20 minutes.

The bus drops you in Fiesole's main square, **Piazza Mino da Fiesole,** named after its most famous son, the sculptor Mino da

Fiesole (1429–1484). Here you'll find the **Duomo,** founded in 1028, its plain 19th-century facade masking an interior enlivened by Bicci di Lorenzo's dazzling high altarpiece (1450) and the Cappella Salutati, right of the choir, which contains an altar frontal and tomb by Mino da Fiesole.

Just behind the Duomo stands the **Museo Bandini** *(Via Dupré 1, tel 055 59 477, closed 1st Tues. of the month),* a small museum devoted mainly to ivories, ceramics, and Florentine paintings. Walk a little farther east, and on Via Marini you'll find the entrance to Fiesole's pretty **archaeological zone,** a pleasantly shady spot in which to while away an hour in the heat of the afternoon. It contains a small museum devoted to some of the Etruscan and Roman finds excavated on the site. Highlights include a 2,500-year-old decorated tombstone, a large lead *cista,* or urn, from about the third or fourth century, and evocative articles such as pearls and silver hairpins removed from skeletons found in tombs around the site. Also in the area is a 3,000-seat Roman theater dating from the first century B.C. It is so well preserved that it is still used to stage performances during the Estate Fiesolana, Fiesole's summer arts and music festival (see p. 325). Also scattered around the site are the remains of a Roman bath complex, temples, and Etruscan walls.

Returning to Piazza Mino da Fiesole, you might want to tackle

Left: Enjoying the sun in Fiesole

Fiesole
△ 227 D3
Visitor information
✉ Piazza Mino da Fiesole 37
☎ 055 598 720
🚌 Bus: No. 7 from Santa Maria Novella railroad station in Florence

Via San Francesco, a steep lane from the piazza's western edge that leads to the churches of San Francesco and Sant'Alessandro, both worth a look; Gothic San Francesco probably occupied the site of the Etruscan acropolis. The main reason for the climb, however, is to enjoy the fine views of Florence, spread out below. Then, instead of retracing your steps to the town center, take the gate in front of San Francesco, which wind into a wooded public park with paths that lead back to the town.

If you have the energy for another modest walk of about 1.75 miles (3 km), then take Via Vecchia Fiesolana from the southern side of Piazza Mino da Fiesole. If you don't want the exercise, then there are usually plenty of cabs on or near the piazza. Dropping steeply, the lane passes the **Villa Medici** *(Gardens closed p.m. & all Sun.),* built by Michelozzo for Cosimo de' Medici. It eventually arrives at the church and convent of **San Domenico.** This was once the home of painter and monk Fra Angelico, and it holds a painting by him of the "Madonna with Saints and Angels" (1425). A five-minute walk down another small lane, Via della Badia, brings you to the beautifully situated **Badia Fiesolana,** the town's cathedral until 1028. Cosimo de' Medici (Cosimo the Elder) had the church altered in the 1460s but left the sublime old Romanesque facade intact. As a result, the old frontage was left picturesquely enclosed by the later, 15th-century church. ■

Fiesole offers sublime vistas of Florence and the hills beyond.

Archaeological zone

- ✉ Via Marini–Via Portigiani
- ☎ 055 59 477
- 🕐 Closed 1st Tues. of month
- 💲 Combined ticket with Museo Bandini: $$$

A drive through the Chianti countryside

This loop drive through vineyards, olive groves, small towns, and wooded hills allows you to see the best of Chianti, Tuscany's most famous region. En route you can stop in tiny villages or buy wine and olive oil from some of the area's many farms.

Whether you follow the loop or drive from Florence, you'll see the best of the Chianti region. The route from Florence (see below) is a much prettier route than the *superstrada* highway between the two cities.

For the loop, leave Siena on the SS2 road (the Via Cassia) to the west, watching for signs to Castellina in Chianti and the Chiantigiana. All manner of diversions are possible, but note that while roads in Chianti are well made, they're also often full of twists and turns. Distances on the ground and journey times are therefore greater than they appear on the map. The region's towns are often relatively unmemorable, making the countryside you travel through Chianti's main attraction. With the countryside come dozens of **vineyards,** producers of Chianti's famous wine (see pp. 272-73). Most of the vineyards are well signposted and open to the public for buying and tasting.

For an introduction to the region's viti-culture you could do worse than pause in **Castellina in Chianti ①,** 16 miles (26 km) from Siena, where local wines and olive oils are sold at the Bottega del Vino Gallo Nero *(Via della Rocca 10).* The Gallo Nero, or Black Cockerel, is one of the most respected federations of Chianti producers. From Castellina head east for 7.5 miles (12 km) on the scenic SS429 to **Radda in Chianti ②.** Radda's modern outskirts are unappealing, though the inner core still retains its medieval aspect. Beyond Radda, continue east a another 7.5 miles (12 km) into the heart of the heavily wooded Monti de Chianti, the Chianti Hills, and to **Badia a Coltibuono ③,** a beautifully located 11th-century abbey now given over to a restaurant and wine cellars. Just south of the abbey the road joins with the SS408, on which you turn right for 4 miles (6.4 km) toward **Gaiole in Chianti ④,** another important wine town with a quaint old center ringed by modern development.

Ignore the turns to Radda and Castagnoli off the SS408 4 miles (6.4 km) south of Gaiole—unless you're in a hurry to get back to Siena. Instead, press on the same distance again to the next main junction. Turn left on the SS484 and follow signs for the **Castello di Brolio ⑤** *(Near San Regolo, tel 0577 747 104 or 0577 747 156, closed L),* a vast crenellated castle that has been in the Ricasoli family since the 12th century. The battlements have sweeping views of the Arbia Valley and the Chianti Hills, and in the on-site *cantina* you can buy the noted wines produced by the castle estate. Several minor roads, most of them gravel-surfaced *strade bianche* (white roads), lead back to the SS408 via either San Felice or Monti and Cacchiano. Once back on the SS408 it's 12.5 miles (20 km) more to Siena.

Alternatively, return from Castello di Brolio to the SS484 and continue 6 miles (10 km) past Villa a Sesta to an intersection beneath **San Gusme ⑥,** one of the region's most picturesque villages. From here the return to Siena is via a minor road for 7 miles (11 km) to Pianella, where you join the SS408 about 7.5 miles (12 km) from Siena.

This tour makes a loop from Siena, but you could follow much of the route on the SS222 road, a specially designated and signposted scenic route known as the Chiantigiana, which goes from Florence toward Siena. Leave Florence on the Via Sienese south, following signs for Galluzzo, 5 miles (8 km) away, where you should see the **Certosa del Galluzzo,** or Florence Charterhouse, an imposing 14th-century monastery *(Closed Mon., donation).* From here, follow signs for 7.5 miles (12 km) to Impruneta, where minor signed roads lead for 6 miles (10 km), by way of Strada in Chianti, to the SS222. Follow the SS222 another 10 miles (16 km) south to Greve in Chianti, and then 15 miles (24 km) farther to Castellina in Chianti, where you can pick up the itinerary to Siena described above. ■

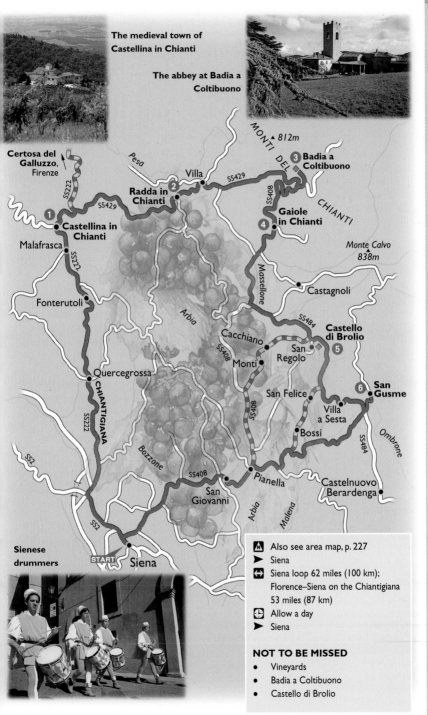

The medieval town of
Castellina in Chianti

The abbey at Badia a
Coltibuono

Certosa del
Galluzzo,
Firenze

Pesa

MONTI DEL ▲ 812m

❸ Badia a
Coltibuono

Villa

SS429

SS222

SS429

❷ Radda in
Chianti

SS408

CHIANTI

❶ Castellina in
Chianti

Malafrasca

❹ Gaiole
in Chianti

SS222

Monte Calvo
838m

Fonterutoli

Massellone

Castagnoli

Arbia

SS484

Cacchiano

Castello
di Brolio ❺

Quercegrossa

SS408

Monti

San
Regolo

CHIANTIGIANA

SS222

San Felice

SS408

❻ San
Gusme

Villa
a Sesta

SS2

Bozzone

Bossi

Ombrone

SS484

SS408

San
Giovanni

Pianella

Castelnuovo
Berardenga

Arbia

Malena

SS2

Sienese
drummers

START   Siena

Also see area map, p. 227

▶ Siena

Siena loop 62 miles (100 km);
Florence–Siena on the Chiantigiana
53 miles (87 km)

🕐 Allow a day

▶ Siena

NOT TO BE MISSED
- Vineyards
- Badia a Coltibuono
- Castello di Brolio

San Gimignano

ONE LOOK AT THE SKYLINE OF SAN GIMIGNANO AND ITS
crop of ancient stone towers is enough to see why the village is often
called a "medieval Manhattan." The towers and the village's picture-
book prettiness make this a much visited spot, yet it is also a place
that retains its charm. It has a fascinating art gallery, a pair of superb
fresco-filled churches, and some beautiful and far-reaching views of
the Tuscan countryside.

San Gimignano
⚏ 226 C2
Visitor information
✉ Piazza del Duomo 1
☎ 0577 940 008

San Gimignano's famous towers
began to appear around 1150. They
had a variety of purposes, some
practical, some fanciful. At their
most basic they provided a readily
defended place of retreat during
attack or periods of civil strife. Yet
they also served as medieval status
symbols: A noble's power and
wealth could be measured by the
height of his tower, especially if it
was higher than those of his rivals.
Yet towers and individual power
were no defense against plague or
constant civil strife, both of which
gradually sapped the strength of the
village. In 1348, fatally weakened, it
placed itself under the protection of
Florence. The move undermined
the power of the nobles, one reason
why so many towers survived; as
they posed no threat, so there was
no need to tear them down.

Many people visit San
Gimignano as a day trip from
Siena, often traveling by either bus
or train. Bus journeys usually
involve a change of bus at
Poggibonsi, an undistinguished and
largely modern town, but you can
buy through-tickets from the TRA-
IN bus company office in Siena's
Piazza San Domenico. Alternatively,
take a train from Siena to Poggibonsi and then walk the short
distance to the TRA-IN bus depot
(exit the railroad station and take
the right turn in the piazza in front
of the station). Total journey time
from Siena to San Gimignano is
about an hour. The route is

straightforward if you're driving,
but be sure to stop off en route at
Monteriggioni (see p. 264) and perhaps Colle di Val d'Elsa (see pp.
263-64). Parking in San Gimignano
can be difficult at busy times. Your
best bet is to use the parking lot at
the southern edge of the village by
Via Roma and walk from there.

Exploring San Gimignano on
foot is easy; you can stroll from one
end of the village to the other in a
matter of minutes. Most of the key
things to see lie in or near the central Piazza del Duomo, but this is a
place where you should devote
plenty of time to casual exploration. Start your tour beyond Via
Roma and Piazzale dei Martiri di
Monte Maggio at the southern
gateway, the Porta San Giovanni,
and then walk north on Via San
Giovanni. This street once formed
part of the Via Francigena, one of
the main medieval pilgrimage roads
between Rome and northern
Europe. San Gimignano's position
on the road was one reason for the
town's early growth and prosperity.
Pop into **San Francesco** midway
up the street on the right, a deconsecrated 13th-century Romanesque
church now given over, like many
places around town, to the sale of
the local Vernaccia white wine. Its
rear terrace has memorable views
over the Tuscan hills.

At the top of the street a
medieval arch, the **Arco dei
Becci,** ushers you into the first of
two linked central squares, Piazza

**Opposite: The
vineyards near
San Gimignano
produce the
celebrated
Vernaccia
white wine.**

della Cisterna and Piazza del Duomo. The first of these is ringed with towers, medieval buildings, and several tempting cafés. The second is home to the village's principal sights: the Collegiata and Museo Civico (see pp. 238-240). Here, too, is the **Museo d'Arte Sacra** *(Tel 0577 940 008, closed Mon.),* a modest museum of sacred art and archaeological finds. The Arco dei Becci formed part of the town's original ring of defensive walls, built before a second set of ramparts was raised in the 13th century to enclose the burgeoning town. **Piazza della Cisterna** takes its

name from the *cisterna* (public well) at its heart, built in 1287 but extended in 1346 on the orders of Guccio de' Malavoli, then the town's Podestà, or ruling magistrate, whose coat of arms is emblazoned on its side. Note the grooves cut over the centuries by ropes used to pull up pails of water.

Off to the left of Piazza della Cisterna lies **Piazza del Duomo.** In front of you here, at the top of the steps, stands the Collegiata. On your left is the Palazzo del Popolo (1288), where the visitor center and Museo Civico are based, and behind you is the Palazzo del

San Gimignano prospered initially thanks to its defensive hilltop position.

Podestà (1239). The Palazzo del Podestà's tower, the Torre della Rognasa, was cited in a civic statute of 1255 as having the maximum height allowed for any privately built tower—167 feet (52 m). Many nobles ignored the law, or subtly subverted it, as in the case of the twin **Torre Salvucci** (to the left of the palace as you face it). Here, the Salvucci family built towers that were below the regulation height, but they placed them so close together that it was obvious their combined height would be greater than anything built by the town council or rival families.

THE COLLEGIATA

The Collegiata was at one time San Gimignano's cathedral, or Duomo, but forsook its title when the village lost its status as a bishopric in 1348. Founded about 1056, the church was consecrated in 1148 and enlarged by the architect and sculptor Giuliano da Maiano between 1466 and 1468.

Beyond a blank facade lies an extraordinary interior almost completely covered in frescoes. Three principal cycles adorn the walls, beginning on the rear (entrance) wall with "Last Judgment" (1410) by leading Sienese painter Taddeo

Wild boar meat is prized in Tuscany, but the animals are becoming pests in the local countryside.

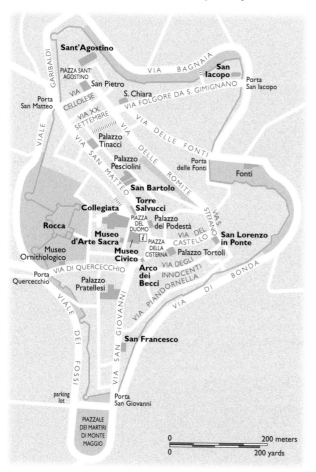

Take a break from sightseeing at a village café, but remember that your drink will cost more if you sit down than if you stand at the bar.

di Bartolo. "Inferno" is portrayed on the right, "Paradiso" on the left. Between these two scenes, which are painted on protruding walls, is a fresco by Benozzo Gozzoli of "St. Sebastian" (1465), a saint invoked against infectious diseases and so often painted during or after plague epidemics. One such epidemic had struck San Gimignano a year before the painting was commissioned. Sebastian was chosen as the subject in such paintings for his immense powers of physical recovery. He miraculously survived his ordeal by arrows—the event usually depicted in paintings of the saint—and was eventually martyred by being crushed to death. The two painted wooden statues flanking the fresco, the "Archangel Gabriel" and the "Madonna Annunciate," are the

work of the 15th-century Sienese master, Jacopo della Quercia.

The church's second fresco cycle fills the north (left) wall and was painted by Bartolo di Fredi (active 1353–1410) with episodes from the Old Testament (main wall) and scenes of the Creation (in the lunettes above). The most celebrated scene, if only because it includes a graphically depicted penis, is the "Drunkenness of Noah" (sixth fresco from the left in the upper of the two main registers as you face the frescoes). Tradition has it that Noah was the first to cultivate the vine, as well as the first to abuse its fruits. Also note the lovely scene portraying the "Creation of Eve" (fourth lunette from the left), in which Eve is shown emerging from Adam's rib. Many of the scenes show the influence of Ambrogio Lorenzetti's "Allegories of Good and Bad Government" in Siena's Palazzo Pubblico (see pp. 200-201), and in particular the painter's love of incidental detail. Several contemporary fishing scenes, for example, are included in the turbulent fresco of "The Passage across the Red Sea" (lower register, fourth from the left).

The cycle of New Testament scenes on the opposite wall is earlier (from about 1333) and is attributed to one of two Sienese artists, Lippo Memmi or Barna da Siena. Here, the scenes are arranged in three levels, with several damaged frescoes from other eras interspersed. Starting at the top and reading from right to left the scenes depicted are as follows: (top register) "Annunciation," "Nativity," "Epiphany," "Presentation in the Temple," "Massacre of the Innocents," and "Flight to Egypt;" (second tier, eight panels, reading left to right) "Dispute in the Temple," "Baptism of Jesus," "Vocation of Peter," "Marriage of Canaan," "Transfiguration," "Resurrection of Lazarus," "Entry of Jesus into Jerusalem," and "The Crowd Meeting Jesus;" (lower register, eight panels, from right to left) the "Last Supper," "Betrayal of Judas," "Jesus in the Garden," "Kiss of Judas," "Jesus in the Pretorian Palace," "Flagellation," "Crown of Thorns," and "Calvary." Among many graphic frescoes here, few are as dramatic as the "Resurrection of Lazarus," which portrays a crowd of awed onlookers watching as Lazarus's tomb is opened to reveal the deceased man—still wrapped in his burial robes—miraculously raised from the dead.

Elsewhere in the church, be sure to admire the **Cappella di San Gimignano** (left of the high altar), which contains an altar by Benedetto da Maiano (brother of Giuliano), and to pay the small admission fee required to enter the **Cappella di Santa Fina** off the south (right-hand) aisle. Benedetto was responsible for the altar, marble shrine, and bas-reliefs in this chapel, which is dedicated to one of San Gimignano's patron saints, St. Fina, the subject of lunette frescoes by the important 15th-century Florentine painter Domenico Ghirlandaio.

St. Fina was born in San Gimignano in 1238. At the age of ten she developed an incurable illness and for the next five years lay on a plank, aiming to bring herself closer to Christ through her increased suffering. Her last days are depicted in the fresco in the right lunette, the "Announcement of St. Fina's Death." Its details include St. Gregory, who told Fina of her death in a vision; a mouse in the gloom to the rear of the picture (Fina was paralyzed in her last days and unable to scare away the mice that tormented her); and the flower-covered board on which she had lain (the flowers appeared miraculously on her death). The more compelling fresco on the left shows the "Funeral of St. Fina," a picture that is said to have greatly impressed Raphael and that portrays the saint on her deathbed with the towers of her native village in the background. Also shown are three miracles associated with the saint: The ringing of San Gimignano's bells by angels on her death; the restoration of a blind boy's sight; and the curing of her nurse's paralyzed hand. Watch, too, for self-portraits of Ghirlandaio (the figure behind the bishop saying Mass) and his assistants (shown to either side)— Davide (Ghirlandaio's brother) and Sebastiano Mainardi (his brother-in-law).

Italian ice cream, unmissable at any price

his brother-in-law, Simone Martini, had completed two years earlier in Siena's Palazzo Pubblico (see p. 199 for more on this type of painting). The Sala del Consiglio is also known as the Sala di Dante, for it was in this room that the poet Dante—then a Florentine diplomat—met representatives of San Gimignano's ruling council to seek their support (see p. 78). Several other small rooms on this floor are given over to temporary exhibits. Upstairs are the four main rooms of the picture gallery proper, crammed with masterpieces by a host of Sienese and Florentine painters, most notably Benozzo Gozzoli and Filippino Lippi.

The best paintings hang in the large room immediately on the right at the top of the stairs, beginning with a painted 13th-century "Crucifix" by Coppo di Marcovaldo, a Florentine painter captured by the Sienese at the Battle of Montaperti in 1260. The work was probably executed while he was in captivity and ranks among the great early Tuscan masterpieces. The top of the painting is adorned with small panels portraying the "Assumption of the Virgin" and "Christ Pantocrater" (Christ in the act of blessing). More small figures around Christ's hands depict scenes from the Passion.

Other exceptional paintings include two tondi, or round paintings (1482), on the opposite wall; they are by Filippino Lippi. One shows the "Angel Annunciate," the Angel Gabriel announcing to Mary that she is to become the mother of a child. The other is a "Virgin Annunciate," or Mary receiving the news, an event that coincided with the Immaculate Conception of Christ. The two episodes are more usually portrayed together in one painting and called the "Annunciation."

A ban on vehicles allows visitors and villagers to enjoy the traffic-free streets.

Museo Civico

✉ Palazzo del Popolo, Piazza del Duomo

☎ 0577 990 312

💲 Museum: $$. Torre Grossa: $$

MUSEO CIVICO

Leaving the Collegiata, your next port of call should be the Museo Civico, San Gimignano's civic museum. This is divided in two: One ticket admits you to the museum proper, another to the **Torre Grossa** (begun 1300), the only one of San Gimignano's towers currently open to the public. You enter both via a pretty courtyard, dotted with archaeological fragments and three frescoes (1513) by Sodoma. Steps lead from here to the ticket office. The museum opens with the **Sala del Consiglio,** dominated by Lippo Memmi's majestic painting of the "Maestà" (1317), or "Madonna Enthroned," a favorite subject among Sienese painters. Memmi's picture was closely modeled on one

Nearby are outstanding paintings by the Umbrian master Pinturicchio—"Madonna Enthroned with St. Gregory and St. Benedict" (1512)—and two pictures by Benozzo Gozzoli of the "Madonna and Child with Saints" (both 1466). One of the saints portrayed is Martha, a woman still held in high esteem by many Tuscans, partly because she is the patron saint of builders, but more particularly because she is also patron saint of cooks.

The other, larger room here contains several multipanel paintings depicting episodes from lives of various saints, all of them fascinating for their incidental narrative detail. If you've visited the Cappella di Santa Fina in the Collegiata, you'll be familiar with some of the episodes in Lorenzo di Niccolò's double-sided scenes from the life of St. Fina (1402). The same artist executed the similar scenes from the life of St. Bartholomew (1401) in the same room, one macabre panel of which shows attempts to martyr the saint by flaying him alive. Another shows his eventual beheading, his flayed strips of skin hampering the work of his executioners. A third painting, by Taddeo di Bartolo, offers a narrative of the life of San Gimignano (1393), painted when the artist was working on the New Testament frescoes in the Collegiata. The work once stood on the church's high altar.

St. Gimignano was born in the northern Italian town of Modena but became associated with San Gimignano when he helped save the village from Attila the Hun. This episode, in which the saint is shown remonstrating with Attila, is one of several depicted on the left of the painting. The other scenes show the saint preventing his followers from being drenched in a leaky church, and St. Severus

officiating at Gimignano's funeral. One extraordinary vignette on the right shows the saint meeting Lucifer as he answers a call of nature and causing the devil to disappear by making the sign of the Cross. The three other episodes here are concerned with the saint's exorcizing of a devil from the daughter of a Byzantine emperor. They show the saint crossing to Constantinople (now Istanbul), miraculously calming storm-tossed waters on this voyage and performing the exorcism of the princess.

A separate room on this floor contains some of Tuscany's most beguiling pictures (reached by turning left rather than right at the top of the stairs). They are the work of a minor local painter, Memmo di Filipuccio, father of the more

Medieval streets provide the perfect backdrop for the range of historical pageants held in San Gimignano during the year.

The "Creation of Eve," by Bartoli di Fredi, is part of a 14th-century fresco cycle in the Collegiata, San Gimignano.

Opposite: "The Martyrdom of St. Sebastian" by Benozzo Gozzoli in the Collegiata

celebrated Lippo Memmi. The early 14th-century panels portray three wedding scenes, including two remarkable vignettes in which the couple share a bath and then a bed. Some say these are innocent narratives celebrating the joy of marriage, others that they are allegorical warnings to men on the wiles of women.

SANT'AGOSTINO

From the museum and Piazza del Duomo you should take a circuitous route to San Gimignano's third major set piece, the church of Sant'Agostino. This enables you to enjoy some of the pretty back streets en route. Try heading west to explore the remains of the **Rocca** (1353), or castle, and its peaceful public gardens; then walk east to

visit the two churches of **San Lorenzo in Ponte** (1240) and **San Iacopo.** The latter was reputedly founded by the Knights Templar in the 13th century, and the former—if you're lucky enough to find it open—has a variety of 15th-century fresco fragments. If you take the more direct route north to Sant'Agostino (on Via San Matteo), watch for the lovely 13th-century Romanesque church of **San Bartolo,** just north of Piazza del Duomo (on the right), and the Palazzo Pesciolini immediately to its left, a house and tower complex built at around the same time as the church.

On entering **Sant'Agostino** (*Piazza Sant'Agostino),* the west wall on your left contains the **Cappella di San Bartolo,** inside which lies the tomb of St. Bartolo, another of San Gimignano's saints. The tomb's reliefs (1495) of three episodes from his life are by Benedetto da Maiano, and in one of them the saint is shown reattaching his leprous toes after they had come off in the hands of a nurse. Working your way down the right (south) wall, you pass a painting of the "Madonna and Child with Eight Saints" (1494) by Pier Francesco Fiorentino (by the first altar) and a nearby figure of "Christ with the Symbols of the Passion" by Bartolo di Fredi. Bartolo worked on the Collegiata's Old Testament frescoes and was also responsible for the frescoes on the life of the Virgin on the walls of the chapel to the right of Sant'Agostino's high altar. Most people miss these pictures, seduced by the more eye-catching fresco cycle around the high altar itself. The work of the Florentine painter Benozzo Gozzoli, a pupil of Fra Angelico, the 17 panels describe episodes from the life of St. Augustine. Like many of Gozzoli's frescoes in Tuscany—you may have seen his paintings in Florence's Palazzo Medici-Riccardi (see pp. 134–37)—these paintings are as charming for their portrayal of 15th-century Italy as for their ostensibly religious subject.

The striking painting on the high altar is "Coronation of the Virgin" by Piero del Pollaiuolo (1441–1496), the brother of the more famous Florentine painter, jeweler, and engraver Antonio del Pollaiuolo. Toward the church's entrance, the north (left) wall contains other artistic oddments, most notably five round reliefs by Tino di Camaino (probably removed from a tomb of St. Bartolo that predated the present sepulcher) and a 15th-century fresco of "St. Sebastian" by Benozzo Gozzoli (third altar). ∎

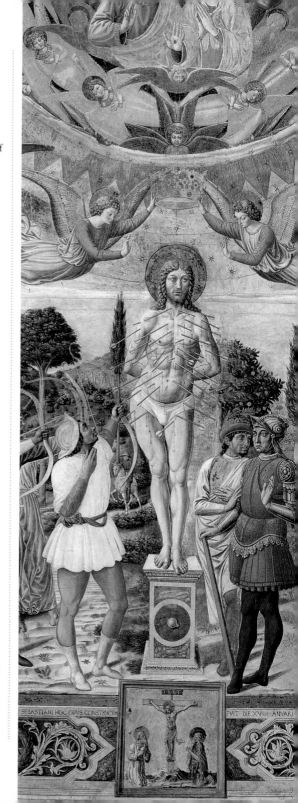

Villas & gardens

It is no surprise to find a wide range of villas and gardens in a place like Tuscany, a region that has been blessed with beautiful countryside, fertile soils, mild climate, and architecturally enlightened patrons with wealth to spare. Many villas are private, some you stumble across by accident, and others are easily accessible from Florence and Lucca.

Rich urban families originally built fortified country houses or castles as refuges from political turmoil in their home cities. Later they commissioned less heavily defended properties as retreats from a city's summer heat. Later still, they turned their houses into showrooms of their wealth and taste, or they transformed them into rural oases of culture and learning. Many exploited the countryside surrounding their villas for agricultural purposes, particularly as Tuscany's textile and other industries began to decline in the 16th and 17th centuries. Houses—and gardens— were also subject to the vagaries of architectural taste and fashion, and many old houses and their gardens were repeatedly modified.

No family's villas exemplify these changes better than those of the Medici. This richest of all Tuscan families had houses across the region, but many of the most famous— inevitably—lie close to Florence, the Medici's home city. The **Villa Medicea La Petraia** (Map 227 D3, Via della Petraia 40, tel 055 451 208, closed 2nd & 3rd Mon. of the month, combined adm. with Villa Medicea di Castello) was built as a castle, turned into a country house in the 1570s by Grand Duke Ferdinando I de' Medici, and then remodeled in the 19th century by the House of Savoy, the Italian royal family. Its parkland is delightful, its garden less so—not something you could say of the nearby **Villa Medicea di Castello** (Map 227 D3, Via di Castello 47, tel 055 454 791; details as for La Petraia above), whose gardens are some of the finest in Tuscany. The house (closed to the public) was bought in 1477 by cousins of Lorenzo the Magnificent, shortly before their uncle bought a lowly farmhouse and turned it into the **Villa Medicea di Poggio a Caiano** (Map 227 D3, Poggio a Caiano, tel 055 877 012, closed 2nd & 3rd Mon. of the month, $), 11 miles (18 km) northwest of Florence. This is the Medici villa to visit if you visit no other, offering a beautiful insight into how life might have been lived in a rural retreat of the day. The gardens, like many in Italy, were remodeled in the 18th century to resemble English-style parkland, the prevailing horticultural fashion of the day.

Much as you can make a tour of these and other estates around Florence (contact the visitor center for details), so you can visit a coronet of villas and gardens around Lucca. Though more modest, these villas suffer less from the creeping urban sprawl that has engulfed the Medicean villas. The best is the **Villa Reale** (Map 226 B3, tel 0583 30 108 or 0583 30 009, guided tours daily March–Nov. on the hour 10 a.m.–12 noon, 3p.m.–6p.m.. except Mon., $$) near the village of Marlia, about 9 miles (14 km) northeast of Lucca. The gardens are charming, as is the 14th-century villa (closed to the public), which Napoleon's sister, Elisa Baciocchi, restored along neoclassic lines in 1806. The environs of the **Villa Torrigiani** (Map 227 C3, tel 0368 320 9614 or 0349 465 7033, closed Nov.–Feb., $$), about 5 miles (8 km) east of Marlia, are more built up, but the gardens and baroque house are still captivating. The 16th-century **Villa Mansi** (Map 226 B3, Segromigno in Monte, Capannori, tel 0583 920 234 or 0583 920 096, closed Mon.) just a mile away (2 km) is also worth a visit, as is the superb formal garden at the **Villa Garzoni** (Map 226 C3, tel 0572 429 590 or a.m. only 0572 429 131) near Collodi, 10 miles (16 km) east of Lucca. On a different note entirely, Collodi is also home to the **Parco di Pinocchio,** a theme park devoted to the children's character Pinocchio, whose creator, Carlo Lorenzini (1826–1890)—known as Carlo Collodi—was born in the village. ∎

The baroque exuberance of the Villa Torrigiani near Lucca (top): Its gardens were remodeled on English lines in the 18th century. The Villa Garzoni (bottom) began life as a fortress. Its gardens are some of the most beautiful in Italy.

Volterra

ON A GLOOMY DAY VOLTERRA CAN SEEM A BROODING, desolate sort of place, a lonely sentinel set amid volcanic hills that seem a world away from Tuscany's more pastoral countryside. English writer D. H. Lawrence (1885–1930) described it in *Etruscan Places* (1932) as a place that "gets all the winds, and sees all the world,...a sort of inland island, still curiously isolated and grim."

The "Descent from the Cross" by Rosso Fiorentino. The mannerist painting is the highlight of Volterra's Pinacoteca.

This said, Volterra is also a majestic town, perched on a craggy summit behind rings of Etruscan and medieval walls, and filled with churches, parks, Roman remains, stone-flagged streets, and one of the region's leading archaeological museums. Sunny weather turns it into a perfect day's outing—despite its peripheral position—from San Gimignano or elsewhere.

The town began as an Etruscan outpost, its lofty site and the presence of mineral and alabaster deposits accounting for its early rise (alabaster products are still available in dozens of shops across town). It was equally important in medieval times for its alum mines, which provided an essential raw material for the dyeing of cloth.

Something of Volterra's medieval prosperity is reflected in the scope of the monuments in **Piazza dei Priori,** the heart of the old town. Buildings here include the Palazzo dei Priori (1208), one of Tuscany's earliest civic palaces, and the slightly later Palazzo Pretorio, best known for its **Torre del Porcellino** (Piglet's Tower), named for the worn, carved boar that sits alongside an upper floor window.

Also in the square is the Duomo, or cathedral, begun in 1120, but much altered over the centuries. Its main treasure is a "Deposition" (1228) in a chapel off the right transept, a rare work that consists of a group of brightly painted wooden figures. On the high altar is a *ciborio,* or marble altarpiece (1471), by Mino da Fiesole, who was also responsible for the flanking angels. Behind the cathedral stands the 13th-century octagonal baptistery, partly decorated in the striped marble bands typical of Pisan-style Romanesque architecture. Its interior highlight

is a baptismal font by Andrea Sansovino (1460–1529).

Just south of the baptistery in Via Roma lies the Palazzo Vescovile, or Bishops' Palace. It is now home to the **Museo Diocesano d'Arte Sacra,** a rich little museum filled with paintings, sculptures, and other precious artifacts. Its principal treasures are a terra-cotta bust of St. Linus, the next pope after St. Peter, by Andrea della Robbia, an anonymous 13th-century painted "Crucifix," and a painting of the "Madonna Enthroned with Saints" (1521) by Rosso Fiorentino, one of Italy's leading mannerist painters.

Another great work by Fiorentino, the "Descent from the Cross"—many consider it a masterpiece of the mannerist tradition—is found in the town's **Pinacoteca e Museo Civico** (art gallery and civic museum), along with excellent paintings by other leading Tuscan artists such as Taddeo di Bartolo and Luca Signorelli (1441–1523).

Another masterpiece from a different era awaits in the **Museo Etrusco Guarnacci** (*Via Don Minzoni 14, tel 0588 86 347, closed p.m. mid-Oct.–mid-Mar.*), one of Italy's best Etruscan museums outside Rome. Etruscan art is not to all tastes—it has many dull painted urns—but few people could fail to be moved by the first-century B.C. statue of "Gli Sposi" ("The Newlyweds"), a vivid sculptural tomb portrait of a married couple, or by the collection's bronze statuettes. The third-century B.C. "Ombra della Sera" ("Shadow of the Evening") is a bronze votive figure, a strange, elongated nude.

Volterra is not just a town of museums, however, and you should try to walk to its eastern margins to see the Rocca (Medici castle) and the **Parco Archeologico,** a lovely area of parkland. Breach the old medieval walls to the north through the Porta Fiorentina and you come to the excavations with an impressive Roman theater, bath complex, and other remains. Leave time to walk to the west of the town to see the famous **Balze,** a series of sheer, eroded cliffs and alabaster mines where the ruins of Volterra's Etruscan walls are still visible. ■

The almost bare hills and deep clefts of the countryside around Volterra typify this part of Tuscany.

Volterra
226 C2
Visitor information
✉ Via G. Turazza 2
☎ 0588 86 150

Museo Diocesano d'Arte Sacra
✉ Via Roma 13
☎ 0588 86 290
🕐 Closed Sun. p.m. & p.m. daily mid-Nov.–mid.-March
💲 $

Pinacoteca e Museo Civico
✉ Via dei Sarti
☎ 0588 87 580
🕐 Closed p.m. Nov.–mid.-March
💲 $

Pisa

MOST PEOPLE KNOW PISA'S FAMOUS LEANING TOWER.
Fewer know that it's just one component in a lovely ensemble of
medieval buildings; fewer still know that the rest of the city—sadly—
is a largely modern place, the result of heavy bombing during World
War II. Allow an hour or so to see the tower and its surroundings, and
about the same again to explore Pisa's other medieval sights.

Pisa began as an Etruscan and then
a Roman colony, and it continued
to thrive under Lombard rule in
the seventh and eighth centuries.
Its period of glory came in the
11th and 12th centuries, when a
thriving port and far-flung trading
links turned it into one of the
Mediterranean's foremost maritime
powers. The wealth from this era
yielded the Leaning Tower and
other key monuments, although the
city's golden age was cut short by a
naval defeat at the hands of the
Genoese in 1284 and by the silting
up of the city's harbor. Florence
assumed control of the city in 1406,
accelerating Pisa's transformation
into a quiet center of science and
learning. A university had been
established in 1343, among whose

alumni was one of the greatest of
all scientists, the Pisan-born Galileo
Galilei. Much of Pisa's heritage was
ravaged in a few weeks, however,
when the city was shelled in 1944
by both Nazi and Allied forces
during World War II.

CAMPO DEI MIRACOLI

The city's **Torre Pendente**
(Leaning Tower) survived the
bombs—a miraculous outcome,
especially as other monuments
within just a few feet were
destroyed. The tower is one element
of the Campo dei Miracoli, or Field
of Miracles, a large, grassy piazza
that also contains Pisa's cathedral,
baptistery, and Camposanto (cemetery). The tower was begun in 1173
as the cathedral's Campanile, or bell

tower, and started to lean almost immediately, the result of the weak, sandy subsoil underpinning its foundations. Attempts to rectify the lean by subsequent architects over the next 180 years—the time it took to complete the tower—ended in failure. Galileo famously made use of the overhang when he dropped metal balls from the tower to show that falling bodies of different weight descend at the same rate. The lean intensified over much of the 20th century, leading to the tower's closure in 1990 and a raft of schemes designed to prevent its collapse. At its worst, the lean was 17.5 feet (5.5 m) from the vertical. In 1999 engineers began tentatively to reverse the process using weights, steel cables, and sophisticated underpinning techniques.

The tower's sheer drama detracts from the Campo's other monuments, which in any other place would be accounted must-see masterpieces. The **Duomo,** or cathedral—among Italy's finest Romanesque buildings—was begun about a century earlier than the tower, in 1064, well before the start of the present-day cathedrals in rival cities such as Florence (1296) and Siena (1179). With its array of pillars, columns, and colored marbles, it would provide the model for similar "Pisan-Romanesque" churches across central Italy, many of which borrowed its use of a striped marble exterior and ornate decorative motifs, a style assimilated by Pisa through its trading links with the Arab, Byzantine, and Levantine worlds.

The carving on the exterior predates the appearance of Pisa's finest sculptors, Nicola Pisano and Giovanni Pisano in the 13th century. Their inspired and often innovative work is found inside the building instead, as well as in the baptistery and other centers across Italy, such as Lucca and Pistoia. In their absence, the exterior's highlight is the **Portale di San Ranieri** (1180), previously the cathedral's main entrance but now tucked away behind the right transept facing the Leaning Tower. The work of a local sculptor, Bonanno Pisano, it consists of 24 bronze panels portraying stories

COMBINED TICKETS

The Duomo, Battistero, Museo dell'Opera, and Camposanto are all open daily between 8 a.m. and 7:30 p.m. (shorter hours in winter). A choice of combined tickets is available for two, three, or four of the sights *(Tel 050 561 820)*. ∎

Romanesque and Gothic styles intermingle in the exterior of the baptistery on Campo dei Miracoli.

from the New Testament. Don't miss the door's surrounds, or architrave, which incorporate fragments of Roman friezes and sculptures from the second century A.D. The entrance for visitors, incidentally, is normally the side door on the right-hand side of the cathedral as you face it from the baptistery.

Some of the cathedral's earliest treasures were lost in a fire in 1595, which means that much of the **interior** dates from the ensuing period of restoration (1602–1616). Two items that survived the blaze were the apse mosaic of "Christ in Majesty" (1302), part of which is by Cimabue, the teacher of Giotto, and Tino di Camaino's tomb (1315) of the Holy Roman Emperor Henry VII (*R*.1308–1313), which you will find high on the left wall of the south (right-hand) transept. The tomb was partly damaged by the fire, and several of its statues were moved to the Museo dell'Opera following restoration (see p. 252). Henry died near Siena, having ransacked the city and then,

**Opposite:
A detail showing the Virgin and the Nativity of Christ from Nicola Pisano's pulpit in the baptistery**

reputedly, eaten a poisoned wafer at Mass. The Pisans, allies of the Emperor, bore his body back to their native city.

Far greater than either of these works is Giovanni Pisano's exceptional **pulpit,** which was stored away after the fire and only restored to public view in 1926. It was the last and finest of the series of pulpits created by Nicola and Giovanni across Tuscany; others are found in Siena and Pistoia. Note how most of the figures crowding its surface are carved almost "free" of the block of stone—a technically demanding discipline. Note, too, the work's immense narrative skill, particularly the manner in which several scenes depicting Christ's Passion—from Judas's betrayal to Christ's scourging—are compressed into a single panel. The inscription on the cornice, incidentally, states that Giovanni knew the "art of pure sculpture…and would not know how to carve base or ugly things, even if he wished to."

An equally staggering pulpit by Nicola Pisano stands in the circular **Battistero** (begun in 1152), a building whose plain interior is in marked contrast to its intricately fashioned exterior. The **pulpit** stands on slender pillars bearing the allegorical figures of the "Virtues," while its main narrative scenes describe the "Annunciation," "Nativity," "Announcement to the Shepherds," "Adoration of the Magi," "Presentation in the Temple," "Crucifixion," and "Last Judgment." Between 1270 and 1297, Nicola and Giovanni were also responsible for much of the exquisite carving on the baptistery's exterior, added after a lull in building caused by financial shortfalls following loss of trade to Genoa. The interior's lovely inlaid font (1246) is by a sculptor from northern Italy, Guido Bigarelli da Como. Notice

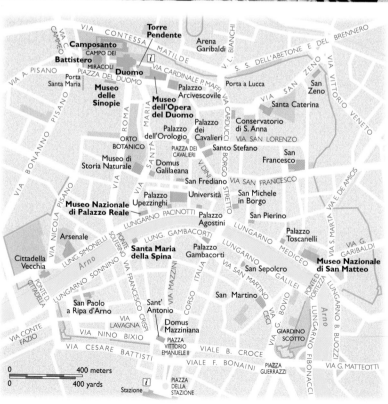

VIA CONTESSA MATILDE

Torre Pendente

Arena Garibaldi

V.L. BIANCHI

S. S. DELL'ABETONE E DEL BRENNERO

VIA CAMMEO

Camposanto

CAMPO DEI MIRACOLI

Battistero

PIAZZA DEL DUOMO

Duomo

VIA CARDINALE P. MAFFI

Porta a Lucca

VIA SAN ZENO

VIA VITTORIO VENETO

VIA A. PISANO

Porta Santa Maria

Museo delle Sinopie

Palazzo Arcivescovile

San Zeno

Santa Caterina

Museo dell'Opera del Duomo

VIA CARDUCCI

VIA SAN LORENZO

Conservatorio di S. Anna

VIA BONANNO PISANO

ROMA

VIA SANTA MARIA

Palazzo dell'Orologio

Palazzo dei Cavalieri

San Francesco

ORTO BOTANICO

PIAZZA DEI CAVALIERI

Santo Stefano

Museo di Storia Naturale

Domus Galilaeana

BORGO STRETTO

VIA SAN FRANCESCO

San Frediano

VDINI

VIA S. MARTA

VIA E. DE AMICIS

VIA NICOLA PISANO

Palazzo Upezzinghi

Università

San Michele in Borgo

Museo Nazionale di Palazzo Reale

LUNGARNO PACINOTTI

Palazzo Agostini

San Pierino

VIA G. GARIBALDI

Arsenale

PONTE SOLFERINO

LUNG. SIMONELLI

Palazzo Toscanelli

Santa Maria della Spina

LUNG. GAMBACORTI

Palazzo Gambacorti

LUNGARNO MEDICEO

LUNGARNO FIBONACCI

PONTE DELLA FORTEZZA

Museo Nazionale di San Matteo

Cittadella Vecchia

Arno

LUNGARNO SONNINO

VIA FRANCESCO CRISPI

VIA MAZZINI

CORSO ITALIA

LUNGARNO GALILEI

San Sepolcro

LUNGARNO B. BUOZZI

PONTE DELLA CITTADELLA

San Paolo a Ripa d'Arno

Sant' Antonio

VIA LAVAGNA

Domus Mazziniana

VIA S. MARTINO

San Martino

VIA G. BOVIO

VIA CECI

Arno

GIARDINO SCOTTO

VIA CONTE FAZIO

VIA NINO BIXIO

PIAZZA VITTORIO EMANUELE II

VIA CESARE BATTISTI

Viale B. CROCE

VIALE F. BONAINI

PIAZZA GUERRAZZI

VIA G. MATTEOTTI

0 — 400 meters

0 — 400 yards

Stazione

PIAZZA DELLA STAZIONE

Saving the Leaning Tower

Pisa's Torre Pendente, or Leaning Tower, was in trouble from the start. Begun in 1173, the tower was built on weak, sandy subsoil that had once been covered by the sea. It had already started to sink when work was abandoned at the third of its planned eight levels in 1178. In 1272, engineers attempted to correct the lean—then already 3 feet from the vertical—by changing the thickness of the marble as they built. In 1370, the upper belfry was added off-center in another attempt to straighten the tower. The result, in the words of one modern engineer, was a structure that "curved like a banana."

British and French engineers conducted tests on the tower in the 19th century—the lean in 1817 was 12 feet 6 inches (3.8 m)—but the first accurate measurements were only made in 1911. By January 7, 1990, the day the tower was finally closed to visitors, the 196-foot (60 m), 16,000-ton tower was 17 feet 6 inches (5.4 m) from the vertical—a lean of 5.5 degrees. Worse, the rate of lean was accelerating. Various interventions in 1935 and 1970 had made things worse by disturbing the already unstable subsoil. At the rate of lean current in 1990, experts foresaw two doomsday scenarios: A gravity-induced collapse would occur within 25 years, or a structural collapse could happen at any time because of the internal pressures exerted on the tower's second story by the imbalance of weight above it.

No fewer than 16 Italian government committees had already pondered the problem. In 1990, an international panel was convened. Endless theories and solutions were proposed: The Russians suggested slicing off the base, the Chinese argued for a second "twin" to the tower to pull on its neighbor, and the Japanese proposed pulling the tower down altogether and rebuilding it straight.

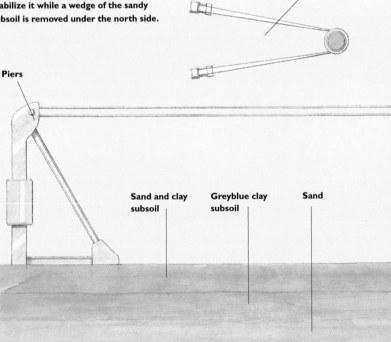

The chosen solution for saving the tower: Steel cables hold the tower in tension to stabilize it while a wedge of the sandy subsoil is removed under the north side.

Aerial view of site

Piers

Sand and clay subsoil

Greyblue clay subsoil

Sand

In the meantime, contingency measures were put in place, including fastening 18 narrow steel belts around sections of the tower to prevent buckling and laying a concrete ring around the base. In 1993, 661 tons of lead weights were fixed to the tower's north side to counterbalance the southward tilt. In six months the tower had straightened—but by just half an inch (1.25 cm).

The chosen solution, budgeted to cost $26.7 million, was begun in 1998. First, vast steel cables were attached to the tower 65 feet (20 m) up and anchored in huge concrete blocks about 100 yards (91 m) away. These were a stabilizing, not a corrective, measure. The real work of correction was to be achieved by the gradual removal of a 26-inch (66 cm) wedge of subsoil from beneath the north side of the tower. This would allow the structure to settle back toward the vertical.

After five months of work the results were impressive. The tower had returned to its position of around 110 years ago, a movement back to the vertical of 5 inches (12.5 cm). Work continues to remove some 14 cubic yards (10 cu m) of soil to arrive at a 10 percent or 17-inch (43 cm) correction by the middle of 2001.

The final stages will involve the reinforcement of the foundations and the removal of the cables, concrete anchors, lead weights, and other external eyesores. In the eyes of visitors the difference will not be noticeable—the Leaning Tower will still lean—but for the tower it should mean salvation for at least another 350 years. Or so the engineers and scientists hope. ∎

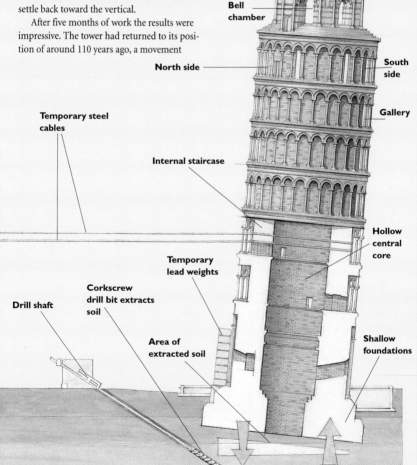

Direction of corrected lean

Bell chamber

North side

South side

Gallery

Temporary steel cables

Internal staircase

Hollow central core

Temporary lead weights

Corkscrew drill bit extracts soil

Drill shaft

Area of extracted soil

Shallow foundations

Bombing in World War II means that Pisa has a largely modern center.

the four tiny fonts inside its main octagonal basin, designed for baptizing very small children.

The Campo's last component, the **Camposanto,** is a medieval cemetery (begun 1278) that takes the form of a large Gothic cloister. According to legend it was filled with earth brought back from the Holy Land during the Crusades, the aim being to allow notable Pisans to be buried in sacred ground. The same legend claimed the soil could reduce a corpse to bones in just 24 hours. The cemetery contains a large range of tombs from different eras (including Roman sarcophagi), and while interesting in their own way, they are a poor substitute for what by all accounts was one of Tuscany's foremost fresco cycles before it succumbed to an Allied incendiary bomb on July 27, 1944. Only a handful of frescoes survived the flow of molten lead that streamed from the burning roof, notably the anonymous "Triumph of Death" in a room opposite the cemetery entrance. Painted in the wake of the Black Death in 1348, it shows three huntsmen confronted

by three coffins, the noxious contents of which force one of the nobles to pinch his nose. Angels and demons bear the souls of the dead to their fate, which is delineated in a nearby fresco of the "Last Judgment," probably the work of the same unknown artist. Some surviving sketches of other frescoes are displayed in the **Museo delle Sinopie** *(Piazza del Duomo)*.

Artistic treasures from both the cathedral and the baptistery can be seen in the **Museo dell'Opera del Duomo** in the Campo's southeast corner. Some of its most captivating works are sculptural, in particular those of Giovanni Pisano, whose masterpiece here is the "Madonna del Colloquio," a carved group of the Madonna and Child with St. John the Baptist and St. John the Evangelist. Removed from above the baptistery's main door in 1935, it takes its name from the intimate, or colloquial, gaze being exchanged by the Virgin and Child. Giovanni was also responsible for the fine ivory "Madonna and Child" in the museum Treasury, which also contains the noted

"Croce dei Pisani," a cross carried by Pisan troops in the First Crusade. Other notable sculptors represented in the museum include Tino di Camaino, who often collaborated with Giovanni Pisano, and who here was responsible for the statues removed from the tomb of Henry VII in the cathedral.

Moving away from Campo dei Miracoli, the highlights of the rest of the town begin with **Piazza dei Cavalieri,** a square ringed by medieval buildings. From here take the Via Dini on the piazza's southeast corner, just off which, on Piazza Vettovaglie, is an enjoyable general market *(Closed p.m. & all Sun.).* At the end of Via Dini you come to Borgo Stretto, home to many of Pisa's leading stores. This street eventually reaches the river past San Michele in Borgo, an 11th-century church on the left. Turn left on Lungarno Mediceo and you come to the **Museo Nazionale di San Matteo** *(Piazza San Matteo, tel 050 541 865, closed Sun. p.m. & all Mon.),* which has a wide-ranging collection of paintings, ceramics, sculptures, and other decorative arts, most of which were collected from Pisa's churches. Amid the lesser artifacts are several genuine gems, namely paintings of the "Madonna and Child" by Fra Angelico, "St. Paul" by Masaccio, a tremendous "Madonna and Child with Saints" by Simone Martini, a "Madonna of Humility" by Gentile da Fabriano, and a bronze bust of "St. Lussorio" by Donatello.

San Matteo is Pisa's principal museum, but you might also visit the **Museo Nazionale di Palazzo Reale** *(Piazza Carrara, Lungarno Pacinotti)* farther west on the banks of the Arno. It houses several private collections left to the city, including a huge range of textiles, ceramics, paintings, prints, sculptures, and other objets d'art. On the other side of the river— cross using the Ponte Solferino— stands **Santa Maria della Spina,** an appealing little 14th-century church on the riverbank at Lungarno Gambacorti. It was built by a merchant who had obtained a thorn *(spina)* from Christ's Crown of Thorns, hence its spiky exterior stonework. ■

The River Arno flows past Pisa's tiny church of Santa Maria della Spina.

Lucca

LUCCA IS ONE OF THOSE HALLOWED HISTORIC PLACES where, in the words of the English essayist Hilaire Belloc (1870–1953), "everything…is good" (*The Path to Rome*, 1902). Within ancient walls, the town is peaceful and urbane, its medieval heart an attractive mix of piazzas, tiny churches, galleries, and cobbled lanes. You will still find it, in the words of American novelist Henry James (1843–1916), "overflowing with everything that makes for ease, for plenty, for beauty, for interest and good example" (*Italy Revisited*, 1877).

The best plan of attack is to start in the central square, Piazza San Michele, work south toward the cathedral, and then walk through the eastern part of the city to visit the sights in the north—the itinerary followed by the account below. There's plenty to see here during a day—you could easily stay overnight—but if time is short be certain to see the church of San Martino in Foro, the Duomo di San Martino (the cathedral), the Casa Guinigi (for the view from its tower), the Museo Nazionale di Villa Guinigi, Piazza Anfiteatro, and the church of San Frediano. Also allow time to walk around part of the city walls.

One thing that quickly becomes clear as you wander the streets is the gridiron plan of its city center, a legacy of the Romans' rational approach to town planning. Under the Goths and Lombards the city later served as the Tuscan capital, and it is widely believed to have been the first center in the region to embrace Christianity. It rose to medieval prominence as a result of a flourishing trade in silk—lingerie is still a major Lucchese money-earner—and during the 14th century the city captured both Pisa and Pistoia. It even came close to conquering Florence. Thereafter, the city declined but maintained an independent status outside the Grand Duchy of Tuscany until the arrival of Napoleon, who presented

Left: A street scene in Lucca

Lucca is easily reached as a day trip from Florence: Trains take about 70 minutes and arrive at the station in Piazza Ricasoli just south of the city's magnificent walls and five minutes' walk from the center. If you're coming by car, park outside these walls; parking in the old center is difficult and there are strict time limits on how long you can stay. One of the bigger parking lots is on the west edge of the old center by Porta San Donato, just five minutes from the main sights. Everything you want to see lies within the walls, and everything can easily be seen on foot. If you've parked by Porta San Donato, you're close to the **visitor center** in Piazzale Giuseppe Verdi, one of several places you can rent bikes, another nice way of seeing the city.

Lucca
- 226 B3
Visitor information
- ✉ Vecchia Porta di San Donato, Piazzale Giuseppe Verdi
- ☎ 0583 419 689

the city to his sister, Elisa Baciocchi. The Bourbons then assumed control until Italian Unification.

Lucca's natural heart is **Piazza San Michele,** the place to start your visit. Few sights are quite as breathtaking as its dazzling center-piece, the church of **San Michele in Foro,** begun in 1070 on the site of the old Roman *foro,* or forum. Its stupendous **facade** combines a distinctive marble-striped veneer with an astounding confection of miniature loggias, blind arcades, and inventively twisted columns. This decorative combination, and the striped marble motifs in partic-ular, is typical of the so-called Pisan style of Romanesque architecture, a style developed in the light of Pisa's trading links with the Orient and the ornate influence of Byzantine

art. In time, the style's influence extended to Siena (the cathedral), Florence (cathedral and baptistery), and beyond. It's an architectural hybrid you'll come across often in Lucca, one of the city's many pleasures being the number of times you round a corner, or stumble on a tiny piazza, to find yourself confronted with a little jewel of a church.

San Michele's plain **interior** is less arresting than the facade, largely because most of the church's funds were lavished on the exterior. It does have one major work of art, however: Filippino Lippi's late 15th-century painting of "SS. Jerome, Sebastian, Roch, and Helena" at the end of the south (right) nave. After seeing the inte-rior, walk round the outside of the

Walkers and cyclists enjoy the town's tree-lined ramparts. The walls run for almost 3 miles.

A view over Lucca's rooftops features the cathedral (center left) and the foothills of the Garfagnana valley and Apuan Alps.

church to look at the tiny windows sunk low on the apse, part of a ninth-century church on the site.

After inspecting the **Casa di Puccini** (see sidebar p. 259), walk back to Piazza San Michele and turn right on Via Vittorio Veneto to Piazza Napoleone. Here the vast building on your right is the **Palazzo della Provincia** (1578–1728), formerly the Palazzo della Signoria, the seat of Lucca's ruling council.

DUOMO

Bear left across the piazza into the linked and smaller Piazza del Giglio, where an alley on the left leads to Piazza San Giovanni and Lucca's cathedral, the **Duomo** dedicated to San Martino *(Piazza San Martino)*. According to tradi-

tion, the first church on the Duomo's site was founded in the sixth century by St. Frediano, an Irish monk, and became the seat of the local bishopric in the eighth century. Anselmo da Baggio, Bishop of Lucca, commissioned the present structure in 1060 and consecrated it ten years later, by which time he had become Pope Alexander II (*R.*1061–1073). Another wonderful **facade** (1060–1241) fronts the building, its effect undiminished by its curious asymmetry. This is the result of its having been squeezed next to the campanile, or bell tower, the lower part of which—originally built as a defensive bastion—was already in place when work began. The facade's most important feature is a series of 13th-century relief carvings around the atrium and the entrance doors. Those on and around the left-hand door are almost certainly the work of the celebrated Pisan sculptor Nicola Pisano, and they depict the "Annunciation," "Nativity," "Adoration of the Magi," and—in the lunette—the "Deposition." The equally captivating panels between the doors are probably the work of the facade's principal architect, Guidetto da Como, who was active in the early 13th century. Some show episodes from the life of St. Martin (San Martino), to whom the cathedral is dedicated; others, the labors and activities associated with the "Twelve Months of the Year." In the latter scenes you can easily make out the labors concerned—winemaking, threshing, a graphic pig-sticking, fruit-picking, and so on. The right-hand door lunette has a relief showing the "Beheading of St. Regolus," a Christian martyr whose relics were honored inside

the church and whose altar was reached via this door (see p. 258).

Unlike San Michele, San Martino's **interior** is filled with points of artistic interest. Immediately on entering, turn around to admire the 13th-century sculpture of "St. Martin on Horseback with the Beggar" to the left of the main door, by an unknown hand. It shows the fourth-century saint sharing his cloak with a poor man, a figure he later recognized as Christ. Above the left door spreads a late 15th-century fresco describing the story of the Volto Santo. Its meaning becomes clearer midway down the nave on the left when you come to the **Tempietto,** a gaudy octagonal chapel designed by the prolific local sculptor Matteo Civitali (1435–1511). It was created to house the much venerated Volto Santo (Holy Face), a cedar-wood crucifix said to be a true likeness of Christ carved by Nicodemus, an

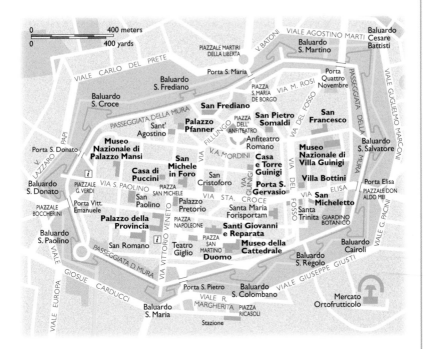

The masterpiece of Sienese sculptor Jacopo della Quercia, it is one of the loveliest sculptures in Italy. Especially touching is the little dog, a symbol of Ilaria's faithfulness. The work is housed in the sacristy off the south (right-hand) side of the church, and a small fee is payable for admission. This admission also allows you to admire a superb painting of the "Madonna and Child with Saints" by the Florentine artist Domenico Ghirlandaio.

Beyond the entrance to the sacristy turn into the right transept, where on the wall immediately on your right is another good work by Civitali, the tomb of Pietro da Noceto, secretary to Pope Niccolò V. Civitali was also responsible for the fine **Altare di San Regolo,** which contains the tomb of San Regolo (St. Regolus), a martyred early bishop of Lucca. It stands on the wall to the right of the main high altar. The cathedral's final outstanding work of art is Fra Bartolommeo's "Madonna and Child with Saints" (1509), housed in the **Cappella del Santuario,** to the left of the high altar.

The ticket for the sacristy also admits you to the **Museo della Cattedrale** outside the cathedral in Piazza Antelminelli (to the left), which has a fine collection of paintings, sculptures, illustrated manuscripts, and religious ephemera. It also allows you into the nearby church of **Santi Giovanni e Reparata,** where excavations have revealed Roman buildings, the remains of Lucca's first cathedral, and—to the rear left of the present church—two early baptisteries from the fifth and eighth centuries (*Sacristy, museum, & church, tel 0583 490 530, closed p.m. Nov.–March*).

WALKING THE WALLS
From the lanes just south of the cathedral climb up to Lucca's

A carving of the "Madonna and Child" is part of the ornate decoration that adorns the church of San Michele in Foro.

Opposite: The use of arches, small pillars, and colored marbles in the facade of San Michele in Foro is repeated in churches across Lucca.

eyewitness to the Crucifixion. In truth it's probably a 13th-century copy of an original 8th-century work. Legend claims the statue miraculously found its way to Lucca of its own accord, journeying by boat and then being carried to the city on oxen guided by Divine Will. Whatever the truth of its arrival, it attracted countless pilgrims to the city, generating enormous wealth for the church in the process. It is perhaps no coincidence that the statue appeared during the reign of Bishop Anselmo (see p. 256), whose career and elevation to the papacy was hardly hurt by its miraculous apparition.

Of greater artistic merit is the tomb of Ilaria del Carretto (1408), second wife of Paolo Guinigi, one of Lucca's leading medieval rulers.

Giacomo Puccini

Lucca's most famous son, the composer Giacomo Puccini (1858–1924), was born a stone's throw from San Michele. His birthplace, the **Casa di Puccini** (*Corte San Lorenzo 9, Via di Poggio 30, tel 0583 584 028, closed Mon. & L Oct.–May*), now contains a music academy and a small museum devoted to the composer. Puccini came from a local family that had provided organists for the city's cathedral for four generations, although in early life he was no more than a chorister at nearby San Michele. Later he went on to become one of Italy's foremost opera composers, responsible for works such as *Tosca, Madama Butterfly,* and *La Bohème.* ■

The curve of the Piazza dell' Anfiteatro follows the line of Lucca's Roman amphitheater.

magnificent walls (1544–1645), which offer a broad, tree-lined 2.5-mile (4.2 km) walk or bike path that you can follow all around the city. The ramparts were begun partly in response to the threat posed by Florence in the early 16th century and partly because the city's old medieval walls (raised in 1198) had been made redundant by recent advances in weapon technology. The resulting defenses were some 100 feet (30 m) wide at the base, 40 feet (12 m) high, and protected by moats over 120 feet (35 m) wide. The effort required to build them was enormous, but the city never had to use them in a conflict. In fact, the only siege the residents ever faced was from the floodwaters of the River Serchio in 1812, when the gates were sealed to prevent the

city's being deluged. Napoleon's sister, Elisa Baciocchi, then the city's governor, returned to Lucca at the last minute and had to be winched over the walls by crane. Beyond the ramparts, a swathe of grass insulates the old center from the modern world, the legacy of a medieval decree that ordered the removal of any vegetation that might offer cover to an enemy. One target you might make for on your walk is the Antico Caffè della Mura, a fine old café-restaurant next to the Baluardo Santa Maria, one of the walls' 11 major bastions. It lies southwest of the cathedral.

Walk east from here and you soon look down on the **Giardino Botanico,** a peaceful botanical garden entered from just off Via del Fosso (*Via del Giardino Botanico*

14, tel 0583 442 160, closed Mon. &
Tues.– Sat. p.m.). Green-thumbed
visitors might also want to explore
the beautiful gardens of the nearby
Villa Bottini, also known as the
Villa Buonvisi *(Via Elisa, tel 0583
442 140, closed p.m. & all Sun.),* a
villa once owned by Elisa Baciocchi.
It lies just north of the Giardino
Botanico, and to reach it, you
follow Via del Fosso (the street
with a canal) north and turn right
(east) on Via Elisa. You soon come
to **San Micheletto,** an ancient
but much altered church. Another,
larger church, San Ponziano, lies a
little farther down the street. The
villa's entrance is close to San
Micheletto on the left.

Retrace your steps, walking back
down Via Elisa and crossing Via del
Fosso. Just past the little church of
Santa Trinita on the left, you come
to the **Porta San Gervasio**
(1260), one of the most impressive
of the city's original medieval
gateways. Follow Via Santa Croce
beyond it and you come to a piazza
containing Santa Maria Forispor-
tam (literally "St. Mary Outside the
Walls"), a charming but unfinished
13th-century Pisan-Romanesque
church that once lay close to the
city's Roman and medieval walls.
From here, walk down Via Santa
Croce, whose side streets contain a
cluster of interesting little churches:
13th-century San Giulio and the
Chiesa del Suffragio lie to the north
(take the first alley on the right
after Via Guinigi), San Benedetto in
Gottella and Santa Maria dei Servi
to the south.

Walk back to the junction of Via
Santa Croce and Via Guinigi, turn
left up Via Guinigi—one of Lucca's
nicest medieval streets—and you
come to the city's strangest sight,
the **Casa Guinigi** *(Via Sant'
Andrea–Via Guinigi 29, tel 0583 48
524, closed for restoration, phone for
details),* a medieval town house

built by the Guinigi, Lucca's preeminent noble family. It's best known
for its **tower**—which has lovely
city views—and the holm oaks
sprouting from its roof.

From the tower walk north on
Via Guinigi and turn right at the
top on Via A. Mordini, following
the street as it bears left to **San
Pietro Somaldi,** a tiny gem of
a church built in the 12th century
over an earlier, 8th-century church.
From here you can take Via della
Fratta to see the immense church
of **San Francesco** (1228), worth
a quick look for its fresco fragments
and fine choir stalls. Beyond it on
the right, another former Guinigi
palace houses the **Museo
Nazionale di Villa Guinigi**
*(Via della Quarquonia, tel 0583 496
033, closed Mon. & p.m. in winter),*

**The Guinigi,
one of Lucca's
most powerful
medieval families,
once owned the
Casa e Torre
Guinigi.**

Elaborate ironwork embellished with caricature figures is a feature of many Tuscan towns.

built in 1418 and today given over to a collection of archaeological displays, medieval paintings, sculptures, textiles, and other applied arts. The highlights are paintings by Fra Bartolommeo and sculptures by Matteo Civitali, an artist whose work you may already have seen in the cathedral.

Walk back to San Pietro and go right, and then take the first left, Via del Portico, to **Piazza dell' Anfiteatro.** The medieval houses of this wonderfully distinctive piazza were built into the oval of Lucca's old Roman amphitheater. Traces of the ancient structure are still visible, woven into the later buildings, although much of the original stone was ransacked during the 12th century for use in Lucca's many Romanesque churches.

A short distance to the northwest, across Via Fillungo, stands **San Frediano** (1112–1147), the third of Lucca's great churches. Its exterior is distinguished not by the columns and reliefs of San Martino and San Michele, but by a striking 13th-century facade mosaic of the "Ascension." Inside, the main highlight is the 12th-century **Fontana Lustrale,** a large font close to the entrance on the south (right-hand) side. It is thought three sculptors were responsible for the work. The first, known as Maestro Roberto, produced the stories of Moses on the outer sections of the main basin (notice the scene of the "Crossing of the Red Sea," in which the Egyptian soldiers are portrayed as chivalric medieval knights); the second, an unknown artist, added the figures of the six Apostles and the Good Shepherd; and the third, also unknown, carved the remaining Apostles and the "Months of the Year" labors above the basin.

Behind the font on the wall are terra-cotta sculptures of the "Annunciation" and a figure of

"St. Bartholomew" by Matteo and Andrea della Robbia respectively. Behind these to the left lies the Cappella Fatinelli, which contains the uncorrupted body of St. Zita, a 13th-century Lucca-born maidservant who became the patron saint of domestic servants. According to one story, she habitually took bread from her master's house to give to the poor. When asked one day what she was carrying in her apron, she replied: "Only roses and other flowers." When examined, the bread had been miraculously transformed.

Moving on, watch for the lovely 12th-century marble pavement around the high altar, which was raised above the body of St. Frediano (see p. 256). Then walk back toward the church entrance. The first chapel on the right, the **Cappella Trenta** (built 1413; fourth from the entrance door), contains an exceptional carved altarpiece (1422) and two worn pavement tombs belonging to the chapel's patron, Lorenzo Trenta, and his wife. All three works are by the Sienese sculptor Jacopo della Quercia. Farther on, the **Cappella di Sant'Agostino** features the church's best frescoes (1508–1509), the work of Amico Aspertini. They portray "St. Frediano Diverting the River Serchio" (and thus saving Lucca) and the "Nativity" on the right wall and the "Baptism of St. Augustine" and the "Arrival of the Volto Santo in Lucca" on the left.

Southwest of the church lie the formal 18th-century gardens of the **Palazzo Pfanner** *(Via degli Asili 33, tel 0583 491 243, open daily, by appt. only in winter)* and—farther west—the **Museo Nazionale di Palazzo Mansi** *(Via Galli Tassi 43, tel 0583 55 570, closed Sun. p.m. & all Mon.),* whose rococo decoration provides the backdrop for a fine collection of paintings. ■

Monteriggioni is one of Europe's most perfect fortified villages. It was built in 1203 to help defend Siena's northern territories against the Florentines.

More places to visit in northern Tuscany

BARGA & THE GARFAGNANA

If you are in Lucca, then consider driving north to the delightful village of Barga, the urban highlight of a little-visited region known as the Garfagnana. The village sits in the lee of the Orecchiella Hills, nestled on green slopes overlooking the Serchio Valley and the jagged peaks of the distant Alpi Apuane. Its highlight is a captivating tenth-century cathedral, a vision of honey-colored stone fronted by a beautiful panoramic terrace. The facade is adorned with reliefs and other carvings, and inside are a huge tenth-century statue of St. Christopher and a carved pulpit by the 13th-century sculptor Bigarelli da Como.

The Serchio Valley and the **Orecchiella** and **Apuane** mountains that flank it are well worth exploring. Both upland areas are crossed by tiny scenic roads, and both have plenty of marked hiking trails. Good maps are available from most local centers, notably **Castelnuovo di Garfagnana,** an unexceptional town just north of Barga.

The towns on the west, or seaward, side of the Alpi Apuane, are known for their marble

quarries and have been scoured for stone by sculptors from Michelangelo to Henry Moore. Most are undistinguished, the notable exception being **Carrara,** which has a fine cathedral, an interesting marble museum, the **Muweo Civilo del Marmo** *(Via XX Settembre, tel 0585 845 746, closed Sat.–Sun.),* and a pretty main square. It's also possible to visit the mines at **Colonnata,** 5 miles (8 km) away; they provide a graphic illustration of the scale of the region's marble deposits and the extraordinary measures required to exploit them. Follow signs from Carrara for Strada Panoramica per Le Cave.

🅰 226 B4 **Visitor information** ✉ Piazza Angelio 4, Barga ☎ 0583 723 499

COLLE DI VAL D'ELSA

Colle di Val d'Elsa is an unfairly neglected town not helped by its new suburbs, which form the lower part of town, known as Colle Basso. The old medieval town on the hill, however—Colle Alto—is a delight and well worth a detour as you travel between Siena and San Gimignano. The town's medieval prosperity was based on abundant supplies of water, which helped foster glass and paper industries, both still mainstays of the local economy.

Little evidence of either, save a few specialist shops, is found in Colle Alto; it consists of barely two streets and a web of small lanes squeezed onto the town's hilly ridge. Follow the main street, Via del Castello, along the ridge to see all the sights and catch the best of the views. Stop off at the **Duomo** *(Piazza del Duomo),* notable for a beautiful marble tabernacle in the right transept attributed to Mino da Fiesole; the **Museo Archeologico** *(Piazza del Duomo, closed Mon.)* next door, a museum of Etruscan and other finds ; and the **Museo Civico e d'Arte Sacra** *(Via del Castello 31, closed Mon. & weekdays Nov.– March),* which contains an array of paintings and other artifacts from different eras.

◩ 227 D2   **Visitor information** ✉ Via Francesco Campana 43   ☎ 0577 922 791

MONTERIGGIONI

Monteriggioni doesn't take long to describe or to see, but no village in Tuscany—not even San Gimignano—presents as perfect a vision of the Middle Ages. It lies just off the main Siena–Poggibonsi road, 8 miles (13 km) south of Poggibonsi. Founded by the Sienese in 1203 as a defensive citadel, it is enclosed by a perfectly preserved set of walls and towers added in 1213, its hilly site untainted by the modern sprawl of buildings that diminishes so many Italian hill towns. Dante described its magnificent towers, added in 1260, as resembling giants in an abyss, and the relevant passage from the poet's *Inferno* greets you as you enter the walls. Inside, there are no sights—just the intrinsic charm of the parish church and a handful of evocative streets.

◩ 227 D2   **Visitor information:** Contact the Siena visitor center (see p. 194)

PISTOIA

Pistoia is a large town in unprepossessing countryside between Florence and Lucca. By any standards other than those of Tuscany, however, this is a town with plenty to recommend it. Start exploring in the central **Piazza del Duomo,** ringed by medieval palaces, several small museums, and the Baptistery and bell tower, and visit the 12th-

century **Duomo,** which contains the famous Dossale di San Jacopo (Altarpiece of St. James), one of Italy's most impressive pieces of silverware, begun in 1287 and completed some 200 years later. It contains 628 sculptured figures, some partially gilded, and weighs close to a ton. A small admission is payable to see the work *(Closed L).*

Among the town's many superb churches, pay special attention to **Sant'Andrea,** site of a magnificent carved pulpit (1297) by Giovanni Pisano. Also search out the **Ospedale del Ceppo** at the end of Via Pacani, a medieval hospital adorned with a colorful terra-cotta frieze (1526–29).

◩ 226 C3   **Visitor information** ✉ Piazza del Duomo 4   ☎ 0573 21 622

VIAREGGIO

Tuscany has a long coastline, but knowing where to go to enjoy a pleasant day on the beach is something of a problem. On the whole, southern Tuscany has less developed resorts and prettier villages than the north of the region, much of whose coast is known as the **Riviera di Versilia.** For the most part this consists of a string of indistinguishable mid-market resorts—**Forte del Marmi** is the nicest—aimed at Italians on their annual vacation. Most are big, modern, and reasonably clean and well-groomed, with lots of restaurants, shops, and nightlife. Out of season (July and August) they are largely dead.

None of these resorts is worth a special journey, with the possible exception of Viareggio, the place to come if you fancy one day by the sea during your time in northern Tuscany. It's the most elegant resort, with lots of big 19th-century hotels, a palm-lined promenade, and the odd hint of art nouveau architecture. It's also just about the closest resort to Florence (a little over an hour away by train), so it's often crowded in summer. The beach is long and broad, and there's plenty of room, but you have to pay for sand and sea: Most of the best parts of the beach are divided into so-called *stabilimenti balneari,* or bathing concessions, where you will find sun chairs, locker rooms, showers, well-groomed sand, and refreshment facilities.

◩ 226 B3   **Visitor information** ✉ Viale Carducci 10   ☎ 0584 962 233 ■

Southern Tuscany is one of Italy's jewels. No other part of the country has its beguiling combination of idyllic landscapes, hidden villages, hilltop towns, superb wines, timeless abbeys, and artistic and architectural wonders.

Southern Tuscany

Chianti Rufina wine

Southern Tuscany

FEW AREAS OF TUSCANY DISAPPOINT, BUT FOR SHEER VARIETY OF landscape, historical interest, and outstanding villages, none quite compare with the area south of Siena. This is quintessential Tuscany, the Tuscany of vineyards, cypress-ringed villas, and olive-cloaked hills. Two of the region's finest abbeys are here, along with several of its loveliest little towns. All are linked by a tangle of quiet roads that cross some of Italy's most beautiful countryside.

The best starting point for a tour is Siena, from which you can drive southeast toward Asciano, a route that leads through the so-called *Crete,* a "badlands" scenery of bare clay hills, sweeping vistas, and summer fields of wheat, flax, and sunflowers. Following scenic minor roads—one of the region's glories—you come to the fresco-filled Monte Oliveto Maggiore, the first of the area's two major abbeys.

From here it's a short hop to picture-perfect Montalcino, a lofty and unspoiled hill town that makes a perfect base for the region. It's ideal for forays to the area's second major abbey, Sant'Antimo, a Romanesque building in some of the prettiest pastoral scenery imaginable. It is also good for more aimless exploration—roads in most directions have their scenic rewards—and produces one of Italy's most

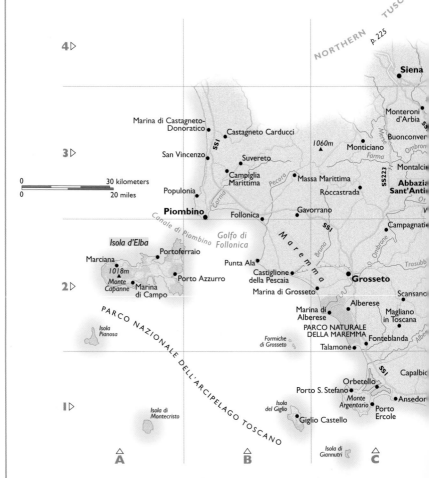

p. 225

Area of
map detail

EMILIA-
ROMAGNA
PARCO NAZIONALE
D. FORESTE CASENTINESI-
MONTE FALTERONA-CAMPIGNA
MARCHE
SS70 Camaldoli Badia Prataglia
S⊳
San Pietro
di Romena Pratovecchio
Poppi La Verna 1283m
Bibbiena Mount
Penna Pieve
Santo
Stefano Badia
Tedalda
1592m Caprese
Michelangelo della Luna Alpe
Loro Ciuffenna Sansepolcro
Arno Anghiari
Chiassa Pieve di
Sovara
☆ Monterchi
Arezzo
1082m
A1
Monte San
Savino SS71 Castiglion Fiorentino
polano
Terme Cortona
rète SS326
sciano Sinalunga Foiano d.Chiana
Abbazia di Monte
Oliveto Maggiore Lago
Trasimeno
Sant'Anna
in Camprena
San
Quirico Pienza Montepulciano
d'Orcia
Bagno Chianciano
ignoni Terme Chiusi
Castiglione
d'Orcia Sarteano
Orcia Bagni San Filippo
UMBRIA
rcidosso Radicofani
1738m Abbadia
Monte Amiata San Salvatore
Santa Fiora
occalbegna Castell'Azzara
Sorano
Sovana Pitigliano
Manciano
LAZIO
Jardino
ei Tarocchi

deservedly praised red wines, Brunello di
Montalcino, in vineyards round the town.

From Montalcino, move on to the villages
of the Val d'Orcia, the verdant valley of the
River Orcia, or head farther south to the little-
known countryside around Monte Amiata and
the villages of Sovana and Pitigliano. Ignore
these if time is short, however, and push on to
Pienza, another gem of a place. A few miles to
the east is Montepulciano, a town as appealing
as Montalcino and Pienza, situated on
Tuscany's eastern periphery.

From here you could loop back to Siena,
but that would be to miss Cortona to the
north, another captivating hill town, and
nearby Arezzo, whose modern outskirts conceal a medieval center and one of Italy's most
famous fresco cycles. From Arezzo, both Siena
and Florence are within range on good roads,
but if you've a day to spare, use it to explore
the back roads of the Casentino and Pratomagno, two almost unvisited scenic enclaves
between Arezzo and the Tuscan capital. ∎

**In Tuscany, grapes are an important crop,
grown by a mixture of small traditional
vineyards and large modern estates.**

D

E

A place of worship has occupied the site of the Abbazia di Monte Oliveto Maggiore for almost 700 years.

Abbazia di Monte Oliveto Maggiore

MONTE OLIVETO MAGGIORE IS THE SECOND OF SOUTHERN Tuscany's great abbeys. Although architecturally less distinguished than Sant'Antimo, its not too distant neighbor (see pp. 274–75), it is just as prettily nestled in timeless countryside and has the considerable artistic bonus of a superb Renaissance fresco cycle.

Abbazia di Monte Oliveto Maggiore

🅰 267 D3

✉ Near Chiusure

☎ 0577 707 061

🕓 Closed L

From whichever direction you approach Monte Oliveto—and it's easily seen on several Tuscan itineraries—you find yourself in lovely countryside. Cypresses, oak woods, and olive groves provide a fine setting for the monastery's cluster of red-stoned buildings. The first retreat here was founded in 1313 by a Sienese aristocrat, Bernardo Tolomei (1272– 1348), who abandoned worldly life after being struck blind and experiencing visions of the Virgin. With two companions he lived as a hermit on land owned by his family, land that was then so lonely and inhospitable it was known as a *deserto,* or desert. Within six years, the Bishop of Arezzo approved the building of a hermitage, and a year later work began on the first abbey building.

In 1344, Pope Clement VI recognized the monks as Olivetans, or White Benedictines, an order that sought to return to the simple ways of the first Benedictines. Ironically, the abbey became immensely powerful over the centuries, only losing its influence when monastic houses were suppressed in the 19th century.

Today, large areas of the abbey are closed to visitors, but what remains on view is more than enough to justify a visit. The key sight is the **Chiostro Grande** (1426–1443), or main cloister. Around its walls is spread a fresco cycle on the life of St. Benedict by Luca Signorelli (1441–1523), a painter from the Tuscan town of Cortona (see pp. 282–84), and the Milanese artist Giovanni Antonio Bazzi, better known by his nickname, Sodoma. Signorelli finished eight frescoes between 1497 and 1498; Sodoma completed the last 27 panels between 1505 and 1508. The sequence starts on the east wall, to the right of a door that leads to the abbey's rather disappointing church, remodeled to dull effect in the 18th century. Only the amazing **choir stalls** (1503–1505) reward attention; they are some of the most intricately crafted works of their kind in Italy.

The fresco cycle's story traces the life of the fifth-century Umbrian founder of Western monasticism, St. Benedict, whose monks—laboring, copying, writing, and recording in Benedictine abbeys across Europe—were partly responsible for preserving the continent's culture through the so-called Dark Ages (the centuries following the fall of the Roman Empire). The frescoes detail events from the saint's life, with a wealth of drama and incidental detail.

Elsewhere in the abbey, it's fun to browse in the monastery shop, full of foodstuffs, potions, soaps,

and elixirs, many made by the monks. Also look into the **Refettorio,** or Refectory, the room in which the monks ate. Its scale gives some idea of Monte Oliveto's importance in its heyday.

Monte Oliveto can easily be seen from **Buonconvento,** a small historic town 5 miles (8 km) to the southwest, whose ugly outskirts conceal a pretty medieval center. The main draw here is the **Museo d'Arte Sacra** *(Via Soccini 18, tel 0577 807 181, closed Mon., also Tues.–Fri. Nov.–mid-March)*, filled with a collection of medieval and Renaissance art out of all proportion to the size of the village. Alternatively, you can drive from Asciano, reached from Siena on the SS438 road. Pause in **Asciano** to visit the **Collegiata di Sant' Agata,** a Romanesque-Gothic church, and the rich collection of medieval Sienese paintings in the **Museo d'Arte Sacra** *(Piazza F. Bandiera, visits arranged through the visitor center, tel 0577 719 510).* ■

Renaissance frescoes by Luca Signorelli and Sodoma, depicting the life of St. Benedict, line the abbey cloister.

Views from
Montalcino
include the
Crete, or clay
"badlands," lying
between the town
and Siena to the
north.

Montalcino

MONTALCINO FROM AFAR IS A PICTURE OF MEDIEVAL
perfection, its pristine hill almost untouched by the modern sprawl
that detracts from many Italian hill towns. Close up, the town is
equally alluring, enclosed by walls, crowned by a fairy-tale castle,
blessed with magnificent views, and edged by vineyards that produce
one of Italy's most magnificent wines.

Montalcino

🗺 266 C3

Visitor information

✉ Costa del Municipio
8, off Piazza del
Popolo

☎ 0577 849 331

🕑 Closed Mon.

There has probably been a settlement on Montalcino's site since
Paleolithic or Etruscan times.The
present town almost certainly takes
its name from the Latin *Mons
Ilcinus* (Mount of the Holm Oak),
hence its coat of arms, a holm oak
atop six hills. The first written reference to the settlement comes in
814, when it features in a list of
lands given to the nearby abbey of
Sant'Antimo by Louis the Pious,

son of Charlemagne (see pp.
274–75). The spur to its early
medieval growth came about 1000,
when it was inhabited by refugees
fleeing Saracen attacks on the
Tuscan coast. The four leading
refugee families settled the town's
four *contrade*, or districts, creating
divisions that survive to this day:
The rival Borghetto, Pianello, Ruca,
and Travaglio hang their flags in the
streets and compete in a twice-

yearly archery tournament. The town's moment of glory came in 1555, when, as the last bastion of the Sienese Republic, it held out for four years against the besieging Florentines.

Many people are lured here by one of Italy's greatest red wines, Brunello di Montalcino, which can be bought, along with Rosso di Montalcino, its cheaper cousin, in many local shops (you get the best deals in the local co-op supermarket). If you're driving, park in the lot just outside the walls off Via Aldo Moro below the **Rocca** or **Fortezza,** a glorious 14th-century castle that has a wine shop and bracing views from its battlements. Parking within the walls is difficult, and from the parking lot and castle it's a short walk to everything you want to see.

The next important sight lies just up the street in front of the castle, the **Museo Civico e Diocesano d'Arte Sacra,** full of superbly displayed medieval paintings and sculptures. Watch for Sano di Pietro's "Madonna dell'Umiltà" ("Madonna of Humility"), a rare subject in which the Madonna is shown sitting or kneeling on a cushion or carpet rather than a throne. This aspect began to appear in Italian art after the new ideas on the importance of humility were promulgated by St. Francis in the early 13th century.

The museum is housed in part of a monastic complex belonging to the church of **Sant'Agostino** (begun 1360), worth seeing for its variety of 14th- and 15th-century Sienese fresco fragments. From the church you could take Via Spagni north to see the 11th-century **Duomo,** or cathedral, rather spoiled by restoration in 1818, and continue on the same street to the **Madonna del Soccorso.** This 17th-century Renaissance church

features a magnificent panorama over half of Tuscany from the gardens to the right of the facade. Alternatively, take the lane down the left side of Sant'Agostino as you face it, and follow the steps through the arch in front of you as the lane bears right. This brings you out a few steps from Montalcino's visitor center (turn right) and narrow main square, the **Piazza del Popolo** (turn left), hunched beneath the tower of the Palazzo dei Priori (1292), seat of

Montalcino's ruling medieval council. The nicest thing to do here is take a break in the hub of town life, the Fiaschetteria Italiana, a café with a pretty 19th-century interior and plenty of outside tables. From here walk down the town's main streets—Via Mazzini to the north, Via Matteotti and Via Saloni to the south—being sure to wander off into the pretty tangle of lanes and alleys to either side. Exploring at random, as ever in Tuscany's medieval towns, brings its own rewards, but particularly good targets include the deconsecrated church of **San Francesco** (turn right off Via Mazzini) and the tiny church of **Sant'Egidio** just off Piazza Garibaldi and Via Boldrini between Via Matteotti and the Rocca (castle). ∎

Right: The Fortezza in Montalcino has a small shop and bar where you can buy or sample local wines.

Fortezza

✉ Piazzale della Fortezza

☎ 0577 849 211

🕐 Closed Mon. Nov.–March

💲 Grounds & shop: free; battlements: $

Museo Civico

✉ Via Ricasoli

☎ 0577 846 014

🕐 Closed Mon.

💲 $

Wine

Time was when Tuscan wine meant Chianti, a thin, tannic red once found in Italian restaurants the world over. Those days are gone. Not only has Chianti improved beyond all measure, but as producers have turned to new methods and new grape varieties, the quality—and variety—of Tuscan wines has been transformed across the region.

Some of the region's wines have always passed muster. There have been good Chiantis for those who knew where to look, and Brunello di Montalcino—produced from a clone of the Sangiovese grape that makes Chianti—has enjoyed an exalted reputation. Vino Nobile di Montepulciano, although less consistent, is another big, bold red that receives plaudits.

Until recently, however, these wines have been known only to the *cognoscenti* of the outside world. And while Italy always produced a lot of wine, most of it was for home consumption. Methods of production, moreover, had hardly changed for centuries.

Matters began to change in the 1970s and 1980s, when younger and more adventurous producers began to take on board the lessons being learned in California and Australia. Modern production methods and new grape varieties were introduced, along with a readiness to blend traditional Tuscan grapes with French and other imports. The result was so-called "super Tuscans"—Tignanello, Sassicaia, Solaia, Sammarco, Tavernelle, and others.

Most of these early innovations blended Sangiovese grapes with Cabernet Sauvignon, the mainstay of the great French wines of Bordeaux. As time has gone by, however, other varieties such as Merlot and Pinot Noir also have been planted. The improvements of these pioneers has had a ripple effect on quality and variety, so that today you have a broad choice of good—and occasionally exceptional—wine. Price is not always a reliable indicator of quality, however, and there's no doubt that many beautifully packaged and over-marketed Tuscan wines cost more than they should.

So what should you drink? One of the strengths of basic Tuscan wines is that they go perfectly with simple Italian food, so don't scorn the humble *vino da tavola,* or table wine, and don't pay too much heed to the "D.O.C." and other official gradings on bottles; Italy's system of wine classifications is currently a mess. You can rarely go wrong with Brunello, but prices can be sky-high. Stick with one of the less exalted producers rather than with the famous names such as Bondi-Santi. Better still, try Brunello's cheaper cousin, Rosso di Montalcino, a wine with many of Brunello's qualities but at a fraction of the price. Chianti can still be very good or very average, and there's huge choice. Wines from the Gallo Nero consortium of producers are usually reliable: Watch for the distinctive Black Cockerel motif on bottles. San Gimignano's ancient white Vernaccia is improving, but too much is still cheap, cheerful wine aimed at tourists.

Perhaps the best way to taste and buy wine is to visit a vineyard. More and more wineries are opening their doors, especially in Chianti. Visitor centers should have details. Or buy in places like Montalcino; you'll find a good selection in most supermarkets. ■

A Tuscan farmer holds a flask used for Chianti wine, now with a plastic, rather than the traditional straw, casing.

Above: Most black grapes grown in Tuscany are the Sangiovese variety.
Below: Winemaking in Tuscany is an industry now, as these presses of Villa Banzi near Montalcino show, but small-scale production still exists at many vineyards.

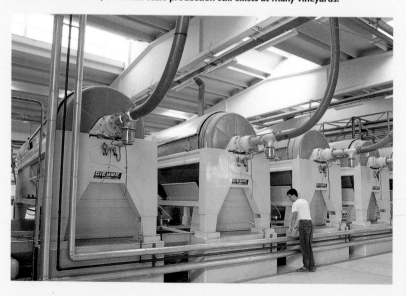

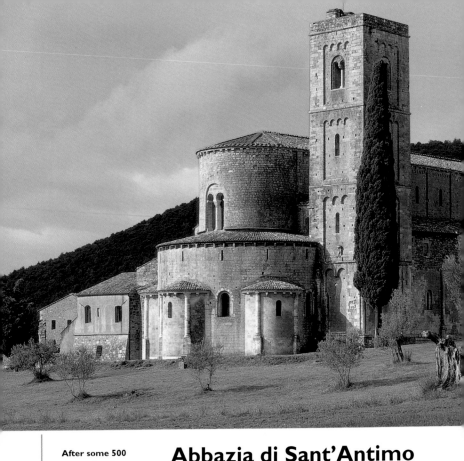

Abbazia di Sant'Antimo

SANT'ANTIMO IS THE MOST BEAUTIFUL OF TUSCANY'S medieval abbeys. Isolated in glorious countryside south of Montalcino, it has a matchless rural setting, a history that dates back to the days of Charlemagne, and artistic and architectural riches that place it in the pantheon of Italy's Romanesque buildings.

Tradition claims the abbey was founded by Charlemagne, who was subsequently crowned the first Holy Roman Emperor. He is said to have stopped close to the abbey's present site on his way north from Rome in 781. His army had been crippled by a mysterious disease, leading Charlemagne to promise God a church, should his men be cured. An angel appeared, telling him to grind a local herb (still called *carolina*) and give it to his

troops with wine. The remedy worked, and Charlemagne duly founded Sant'Antimo. More concrete evidence of Charlemagne's involvement comes from the fact that in 781 the pope had also presented him with the relics of St. Antimo, a bishop martyred around A.D. 305—the same relics venerated at the abbey that took his name.

It is also known that the abbey existed in 814, when Louis the Pious, Charlemagne's son, enriched

Abbazia di Sant'Antimo

- 267 D3
- Near Castelnuovo dell'Abate
- No phone
- Closed 2–3 hours L

Above right: The Romanesque interior of Sant'Antimo was inspired by the Cistercian churches and abbeys of France.

it with lands in a charter of that year. Over the next two centuries it became the second richest abbey in Tuscany, thanks in part to its position astride several vital trade and pilgrimage routes. These included an old sunken Etruscan road between the coast and the Tuscan heartland (traces can be seen in the fields in front of the abbey), the old Roman Via Clodia, the Strada Pecorile (an ancient track used to drive sheep to the mountains), and—most importantly—the Via Francigena, the main pilgrimage route between Rome and northern Europe.

In 1118 the abbey expanded further after receiving a vast bequest, the terms of which are still engraved on the steps of the main altar. In time, Sant'Antimo's funds began to run dry, partly because benefactors began to bestow their gifts on new religious orders such as the Cistercians, and partly because the growing power of Siena began to strip the abbey of its lands. By 1293 it retained just a fifth of its original territories; in 1439 the abbot was imprisoned for

"villainy"; and in 1462 the abbey was suppressed for good.

The abbey's appeal for visitors is partly its setting: The drive, if you're coming from Montalcino, is delightful. The surroundings are perfect, from the cypress-dotted hills and fields to the great single tree that stands sentinel alongside the church bell tower. The abbey's interior is similarly impressive, a picture of honey-colored stone and fine medieval carving. Its French-inspired form—a single nave with an ambulatory (a walkway around the high altar)—is unique in Tuscany and found in only a handful of churches elsewhere in Italy.

Among the fine Romanesque carvings—many of which are in subtly hued alabaster—the capital on the second pillar on the right side of the nave is well worth a close look. It depicts a graphic representation of "Daniel in the Lion's Den," the work of the Master of Cabestany, a sculptor of French or Spanish origin whose work has been identified in several major Benedictine abbeys across Western Europe. ∎

Pienza

PIENZA WAS A SLEEPY HAMLET KNOWN AS CORSIGNANO
until 1459, the year Pope Pius II decided to transform his birthplace
into a model Renaissance city. Pius died soon afterward, but not
before creating a cathedral, a papal residence, and a palace-ringed
central piazza. This hint of city still survives, forming the heart of one
of Italy's most charming villages.

Pienza

🄰 267 D3

Visitor information

✉ Palazzo Comunale,
Piazza Pio II, Corso
Rossellino 59

☎ 0577 749 071

Although there's little specific to see
here, you'll probably remember the
flower-hung streets and magnificent vistas—the views extend over
some of the region's loveliest countryside—long after other Tuscan
memories have faded. Pienza also
has a good central hotel (see p. 318)
and several pleasant restaurants,
making it an excellent base for
exploring the region.

You won't get lost here. Roads
outside the walls meet in Piazza
Dante, from which a single main
street, Corso Rossellino, leads to
Piazza Pio II, the heart of Pius's
model "city." The Corso takes its
name from Bernardo Rossellino,
the architect commissioned by Pius
to realize his dream. He began work
in 1459, less than a year after his
patron became pope. Pius was

christened Enea Silvio Piccolomini, and it was to him that another sight you may have seen, the magnificent library in Siena cathedral, was dedicated (see p. 207). Pius's coat of arms is enclosed by a large garland of fruit on the facade of the **cathedral,** the piazza's obvious centerpiece. Inside the church, notice the tall windows—requested by Pius to let in a flood of light—designed to symbolize humanist enlightenment. Pius also commissioned the interior's five major altarpieces, demanding that the painters should be Sienese rather than Florentines, despite the fact that most Florentine painters were then more advanced than their Sienese counterparts. This said, the pictures are still outstanding, the best being Vecchietta's "Assumption with Pius I and Saints Agatha, Callistus and Catherine of Siena" (in the fourth chapel as you work around the church from the right). Pius's insistence on having the cathedral built on its cramped site, however, means the future of these paintings and other interior treasures is doubtful, for the building is very obviously slipping down the hillside to the rear—as the ominous cracks and measuring devices on the walls make clear.

To the cathedral's left, as you face it, stand two palaces. The Palazzo Borgia, or Palazzo dei Vescovi, houses the **Museo Diocesano** (*Corso Rossellino 30, tel 0578 749 905, closed Tues., $*) and its collection of medieval paintings, sculptures, miniatures, illuminated manuscripts, portrait busts, tapestries, and other artifacts. The star turn is a 14th-century *piviale*, or cope, a wondrously embroidered English-made cloak—it bears the words *Opus Anglicanum* (An English Work)—from Pius's papal wardrobe. Almost equally remarkable are the paintings, which

include an anonymous "Madonna dell'Umilità," a "Madonna della Misericordia" (1364) by Bartolo di Fredi (his first signed and dated work), Vecchietta's "Madonna and Child with Saints" (1462), and—most interesting of all—an anonymous work in 48 panels whose

miniature paintings portray scenes from the life of Christ. The last is one of only a handful of surviving "portable" paintings once carried around the countryside by monks, who used them as aids when preaching to illiterate congregations.

To the cathedral's right lies the **Palazzo Piccolomini** (*Piazza Pio II, tel 0578 748 503, closed Mon., $*), built by Rossellino on the site of a former Piccolomini family house. Rossellino spent five times his allotted budget on the project, a sum he was liable to repay, but Pius was so pleased with the palace he forgave him the extravagance. Admire the courtyard and the view from the rear loggia, and then join one of the guided tours around Pius's former state apartments, where the

Right: Sheep around Pienza are mainly kept for their wool; their milk is used to make a renowned pecorino cheese.

The courtyard of the Palazzo Piccolomini. Family descendants of the original owner, the 15th-century Pope Pius II, occupied the palazzo until 1968.

highlights are the papal bedroom and the weapon-filled armory.

After seeing the sights on Piazza Pio II, be sure to walk along the little streets and alleys behind and to the east of the square (that is, to the left as you face the cathedral). Not only are these pretty, but they have remarkable views over the surrounding countryside. Then walk east on the main street, Corso Rossellino, where you come to the church of **San Francesco,** a survivor from pre-Pius Pienza. Inside, it has traces of 14th-century frescoes on the life of St. Francis. Beyond lies Piazza Dante, from which a tempting small lane runs along the old walls for more sensational views. This short stroll is highly recommended, as is the ten-minute walk down the road from

the piazza's lower-left (southwest) corner, signposted to **Pieve di Corsignano,** the lovely tenth- to eleventh-century parish church. Among the church's rare and precious features are an unusual tower—used to shelter townspeople during bandit raids—and the Romanesque carvings above the main and side doors. The farm next door holds the key to the interior *(leave a tip),* which contains, among other things, the font used to baptize Pius II.

Two slightly longer excursions from Pienza are also highly worthwhile. One takes you to the little-known abbey of **Sant'Anna in Camprena,** 5 miles (8 km) away, reached by taking the road for San Quirico for a mile (2 km) and then bearing north on a signed secondary road. The abbey's refectory contains important frescoes (1502–1503) by Sodoma, whose work you may have seen at Monte Oliveto Maggiore (see pp. 268–69). The frescoes are generally open to view daily in summer, afternoons only the rest of the year, but check with the visitor center in Pienza for current details. It won't matter if the frescoes are closed to view when you arrive, for the countryside en route is ravishing. The same goes for the scenery elsewhere around Pienza, notably that along the good *strada bianca,* or white road (named after its pale gravel surface) toward Montepulciano to the east. After 3 miles (5 km) you come to the sleepy walled village of **Monticchiello,** worth a short pause to wander its streets and admire its fresco-dotted parish church (Santissime Leonardo e Cristoforo). Rummage in the old-fashioned shop close to the church (on the corner to the right as you stand in front of the facade): It sells some of Tuscany's most beautiful handmade fabrics. ■

Montepulciano

MONTEPULCIANO IS THE SORT OF CLASSIC HILL TOWN YOU want to roll up and take home. Ranged over a narrow volcanic outcrop, it has art and architecture galore, sweeping views over Tuscany and the hills of nearby Umbria, a velvety red wine—Vino Nobile—an easygoing air, and one of Tuscany's most lauded Renaissance churches.

It also makes a good base for much of southern Tuscany and a logical stop-off after Pienza as you journey between Siena, Arezzo, and Florence. Arriving by car can be a confusing business, however, for the twisting approach roads do their best to keep you from the old town high on the hill. Parking, needless to say, is difficult, but try to leave your car as near to the walls or as high as possible, preferably at the southern end of town by the Fortezza (castle). Failing that, park at the lowest part of town near Piazza Sant'Agnese.

Wherever you start exploring, you're going to have to climb at some point, for Montepulciano effectively consists of a single main street—known as the **Corso**—that ascends from Piazza Sant'Agnese to the Fortezza, passing the town's theatrical main square, Piazza Grande, en route. Unless you take a cab one way, you'll have to follow the street in both directions. The account below assumes you start at the bottom and work up.

Things to watch for include a string of late-Renaissance and baroque palaces, Montepulciano having received a thorough architectural makeover during the 16th century. Before that, the town had oscillated between independence and submission to either Florence or Siena. Florence took permanent control in 1511 and dispatched the architect Antonio da Sangallo the Elder (1455–1534) to rebuild the town's defenses. His employers were so pleased with the result that they commissioned him to remodel

The Palazzo Nobili-Tarughi on Piazza Grande is one of several palaces in Montepulciano designed by the architect Antonio da Sangallo.

Montepulciano
🅜 267 D3
Visitor information
✉ Via Graciano del Corso 26
☎ 0578 715 322

many of the town's churches and palaces, a process continued by Jacopo Vignola (1507–1573), Baldassare Peruzzi (1481–1536), Ippolito Scalza (1532–1617), and other architects of the time.

Before starting your climb, spend a moment or two in the 1306

church of **Sant'Agnese** *(Piazza Sant'Agnese),* where the first chapel on the right contains a frescoed Madonna attributed to Simone Martini or his school, and the second altar on the left holds a 14th-century painting of the "Madonna del Latte" ("Madonna of the Milk"). The latter shows a breast-feeding Virgin, a frequent subject in Tuscan painting. The Virgin's milk symbolized the fount of Eternal Life, and many Tuscan churches claimed to possess actual "drops" of it.

Walking past the **Giardino di Poggiofanti** on your left, gardens laid out in 1866, you enter the old town proper through Sangallo's Porta del Prato gateway. The first square beyond this features the **Colonna del Marzocco,** a column bearing Florence's heraldic

lion *(marzocco),* raised after the town fell to the Tuscan capital in 1511. Palaces to watch for thereafter include Palazzo Avignonesi (No. 91) and Palazzo Tartugi (No. 82), both probably designed by Vignola; Sangallo's Palazzo Cocconi (No. 70); and the Palazzo Bucelli (No. 73), the last easily recognizable from the Roman and Etruscan remains built into its base. (Pietro Bucelli, the 17th-century owner, was a keen collector of antiquities.)

Just beyond these palaces on the right stands the church of **Sant' Agostino,** founded in 1285; its facade was remodeled in the 15th century by Michelozzo, who also carved the delicate terra-cotta "Madonna and Child with Saints" above the door. Inside, the key work is Sangallo's wooden crucifix above the high altar, a work long attributed to Donatello. Almost opposite the church, the **tower house** is a rare survivor of medieval Montepulciano, mounted on which is a clock whose hours are struck by the figure of Pulcinella, the stock clown character of early Italian plays.

About 100 yards farther up the Corso you come to **Piazza dell' Erbe,** long the site of the town's market, with the distinctive arches of the Loggia del Grano (1570) on your right. Here you should turn right and then dogleg immediately left up Via Poggiolo: This offers the most direct route to Piazza Grande. Take the lane that strikes off right from the dogleg and you come to a pretty little square fronting the baroque church of **Santa Lucia** (1633). Return to Via di Poggiolo and continue upward. Pass the church of **San Francesco** on the right, beside which there's a good view of the countryside to the west of Montelpulciano. The street then becomes Via Ricci, passing the **Museo Civico** *(Via Ricci 10, tel 0578 715 322, closed Mon., & p.m. in*

Left: When San Biagio was begun in 1518, the only larger church in Italy was St. Peter's in the Vatican.

winter), a modest collection of medieval paintings and sculptures.

At the top of the climb you come to **Piazza del Duomo,** a wonderful square ringed by palaces and dominated by the Duomo, or cathedral. The palace on its right (west) flank is the 14th-century **Palazzo Comunale.** Be certain to climb its tower *(Closed p.m. & all Sun.)* for sensational views as far as Siena and Lake Trasimeno in Umbria. The palace on the opposite flank, **Palazzo Cantucci,** is one of several places where you can sample and buy Vino Nobile di Montelpulciano, one of Tuscany's traditional "big three" wines.

Dominating the square is the **Duomo** (rebuilt after 1680), known for Taddeo di Bartolo's astounding high altarpiece of the "Assumption" (1401), perhaps the loveliest rendition of a subject that was a favorite of Sienese artists. The baptistery, the first chapel on the north (left) wall, is filled with fine art: The eye-catching plethora of glazed terra-cotta, known as the "Altar of the Lilies," is by Andrea della Robbia; the marble bas-relief it frames is by Benedetto da Maiano; the niche statues of Saints Peter and John the Baptist are attributed to Mino da Camaino; and the font and six bas-reliefs are the work of Giovanni d'Agostino.

Explore the streets beyond and below Piazza Grande to the east, but leave time to backtrack down Via Ricci and follow the signs down Via di San Biagio to **San Biagio,** a harmonious Renaissance church begun by Sangallo in 1518. ■

Vineyards slope down from Montepulciano to the rolling Tuscan countryside.

Cortona

CORTONA IS ONE OF THE MOST ANCIENT OF ALL TUSCAN hill towns. Chroniclers in the Middle Ages believed it was as old as Troy, and it was a flourishing center under the Etruscans in the eighth century B.C. Today, its appearance is largely medieval, something that when added to two excellent small museums, a medley of fine churches, and sweeping views from its hilltop ramparts makes it one of Tuscany's most pleasant—and still little-visited—small towns.

Most people approach Cortona from the village of Camucia, following a road through olive groves and vineyards that takes them past the area's most celebrated church, **Santa Maria del Calcinaio,** 1.5 miles (2.5 km) from Cortona's walls. An austere creation built on a Greek Cross plan, it was begun in 1485 and—with the similar church of San Biagio in Montepulciano— is often considered the finest of Tuscany's Renaissance churches. There's little to see inside, but its scenic impact is considerable.

Closer to town, park at one of several lots outside the walls and walk to the main square, **Piazza della Repubblica.** From here it's a short stroll through Piazza Luca Signorelli—named after the Cortona-born Renaissance painter—to a lackluster cathedral and the town's chief attraction, the **Museo Diocesano** (*Piazza del Duomo, tel 0575 62 830, closed Mon.*). The latter is dominated by two compelling paintings by Fra Angelico, who spent ten years in the town's Dominican convent. His "Annunciation" here is one of Italy's supreme Renaissance masterpieces, although his second work, a "Madonna and Child with Saints," barely suffers by comparison. Other paintings in this hallowed company include several works by Signorelli, an "Assumption" (1470–75) by Bartolomeo della Gatta, and a fetching "Madonna dell'Umilità" (1435) by the Sienese artist Sassetta. Don't miss the museum's major archaeological exhibit, a second-century Roman sarcophagus carved with reliefs showing "Dionysus and the Amazons."

Not far from the gallery stands Cortona's second major museum, the **Museo dell'Accademia Etrusca** (*Via Porsenna 17, tel 0575 637 235, closed Mon.*). Its collection embraces a wide variety of paintings, sculptures, and other artifacts, but its most appealing exhibits are those connected with Cortona's Etruscan heritage. Of special note is the "Lampadario Etrusco," an enormous fifth-century B.C. bronze

Left: **Santa Maria del Calcinaio** was built to enshrine a miraculous image of the Virgin found by a lime burner, or *calcinaio.*

Cortona
🄰 267 D3
Visitor information
✉ Via Nazionale 42
☎ 0575 630 352

lamp whose design and extravagance would have been striking in any era. Much the same can be said of the museum's beautiful collection of Etruscan jewelry, but not, perhaps, for its dull collection of urns and vases, the curse of many an Italian Etruscan museum. More prepossessing are the remains from a local tomb, the Melone II del Sodo, part of which has been reconstructed on the gallery's top floor. Other exhibits include Renaissance medallions, gold and silverware, a modest collection of medieval paintings, and mummies and other ancient Egyptian artifacts (part of a local collection donated to the museum).

As in most medieval Italian towns, it's as much fun simply wandering Cortona's streets as it is seeing the museums. Brave the streets' steep grades to reach the town's upper levels and the ruined 1556 **Fortezza Medicea** (Medici Fortress), in particular, where the views are sensational. From here you can look over the town and out to Lake Trasimeno and the hills of Umbria, Tuscany's neighbor. The sanctuary of **Santa Margherita** just below the fortress (rebuilt in the 19th century) houses the body of Margherita di Cortona, the town's patron saint, but there is little to recommend it save the saint's tomb (1362) housed in a chapel left of the high altar.

Other churches around town more worthy of a visit include **San Cristoforo**, a rough-hewn little Romanesque chapel just off Piazza della Pescaia, and **San Niccolò**

The Palazzo Communale, with its huge flight of steps, commands the Piazza Luca Signorelli.

"Annunciation"
by Fra Angelico

off Via San Niccolò, both of which are easily seen as you walk to or from the Fortezza. The latter has an intriguing double-sided altarpiece by Luca Signorelli. Another work by the same painter is found in **San Domenico,** which also has a poetic "Coronation of the Virgin" (1402) by Lorenzo di Niccolò Gerini. The church stands near the **public gardens** off Piazza Garibaldi, whose long "Passeggiata in Piano" walkway has more glorious views. ■

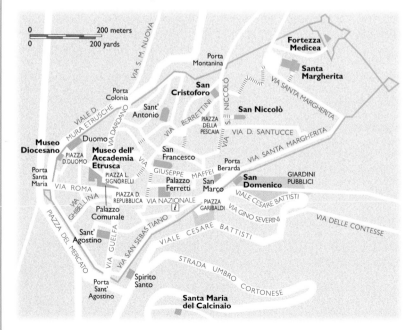

Arezzo

AREZZO TODAY IS VISITED MOSTLY FOR ITS MEDIEVAL CENTER and Piero della Francesca's "The Legend of the True Cross," one of Tuscany's most celebrated fresco cycles. Art aside, it is also a prosperous town, thanks in large part to its jewelry and gold-working industry—the world's largest—a tradition that developed in Etruscan, Roman, and medieval times, when the ancient settlement flourished as a result of its position on the trade routes across the Apennines.

This strategic position also invited bombing in World War II, and as a result the outskirts are largely modern. Don't be put off, however, for the 20th-century veneer conceals an almost perfect historic core. The town is well connected by road and rail to the rest of Tuscany: Florence is only an hour away by train.

Most visitors spend a few moments in the excellent visitor center outside the railroad station and then walk straight to the church of **San Francesco** (begun in 1318) in Piazza San Francesco, where Piero della Francesca's famous frescoes (1453–1466) adorn the walls of the apse. Their theme is

the "The Legend of the True Cross," a complicated story that follows the story of the wood used to build the Cross on which Christ was crucified.

The source for the story was the *Legenda Aurea (Golden Legend)* of Jacopo da Varagine, a 13th-century tract that had returned many apocryphal and other stories to the public domain. Piero is less concerned with simple narrative, however—the story is not told sequentially—than with the rigid sense of symmetry and artistic proportion that infused many of his unsettling and almost mystical paintings. For example, the cycle's

The church of Santa Maria (left) and the Fraternità dei Laici (right) tower above Arezzo's Piazza Grande.

Arezzo
🅰 267 D4
Visitor information
✉ Piazza della Repubblica 22
☎ 0575 377 678

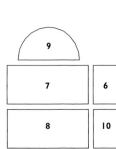

Opposite and above: "The Legend of the True Cross" by Piero della Francesca

two battle scenes (5 and 8 on the plan shown above) are placed facing one another across the apse—not where their position in the narrative demands—while the retinue of the Queen of Sheba is shown twice in a mirror image.

In the plan above:
1a. Adam foretells his death and asks his son Seth to seek the "oil of mercy" from the Angel of Eden.
1b. Instead, the Angel gives Seth a shoot from the "Tree of Knowledge." Seth plants it in Adam's mouth, from which will grow the tree that will become Christ's Cross.
2a. King Solomon has a bridge built from this tree. The Queen of Sheba, visiting Solomon, senses the wood's holiness and kneels in prayer.
2b. The queen foresees the wood will be used in a crucifixion. She tells Solomon of the vision.
3. Solomon has the wood buried by three men.
4. Constantine, the first Christian Roman emperor, asleep in his tent before battle in A.D. 313, dreams of

3	2a and 2b
4	5

the Cross and is told by an angel that "under this sign you shall be victorious."

5. Constantine defeats his rival, Maxentius, next morning and is baptized.

6. Under torture, the Levite Jew, Judas, reveals to Helena, Constantine's mother, the burial place of the three crosses of Golgotha, stolen and buried after the Crucifixion.

7. Judas digs up the Cross in front of Helena and her court. Its authenticity is confirmed when it revives

a dead man as Helena kneels in wonder. Arezzo is painted (left) in place of Jerusalem, the scene's setting.

8. The seventh-century Persian king Chrosroes, who had stolen the Cross and incorporated it into his throne (shown right), is defeated in battle by the Emperor Heraclius. He awaits his execution (right).

9. Heraclius returns the Cross to Jerusalem.

10. The Annunciation, or the Apparition of an Angel to Helena.

San Francesco

✉ Piazza della Repubblica

☎ 0575 900 404

🕐 Closed Sun a.m. Visits every half hour Mon.–Sat., max. 25 people at a time. Reservations essential.

💲 SS

The Piero trail

Devotees of Piero della Francesca (1416–1492), an influential and enigmatic Renaissance painter, may wish to visit the village of Monterchi, 20 miles (33 km) east of Arezzo, where the old school building contains his strange painting of the pregnant Madonna, the "Madonna del Parto." The town museum in nearby Sansepolcro (11 miles, 18 km, northeast) contains two further paintings by the artist: the "Resurrection" and "Madonna della Misericordia." ■

Most of Arezzo's other high-lights lie on or close to the **Piazza Grande,** the town's oddly sloping main square. At the top of its incline stands the **Palazzo delle Logge** (1573), fronted by a Renaissance loggia designed by the Arezzo-born artist and art historian Giorgio Vasari. In the square's top left-hand corner as you face uphill stands the **Fraternità dei Laici,** a Gothic palace renowned for its doorway and beautiful lunette sculptures (1434), the latter the work of Bernardo Rossellino. Lower down the square is the rear apse of **Pieve di Santa Maria,** a magical 12th-century Romanesque church whose entrance lies around the corner on Corso Italia. Its ornate Pisa-Romanesque style, with its distinctive tiny columns and arcades, is rarely found in eastern Tuscany. Note the lovely carvings around the

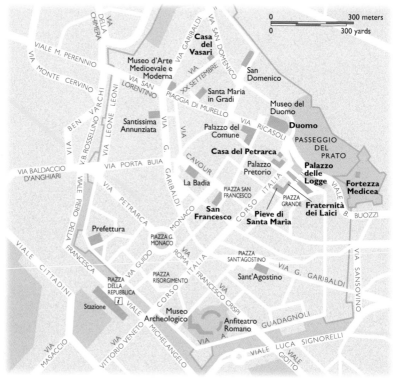

doors, especially the four little panels containing allegories of the months of the year. Step inside to admire Pietro Lorenzetti's high altarpiece painting of the "Madonna and Saints" (1320). The saint on the painting's far left is St. Donatus (San Donato), Arezzo's patron saint, who was martyred in the fifth century and whose relics lie in the gold reliquary (1346) on the altar, a consummate example of Arezzo's superb gold-working tradition.

As you leave the church, notice the carved "Epiphany" to the right of the main door on the rear wall, a lovely 11th- or 12th-century sculpture that probably once formed part of a pulpit.

North of the square stretches the **Passeggio del Prato,** a pleasant public park flanked by the cathedral and the remnants of the **Fortezza Medicea,** a 16th-century castle built by Florence's Medici rulers (Florence captured Arezzo in 1384). The **Duomo** with

gothic columns and pointed arches warrants a visit for its lovely stained glass windows (1523) by French artist Guglielmo di Marcillat, who settled in Arezzo, and a fresco of "Mary Magdalene" by Piero della Francesca in the north (left-hand) aisle beyond the organ. Another treasure is the tomb (1330) of Guido Tarlati (next to Piero's fresco), the 14th-century Bishop of Arezzo who commissioned Lorenzetti's painting in Santa Maria. Also worth seeking out is the Cappella di Ciuccio Tarlati, the last chapel on the south (right) wall before the high altar, which has an eye-catching sculpture (1334) and a series of mid-15th-century frescoes, both by unknown hands.

Literary pilgrims may want to see the house of Giorgio Vasari, the architect and art historian, the **Casa dei Vasari,** (*Via XX Settembre 55),* and the **Casa dei Petrarca,** (*Via dell'Orto 28),* reputed to have been the birthplace of the poet Petrarch in 1304. ∎

The Giostra del Saracino recalls the days when Saracen pirates menaced Tuscany and the Italian coast. The festival is traditionally held on the first Sunday in September.

A drive through the Casentino

This loop drive from Arezzo takes you through some of Tuscany's least-traveled but most picturesque countryside. Or you could make it a scenic alternative to the A1 highway between Arezzo and Florence.

Many Tuscan visitors explore the landscapes of southern Tuscany. Few, however, see two of the region's other areas of outstanding countryside—the Casentino and Pratomagno, two linked enclaves of wild hills, high mountains, remote abbeys, and ancient forests.

The area's scenic highlight is the Parco Nazionale delle Foreste Casentinesi, a national park that protects the best of the area's mountains and forests. Visit Arezzo's visitor center (see p. 285) for more details of the park (including marked hiking trails). Shorten the drive if necessary by traveling directly to Poppi or Pratovecchio, gateways to the park.

From Arezzo take the SS71 road 4 miles (7 km) north to Ponte alla Chiassa and turn right, following signs to Chiassa and **Anghiari,** 12.5 miles (20 km). About a mile (2 km) before Anghiari, watch for a minor road signposted to the **Pieve di Sovara ❶,** a ninth-century Romanesque church. Pause in Anghiari to see its tiny medieval center and the art of the **Museo di Palazzo Taglieschi** (*Piazza Mameli 16, closed Sun. p.m. & winter*). From Anghiari take the only road north for 11 miles (18 km) to **Caprese Michelangelo ❷,** the birthplace of Michelangelo. The cliff-top village is pretty, but the sculptor's former home has only a modest museum (*Casa del Podestà*). From Caprese take the mountain road through Chiusi della Verna to the junction with the SS208, 8 miles (13 km) northwest of Caprese. Signs here lead you 2.5 miles (4 km) to **La Verna ❸,** one of Italy's most important Franciscan abbeys. Here St. Francis received the stigmata, the wounds of Christ. Pilgrims flock to the shrine but do not spoil its charm. The mountain setting is superb, and above the sanctuary you can take a trail to the summit of Mount Penna, 4,209 feet (1,283 m) high, for superlative views.

Return to the SS208 and turn right for the town of Bibbiena, 16 miles (24 km) west. Here, pick up the SS71 then SS70 and head north for 2 miles (5 km) to **Poppi ❹,** where

you should see the Palazzo dei Conti Guidi (*off Piazza Amerighi, closed Mon.*), a large fortress, and the 12th-century church of San Fedele. Just before Poppi is a signed turning to the right for **Camaldoli ❺,** 10 miles (16 km), which, as well as being near another monastery (the Eremo), is also at the heart of the **Parco Nazionale delle Foreste Casentinesi.** Many walks start at Camaldoli and from Badia Prataglia, 6 miles (10 km) east, but you can also enjoy the scenery by following minor roads that crisscross the area.

From close to the monastery, take the only road west to Pratovecchio, from where you should drive 1.5 miles (3 km) on the minor road to the southwest signed to "Firenze" (Florence) and see **San Pietro di Romena ❻,** a beautiful eighth-century church set in lovely countryside. A road from the church leads to the **Castello di Romena,** a castle that offers magnificent views.

From Pratovecchio you can drive the 28 miles (46 km) to Arezzo on the SS310/SS70/SS71. Alternatively, you could continue to Florence by driving beyond San Pietro to the SS70 road and going west for 20 miles (32 km) toward Pontassieve. If you have time, turn left after 5 miles (8 km) for **Vallombrosa,** 11 miles (18 km) farther on, another celebrated monastery. Return to the SS70 via Tosi and Pelago, a longer but more scenic route. From Pontassieve the SS69 road follows the Arno valley for 11 miles (18 km) to Florence. ■

🏔   Also see area map, p. 267
▶   Arezzo
🔄   130 miles (208 km)
🕐   Allow 1–2 days
▶   Arezzo

NOT TO BE MISSED
- La Verna
- Camaldoli
- Parco Nazionale delle Foreste Casentinesi

1654m
Monte
Falterona
Passo
la Calla
SS310

Lago di
Ridracoli

PARCO NAZIONALE
D. FORESTE CASENTINESI-
MONTE FALTERONA-
CAMPIGNA

Papiano
Arno
Stia
Pratovecchio
SS70
To Firenze
(Florence),
Vallombrosa

Eremo di
Camaldoli
Camaldoli ⑤
**Castello di
Romena**
**San Pietro
di Romena** ⑥
Moggiona

Badia
Prataglia

Casentino Forest National Park

Borgo alla
Collina
④
Poppi
SS310
SS70

Soci
SS71

C A S E N T I N O

Mount Penna
La ③ ▲ 1283m
Verna
SS208

Montalone
SS208

Pieve
Santo
Stefano

P R A T O M A G N O

Bibbiena
Quota

Castel
Focognano
Rassina
Pieve
Socana
SS71

Chiusi della
Verna

Chitignano

**Caprese
Michelangelo** ②

A L P E
D I
C A T E N A I A

Manzi

Singerno

Tevere

Talla
Salutio
SS71

Arno

Subbiano

San Giustino
Valdarno

Castelnuovo

Chiassa

Ponte alla
Chiassa
SS71

Tavernelle
Anghiari
①
**Pieve di
Sovara**

Le Ville
SS73
Cerfone

START
Arezzo

The hill town of Anghiari

Viciomaggio ●
● Olmo
SS73
Canal Maestro
d. Chiana
SS71

| 0 | | 6 kilometers |
| 0 | | 4 miles |

Medieval costumed festival in Arezzo

Elba

THE ISOLA D'ELBA IS A WORLD UNTO ITSELF IN TUSCANY, an island that many European visitors treat as a vacation destination in its own right. Most people come here for the beaches and sapphire seas; the resorts teem with over a million visitors in summer. But the island also has its picturesque and historical side, not least its associations with Napoleon, the French emperor exiled here in 1814.

Elba is the largest of several off-shore islands making up the so-called Tuscan Archipelago. It measures just 17 miles by 11 miles (27 km by 18 km), and it is about 9 miles (14 km) from the mainland port of Piombino (which offers regular car and passenger ferries). Most boats dock at **Portoferraio,** the island's capital, whose modern docks give way to the more alluring old town, rebuilt by the Medici Grand Duke Cosimo I in 1548. Island legend has it that Napoleon was attracted here, after being forced to renounce the thrones of France and Italy, by "the gentleness of the climate and its people." In fact, the victorious forces chose his place of exile, while allowing that

the tiny domain would be a "separate principality for his lifetime, held by him in complete sovereignty." Napoleon remained on the island for just nine months in 1814 and 1815, during which time he is remembered for improving roads and drainage, clearing land, repairing defenses, and improving education and the legal system. Intrigue and unrest in France, however, enabled him to escape, whereupon he embarked on the 100-day adventure that would culminate in his final defeat at the Battle of Waterloo.

In Portoferraio you can visit the emperor's former home, the **Villa dei Mulini** (*Via Garibaldi, closed Sun p.m.*). The ticket also allows

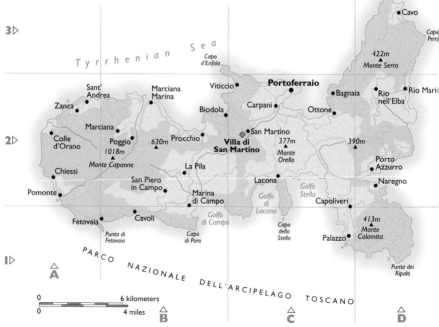

entry to the emperor's less appealing summer home—the **Villa di San Martino**—some 4 miles (6 km) out of town, south of the road to Marciana.

If you've come to Elba for the beaches then it's best to have reserved accommodations well in advance in summer. Most hotels are filled with visitors on prepaid package vacations, and they often only accept casual visitors for stays of more than one night. Perhaps the best approach if you want to see Elba as part of a longer Tuscan itinerary is to cross over for the day. If you want a swim, you'll find plenty of beaches as you drive, but don't expect to find any undiscovered corners. **Marina di Campo** has the largest stretch of sand but is also the most developed town after Portoferraio, with bars, hotels, restaurants, and lively nightlife.

The island's most attractive region is the western interior and the forest and scrub-covered countryside around the island's main peak, **Monte Capanne.** You can hike to the mountain's summit at 3,308 feet (1,018 m) from several

points, notably the village of Poggio on its northeast flanks. Hiking maps showing paths across the island marked for walkers by the Italian Alpine Club (C.A.I.) are available from most villages and visitor centers. If you don't want to walk, a cable car runs to the top from the hill village of **Marciana,** Elba's oldest settlement (a mile or so west of Poggio).

The west end of the island also has some of the best coastal scenery and, relatively speaking, some of its less busy beaches and resorts. The settlements of **Chiessi** and **Pomonte** have stony beaches, little development, and crystal-clear waters; **Fetovaia** to the south has good sand but more people, as does **Cavoli,** farther east.

Don't overlook the eastern part of the island: **Porto Azzurro** is a fashionable retreat overlooking a pretty bay (but with poor swimming); **Capoliveri,** in the hills is a relatively unspoiled village; and tiny upland roads near Bagnaia, 6 miles (10 km) east of Portoferraio, or Ottone and Rio nell'Elba, offer the best of the scenery. ■

Sun, sea, and sand—such as that found at Morcone's beach in southeast Elba—are the reasons most people visit the island.

Elba
🗺 266 A2
Visitor information
✉ Calata Italia 26, Portoferraio
☎ 0565 914 671

More places to visit in southern Tuscany

BAGNO VIGNONI

Bagno Vignoni is a slip of a village, but one with a unique attraction that shouldn't be missed. It can easily be incorporated into a tour of the area around Montalcino, Sant'Antimo, and the Val d'Orcia (see p. 296). The village is famous for its main square, which is not a square at all, but a large open *piscina*, or pool, which bubbles with waters from sulphurous hot springs below. If you can, try to be here first thing on a cool morning, when the steaming square provides one of Tuscany's most magical sights. The Romans bathed here, as did the Medici, among others. The latter built the pretty Renaissance arcade that surrounds the springs. The pool is now out of bounds, but you can bathe in waters from the same source in the nearby Posta Marcucci Hotel for a fee. The rest of the village can be seen in an instant. Follow some of the little lanes and paths that radiate from the village: All quickly lead to pretty countryside.

🅰 267 D3 **Visitor information:** Contact the visitor center at Via Dante Alighieri 33, San Quirico d'Orcia.

The beach at Castiglione della Pescaia, a fishing village and one of the most pleasant small resorts on the Maremma coast

THE MAREMMA

The Maremma is a region that embraces Tuscany's southerly coastal margins, encompassing the dismal town of Grosseto and the more enticing medieval charms of **Massa Marittima,** the one town in the region worth a special visit (the cathedral is magnificent). Once an area of wetland and coastal flats, the region was drained by the Etruscans and Romans, but in later centuries it slipped back to its original marshy state.

The landscape of coastal lowlands and occasional hills has a rather melancholy character. If you do come here, it'll be for the Parco Naturale (see p. 295) and the coastline, which is dotted with a variety of small resorts and beaches. The best of these are the undeveloped sands at **Marina di Alberese** (southwest of Grosseto), the pretty fishing village of **Castiglione della Pescaia,** and the chic resorts of **Porto Ercole** and **Porto Santo Stefano** on Monte Argentario, a spectacular rocky promontory. If you want to swim or sunbathe on the Tuscan coast, these are the best places to do so. The nicest beach

Ancient tunnels and caves riddle the tufa rock of Pitigliano's dramatic volcanic ridge. The Etruscans were among the first attracted here.

that can easily be reached is the one at **Marina di Alberese,** where the views to Monte Argentario are memorable, the water is perfect for swimming, and the trees come down to the sand in the manner of a tropical island.

The best of the coastal scenery is protected by the glorious **Parco Naturale della Maremma.** Visit it from **Talamone,** another pretty little resort village, or by special shuttle bus from Alberese south of Grosseto (the park is closed to automobiles; check current park opening times and bus schedules with the park visitor center at Alberese). The bus makes the best approach, dropping you on one of Italy's finest tracts of virgin coastline. You can walk on the beach, stroll at will through the beautiful *pineta* (pine wood), or follow one or more of the four easy marked

trails through the park's wide variety of natural habitats, including the typical Mediterranean *macchia* of myrtle and juniper bushes.

If you're in the area, the isolated inland village of **Capalbio,** with its hilltop maze of old streets, is also worth a detour, as is the extraordinary **Giardino dei Tarocchi** *(Garavicchio, near Pescia Fiorentina; tel 0564 895 122; closed a.m. & all Sun., winter open 1st Sat. of the month, a.m. only)* southeast of the village. The Giardino is a monumental sculpture garden based on the cards of the Tarot created by the modern sculptor Nicki de Saint Phalle. Opening times may vary.

Massa Marittima 🗺 266 B3 **Visitor information** ✉ Via Parenti 22 ☎ 0566 902 756 **Parco Naturale della Maremma** 🗺 266 C2 **Visitor information** ✉ Centro Visite, Via del Fante, Alberese ☎ 0564 407 098

MONTE AMIATA

If you want to see parts of Tuscany still virtu-ally unknown to most foreign visitors, then head for the swathe of countryside south of Montalcino and the Val d'Orcia. The best of the area is inland; the coastal Maremma is generally less enticing (see pp. 294–95). Don't expect the cultural riches of the area around Siena, however. Here the rewards are fewer and farther between. Heading south, you reach **Monte Amiata,** 5,702 feet (1,738 m) high, a mountain whose looming peak dominates many southern Tuscan vistas. You can drive almost to the summit—spoiled by a cluster of cafés—through beech woods laced with marked hiking trails; or tour the little-known villages on the mountain's flanks—Santa Fiora, Pescina, Piancastagnaio, and Castel del Piano. Be sure to visit the village of **Abbadia San Salvatore,** named after its stunning 11th-century abbey church.

Abbadia San Salvatore 🅰 267 D2
Visitor information ✉ Via Adua 25
☎ 0577 775 811

PITIGLIANO & SOVANA

Well south of Monte Amiata, near Tuscany's neighboring region of Lazio, lie two excep-tional villages, **Pitigliano** and **Sovana.** Pitigliano is a village of Etruscan vintage superbly located on a narrow rocky ridge, its old castle and medieval houses perched pre-cariously above the encircling ravine. There are a couple of modest museums here, but the setting is by far the main attraction. Tiny Sovana, by contrast, has two major artistic lures: The parish church of Santa Maria, in the tiny main square (the village has just a couple of streets), has a rare and beautiful stone altar canopy; the venerable cathedral has walls and a main door that are graced with some of Tuscany's finest Lombard-Romanesque carvings. All around the village lie numerous well-signed Etruscan tombs; the most impor-tant is the Tomba Ildebranda. Other tombs can be seen en route for Saturnia to the west or the neighboring village of **Sorano** to the east, whose ancient approach road is lined with niche tombs cut deep into the soft volcanic stone.

🅰 267 D2 **Visitor information** ✉ Via Roma, Pitigliano ☎ 0564 614 433

SAN QUIRICO D'ORCIA

Some 3.5 miles (6 km) north of Bagno Vignoni lies the village of **San Quirico d'Orcia,** a curious mixture of the medieval and modern known primarily for the Collegiata, an outstanding Romanesque church just off Piazza Chigi. Built in the 12th century, the church is renowned for its earlier main portal (1080), considered the region's finest work of its kind. The interior is almost as admirable; be sure to see Sano di Pietro's 15th-century Sienese painting of the "Madonna and Saints" in the north transept. Also visit the Horti Leonini by the Porta Nuova, a simple Renaissance garden, and the little 11th-century church of Santa Maria Assunta in Via Dante Alighieri.

🅰 267 D3 **Visitor information** ✉ Via Dante Alighieri 33 ☎ 0577 897 211 🕐 Closed Nov.–March

VAL D'ORCIA

The Val d'Orcia is a picturesque valley south of Montalcino and Sant'Antimo. Make a big effort to incorporate its lonely roads and little villages into a tour, for its quintessential pastoral landscapes are some of Tuscany's most beautiful.

Assuming you're approaching from the north, drive on the lovely country road from the abbey of Sant'Antimo southeast to **Castiglione d'Orcia,** 12 miles (19 km) from the abbey, a village huddled around an imposing fortress. From here meander on country roads through hamlets to the south—Campiglia d'Orcia, Vivo d'Orcia, Bagno San Filippo, and the imposing fortress village of Radicofani. You may become a little lost, but you won't be disappointed. Most routes and signposts eventually bring you to the main SS2 highway, the old Roman Via Cassia road to Siena. Take this road north (toward Siena), visiting Bagno Vignoni and San Quirico d'Orcia en route (see above). From the latter you can return to Montalcino or press on to Pienza and Montepulciano to the east.

Castiglione d'Orcia 🅰 267 D3 **Visitor information** ✉ Via Marconi 13 ☎ 0577 887 363 🕐 Closed Oct.–Easter
Radicofani 🅰 267 D2 **Visitor information** ✉ Via R. Magi 25 ☎ 0578 55 684 🕐 Closed p.m. & Sept.–May ■

Travelwise

Law and order with a smile

TRAVELWISE INFORMATION

PLANNING YOUR TRIP

WHEN TO GO

Deciding when to visit Florence and Tuscany depends on your chosen vacation. The country-side is at its best in spring, April to June, which is also a good time for sightseeing. In fall, late September to October, the countryside has been parched by the sun, but the weather is still good enough for sightseeing. Summer, July and August, is extremely busy and unpleasantly hot in the towns and cities; winter, January to March, is good for cultural tours, with fewer lines and lower prices. Easter, however, is always busy. Many festivals take place in summer, but others are scattered throughout the year (see p. 326). You might want to plan your trip around one of these artistic, religious, or cultural events.

Further help in planning your trip is available from Italian State Tourist Offices outside Italy (see p. 304). Some organizations also have useful websites.
www.alitalia.it
(routes and schedules for Italy's national airline)
www.beniculturali.it
(website for Italy's Ministry of Art and Culture)
www.fionline.it
(general information from a Florentine service-provider)
www.uffizi.firenze.it
(the Uffizi's official site)
www.fs-on-line.com
(Italian State Railroads)

CLIMATE

As a general rule, Tuscany has mild winters and hot summers, but its varied topography pro-duces a wide range of climatic conditions. Winters in the Apennines and mountainous areas can be severe, with snow and temperatures below freezing. Winter across the rest of the region is broadly compa-rable to the colder climate of northern Europe. Spring tends to be short; fall is more drawn out.

Winter daytime temperatures in Tuscany range from around 15° to 59°F (-10° to +14°C), and summer temperatures from 65° to 90°F (18° to 33°C), although temperatures may often exceed these extremes. Italy uses degrees Celsius (°C) as its unit of temperature.

WHAT TO TAKE

You should be able to buy anything you need in Florence and Tuscany except in the smallest towns. Pharmacies offer a wide range of drugs, medical supplies, and toiletries, along with expert advice, but you should bring any prescription drugs you might need. Many brand-name drugs are different in Italy. A pharmacy (una farmacia) is shown by a green cross outside the store. It is sensible to bring a second pair of glasses or contact lenses if you wear them. Don't forget sunscreen and mosquito repellents in summer.

Clothing will depend on when you travel and any activities you plan: You will only really need to dress up for the grandest restaurants. Don't be too casual, however, as Italians generally dress more smartly than most U.S., Canadian, and northern European visitors. Make some effort for any meal out, and always dress appropriately in churches—ideally no bare shoulders or shorts for women. Note, too, that dress codes are more conservative in most rural areas. Bring a sweater, even in summer, for evenings can be chilly. Come prepared for some rain and cool temperatures any time outside high summer. Hiking, camping, and other sports equipment can easily be bought or rented, but bring more personalized equipment such as hiking boots.

Lastly, don't forget the essentials: passport, driver's license, tickets, travelers' checks, and insurance documentation.

INSURANCE

Make sure you have adequate travel and medical coverage for treatment and expenses, including repatriation and baggage and money loss. Keep all receipts for expenses. Report losses or thefts to the police and obtain a signed statement (una denuncia) from police stations to help with insurance claims.

ENTRY FORMALITIES

U.S. and Canadian citizens require a passport to enter Italy for stays of up to 90 days. No visa is required. U.K. citizens require a passport.

FURTHER READING

Florence and Tuscany have spawned much poetry, fiction, and non-fiction from native and foreign writers. One essential read before or during your trip is The Italians, by Luigi Barzini (Simon & Schuster, 1996). It was first published in 1964, but no one before or since has produced a better-written analysis of Italy and the Italians.

HOW TO GET TO FLORENCE & TUSCANY

AIRLINES

Most major airlines have flights to Italy, and many arrange package tours or offer budget-price flights. Alitalia, the main Italian carrier, has reservation offices abroad in most major cities. Direct scheduled flights from North America fly either to Milan or Rome. Rome is the most convenient hub for Florence and Tuscany. It is worth considering flights to London's Heathrow Airport, where you can connect with British Airways and several low-cost airlines that fly to Pisa. This airport is convenient for most of Tuscany and offers an easy 60-mile (95 km) drive to Florence. Florence also has a small airport, Peretola, serviced by two daily flights with Meridiana (see below) from London's Gatwick Airport.

Flying time to Rome is about 8–9 hours from New York, 10–11 hours from Chicago, and 12–13 hours from Los Angeles. Flying time from London to Pisa or Florence is about two hours.

You can fly to Rome, Pisa, Florence, or Bologna from the U.K. on scheduled flights with British Airways, Alitalia, Meridiana and a host of smaller cut-price carriers from Heathrow, Gatwick, Stansted, Luton, and Manchester.

Driving to Italy from the U.K. takes up to 24 hours. Routes go through France or Germany and Switzerland.

Useful numbers
In Italy:
Alitalia (Rome), tel 06 65 621 or 06 65 643; 1478 65643 (toll free)
American Airlines, tel 02 6791 4400
British Airways tel 1478 12266 (toll free)
Continental, tel 06 487 711
Delta, tel 800 864 114
TWA, tel 06 47 211
United, tel 02 482 9800
In the U.S. and Canada:
Alitalia (U.S.), tel 800/223-5730 (Canada), tel 514/842-8241
American Airlines, tel 800/433-7300
Continental, tel 800/231-0856
Delta, tel 800/241-4141
TWA, tel 800/892-4141
United, tel 800/538-2929
In the U.K.:
Alitalia, tel 020 7602 7111
British Airways, tel 0345 222111
Meridiana, tel 020 7839 2222
Ryanair, tel 0541 569569

GETTING AROUND

AIRPORTS

You will arrive in Italy from the U.S. and Canada at Rome's Leonardo da Vinci airport (better known by its colloquial name of Fiumicino). If you fly from London, you will land at either Pisa's Galileo Galilei airport or Florence's Peretola (or Amerigo Vespucci) airport.

Fiumicino-Leonardo da Vinci

Fiumicino is 19 miles (30 km) west of Rome's city center. If you are renting a car to drive to Tuscany, the rental desks are across the raised walkway from above the main international departure terminal (follow signs for the FS railroad station). Driving from the airport, follow signs for "Roma" and "Centro" and then watch for the "Firenze" turnoff after about 6 miles (10 km)—the turn comes suddenly. This takes you onto the Rome ring road, Grande Raccordo Anulare (G.R.A.). Follow the ring road for about 11 miles (18 km), looking out for the Firenze–A1 turnoff (intersection 10): Then follow the A1, Italy's main expressway, north to Florence (about 150 miles/240 km). Road tolls are payable on the A1.

The best way into Rome if you wish to catch a train to Florence or other parts of Tuscany (see below) is on the special airport express rail service, which leaves the airport hourly between about 7:30 a.m. and 10 p.m., taking 30 minutes to reach Stazione Termini, Rome's principal railroad station. Onward rail connections to Florence (2 hours), Pisa (3 hours), and other parts of the country leave from Termini. Tickets for the rail service can be bought from automated machines in the airport arrivals (Arrivi) terminal or from a small ticket office (biglietteria) on the right as you face the railroad

station platforms. The same office also sells tickets for the state (FS) network: Buying tickets here saves waiting in long lines at Termini.

Galileo Galilei Airport

Most scheduled and charter flights fly to Pisa's airport (Tel 050 500 707), 60 miles (95 km) west of Florence. Getting to Florence from the airport couldn't be simpler. Direct trains for Florence leave every hour from a platform at the left-hand end of the airport concourse as you face the exit, 150 yards (140 m) from arrivals. The journey time is an hour. Tickets can be bought from an office midway down the concourse on the right. It is compulsory to validate your ticket in the machines on the platform before you board the train.

Note that on the return journey there's a check-in desk for most airlines by platform 5 at Santa Maria Novella, Florence's main railroad station. Bags have to be checked in at least 30 minutes before the departure of the train, which must arrive at Pisa airport at least 30 minutes before the departure of the flight. When catching the train, double check it runs through to Pisa Aeroporto—some go no farther than Pisa's central station, Pisa Centrale.

Peretola-Amerigo Vespucci

A limited number of inter-national carriers use Florence's Peretola airport (Tel 055 373 498), 3 miles (6 km) northwest of the city center (the airport is also known as Amerigo Vespucci airport). The airport has a small arrivals hall, with foreign exchange machine, several car rental desks, a lost baggage counter, and a small visitor center (Tel 055 315 874; open daily 8:30 a.m.–10:30 p.m.).

Light blue SITA buses (Tel 055 478 2231) provide roughly hourly shuttles to and from the airport from immediately outside the arrivals area. Tickets can be bought on board the bus. In Florence, buses arrive and depart from the main bus terminal on Via di Santa Caterina da Siena, just a few steps west of Santa Maria Novella railroad station. Cabs are also available. The journey by bus or taxi takes 15 to 30 minutes depending on the traffic.

TRAVELING IN FLORENCE & TUSCANY

BY BUS

Most of central Florence is easily explored on foot. If you do need to use public transportation, the city's ATAF company runs orange city buses. Florence has no subway. Tickets (biglietti) are valid for any number of journeys for either 60 minutes or three hours. They must be bought before boarding a bus from shops and bars displaying an ATAF sticker, from the automatic machines situated around the city, or from the main ATAF ticket and information office in the bus bays immediately east of the Santa Maria Novella railroad station. Tickets at a flat fare may be bought on board only between 9 p.m. and 6 a.m. Four 60-minute tickets bought in a block (un biglietto multiplo) and 24-hour passes offer savings on the basic rate tickets. Two-, three-, and seven-day passes are also available. All tickets must be stamped on board buses, in the machines provided, at the beginning of your first journey. Spot fines are levied by roving inspectors if you travel without a ticket or with an unvalidated ticket.

Around Tuscany, trains are usually quicker and cheaper than inter-town buses (pullman or corriere), but in more remote areas such buses (usually blue in color) may be the only viable means of public transportation. Services are operated by many different companies, but usually depart from a town's major

square, outside the railroad station, or a bus depot.

In Florence, the main SITA bus company depot for most Tuscan connections (including the Peretola airport bus) is just west of Santa Maria Novella railroad station at Via Santa Caterina da Siena 17. Other companies operate from Piazza Stazione (LAZZI and CLAP buses to Lucca, Pisa, Pistoia, Prato, Viareggio, and Lucca province); and Via Fiume 2 (CAT services to Arezzo and Sansepolcro). Tickets in Florence and other towns must generally be bought before boarding the bus, usually from the depot or the nearest bar or station kiosk. Inquire at local visitor centers for precise details.

BY TRAIN

Trains are an excellent way of traveling around Tuscany. Fares on the state-run railroad network (the Ferrovie dello Stato, or FS) are inexpensive, and service and comfort are improving. Key lines run from Florence, a major railroad hub, to Siena (direct services or change at Empoli); Pisa; Lucca (via Prato and Pistoia); Viareggio; and Arezzo. Smaller scenic lines run from Siena to Grosseto; Lucca to Aulla (via the Garfagnana); and Arezzo to Stia (in the Casentino).

Tickets can be bought at stations and some travel agents, and are issued in first (prima) or second class (seconda classe). On fast InterCity (I.C.) trains an extra supplement (supplemento) must be paid at the time you pay for your ticket or (for a higher fee) on the train. On the super-fast Pendolino or Eurostar services between Florence and Rome, or Florence and Bologna, you must pay a supplement and make seat reservations in advance. Seats can often be reserved until a few minutes before a train's departure.

The FS issues two main rail passes for non-resident visitors

to Italy, but these are not good value if you are only traveling within Tuscany. Before traveling you must validate all tickets in the special machines (small gold or yellow boxes) on platforms and station ticket halls: A heavy fine is payable if you travel with a non-validated ticket. If you intend to travel extensively on trains, then buy the Pozzorario, a cheap biannual schedule available from bookstores and station kiosks.

BY CAB

Florentine taxies are white with a yellow trim. It's easier to pick up cabs at a taxi stand than to hail them on the street. Central stands can be found at the railroad station, Piazza della Repubblica, Piazza del Duomo, Piazza Santa Maria Novella, Piazza San Marco, Piazza Santa Croce, and Piazza Santa Trinita. When you pick up a cab check that the meter is set at zero. When you set off it will jump to the current minimum fare for the first 220 yards (200 m) and then rise quickly. Supplements to the meter fare are charged on Sundays, and public holidays, for fares between 10 p.m. and 7 a.m., and for each individual item of luggage placed in the trunk. All current supplements should be posted on a list inside the cab. Take a cab driver's name and number if you suspect that he has been dishonest. Making clear to the driver that you are doing this is often enough to set matters right. Report any complaint to a visitor center or, in serious cases, to the police (see p. 305).

The best to way to be sure of a cab is to phone for one. Most operators speak a little English: Otherwise, ask your hotel to call for you. When you call, give the address of where you wish to be picked up. The operator will then give you a taxi-code number (always a geographical location followed by a number), plus the time you will have to wait: For example, "Parigi dodici in cinque minuti" (Paris 12 in five minutes). Meters run from the moment a taxi sets off to pick you up. Cabs can be called on the following numbers: tel 055 4798, 055 4242, 055 4499, or 055 4390.

BY CAR

Tuscany's town and city centers may be congested, but the rest of the region has an excellent network of clearly signposted and numbered roads, from the ordinary highway—known as a *Nazionale* (N) or *Strade Statale* (S or SS)—to the fast four- or six-lane expressways known as *autostrade*. Tolls are payable on autostrade. Sometimes you pay a fixed rate, but usually you take a card from automated machines on joining the road and then pay at a manned booth (*Alt Stazione*) when exiting.

Gravel-surface roads known as strade bianche (white roads) are common in rural areas but are intended for automobiles and are usually marked on maps. You may have to drive slowly on them, but they are passable and often very attractive. Maps are widely available from book and other stores. The best motoring map is the Touring Club of Italy (T.C.I.) Toscana 1:200,000 sheet.

Renting a car

It's easy to rent a car in Florence or larger Tuscan towns such as Siena, Pisa, Lucca, and Arezzo. Leading international companies also have offices in some railroad stations and Pisa and Peretola airports. Costs are high by North American and U.K. standards, and it can be worth arranging car rental through a travel agent before leaving home.

Cheaper deals in Tuscan centers can often be obtained through smaller local companies: Contact visitor centers for details or look under *"Autonoleggio"* in Yellow Pages (*Pagine Gialle*). Drivers must be over 21 and hold a full license to rent a car. Rental companies in Florence include the following:

Avis, Borgo Ognissanti 128r (Tel 055 213 629) and Peretola airport (Tel 055 315 558); **Hertz,** Via Maso Finiguerra 23r (Tel 055 239 8205); and **Thrifty,** Borgo Ognissanti 134r (Tel 055 287 161).

Motoring information

Accidents See p. 305.

Breakdowns Put on hazard lights and place a warning triangle behind the car. Call the Automobile Club d'Italia (A.C.I.) emergency number (Tel 116), giving your location, car make, and registration. The car will be towed to the nearest A.C.I.-approved garage. Car rental firms often have their own arrangements for breakdowns and accidents: Inquire when renting.

Busy periods Tuscan and most other Italian roads are especially busy on Friday and Sunday evenings, and in the run up to, and aftermath of, major public vacations such as August 15. The first and last weekends of August, when many Italians begin and end their vacations, are also busy. City traffic builds up in the early morning, evening, and pre-lunch periods.

Distances All distances on signposts in Italy are shown in kilometers (1 km = 0.62 mile).

Gas In Italy gas (*benzina*) is expensive and priced by the liter (0.26 U.S. gallons). Gas stations on autostrade are open 24 hours and generally accept credit cards. Other gas stations may close from around 1 p.m. to 4 p.m., after 7 p.m., and all day Sunday: Smaller stations may accept cash only. Be sure all pump meters are set to zero before the attendant starts filling your tank. Some gas stations have automatic dispensers that take L10,000 or L50,000 notes to use when no attendant is present.

Licenses U.S., Canadian, and U.K. drivers in Italy require a valid driver's license (*patente*) or International Driver's License (Permit). They are also legally bound to carry a translation of the license to help police, but this obligation is rarely enforced. For details of current regulations and how to obtain translations and an International Driver's License contact any branch of the American Automobile Association, Canadian Automobile Association, or A.A., in the U.K.

Parking Parking is often extremely difficult in Florence and in Tuscany's major towns. Most street spots and parking lots (*parcheggi*) will be filled by locals. Many historic centers, notably Florence and Siena, have "blue zones" (*zona blu*) or similar areas that are closed to traffic: Some towns have restrictions at busy times of day. Metered parking (*parcometro*) is being introduced in some cities. Try to park your car in a supervised lot, and never leave valuables or luggage in a parked vehicle. Illegally parked cars, especially those left in a removal zone (*zona rimozione*), may be towed away or receive a ticket.

Rules of the road Most regulations in Italy are similar to the U.S., notably the fact that you drive on the right. Passing is on the left only. Seat belts are compulsory in front and back seats, and licenses, insurance, and other documentation must be carried at all times. Drunk-driving penalties are severe, with heavy fines and the possibility of six months' imprisonment. A red warning triangle for use during breakdowns or accidents must be carried by law.

Speed limits The limit in built-up areas is 50 kph (31 mph) and 110 kph (70 mph) outside them, unless marked at 90 kph (56 mph). Autostrade limits are 130 kph (80 mph) and 110 kph (70mph) for vehicles with engine capacity under 1100 cc.

PRACTICAL ADVICE

COMMUNICATIONS

POST OFFICES

Stamps (francobolli) can be bought from a post office (ufficio postale) or most tobacconists (tabacchi), the latter indicated by a blue sign with a white "T." Most offices are generally open from about 8 or 9 a.m. to 2 p.m., Monday through Friday, 8 a.m. to noon on Saturday. Main post offices in larger towns and cities usually open from 8 or 9 a.m. to 7 or 8 p.m., Monday through Saturday. The Italian mail system can be slow: Allow 15 days for letters between Italy and North America, longer for postcards. Use fax for hotel bookings.

Mail boxes Small red mail boxes are found outside post offices or on walls in towns and cities. They are marked "Poste" and usually have two slots: One marked "Per La Città" (City Mail), the other "Per Tutte Le Altre Destinazioni" (Other Destinations).

Receiving mail You can arrange to have mail sent to you in Italy poste restante (fermo posta in Italian). Mail must carry your name and be addressed to the "Ufficio Postale Centrale, Fermo Posta" plus the name of the town or city. Collect it from the town's main post office. You will need to present a passport or photo ID and pay a small fee. American Express also has a general-delivery service: Its Florence office is at Via Dante Alighieri 22r (Tel 055 50 981, fax 055 509 8220).

Florence's main central post offices are at Via Pellicceria 8 (near Piazza della Repubblica) and Via Pietrapiana 5355.

TELEPHONES

Italy's telephone network is operated mainly by Telecom Italia (TI). Public phones are found on the streets, bars, restaurants, and TI offices in larger towns. Look for red or yellow signs showing a telephone receiver or receiver and dial. Most take coins and cards (schede telefoniche), the latter available from tabacchi and newsstands in L500, L10,000, and L15,000 denominations. Cards have a small perforated corner that must be removed before use.

To make a call, simply pick up the phone, insert money or card, and then dial the number. Most call boxes have instructions in English. All calls can be made direct, without operator (call 10 if you do need the operator) or long-distance connections. Telephone numbers may have anything between seven and eleven digits. Call 12 for directory enquiries, 176 for information in English, 170 for the intercontinental operator (15 for Europe), and 172-1011 to make collect calls. Calling rates are lowest on Sundays and between 10 p.m. and 8 a.m. weekdays. Hotels always add a significant surcharge to calls made from rooms.

To call an Italian number within Italy use the full number, including the town or city code (for example, 055 in Florence). The code must also be used when calling within a city. Thus in Florence you still add the 055 code when calling another number in the city. To call an Italian number from abroad, dial the international code (011 from the United States and Canada, 00 from the U.K.) then the code for Italy (39), followed by the city code (including the initial 0) and number.

CONVERSIONS

1 kilo = 2.2 lbs
1 liter = 0.2642 U.S. gallons
1 mile = 1.6 km

Women's clothing

U.S.	8	10	12	14	16	18
Italian	40	42	44	46	48	50

Men's clothing

U.S.	36	38	40	42	44	46
Italian	46	48	50	52	54	56

Women's shoes

U.S.	6-6½	7-7½	8-8½	9-9½
Italian	38	39	40-41	42

Men's shoes

U.S.	8	8½	9½	10½	11½	12
Italian	41	42	43	44	45	46

ELECTRICITY

Electricity in Italy is 220 volts, 50 Hz, and most plugs have two (sometimes three) round pins. If you bring electrical equipment you will need a plug adapter plus a transformer for appliances.

ETIQUETTE & LOCAL CUSTOMS

Italians may have a reputation for being passionate and excitable, but they are also generally polite and considerate in social and public situations. On meeting people, or entering or leaving stores, bars, hotels and restaurants, use a simple buon giorno (good day) or buona sera (good afternoon/evening). Do not use the informal ciao (hi or goodbye) with strangers. "Please" is per favore, "thank you" grazie, and prego "you're welcome." Before a meal you might say buon appetito (eat well), to which the reply is grazie, altrettanto (thank you, and the same to you). Before a drink, the toast is salute (good health) or cin cin. Say permesso when you wish to pass people, and mi scusi if you wish to apologize, say "excuse me," or stop someone to ask for help. A woman is addressed as signora, a young woman signorina, and a man as signore.

Kissing on both cheeks as a greeting is common for men and women when you know someone well. Dress appropriately in churches, respect those at worship, and do not enter churches when services are in progress. Italians dress conservatively for almost all occasions, and unusual dress will be noticed. For help with tipping see p. 304.

Italians are generally more assertive in lines, when they form them at all, and in stores, banks, and other offices you should not expect "fairness" or for people to "wait their turn." You should be equally assertive in such situations—such pushiness is not generally considered rude in Italy.

Smoking in public places is common and generally not subject to the restrictions found in the U.S.

HOLIDAYS

Stores, banks, offices, and schools close on the following national holidays:

January 1 (New Year's Day)
January 6 (Epiphany)
Easter Sunday
Easter Monday
April 25 (Liberation Day)
May 1 (Labor Day or May Day)
August 15 (Ferragosto or Assumption)
November 1 (All Saints' Day)
December 8 (Immaculate Conception)
December 25 (Christmas)
December 26 (St. Stephen's Day)

Some cities have special holidays when businesses may close. In Florence the main city holiday is June 24 (St. John's Day).

LIQUOR LAWS

Liquor laws are far more relaxed in Italy than in North America—most bars stay open all day and late into the night—but restrictions on drunk-driving are strict and transgressions are heavily punished.

MEDIA

USEFUL PUBLICATIONS
Most Italian newspapers are sold from a street newsstand (edicola), many of which in larger cities and tourist centers also stock American, British, and other foreign language newspapers and periodicals. The International

Herald Tribune, USA Today, and most U.K. papers are available on the day of issue after about 2 p.m. Airports and railroad stations often have the largest selection of foreign publications.

Italy has a buoyant newspaper market. Among national papers, Corriere della Sera is one of the most authoritative publications, while the more populist La Repubblica is also widely read. The best-selling papers of all, however, are sports publications such as the pink Corriere dello Sport. Many papers have strong city or regional links. Florence and Tuscany's "local" paper is La Nazione. People often read a regional or city paper in preference to a national one. Local newspapers are a good source of information on forthcoming events, museum opening times, and so forth.

TELEVISION
Italian television has three main state channels—RAI 1, 2, and 3—three prominent privately owned channels (Rete Quattro, Canale 5, and Italia Uno), and a plethora of cable, local, and other private channels. In most parts of the country you can expect to have 15 or more channels. Foreign movies and shows are almost always shown dubbed into Italian, never with English subtitles, but better hotels provide access to CNN, Sky, BBC World, and other foreign stations via cable and satellite. The main RAI 1 news bulletin is at 8 p.m.

RADIO
Italian radio is generally of poor standard, although the number of stations, particularly FM music stations, is enormous. The only English-language broadcasts are those of the BBC World Service and similar organizations.

MONEY MATTERS

On January 1, 1999, the euro became the official currency of Italy, and the Italian lira (L)

became a denomination of the euro. Lira notes and coins continue to be legal tender during a transitional period. Euro bank notes and coins are to be introduced by January 2002.

Lira coins are issued in denominations of L50, L100, L200, L500, and L1000. Notes are issued in L1000, L2000, L5000, L10,000, L50,000, L100,000, and L500,000 denominations.

Most major banks, airports, and railroad stations have ATMs (Bancomat in Italian) for money cards and international credit cards (carta di credito) with instructions in a choice of languages. Arrange the four-digit "PIN" number needed to access these ATMs with your credit card company before leaving home. Currency and travelers' checks—best bought in Italian lire before you leave—can be exchanged in most banks and Bureaux de Change (cambio), but lines are often long and the procedures slow. ATMs and cambio facilities are rarer—sometimes nonexistent—in rural areas and small towns. Credit cards are accepted in hotels and restaurants in most major towns and cities. Look for Visa, Mastercard, or American Express stickers, (Diners Card is less well-known), or the Italian "Carta Sì" (Yes to Cards) sign. Many businesses still prefer cash, however, and smaller stores, hotels, and so forth, especially in rural areas, may not take cards: Always check before eating a meal or reserving a room.

American Express
Florence Via Dante Alighieri 22r, tel 055 50 981

OPENING TIMES

Opening times are a problem in Florence and Tuscany. There are few hard and fast rules, and opening times of museums and churches, in particular, can change with little or no notice. Stores, banks, and other institutions in big cities are also increasingly moving to northern European hours—that is, with no lunch and afternoon closing: Look for the words *orario continuato*. Treat the following times as a general guide only:

Banks 8:30 a.m.–1:30 p.m. Monday–Friday. Major banks may also open for an hour in the afternoon and Saturday morning. Hours are becoming longer and more flexible.

Churches 8 or 9 a.m.–noon and 3 or 4–6 or 8 p.m. excluding services; many churches close on Sunday afternoons.

Gas stations 24 hours on autostrade; store hours elsewhere (see below).

Post offices 8 or 9 a.m.–2 p.m., Monday–Saturday, but larger offices 8 or 9 a.m.–6 or 8 p.m. Monday–Saturday.

Museums State-run national museums usually close Sunday afternoon and all day Monday. Most close for lunch (1 p.m.–3 or 4 p.m.), although major museums are increasingly open 9 a.m. to 7 p.m. Winter hours are usually shorter.

Restaurants Many bars and restaurants close on Sunday evening and all day Monday or one other statutory closing day a week (*la chiusura settimanale*). Many close in January and periods in July or August.

Stores Generally 8:30 or 9 a.m.–1 p.m. and 3:30 or 4–8 p.m. Monday to Saturday. Many stores close Monday morning and another half-day a week. A few department stores and major city stores may stay open seven days a week from 9 a.m. to 8 p.m. or later (10 p.m.).

RESTROOMS

Few Italian public buildings have restrooms. Generally you need to use facilities in bars, railroad stations, and gas stations, where

standards are generally low. Ask for *il bagno*, take a few tissues to be sure, and don't confuse *Signori* (Men) with *Signore* (Women). Tip any attendants L200–500.

TIME DIFFERENCES

Italy runs on CET (Central European Time), one hour ahead of Greenwich Mean Time and six hours ahead of Eastern Standard Time. Noon in Italy is 6 a.m. in New York. Clocks change for daylight saving in May (1 hour forward) and late September or October (1 hour back). Italy uses the 24-hour clock.

TIPPING

In restaurants where a service charge (*servizio*) is not levied leave 10–15 percent: Even where it is, you may wish to leave 5–10 percent for the waiter. In bars, tip L100 or L200 for drinks consumed standing up, and L500–1000 for waiter service. In hotel bars be slightly more generous. Cab drivers merit around 10 percent. Service is included in hotel rates, but tip chambermaids and doormen about L1000 (L2000 for calling a cab), the bellhop L3000–5000 for carrying your bags, and the concierge-porter (*portiere*) about L5000–15,000 if he has been helpful. Double these figures in the most expensive hotels. Tip restroom and checkroom attendants up to L500. Porters at airports and railroad stations generally work to fixed tariffs, but tip L1000–3000 extra at your discretion. Barbers merit around L3000–4000, a hairdresser's assistant L3000–8000 depending on the level of establishment. Tip church or other custodians L2000–4000.

VISITOR CENTERS

Every Tuscan city and town—plus many villages—has a visitor center. These usually provide maps, lists of accommodations (but no reservation service),

leaflets on local sights, and lists of festivals and local cultural and other events.

The main Florence visitor center is just north of the cathedral (Duomo) at Via Cavour 1r (Tel 055 290 832 or 055 290 833, closed Sunday p.m.). There are centers just southwest of the Santa Croce church at Borgo Santa Croce 29r (Tel 055 234 0444, closed Sunday) and on the east side of the Santa Maria Novella railroad station in Piazza della Stazione (Tel 055 212 245, closed Sunday and p.m. daily). Details of local visitor centers are given in the main text of this guide.

ITALIAN STATE TOURIST OFFICES

UNITED STATES
New York
630 Fifth Avenue, Suite 1565, New York, NY 10111, tel 212/245-4822, fax 212/586-9249

Chicago
500 North Michigan Avenue, Suite 2240, Chicago, Il 60611, tel 312/644-0990, fax 312/644-3109

Los Angeles
12400 Wilshire Boulevard, Suite 550, Los Angeles, CA 90025, tel 310/820-0098, fax 310/820-6357

CANADA
Montréal
1 Place Ville-Marie, Suite 1914, Montréal PQ H3B 2C3, tel 514/866-7667, fax 514/392-1492

UNITED KINGDOM
London
1 Princes Street, London W1R 8AY, tel 020 7408-1254, fax 020 7493-6695

TRAVELERS WITH DISABILITIES

Museums, galleries, and public buildings across Italy are making great strides in providing wheelchair access, but there remains much to be done. Few buses or trains have dedicated facilities, and virtually no cabs.

Many historic cities with narrow streets and old buildings present special problems. Only hotels in higher star categories provide dedicated rooms, but hotels and restaurants will usually provide help if you call in advance. Consult your nearest Italian embassy or consulate for details of the special procedures required to bring a Seeing Eye dog into Italy.

Useful contact bodies in North America include Wheels Up! (Tel 888/389-4335), which offers discounted air fares and other travel arrangements; Access First (Tel 800/557-2047 or 617/397-8610), which specializes in Italian vacations; and information agencies dealing with travel for visitors with disabilities such as AccessAbility Travel (Tel 800/ 610-5640 or 800/228-5379), SATH (Tel 212/ 447-7284 or 447-0027), and Twin Peaks Press (Tel 206/694-2462).

EMERGENCIES

EMBASSIES IN ITALY

U.S. Embassy Via Vittorio Veneto, Rome, tel 06 46 741
U.S. Consulate Lungarno Vespucci 38, Florence, tel 055 239 8276
U.S. Consulate Via Principe Amadeo 2, Milan, tel 02 290 351
Canadian Embassy Via Zara 30, Rome, tel 06 445 981
Canadian Consulate Via Pisani 9, Milan, tel 02 67 581
U.K. Embassy Via XX Settembre 80/A, Rome, tel 06 482 5441

EMERGENCY PHONE NUMBERS

112 Police
113 Emergency Services
116 Car breakdown
118 Ambulance

For legal assistance in an emergency, contact your embassy or consulate (see above) for a list of English-speaking lawyers.

WHAT TO DO IN A TRAFFIC ACCIDENT

Put on hazard lights and place a warning triangle 165 feet (50 m) behind the car. Call the police (Tel 112 or 113) from a public phone box (see p. 302): Autostrade have emergency telephones at regular intervals. At the scene, don't admit liability or make potentially incriminating statements to police or onlookers. Ask any witnesses to remain, make a police statement, and exchange insurance and other relevant details with the other driver(s). Call the car rental agency, if necessary, to inform them of the incident.

LOST PROPERTY & CRIME

If you lose anything, go first to the local visitor center and ask for assistance. Bus, tram, train, and subway systems in cities usually have special offices to deal with lost property, but they can be hard to find and usually only open a few hours a day. Ask for directions at visitor centers, and try bus depots and railroad stations. Hotels should also provide assistance.

To report a more serious loss or theft, go to the local police station or Questura. In Florence this is at Via Zara 2 (tel 055 49 771) and in Siena in Via del Castoro, east of the cathedral.

Many police stations have special English-speaking staff to deal with visitors' problems. You will be asked to help fill in and sign a form (una denuncia) reporting any crime: Keep your copy for any possible insurance claims. Report the loss or theft of a passport to the police and then notify your embassy.

HEALTH

Make sure that your health insurance covers visits to Italy and that any travel insurance also includes sufficient medical coverage. For minor complaints visit a drugstore or pharmacy (una farmacia), indicated by a green cross outside the store. Staff are well trained and will be able to advise, as well as help in finding a doctor (un medico) if necessary. Or consult your hotel, the Yellow Pages (Pagine Galle), or visitor centers for help in finding or choosing a doctor or dentist (un dentista). The private Tourist Medical Service (Tel 055 475 411) has doctors on call 24 hours a day.

Bring enough prescription medicine (medicina) to cover your journey—brand names may be different in Italy, leading to confusion at pharmacies. If you need a prescription, pharmacies will direct you to a doctor.

For more serious complaints go to a hospital (un ospedale). Immediate treatment is provided at the Pronto Soccorso. Italian hospitals often look run down, but the standards of treatment are generally good.

Before leaving home consider contacting the International Association for Medical Assistance to Travelers (IAMAT), a nonprofit-making organization that anyone can join free of charge. Members receive a directory of English-speaking IAMAT doctors and are entitled to services at set rates (Tel 716/754-4883 in the U.S. and 416/652-0137 in Canada).

The most common minor complaints in Italy are likely to be too much sun, stomach aches, and insect bites. Italy does have poisonous snakes (vipere), although bites are generally only fatal if you have an allergic reaction. Faucet water is safe across the country, unless marked acqua non potabile. Milk is pasteurized and safe.

Hospital
Florence Santa Maria Nuova, Piazza Santa Maria Nuova 1 (Tel 055 27 581).

HOTELS & RESTAURANTS

HOTELS

Grading system

Italian hotels are officially graded from one star, the simplest accommodations, to five star (luxury). Grading criteria are complex, but in a three-star establishment and above, all rooms should have private baths, a phone, and a TV. Most two-star hotels also have private bathrooms. Note that in even the smartest hotels, bathrooms may only have a shower (una doccia) and no tub (una vasca). Always ask to see a selection of rooms—you may be shown the worst first. Rooms are often small by U.S. standards, even in smart hotels. All-day room service and air-conditioning are also comparatively rare.

Recommended hotels have a restaurant unless stated otherwise. A restaurant symbol is given where the restaurant is outstanding in its own right. Note that the term pensione, referring to private rooms or the simplest hotels, is still seen, but is no longer in use as an official designation.

Location

Hotels have been selected to provide the best centrally placed accommodations within a town or city. Noise can be a problem in many urban areas, however, and a quiet, out-of-town option is therefore often provided.

Hotels are also chosen where possible for the character, charm, and historical associations. In country areas the emphasis is on period villas and restored historic properties with pools, grounds, and gardens. Choice and quality of accommodations are generally poorer in more remote rural areas.

Reservations

It is advisable to reserve all hotels in advance, especially in the major towns, and particularly in high season (June–Aug.). Note that in Florence "high season"

often means Christmas, New Year, and Easter through October.

Reservations should be made by phone and followed by a faxed confirmation. It is also a good idea to reconfirm reservations a couple of days before arrival. Hoteliers are obliged to register every guest, so on checking in you have to hand in your passport. Usually it is returned within a few hours or on the day of departure.

Check-out times range from around 10 a.m. to noon, but you should be able to leave luggage at reception for collection later in the day.

Prices

All prices are officially set, and room rates must be displayed by law at reception and in each room. Prices for different rooms can vary within a hotel, but all taxes and services should be included in the rate.

Hotels often levy additional charges for air-conditioning and garage facilities, while laundry, drinks from mini-bars, and phone calls made from rooms invariably carry large surcharges. Price categories are for double (una matrimoniale) or twin (una camera doppia) rooms, and are given for guidance only. Seasonal variations often apply, especially in coastal resorts, where high season (summer) rates are usually higher.

At busy times there may also be a two- or three-day minimum stay policy, and you may be obliged to take full- or half-board packages. Half-board (mezza pensione) includes breakfast and lunch; full-board (pensione completa) includes all meals. Such packages are usually priced on a per person basis. Prices usually include breakfast (colazione), but where breakfast is optional (see rate cards in rooms), it always costs less to eat at the nearest coffee shop. Breakfasts in better hotels are improving—U.S.-style buffets are

now more common—but for the most part colazione means a "continental" breakfast—a coffee, a roll, and jelly.

Credit cards

Many large hotels accept all major credit cards. Smaller ones may only accept some, as shown in their entry. Abbreviations used are AE (American Express), DC (Diners Club), MC (Mastercard), V (Visa). Look for individual card symbols outside establishments or the Italian "Carta Si" (Card Yes) sign. As a general rule, AE and DC are less widely accepted than V and MC.

RESTAURANTS

Tuscany enjoys a great cuisine, and the pleasures of Italian food and wine are as much a part of a visit to the region as museums and galleries. Restaurants of different type and quality are found in every town or village, from the humble pizzeria to the venerable classics of Florence.

Our selection includes restaurants that reflect the best regional cooking available, but don't be afraid to experiment, especially in small towns. If in doubt, look for somewhere where local people are eating.

PRICES

HOTELS
An indication of the cost of a double room without breakfast is given by $ signs.

$$$$$	Over $300
$$$$	$220– $300
$$$	$160–$220
$$	$80–$160
$	Under $80

RESTAURANTS
An indication of the cost of a three-course dinner without drinks is given by $ signs.

$$$$$	Over $80
$$$$	$50–$80
$$$	$35–$50
$$	$20–$35
$	Under $20

KEY   🏨 Hotel   🍴 Restaurant   ① No. of bedrooms   ✚ No. of seats   🚌 Bus   🅿 Parking   🕐 Closed

Types of restaurant

Categories of restaurants in Italy are increasingly blurred. Once an *osteria* was a simple inn, a *trattoria* was a neighborhood eating place, and a *ristorante* was a smart establishment with culinary pretensions. Now some of the best places to eat can be *osterie*, increasingly being revamped as informal restaurants with an innovative approach to cooking. Old-fashioned trattorias with checked tablecloths are also largely things of the past—except in smaller towns off the beaten track—while *ristorante* is a term now applied to just about any eating place. A pizzeria *(una pizzeria)* remains the one constant—a simple place that often serves basic pastas, main courses, and desserts as well as pizzas. Wherever you eat, remember that neither price nor a restaurant's smartness necessarily reflect the quality of the food. A pizza in a boisterous pizzeria may be every bit as good—and as memorable—as a five-course feast in a sleek Florentine hotel restaurant full of businesspeople.

Dining hours

Breakfast *(colazione)* is usually a cappuccino and a bread roll or sweet pastry *(una brioche)* taken standing up in a bar between 7 and 9 a.m. Lunch *(pranzo)* starts around 12.30 p.m. and finishes at about 2 p.m.—the long lunch and siesta are increasingly a thing of the past. Dinner *(cena)* begins about 8 p.m., with last orders around 10 p.m., although dinner hours may be earlier in rural areas and smaller towns.

Pizzerias often only open in the evenings, especially those with wood-fuel ovens *(forno a legno)* that take time to fire. Most eating places close one day a week *(la chiusura settimanale)*, and many take long vacation breaks *(ferie)* in July or August.

Meals

Italian meals traditionally start with appetizers *(antipasti*—literally "before the meal"), a first course of soup, pasta, or rice *(il primo)*, and a main course of meat or fish *(il secondo)*. Vegetables *(contorni)* or salads *(insalata)* are often served separately, with or after the secondo. Desserts *(dolci)* may include, or be followed by, fruit *(frutta)* and cheese *(formaggio)*. You needn't indulge in every stage, of course—a primo and salad is acceptable in all but the smartest restaurants. Many Italians choose to go to an ice-cream parlor *(gelateria)* as part of an after-dinner stroll instead of dessert.

Meals are usually accompanied by bread and mineral water, for which you pay extra.

Set menus

The menu in Italian is *il menù* or *la lista*. Set-price menus are available in many restaurants in tourist areas. The *menù turistico* usually includes two courses, a simple dessert, and half a bottle of wine and water per person. Quantities and quality of food are invariably poor. Of better value in more upscale restaurants is the *menù gastronomico*, where you pay a set price to sample a selection of the restaurant's special dishes.

Bars, cafés, & snacks

Bars and cafés are perfect for breakfast and often provide snacks such as filled rolls *(panini)* or sandwiches *(tramezzini)* through the day. A few may offer a light meal at lunch. Kiosks or small stores selling slices of pizza are common and good for food on the go.

It always costs less to stand at the bar. Specify what you want and pay at the separate cash desk *(la cassa)*, then take your chit *(lo scontrino)* to the bar and repeat your order. A small coin as a tip placed on the bar often helps secure prompt service. Where a bar has a waiter and tables, especially outside tables, you pay more to sit and give your order to the waiter. Only in small rural bars can you pay at the bar and then sit down.

Wine bars *(enoteche)* are becoming more common. All serve wine by the glass or bottle, often in informal surroundings, and most provide bread, cheeses, other snacks, and light meals. A *birreria*, or beer cellar, is similar, but usually appeals to a younger generation.

Paying

The check *(il conto)* must be presented to you by law as a formal receipt. A price scrawled on a piece of paper is illegal, and you are within your rights to demand an itemized *recevuta*. Bills once included a cover charge *(pane e coperto)*, a practice the authorities are trying to outlaw. Many restaurants attempt to get around the law by charging for bread brought to your table whether you want it or not. Smaller and rural restaurants are less likely to accept credit cards, and it can be worth checking if your card is acceptable, even in places with card signs outside.

Tipping & dress

Tip between 10 and 15 percent where service has been good and where a service charge *(servizio)* is not included. As a rule, Italians dress well but informally to eat out, especially in better restaurants. A relaxed casual style is a good rule of thumb: Jacket and tie for men are rarely necessary, but often the better dressed you are, the better service you can expect.

Smoking

Smoking is common in Italy, and there are very few nonsmoking areas in restaurants. Italians will be unlikely to move or desist from smoking if you protest.

The hotels and restaurants listed here have been grouped first according to their area (in Florence) or region, then listed alphabetically by price category. For disabled access, check with the establishment to verify the extent of their facilities.

L = lunch   D = dinner

FLORENCE

PIAZZA DEL DUOMO

HOTELS

🏨 BRUNELLESCHI
$$$$–$$$$$ ✪✪✪✪
PIAZZA SANTA ELISABETTA 3
TEL 055 290 311
FAX 055 219 653
The location of this fascinating hotel, just off the main Via dei Calzaiuoli, could hardly be more central. Designed by leading Italian architect Italo Gamberini, it has been stylishly converted from a Byzantine chapel and fifth-century tower (the latter is one of the city's oldest surviving structures). Old brick and stone have been preserved in the public areas and complemented by the tasteful use of wood, while the rooms are bright, airy, and comfortable.
🛏 88 + 8 suites 🚌 23, A 🅿 🔄 🔲 All major cards

🏨 CASCI
$$ ✪✪
VIA CAVOUR 13
TEL 055 211 686
FAX 055 239 6461
This excellent two-star hotel is the best in its class and enjoys a perfect position just two minutes' walk north of the cathedral. Rooms are modest in size, but immaculate and modern, and the courtesy and welcome of the multi-lingual family owners is faultless. Buffet breakfast but no restaurant.
🛏 25 🚌 1, 6, 7, 14, 23 🔄 🔲 All major cards

RESTAURANTS

🍽 CAFFÈ GILLI
$
PIAZZA DELLA REPUBBLICA 36–39r
TEL 055 213 896
Piazza della Repubblica is a vast, characterless square distinguished only by its four historic cafés, of which Gilli is the best. Founded in 1733, it moved to its present corner site in 1910, the date of its magnificent belle epoque interior. Its large terrace is a fine place for an aperitif as you watch the Florentines on early evening parade.
🚌 A 🕐 Closed Tues. 🔲 All major cards

🍽 CANTINETTA DEI VERRAZZANO
$
VIA DEI TAVOLINI 18–20r
TEL 055 268 590
An unmissable place just off the main Via dei Calzaiuoli for take-out snacks, cakes, or slices of pizza, or a more leisurely lunch and glass of wine at the tables to the rear. Choose from the array of food under the huge glass-fronted display. The Cantinetta is owned by a notable Chianti vineyard, so the wines are as good as the food.
🚌 A 🕐 Closed Sun. & Aug. 🔲 All major cards

🍽 PERCHÈ NO!
$
VIA DEI TAVOLINI 19r
TEL 055 239 8969
The only serious alternative to Vivoli (see p. 309) for ice cream in Florence. It's been in business since 1939 and has a varying menu of around 30 flavors from a repertoire of almost 60.
🚌 A 🕐 Closed Tues. in winter, Tues. p.m. in summer

EASTERN FLORENCE

HOTELS

🏨 J & J
$$$$ ✪✪✪✪
VIA DI MEZZO 20
TEL 055 234 005
FAX 055 240 282
This converted 15th-century convent appears bland from the outside, but within reveals itself as a beautifully romantic little hotel. Patches of old fresco and vaulted ceilings distinguish the public areas, while the rooms—which vary in size and decor—combine fine fabrics, modern fittings, and an array of antiques. The hotel is located away from the throng in the Sant'Ambrogio district, but within easy walking distance of all the sights. No restaurant.
🛏 14 + 5 suites 🅿 🔲 ♿ 🔲 All major cards

🏨 MONNA LISA
$$$$ ✪✪✪✪
BORGO PINTI 27
TEL 055 247 9751
FAX 055 247 9755
A somber facade conceals a marvelous 14th-century palazzo complete with sweeping staircase, frescoed ceilings, and terra-cotta floors. Rooms vary in size but preserve an aristocratic, old-world feel, with oil paintings and antiques. Some overlook a peaceful rear garden, others an inner courtyard.
🛏 30 🚌 14, 23, A 🅿 🔲 🔲 All major cards

RESTAURANTS

SOMETHING SPECIAL

🍽 ENOTECA PINCHIORRI
Florence's best and most expensive restaurant has two Michelin stars and—at over 80,000 bottles—one of Europe's finest wine cellars. The setting—a Renaissance palazzo with lofty frescoed ceilings—and Tuscan-international cuisine are predictably chic and sophisticated, although the formality and ceremony may not be to all tastes. Food is exquisite but comes in modest portions. Jacket and tie recommended for men.
$$$$$
VIA GHIBELLINA 87
TEL 055 242 777
🪑 80 🚌 14 🕐 Closed Sun., Mon., & Wed. L, & Aug. 🔲 All major cards

---

❚❙ ALLE MURATTE
$$$$
VIA GHIBELLINA 52R
TEL 055 240 618

Don't be put off by an initial reception that can border on the brusque, for once inside this intimate restaurant you are treated to some of the city's most innovative cooking. Standards can vary, and some dishes are more successful than others—eat à la carte or opt for one of two set "gastronomic menus." Desserts are especially good—so leave room—as is the wine list, which contains some 150 mainly Tuscan vintages.

🍴 65 🛏 14 🕐 Closed Mon. ❄ 💳 All major cards

❚❙ CIBREO
$$$–$$$$
VIA DE' MACCI 118
TEL 055 234 1100

Cibreo is the first choice of most Florentine gastronomes and the best place in the city to enjoy creative interpretations of traditional Tuscan dishes such as *trippa in insalata* (a cold tripe salad—better than it sounds) and the celebrated *fegato brasato* (braised liver). The dining room is plain, with simple wooden tables and painted walls, and the service and atmosphere are relaxed and informal. Prices are set for each course—be sure to leave room for the mouthwatering desserts. Reservations several days in advance are essential.

🍴 70 🛏 14, A 🅿
🕐 Closed Sun. & Mon. ❄
💳 All major cards

❚❙ PAOLI
$$$
VIA DEI TAVOLINI 12r
TEL 055 216 215

A tempting place to eat at the very heart of the city (just off Via dei Calzaiuoli), although the temptation is not so much the food, which is a mixture of Tuscan grilled meats, pastas

and soups, as the beautiful frescoed dining room—one of the oldest and most beautiful in the city.

🍴 85 🛏 A 🕐 Closed Tues. & Aug. ❄ 💳 All major cards

❚❙ BALDOVINO
$$–$$$
VIA SAN GIUSEPPE 22r
TEL 055 241 773

This bustling, innovative, and pleasantly chic restaurant just behind Santa Croce offers pizzas made in traditional Neapolitan style in wood-fired ovens or a choice of well-cooked Tuscan pasta and meat dishes. Its success is the more remarkable given that it is run by foreigners—a young Scottish couple who has also opened a wine bar and food store across the street.

🍴 130 🛏 14, 23 🕐 Closed Mon. 💳 All major cards

❚❙ CAFFÈ ITALIANO
$$–$$$
VIA ISOLE DELLE STINCHE 11–13r
TEL 055 289 368

This restaurant divides into three: A formal restaurant, a wine bar for snacks and lighter meals, and a simple trattoria for lunches and less formal dining. All serve well-priced Tuscan food and have a fine medieval setting, with vast beams, brick vaults, terra-cotta floors, and pretty wooden cabinets.

🍴 50–120 🛏 23
🕐 Closed Mon. 💳 All major cards

❚❙ OSTERIA DE' BENCI
$$
VIA DE' BENCI 13r
TEL 055 234 4923

A busy dining room painted in pastel colors that give a fresh, modern air. Staff are young, energetic, and informal, and the food offers well-cooked takes on Tuscan staples such as *zuppa di verdura* (vegetable soup) and *agnello scottaditto* (grilled lamb).

🍴 50–80 🛏 13, 23, B
🕐 Closed Sun. & some of Aug. ❄ 💳 All major cards

❚❙ CAFFÈ RIVOIRE
$
PIAZZA DELLA SIGNORIA 55
TEL 055 214 412

Rivoire was founded in 1827 as a bar specializing in hot chocolate. Today, it is the city's premier central café, its position on Piazza della Signoria ensuring it is constantly full. High prices and mass tourism, however, have somewhat tarnished its allure.

🛏 A 🕐 Closed Mon.

❚❙ RUGGINI
$
VIA DEI NERI 76r
TEL 055 214 521

A bar and *pasticceria* (pastry shop) with a sensational selection of chocolates, cakes, and other goodies. At the bar (no seating) you can buy bowls of pasta at lunch.

🛏 B 🕐 Closed Sun. p.m. & Mon.

❚❙ VIVOLI
$
VIA ISOLE DELLE STINCHE 7r
TEL 055 292 334

A visit to this *gelateria*—a Florentine institution—is as essential as a visit to the Uffizi. Many claim its ice cream is the best in Italy, and if that's per-haps pitching things too high, there's no disputing its posi-tion as the best in Florence. It lies in a hard-to-find little street off Via Ghibellina just west of Piazza Santa Croce.

🛏 23 🕐 Closed Sun. p.m. & Mon.

NORTHERN FLORENCE

HOTELS

🏨 LOGGIATA DEI SERVITI
$$$ 000
PIAZZA SS ANNUNZIATA 3
TEL 055 289 592
FAX 055 289 595

🛗 Elevator ❄ Air-conditioning 🏊 Indoor/🏊 Outdoor swimming pool 💪 Health club 💳 Credit cards   **KEY**

This hotel occupies a former convent building in a distinguished square designed by leading Renaissance architect Filippo Brunelleschi. Rooms vary in style, but all have tasteful, understated lines and decor that recalls the simplicity of the original structure. Some have vaulted ceilings and canopy beds, and all are enlivened by rich fabrics and pieces of period furniture.

ⓘ 25 + 4 suites 🚌 6, 31, 32 🅿 🔄 ♿ ⛰ All major cards

🏨 MORANDI ALLA CROCETTA
$$$ ✿✿✿
VIA LAURA 50
TEL 055 234 4747
FAX 055 248 0954
A quiet and intimate hotel—part of a former monastery—near Piazza SS Annunziata. This is a gem, thanks to both the charm and friendly welcome of the owner, and the considerable style with which she has decorated individual rooms and public spaces. Colorful rugs cover polished wooden floors, and old prints and antiques decorate the walls. No restaurant. Reserve well in advance.

ⓘ 10 🚌 6, 31, 32 ♿ ⛰ All major cards

🏨 HOTEL BELLETTINI
$$ ✿✿
VIA DEI CONTI 7
TEL 055 213 561
FAX 055 283 551
More than a hint of the 19th century pervades this central and friendly hotel, with the type of terra-cotta floors and wood-beamed ceilings you would expect of a period Florentine town house. Rooms can be a little spartan but are spotless—the two on the top floor have views—and the staff are unfailingly helpful.

ⓘ 28 🚌 11, 12 🅿 🔄 ♿ ⛰ All major cards

RESTAURANTS

🍴 CASA DEL VINO
$
VIA DELL'ARIENTO 16r
TEL 055 215 609
Although close to busy San Lorenzo market and the Mercato Centrale, few foreigners frequent this lively wine bar. But the locals are friendly, so come here for a glass of wine with a selection of rustic snacks (breads, ham, sandwiches, and cheeses).

🚌 7, 10, 11, 12, 25, 32, 33 to Via Nazionale 🔄 Closed Sat. p.m., Sun.

🍴 NERBONE
$
MERCATO CENTRALE
TEL 055 219 949
Nowhere is better than Nerbone for a taste of local color and robust Florentine food. This little place is a combination of food stall and diner, and has been in business in a corner of the Mercato Centrale, the city's main covered market, since 1872. It's always full of market traders and shoppers.

🚌 7, 10, 11, 12, 25, 32, 33 to Via Nazionale 🔄 Closed Sun. & p.m. Mon.–Sat.

WESTERN FLORENCE

HOTELS

🏨 EXCELSIOR
$$$$$ ✿✿✿✿✿
PIAZZA OGNISSANTI 3
TEL 055 264 201
FAX 055 210 278
Florence's second grandest hotel is undermined only by its position on one of the city's less attractive piazzas. Otherwise the antique-filled rooms are visions of traditional elegance, while the public areas—all marble columns and ornate ceilings—are on a sumptuous scale. More regal and old-world than the Grand, the rival hotel right across the square.

ⓘ 146 +7 suites 🚌 12, B 🅿 🔄 ♿ ⛰ All major cards

🏨 HELVETIA & BRISTOL
$$$$$ ✿✿✿✿✿
VIA DEI PESCIONI 2
TEL 055 287 814
FAX 055 288 353
First choice in Florence if money is no object. Luxurious and exclusive, this superb hotel has been in business since the 18th century. Facilities and bathrooms are state of the art, but rooms are in a more sober, traditional style with antiques and old paintings. Some rooms are relatively small.

ⓘ 34 + 18 suites 🚌 A 🅿 🔄 ♿ ⛰ All major cards

🏨 HERMITAGE
$$$ ✿✿✿
VICOLO MARZIO 1–PIAZZA DEL PESCE
TEL 055 287 216
FAX 055 212 208
This is one of Florence's most popular small hotels, thanks largely to its position close to the Ponte Vecchio, friendly service, and good facilities. Rooms are cozy and intimate—bathrooms can be a touch small—and adorned

with the occasional antique. Some rooms enjoy river views but can be noisy, despite double-glazing. The garden roof terrace where you can take breakfast in summer is a major plus.

[I] 28 [B] [P] [⇄] [S]
[S] All major cards

[m] PORTA ROSSA
$$–$$$ ❊❊❊
VIA PORTA ROSSA 19
TEL 055 287 551
FAX 055 282 179
One of Italy's oldest inns, dating from 1386, has played host to the likes of poet Lord Byron and French writer Stendhal. Today, you are paying for a good central location and sense of history, as the rooms, while large, are relatively plain. The vaulted lobby has period leather couches and stained glass.

[I] 85 [B] [P] [⇄] [S] All major cards

RESTAURANTS

[¶] OLIVIERO
$$$
VIA DELLE TERME 51R
TEL 055 212 421
Oliviero shares with Cibreo (see p. 309) a reputation for excellent regional cooking with a twist, but unlike its rival it also offers fish and seafood. Typical dishes might include *tagliatelle all'ortica* (pasta with a green nettle sauce) or pigeon with a purée of peas and potato. The ambience has a strangely dated feel, but it is warm and welcoming.

[¶] 80 [B] [C] [S] Closed Sun. & Aug. [S] [S] All major cards

[¶] BELLE DONNE
$–$$
VIA DELLE BELLE DONNE 16r
TEL 055 238 2609
The tiny Belle Donne is a good spot for lunch. Cascades of fruit and flowers provide a backdrop to a handful of shared paper-covered tables. Daily specials, Tuscan to a

fault, are posted on a blackboard. The service is informal, the atmosphere lively.

**[¶] 55 [6, 11, 36, 37 [P]
[C] Closed Sat., Sun. & Aug.
[S] All major cards**

[¶] ROSE'S
$–$$
VIA DEL PARIONE 26r
TEL 055 287 090
Imagine a sleek, New York designer bar given a Florentine makeover and you have Rose's, a perfect place for lunch, coffee, afternoon tea, light supper, or late-night drinks. It provides a welcome contrast to the wood and terra-cotta interiors of many Florentine restaurants.

[¶] 60 [A, B [C] Closed Sun. [S] All major cards

[¶] CAFFÈ AMERINI
$
VIA DELLA VIGNA NUOVA 63r
TEL 055 284 941
The interior at Amerini combines modern splashes of color and design with art deco mirrors and medieval brick ceilings. Customers are eclectic—elderly locals, shoppers, students—attracted by the excellent lunch salads, snacks, and sandwiches.

**[6, 11, 12, 36, 37
[C] Closed Sun.**

[¶] CAFFÈ MEGARA
$
VIA DELLA SPADA 15–17r
TEL 055 211 837
The Megara is similar to the Amerini (see above), in that it attracts a local crowd at lunch. Breakfast is good here, as are the snacks and Happy Hour cocktails (5–8 p.m.), but the main attractions are the light lunches. Open until 2 a.m.

**[6, 11, 12, 36, 37
[C] Closed Sun.**

[¶] CAPOCACCIA
$
LUNGARNO CORSINI 12–14r
TEL 055 210 751
A smart combination of café, bistro, and bar—and a haunt of

stylish and cosmopolitan locals by day and night—it's been voted the Florentines' favorite night-time rendezvous. Don't be put off by the busy roadside position. Coffee, drinks, snacks, and light meals are available in the pretty wood and blue-tiled interior.

[B] [C] Closed Mon. p.m.

[¶] GIACOSA
$
VIA DE' TORNABUONI 83r
TEL 055 239 6226
Take a break from shopping in Giacosa, once the favored retreat of Florence's 19th-century beau-monde, and still stylish. A sister café to Rivoire (see p. 309), it serves the same excellent chocolate and cakes, although it is best known for its Negroni cocktail.

**[6, 11, 12, 36, 37
[C] Closed Sun.**

[¶] ZANOBINI
$
VIA SANT'ANTONINO 47r
TEL 055 239 6850
Like the nearby Casa del Vino (see p. 310), this is an old wood-paneled wine bar that sees few foreign visitors. Sip a glass of wine with a rough and ready hunk of bread and cheese, or buy a bottle at the rear of the bar.

[7, 10, 11, 12, 25, 32, 33 to Via Nazionale [C] Closed Sun.

OLTRARNO

HOTELS

[m] LUNGARNO
$$$$ ❊❊❊❊
BORGO SAN JACOPO 14
TEL 055 27 261
FAX 055 268 437
The Lungarno, as its name suggests, stands on the banks of the Arno in the Oltrarno district, but not all rooms enjoy river views (request these when you reserve). The bar, restaurant, and sitting

area, however, have views of the water. Bedrooms are not large but are tastefully decorated: Those in the hotel's medieval tower have rugged stone walls.
🛈 57 + 12 suites 🚌 11, 36, 37 🅿 🔄 🛗 🚭 All major cards

RESTAURANTS

🍴 ALLE VECCHIA BETTOLA
$$–$$$
VIALE LUDOVICO ARIOSTO 32–34r
TEL 055 224 158
Historically, a *bettola* was a simple Florentine eating place. Opened in 1979, this family-run restaurant continues the tradition, with plain Tuscan cuisine—hearty soups, pastas, and grilled meat—in rustic surroundings (tiled walls and lots of hanging fruits and hams). You sit on benches, eat off marble tables, and pay for wine from the flask by the amount you drink. The menu changes daily, but among the regulars the cured hams and *carpaccio* (sliced beef) are outstanding. Ice cream comes from Vivoli (see p. 309).
🪑 50–85 🚌 6, D 🕐 Closed Sun., Mon., & 3 weeks Aug. 🚭 All major cards

🍴 ANGIOLINO
$$–$$$
VIA SANTO SPIRITO 36r
TEL 055 239 8976
Angiolino is an old school trattoria: festoons of dried flowers, chilies, and pumpkins hang from the ceiling; wicker-covered Chianti bottles and red-checked tablecloths add another traditional touch. Cooking is good, and Florentine in flavor, with appetizers such as *crostini* (small toasts with liver or olive paste) and hearty soups such as *ribollita* and *pappa al pomodoro*.
🪑 95 🚌 11, 36, 37 🕐 Closed Mon. 🛗 🚭 All major cards

🍴 BECCOFINO
$$–$$$
PIAZZA DEGLI SCARLETTI 1
TEL 055 290 076
The success of Baldovino (see p. 309) has prompted owner David Gardner to open this new restaurant on a small square near the Arno in a building that had previously been a gallery and mosque. The approach here is the same as at Baldovino: Good, modern Tuscan cooking—anything from a gourmet salad to steaks and organic coffee and homemade cakes—fair prices, and lively and informal surroundings. There is also a wine bar with a good choice of snacks, sandwiches, and wines by the glass.
🪑 100 🚌 6, D 🛗 🚭 All major cards

🍴 FUORI PORTA
$
VIA MONTE ALLE CROCI 10r
TEL 055 234 2483
This celebrated wine bar—Florence's most famous—is perfectly situated in the Oltrarno as a refreshment stop on the walk to the church of San Miniato al Monte (see pp. 182–83). It's always busy, thanks to over 600 wines by the bottle, 40 by the glass (the selection changes regularly), and the excellent range of snacks and Tuscan bread laden with a variety of savory toppings.
🚌 12, 13 🕐 Closed Sun.

🍴 HEMINGWAY
$
PIAZZA PIATTELLINA 9r, OFF PIAZZA DEL CARMINE
TEL 055 284 781
This café in the Oltrarno breaks the Florentine mold with its modern and stylish decor. It specializes in all forms of chocolate, plus more than 20 different coffees and many teas, including cream teas and tea cocktails such as Victoria Tea—milk, vanilla tea, and Southern Comfort.
🚌 D

🍴 LE VOLPI E L'UVA
$
PIAZZA DEI ROSSI 1r
TEL 055 239 8132
A discreet wine bar tucked away just off Piazza Santa Felicità a little way south of the Ponte Vecchio. It offers a well-chosen and interesting selection of regularly changing wines and a first-rate selection of cheese and snacks as an accompaniment.
🚌 B, D 🕐 Closed Mon. & 1 week in Aug. 🚭 AE, MC, V

OUTER FLORENCE

🏨 GRAND HOTEL VILLA CORA
$$$$$ 😊😊😊😊😊
VIALE NICCOLÒ MACHIAVELLI 18
TEL 055 229 8451
FAX 055 229 086
This is a luxury hotel in the grand old style and was once home to Napoleon III's wife, the Empress Eugénie. Its modest size, 19th-century villa interior—full of rich stucco and glass chandeliers from Murano—and pretty gardens enable it to preserve the feel of a private country house. It lies close to the Porta Romana to the south of the city. A courtesy car service to the center is provided. Rooms vary in style from lavish and ornate, with richly draped beds, to the more classical and restrained.
🛈 33 + 15 suites 🚌 12,13 🅿 🔄 🛗 🏊 🚭 All major cards

🏨 TORRE DI BELLOSGUARDO
$$$–$$$$$ 😊😊😊😊
VIA ROTI MICHELOZZI 2
TEL 055 229 8145
FAX 055 229 008
Florence's finest hotel if you wish to be away—but not too far away—from the city center. This Renaissance villa hotel lies among hill-top gardens with lovely views, about five minutes' drive south of the Oltrarno. The

lofty public spaces are vaulted, frescoed, and dotted with vast stone fireplaces, creating a historic atmosphere, while the spacious rooms are individually decorated in a suitably old-fashioned manner. Breakfast and light meals served, but no restaurant.
ⓘ 10 + 6 suites 🅿 ⬍
🅢 3 rooms only 🖼 🅢 All major cards

TUSCANY

SIENA

SOMETHING SPECIAL

🏨 CERTOSA DI MAGGIANO
Favored by honeymoon and anniversary couples, this magnificent converted 14th-century abbey on beautiful grounds 2 miles (3 km) east of Siena is one of central Italy's finest and most romantic hotels. Antiques and paintings grace the elegant rooms and the atmosphere is unhurried and relaxing.
$$$$$ ✦✦✦✦
STRADA DI CERTOSA 82
TEL 0577 288 180
FAX 0577 288 189
ⓘ 6 rooms + 11 suites 🅿
🅢 🖼 🅢 All major cards

🏨 VILLA SCACCIAPENSIERI
$$$$ ✦✦✦✦
VIA DI SACCIAPENSIERI 10
TEL 0577 41 441
FAX 0577 270 854
This peaceful hotel occupies a 19th-century hilltop villa about 2 miles (3 km) north of the city. Facilities include tennis courts and swimming pool, and there are lovely gardens.
ⓘ 27 + 4 suites 🅿 ⬍
🅢 🖼 🅢 All major cards

🏨 ANTICA TORRE
$$–$$$ ✦✦✦
VIA FIERAVECCHIA 7
TEL 0577 222255
FAX 0577 222255

Siena's most appealing small hotel has just eight rooms squeezed into an old medieval tower *(torre)* a few minutes' walk southeast of the historic center. No restaurant.
ⓘ 8 🅢 All major cards

🏨 DUOMO
$$–$$$ ✦✦✦
VIA STALLOREGGI 38
TEL 0577 289 088
FAX 0577 43 043
Siena has few good, central hotels in the upper and mid-range. Rooms here are unexceptional, but the position is perfect. No restaurant.
ⓘ 23 ⬍ 🅢 🅢 All major cards

🏨 PALAZZO RAVIZZA
$$–$$$ ✦✦✦✦
VIA PIAN DEI MANTELLINI 34
TEL 0577 280 462
FAX 0577 221 597
Siena's most charming mid-range hotel occupies an 18th-century palace on the edge of the center. It retains many old features and original antiques.
ⓘ 38 🅿 ⬍ 🅢 🅢 All major cards

🍴 ANTICA TRATTORIA BOTTEGANOVA
$$$$
VIA CHIANTIGIANA 29
TEL 0577 284 230
A formal restaurant whose sublime food has earned a Michelin star, but you have to go just beyond the city walls to enjoy it. Signature dishes include *tortelli di pecorino con fonduta di parmigiano e tartufo*, cheese-filled pasta topped with truffle-scented sauce. Less expensive at lunch.
🍴 50 🅿 🕐 Closed Mon. 🅢 🅢 All major cards

🍴 AL MANGIA
$$$
PIAZZA DEL CAMPO 42
TEL 0577 281 121
The best of the mostly over-priced restaurants on Italy's greatest piazza. The setting here takes precedence over all culinary concerns.

🍴 40–150 🕐 Closed Feb., Mon. except April–Oct.
🅢 All major cards

🍴 ANTICA TRATTORIA PAPEI
$$–$$$
PIAZZA DEL MERCATO 6
TEL 0577 280 894
Good food at reasonable prices is served at this little trattoria in the market square behind the Campo.
🍴 100 inside, 100 outside
🕐 Closed Mon. 🅢 All major cards

🍴 CAMPANE
$$–$$$
VIA DELLE CAMPANE 6
TEL 0577 284 035
Voted the city's favorite restaurant in a readers' poll in the local newspaper. It's unusual for Siena, in offering fish and seafood dishes.
🍴 40–60 🕐 Closed Mon. in winter 🅢 🅢 All major cards

🍴 LE LOGGE
$$–$$$
VIA DEL PORRIONE 33
TEL 0577 48 013
No Sienese restaurant is prettier than this former medieval pharmacy just off the Campo, complete with period furniture and fittings. Innovative but occasionally hit-and-miss Sienese cuisine.
🍴 40–80 🕐 Closed Sun., plus some of June & Nov.
🅢 🅢 AE, DC

🍴 MARSILI
$$–$$$
VIA DEL CASTORO 3
TEL 0577 47 154
This attractive old restaurant has medieval touches in its large, formal dining room and reliable regional cooking.
🍴 80–140 🕐 Closed Mon.
🅢 🅢 All major cards

🍴 IL GHIBELLINO
$$
VIA DEI PELLEGRINI 26
TEL 0577 288 079
A simple and stylish trattoria,

HOTELS & RESTAURANTS

with marble-topped tables, terra-cotta tiles, and wooden beams, that serves Tuscan food in a relaxed setting. Fish is a specialty on Thursdays and Fridays.
🍴 60 🕐 Closed Mon. 🖪 All major cards

NORTHERN TUSCANY

CHIANTI

🏨 CASTELLO DI 🍴 SPALTENNA
$$$-$$$$ ✪✪✪✪
PIEVE DI SPALTENNA, GAIOLE IN CHIANTI
TEL 0577 749 483
FAX 0577 749 269
A splendid former castle-monastery on the outskirts of Gaiole. Buildings and rooms retain many medieval features. The first-rate restaurant occupies the old refectory.
🛏 26 🅿 🕐 Closed Jan.–mid-March, restaurant closed Mon. L 🖪 🚌 🖪 All major cards

🏨 RELAIS FATTORIA VIGNALE
$$$-$$$$ ✪✪✪✪
VIA PIANIGIANI 8, RADDA IN CHIANTI
TEL 0577 738 300
FAX 0577 738 592
A roadside setting makes this hotel less enticing than some Chianti hotels, but the gardens and rooms in the old farm-house with their simple country furniture more than compensate. No restaurant.
🛏 34 🅿 🕐 Closed Jan.–March 🖪 🚌 🖪 All major cards

🏨 TENUTA DI RICAVO 🍴
$$$-$$$$ ✪✪✪✪
LOCALITÀ RICAVO 4, CASTELLINA IN CHIANTI
TEL 0577 740 221
FAX 0577 741 014
In the country 2 miles (3 km) outside Castellina, this lovely converted medieval hamlet is perfect as a place to relax. The Pecora Nera restaurant

serves refined Tuscan cuisine.
🛏 23 🅿 🕐 Closed Oct.–April, restaurant closed Tues. & Wed. 🚌 🖪 All major cards

🍴 BADIA A COLTIBUONO
$$$
BADIA A COLTIBUONO (3 MILES/5 KM NE FROM GAIOLE)
TEL 0577 749 031
Housed in the refectory of a restored monastery (founded 770), this famous restaurant forms part of a family-owned Chianti vineyard and estate.
🍴 65–110 🅿 🕐 Closed Jan.–Feb. plus Mon. in winter 🖪 🖪 All major cards

COLLE DI VAL D'ELSA

🏨 ARNOLFO 🍴 $$$
VIA XX SETTEMBRE 52
TEL 0577 922 020
FAX 0577 922 324
The cooking here has earned a Michelin star. In summer eat the sophisticated Italian food on the terrace with lovely views of the surrounding hills.
🛏 4 🍴 24–36 🅿 🕐 Closed Tues. & some of Jan., Feb., & Aug. 🖪 🖪 All major cards

FIESOLE

SOMETHING SPECIAL

🏨 VILLA SAN MICHELE
One of Tuscany's finest hotels, this is a good alternative to staying in Florence. The villa was supposedly designed by Michelangelo, and most of the antiques are 17th-century originals. Lovely parks and gardens, and sweeping views of the countryside.
$$$$$ ✪✪✪✪
VIA DOCCIA 4
TEL 055 59 451
FAX 055 598 734
🛏 25 + 15 suites 🅿 🕐 Closed Nov.–mid-March 🖪 🖪 🚌 🖪 All major cards

PRICES

HOTELS
An indication of the cost of a double room without breakfast is given by $ signs.
$$$$$	Over $300
$$$$	$220–$300
$$$	$160–$220
$$	$80–$160
$	Under $80

RESTAURANTS
An indication of the cost of a three-course dinner without drinks is given by $ signs.
$$$$$	Over $80
$$$$	$50–$80
$$$	$35–$50
$$	$20–$35
$	Under $20

LUCCA

🏨 LOCANDA L'ELISA
$$$$$ ✪✪✪✪✪
VIA NUOVA, MASSA PISANA
TEL 0583 379 737
FAX 0583 379 019
A superlative luxury hotel in a neoclassic villa 2 miles (3 km) south of Lucca on the road to Pisa. It has just two rooms and eight sumptuous suites, plus lush gardens, discreet service, and a dazzling collection of antiques and furniture.
🛏 10 🅿 🖪 🚌 🖪 All major cards

🏨 LA LUNA
$$ ✪✪✪
VIA FILLUNGO-CORTE COMPAGNI 12
TEL 0583 493 634
FAX 0583 490 021
A family-run hotel in a sleepy courtyard just off old Lucca's main street. No restaurant.
🛏 30 🅿 🕐 Closed some of Jan. 🖪 All major cards

🏨 PICCOLO HOTEL PUCCINI
$$ ✪✪✪
VIA DI POGGIO 9
TEL 0583 55 421
FAX 0583 53 487

Bright, tasteful rooms in a Renaissance palace at the heart of the old city. Private parking must be requested in advance. No restaurant.
🛈 14 🅿 🚫 All major cards

🍴 LA MORA
$$$
VIA SESTO DI PONTE A MORIANO 1748
TEL 0583 406 402
A Michelin star underlines the quality of La Mora's cooking, the region's best. To enjoy its sublime Lucchese dishes travel 5 miles (8 km) northwest of Lucca to the hamlet of Ponte a Moriano.
🍴 40–60 🅿 🕐 Closed Wed. plus some of Jan. & June 🚫 All major cards

🍴 BUCA DI SANT'ANTONIO
$$
VIA DELLA CERVIA 3
TEL 0583 55881
Established in 1787, this is the best of Lucca's city-center restaurants. Cooking is based on old Lucchese traditions but is unafraid of innovation. Try the celebrated *semifreddo buccellatto*, a mix of chilled cream and wild berries.
🍴 90 🕐 Closed Sun. D, all Mon., & some of July 🔆 🚫 All major cards

🍴 OSTERIA BARALLA
$$
VIA ANFITEATRO 59
TEL 0583 440 240
Lighter cooking here than in some Lucchese restaurants: The *antipasti* (appetizers) are good, as are the grilled meats and chocolate tart (*crostata*).
🍴 80 🕐 Closed Sun. 🚫 All major cards

🍴 CAFFÈ DI SIMO
$
VIA FILLUNGO 58
TEL 0583 496 234
Lucca's loveliest café has a fine belle époque interior that has played host to many famous names, among them Puccini.

Wonderful for cakes, pastries, coffee, and light snacks and sandwiches.
🕐 Closed Mon. 🔆 🚫 All major cards

PISA

🏨 ROYAL VICTORIA
$$–$$$ ◗◗◗
LUNGARNO PACINOTTI 12
TEL 050 940 111
FAX 050 940 180
The Royal stands out among Pisa's mostly modern hotels. Beside the Arno, ten minutes' walk from the Leaning Tower, it has been in the same family for five generations. Service is courteous and attentive, and the atmosphere and fine rooms recall times past.
🛈 48 🅿 🛗 🚫 All major cards

🏨 HOTEL AMALFITANA
$$ ◗◗◗
VIA ROMA 44
TEL 050 29 000
FAX 050 25 218
A good mid-range choice on a street just south of the Leaning Tower. Rooms are modern and well-equipped.
🛈 21 🅿 🛗 🔆 🚫 All major cards

🍴 RISTORO DEI VECCHI MACELLI
$$$–$$$$
VIA VOLTURNO 49
TEL 050 20 424
Pisa's most noted restaurant lies close to the Arno on the city's western fringe. Dishes that brought it fame include *verde con i frutti di mare* (green pasta with mixed seafood).
🍴 45 🕐 Closed Sun. L, Wed., & 2 weeks Aug. 🔆 🚫 All major cards

🍴 OSTERIA DEI CAVALIERI
$$
VIA SAN FREDIANO 16
TEL 050 580 858
A plain but welcoming trattoria in the old city. The well-priced classic Tuscan dishes include wild boar

(*cinghiale*) plus other adventurous meat and fish dishes.
🍴 60 🕐 Closed Sat. L, Sun., & Aug. 🔆 🚫 All major cards

🍴 TAVERNA KOSTAS
$$
VIA DEL BORGHETTO 39
TEL 050 571 467
Despite the Greek name (from a previous owner), this restaurant serves refined Tuscan food. Try the *tortino di patate e porcini*, a tartlet of potato and wild mushrooms.
🍴 55 🕐 Closed Sun. L, Mon., & Aug. 🔆 🚫 All major cards

🍴 LA MESCITA
$–$$
VIA CAVALCA 2
TEL 050 544 294
An attractive trattoria in the Vettovaglie market..
🍴 35 🕐 Closed Mon. & Aug. 🔆

🍴 PASTICCERIA SALZA
$
BORGO STRETTO 46
TEL 050 580 144
The most celebrated of Pisa's cafés. Ideal for coffee, cakes, snacks, or an evening aperitif.
🕐 Closed Mon.

PISTOIA

🍴 TRATTORIA DELL'ABBONDANZA
$$
VIA DELL'ABBONDANZA 1014
TEL 0573 368 037
Prices at this restaurant just off Piazza del Duomo are a bargain, given the quality of the fine regional cooking. Be sure to reserve for evening.
🍴 35 + 35 outside 🕐 Closed Wed. & some of Aug.

SAN GIMIGNANO

🏨 LA COLLEGIATA
🍴 $$$$$ ◗◗◗◗
LOCALITÀ STRADA 27
TEL 0577 943 201
FAX 0577 940 566

HOTELS & RESTAURANTS

A dazzlingly stylish hotel with a good restaurant housed in a converted 16th-century convent 1 mile (2 km) from the town walls. Fine views of San Gimignano and its towers.

🏨 20 🅿 ⬛ 🔳 ⬛
🃏 All major cards

🏨 LA CISTERNA
🍴 $$ ⬖⬖⬖⬖
PIAZZA DELLA CISTERNA 24
TEL 0577 940 328
FAX 0577 942 080
The village's oldest established hotel has a central location on the main piazza. Rooms with a view command higher prices.
🏨 46 🅿 🕐 Closed
Jan.–Feb. ⬛ 🃏 All major cards

🏨 LEON BIANCO
$$ ⬖⬖⬖
PIAZZA DELLA CISTERNA 13
TEL 0577 941 294
FAX 0577 942 123
This hotel shares the Cisterna's perfect location but is smaller and more intimate.
🏨 19 🅿 🕐 Closed mid-Jan.–Feb. ⬛ 🔳 🃏 All major cards

🍴 DORANDÒ
$$$–$$$$
VICOLO DELL'ORO 2
TEL 0577 941 862
An intimate restaurant in a medieval setting but with a modern ambience. Unusually, it re-creates ancient recipes from Etruscan, Medici, and early medieval periods
🍴 35 🕐 Closed mid-Jan.–mid-March & Mon. in winter
🔳 🃏 All major cards

🍴 LE VECCHIE MURA
$–$$
VIA PIANDORNELLA 15
TEL 0577 940 270
Tasty pizzas and honest, fairly priced food. Set in converted stables built into the walls.
🍴 65–120 🕐 Closed Tues.
🃏 All major cards

🍴 GELATERIA DI PIAZZA
$
PIAZZA DELLA CISTERNA 4

TEL 0577 942 244
San Gimignano's best ice cream palor.
🕐 Closed Nov.–Feb.

VOLTERRA

🏨 SAN LINO
$$ ⬖⬖⬖⬖
VIA SAN LINO 26
TEL 0588 85 250
FAX 0588 80 620
A converted convent is Volterra's best central option but is not as polished as some four-star Italian hotels.
🏨 43 🅿 ⬛ 🔳 ⬛
🃏 All major cards

🍴 SACCO FIORENTINO
$–$$
PIAZZA XX SETTEMBRE 18
TEL 0588 88537
A central restaurant and wine bar offering innovative creations such as *coniglio in salsa di aglio e Vin Santo*— rabbit in a garlic and sweet wine sauce—along with more traditional dishes such as *salsicce e fagioli* (Tuscan sausages and beans). Light meals and snacks also.
🍴 50 🕐 Closed Fri., 10 days June, & mid-Nov.–March
🔳 🃏 All major cards

SOUTHERN TUSCANY

AREZZO

🏨 CASTELLO DI
🍴 GARGONZA
$$–$$$ ⬖⬖⬖
CASTELLO DI GARGONZA, MONTE SANTO SAVINO
TEL 0575 847 021
FAX 0575 847 054
A converted medieval castle, in a hamlet 4 miles (6 km) west of Monte San Savino, a village 10 miles (16 km) southwest of Arezzo. Rooms must be taken for a minimum of three nights. Flats and cottages in the hamlet for weekly rental.
🏨 32 🅿 🕐 Closed Nov. & some of Jan. ⬛ 🃏 All major cards

🏨 PALAZZO CAVALIERE
$$ ⬖⬖⬖⬖
VIA MADONNA DEL PRATO 83
TEL 0575 26 836
FAX 0575 21 925
The Cavaliere Palace provides the best available accommodations in its modern rooms. Near the station, and within walking distance of the sights.
🏨 27 🕐 Closed some of Aug. ⬛ 🔳 🃏 All major cards

🍴 BUCA DI SAN FRANCESCO
$$–$$$
VIA SAN FRANCESCO 1
TEL 0575 23 271
The central Buca has been serving simple Tuscan staples such as thick *ribollita* vegetable soup and roast lamb (*agnello*) since 1929. The attractive dining room has an ancient floor and medieval paintings.
🍴 60 🕐 Closed Mon. D, Tues., & July 🃏 All major cards

🍴 ANTICA OSTERIA L'AGANIA
$$
VIA MAZZINI 10
TEL 0575 295 381
No reservations are accepted in this busy osteria, so arrive early. The Tuscan food is simple but expertly cooked by a group of women who have worked here for years. The decor is an eccentric mix of old photos, pictures, and strings of garlic and peppers.
🍴 100 🕐 Closed Mon. & some of June 🃏 All major cards

🍴 TRATTORIA IL SARACENO
$–$$
VIA MAZZINI 6A
TEL 0575 27 644
Just a few steps east of the church of San Francesco this restaurant offers food of a quality you don't normally find in this price range.
🍴 120 🕐 Closed Wed., 2 weeks Jan., & 2 weeks July or Aug. 🃏 All major cards

KEY   🏨 Hotel 🍴 Restaurant 🏨 No. of bedrooms 🍴 No. of seats ⬛ Bus 🅿 Parking 🕐 Closed

IL GELATO
$

VIA DEI CENCI 24

TEL 0575 23 240

The best ice cream for miles
—handmade, using only fresh
ingredients and real fruit.
Closed Wed. & some of
Nov. or Feb.

CASENTINO

GLI ACCANITI
$$

VIA FIORENTINA 12,
PRATOVECCHIO

TEL 0575 583 345

This tiny restaurant (be sure
to reserve) offers regional
cooking and is a good stop
as you explore the Casentino.
If you merely want a snack
or a sandwich, try the village
bar, L'Osteria di Giovanni
Petraglia, Via Roma 57 (closed
Thurs.).
35 Closed Tues. & 3
weeks Nov. AE, MC, V

CORTONA

IL FALCONIERE
$$$–$$$$ ◊◊◊◊

LOCALITÀ SAN MARTINO A
BOCENA 370

TEL 0575 612 679

FAX 0575 612 927

A beautifully restored 17th-
century villa about 2 miles (3
km) off the SS71 road for
Arezzo. Rooms are exquisitely
furnished in period style—
some retain original frescoes.
The restaurant offers fine
meat and fish dishes, and
boasts a good wine list.
10 + 2 suites 55
inside, 40 outside
Hotel closed some of
Nov., restaurant closed Mon.
Nov.–March All
major cards

SAN MICHELE
$$–$$$ ◊◊◊◊

VIA GUELFA 15

TEL 0575 604 348

FAX 0575 630 147

Converted Renaissance
palace in the town's historic
heart. The building retains

many original features. The
room in the tower is a gem.
34 Closed mid-
Jan.–Feb. All
major cards

LA LOGGETTA
$$

PIAZZA PESCHERIA 3

TEL 0575 630 575

A centrally placed restaurant
with a simple brick-vaulted
medieval interior, white walls,
and honest Tuscan cooking.
60 Closed Nov. &
Mon. Sept.–June All
major cards

TONINO
$–$$

PIAZZA GARIBALDI 1

TEL 0575 630 500

Tonino is not to all tastes: It's
big, busy, modern, and noisy,
but that's how many Italians
like their restaurants. Locals
flock here for the famous
"antipastissimo" (15 different
appetizers) and the views
across the Val di Chiana.
200 Closed Mon. D,
Tues. All major cards

ELBA

VILLA OTTONE
$$$–$$$$ ◊◊◊

OTTONE, PORTOFERRAIO

TEL 0565 933 042

FAX 0565 933 257

An elegant hotel built around
an 18th-century villa, about 6
miles (10 km) southeast of
Portoferraio, Elba's main town.
It makes a good base from
which to explore the island.
75 + 2 suites
All major cards

LA CANOCCHIA
$$–$$$

VIA PALESTRO 3, RIO MARINA

TEL 0565 962 432

Classic Tuscan cooking with an
emphasis on fish and seafood
characterize this polished
restaurant in Rio Marina, a
port on Elba's east coast.
50 Closed Nov.–Feb.
& Mon. except July–Aug.
All major cards

PUBLIUS
$$–$$$

PIAZZA XX SETTEMBRE 67,
POGGIO

TEL 0565 99 208

Family-run Publius lies up in
the hills above Marciana, in
the west of Elba. Its outdoor
terrace offers exceptional sea
views. Fish and seafood
dominate the menu, but meat
and other dishes are available.
90 Closed Nov.–late
March & Mon. except July–
Aug. All major cards

MONTALCINO

DEI CAPITANI
$$ ◊◊◊

VIA LAPINI 6

TEL 0577 847 227

FAX 0577 847 227

A modern hotel in an old
town house with a terrace,
bar area and swimming pool.
No restaurant.
29 All
major cards

TAVERNA DEI BARBI
$$–$$$

FATTORIA DEI BARBI,
LA CROCE,
LOCALITÀ PODERNOVI

TEL 0577 849 357

Annexed to a well-known
Brunello vineyard 3 miles (5
km) southeast of Montalcino,
this wonderful restaurant
serves superb local dishes
and home-produced wine. A
huge stone fireplace dominates the rustic dining room.
80 Closed Jan., 2
weeks July, Tues. D, & Wed.
except in Aug. All major
cards

GRAPPOLO BLU
$$

VIA SCALE DI MOGLIO 1

TEL 0577 847 150

In a stepped alley off the
main Via Mazzini, the cool,
stone walls of the medieval
interior house two small
dining rooms. The high-quality
pasta dishes are all good.
35 Closed Fri. All
major cards

HOTELS & RESTAURANTS

MONTE AMIATA

SOMETHING SPECIAL

🔢 SILENE

🔢 People travel for miles to eat in this restaurant, just outside Pescina, one of the tiny villages ringing Monte Amiata. Many dishes use produce from local woods—wild mushrooms, wild asparagus, roebuck, wild boar, truffles, and snails. There's nothing rustic about the cooking, however, which is refined and often elaborate. Rooms in the hotel need to be reserved in advance, as do places for both dinner and Sunday lunch.

$$-$$$ ✪✪✪
SIGNED FROM PESCINA, 2
MILES (4 KM) EAST OF
SEGGIANO
TEL 0564 950 805
FAX 0564 950 553
🛏 7 🍽 80 🕐 Closed Mon.
& Nov. 💳 AE, MC, V,

MONTEPULCIANO

🏨 DUOMO
$$ ✪✪✪
VIA SAN DONATO 14
TEL 0578 757 473
FAX 0578 757 473
A few steps from the town's cathedral and main piazza, this hotel is a family-run place with bright, straightforward rooms.
🛏 13 🍽 💳 All major cards

🍽 LA CHIUSA
🏨 **$$$$**
VIA DELLA MADONNINA 88,
MONTEFOLLONICO
TEL 0577 669 668
FAX 0577 669 593
For the best food close to Montepulciano drive 5 miles (8 km) northwest of the town to Montefollonico to this former mill, now a select, Michelin-starred restaurant with rooms. Meals are expensive but outstanding: A light creative touch informs the mostly Tuscan cuisine.
🛏 14 🍽 35 🅿 🕐 Closed

Tues. & mid-Jan.–mid-March
💳 All major cards

🍽 LA GROTTA
$$
LOCALITÀ SAN BIAGIO
TEL 0578 757 607
La Grotta is a convenient place for lunch, thanks largely to its location directly opposite the noted church of San Biagio.
🍽 45 🅿 🕐 Closed Wed. & Jan.–Feb. 💳 All major cards

PIENZA

🏨 IL CHIOSTRO
$$$ ✪✪✪
CORSO ROSSELLINO 26
TEL 0578 748 400
FAX 0578 748 440
The central Chiostro takes its name from the cloister (chiostro) of the 15th-century convent from which it was converted. Simple but elegant rooms retain the evocative flavor of the old building.
🛏 28 🅿 🍽 🏊 💳 All major cards

🍽 LATTE DI LUNA
$$
VIA SAN CARLO 2–4
TEL 0578 748 606
A family-run trattoria in the village center. Simple but appetizing food: Try the daily specials or local pici all'aglione, pasta in a rich garlicky tomato sauce. Be sure to reserve.
🍽 35 + 20 outside
🕐 Closed Tues. & some of Feb. & July 💳 MC, V

🍽 FALCO
$–$$
PIAZZA DANTE 3
TEL 0578748 551
A trattoria with a medieval interior and robust country cooking on a square just outside the village, frequented by locals as well as visitors. Try the famed local pecorino cheese melted and wrapped in prosciutto (ham).
🍽 80 🅿 🕐 Closed Fri. 💳 All major cards

SOVANA

🏨 HOTEL-RISTORANTE
🍽 **ETRUSCA**
$$ ✪✪
PIAZZA DEL PRETORIO 16
TEL 0564 616 183
FAX 0564 614 193
A simple but beautiful interior in a building dating from 1241 provides an elegant setting for this restaurant run by a charming Colombian who has lived in Italy for over 30 years. Rooms in the hotel are simple but comfortable.
🛏 10 🍽 90 🕐 Closed Mon. 🅿 💳 AE, MC, V

VAL D'ORCIA

🏨 CASTELO DI RIPA DORCIA
$$$ ✪✪✪
VIA DELLA CONTEA 116, RIPA DORCIA, 4 MILES (7 KM) SW OF SAN QUIRICO DORCIA
TEL 0577 897 376
FAX 0577 898 038
This hotel is built around a mighty borgo, or fortified village, that dates from the 13th century. A stay here provides a highly memorable rural escape. Peace and quiet are assured, the views are wonderful, and you can make easy hikes into the country. Rooms and apartments are spacious but simply furnished.
🛏 6 + 7 suites 🅿 💳 All major cards

🍽 CANTINA IL BORGO
🏨 **$$**
BORGO MAESTRO 37,
ROCCA D'ORCIA
TEL 0577 887 280
The village of Rocca d'Orcia is tiny, just 50 or so inhabitants., The restaurant's vaulted main room dates from the 18th century and retains its bare stone walls and terra-cotta floors. The menu revolves around Tuscan staples such as ribollita soup and grilled meat. There are also three rooms.
🍽 45 + 16 outside
🕐 Closed Mon., Jan.–Feb. 💳 AE, MC, V

MENU READER

PASTA & SAUCES

agnolotti large filled pasta parcels
al pomodoro tomato sauce
amatriciana with tomato and bacon
arrabbiata spicy chili tomato sauce
bolognese veal or beef sauce
burro with butter
burro e salvia with sage and butter
cannelloni filled pasta tubes
carbonara with cream, ham, and egg
farfalle butterfly-shaped pasta
gnocchi potato dough dumplings
pasta e fagioli pasta and beans
peperoncino with oil, garlic, and chilli
puttanesca with tomato, anchovy, oil, and oregano
ragù any meat sauce
vongole with wine, clams, and parsley

MEATS

agnello lamb
anatra duck
bistecca beef steak
carpaccio thin slices of raw beef
cinghiale wild boar
coniglio rabbit
fagiano pheasant
fegatini chicken liver
fegato liver
fritto misto mixed grill
involtini rolled and stuffed meat slices
lepre hare
maiale pork
manzo beef
pancetta pork belly/bacon
pollo chicken
polpette meatballs
salsiccia sausage
tacchino turkey
trippa tripe
vitello veal

FISH & SEAFOOD

acciughe anchovies
calamari squid
capesante scallops
cozze mussels
gamberetti shrimps
gamberi prawns
granchio crab
merluzzo cod
ostriche oysters
pesce spada swordfish
polpo octopus
salmone salmon
sarde sardines
seppie cuttlefish
sgombro mackerel
sogliola sole
tonno tuna
vongole clams

VEGETABLES & HERBS

aglio garlic
carciofi artichokes
cavolo cabbage
cetriolo cucumber
cipolle onions
fagioli beans
finocchio fennel
funghi mushrooms
insalata salad
melanzane egg plant
patate fritte french fries
piselli peas
pomodoro tomato
rucolo/rughetta rocket

FRUIT

albicocca apricot
ananas pineapple
arancia orange
ciliegie cherries
cocomero water melon
ficchi figs
fragole strawberries
mela apple
melone melon
pera pear
pesca peach
pompelmo grapefruit
prugna plum
uva grapes

DRINKS

acqua water
acqua minerale mineral water
una birra beer
una bottiglia bottle
caffè coffee
caffè Hag/caffè decaffeinato decaffeinated coffee
cioccolata calda hot chocolate
ghiaccio ice
latte milk
mezza bottiglia half-bottle
secco/dolce dry/sweet
una spremuta fresh fruit juice
spumante sparkling wine
un succo di frutta bottled juice
tè tea
vino della casa house wine

Useful words & phrases
(see also p. 324)

breakfast *la colazione*
lunch *il pranzo*
dinner *la cena*
waiter *il cameriere*
menu *il menù/la lista*
tourist menu *menù turistico*
tasting menu *menù degustazione*
wine list *la lista dei vini*
knife *un coltello*
fork *una forchetta*
spoon *un cucchiaio*
bread *pane* (brown: *integrale*)
bread roll *panino*
butter *burro*
oil *olio*
vinegar *aceto*
cream *panna*
meat/fish *carne/pesce*
seafood *frutti di mare*
rice *riso*
eggs *uova*
salt/pepper *sale/pepe*
sugar *zucchero*
appetizers *antipasti*
first courses *primi*
soup *zuppa/minestra*
main courses *secondi*
vegetables *contorni*
cheeses *formaggi*
puddings *dolci*
without meat *senza carne*
rare/medium (steaks)
  al sangue/al punto
well done *ben cotto*
raw/cooked *crudo/cotto*
cover charge *coperto*
service charge *servizio*
I'd like to reserve a table
  Vorrei prenotare una tavola
Have you a table for two?
  Avete una tavola per due?
I'd like to order *Vorrei ordinare*
I'm a vegetarian
  Sono vegetariano/a
It's good *È buono*
The check, please
  Il conto, per favore
Is service included?
  Il servizio è incluso?

At a hotel

a room *una camera*
with private bathroom *con bagno*
Do you have rooms free?
  Avete camere libere?
I have a reservation
  Ho una prenotazione
elevator *ascensore*
key *la chiave*

SHOPPING

Shopping is one of the great pleasures of visiting Florence and Tuscany. From the smallest town to the grandest city street, stores offer arrays of food and wine, wonderful clothes, inspired design, beautiful fabrics, precious jewelry, exquisite shoes, leatherware and accessories, precious antiques, objets d'art, and a host of craft items.

STORES

Most Tuscan stores are small, family-run affairs. Many neighborhoods still have a baker (panificio), pastry store (pasticceria), butcher (macellaio), and food shop (alimentari). Department stores and supermarkets are gradually gaining ground, but malls are still almost unknown.

MARKETS

Large towns have at least one street market (mercato). Most open daily except Sunday, from dawn until early afternoon. Times are the same in smaller towns, but markets are usually held just once a week. Many larger towns also hold antique fairs, usually once monthly or on a weekend, or special events devoted to local food or a craft product. These are the only places you might try to bargain: Haggling in food markets or other stores is not appropriate.

WHAT TO BUY

Many Tuscan products are unique to one part of the year. Fruit and vegetables appear in stores when they're in season, so don't expect to find grapes in spring or cherries in fall. Some towns have their own food and wine specialties, such as the spicy panforte cake of Siena, or handicraft specialties such as leatherware in Florence or alabaster in Volterra.

Food delicacies are obvious purchases, but check import restrictions of meat and other products into North America. Lingerie, silks, lace, linens, soaps, shoes, bags, wallets, marbled paper products, and jewelry are all easily transportable items. Also leave space for wine, clothes, and design objects, particularly kitchenware, an area in which Italian designers excel. Many stores should be able to arrange shipping for larger items such as ceramics, furniture, and antiques.

OPENING HOURS

Most small stores open Tuesday through Saturday from about 8 a.m. to 1 p.m. and 3:30 to 8 p.m., and close on Monday morning or one other half day a week. Hours often alter slightly in summer, with a later afternoon opening to avoid the heat of the day. In Florence and larger towns, especially in clothes and department stores, there's a move toward full-time opening (orario continuato) from 9 a.m. to 8 p.m., Monday through Saturday (and occasionally Sunday).

PAYMENT

Supermarkets and department stores usually accept credit cards and traveler's checks, as do clothes and shoe stores. Cash is required for transactions in small food and other stores.

EXPORTS

Most Italian luxury items and clothing purchases include a value-added goods and services tax of 19 percent (known as IVA in Italy). Non-European Union residents can claim an IVA refund for purchases over L300,000 (before tax) made in one store. Shop with your passport and ask for invoices to be made out clearly, showing individual articles and tax components of prices. Department stores often have special counters for this purpose. Keep all receipts and invoices and have them stamped at the customs office at your departure airport, or the last exit from the EU if you are traveling beyond Italy. Then mail the invoice to the store within 90 days of arriving home for your rebate. Many stores are members of the Tax-Free Shopping System and issue a "tax-free check" for the rebate, which can be cashed at special tax-free counters at airports or rebated to your bank or credit card account.

FLORENCE

Florence is a great city for luxury goods. Leather, clothes, jewelry, and antiques are top buys, but less expensive gift possibilities include marbled paper and goods from the city's thriving markets. Most clothes and other luxury goods stores are found on and around Via de' Tornabuoni. Antique stores group together in the Oltrarno on and around Via Maggio. Jewelers congregate on the Ponte Vecchio.

To ship large goods home, contact either Fracassi, Via Santo Spirito 11 (Tel 055 283 597), or Gondrand, Via Baldanzese 198 (Tel 055 882 6376). Neither accepts credit cards.

ARTISTS' MATERIALS
Zecchi Via dello Studio 19r, tel 055 211 470. It's no surprise that a city with Florence's artistic pedigree has a store of this quality: Zecchi is an Aladdin's cave of pens, paints, pencils, oils, gold leaf, and other items.

BOOKS
Feltrinelli Internazionale Via Cavour 12–20r, tel 055 219 524. A modern bookstore just north of Piazza del Duomo with a large selection of English-language titles, including guides.

CAMERAS & FILM
Bongi Via Por Santa Maria 82–84r, tel 055 239 8811. Try well-stocked Bongi if you need any item of camera or related equipment. For film processing, try **Fontani** Viale Strozzi 18–20, tel 055 470 981, or **Foto Levi** near the Ponte Vecchio at Vicolo dell' Oro 12–14r, tel 055 294 002.

COFFEE

Piansa Borgo Pinti 18r, tel 055 234 2362. Piansa is Florence's main coffee roaster, and bars across the city use its products. This is its city-center outlet and sells different coffees as well as operating as a normal bar, with light meals also available.

DEPARTMENT STORES

COIN Via de' Calzaiuoli 56r, tel 055 280 531. Florentines crowd this central mid-range store, which sells a wide variety of quality goods.

Rinascente Piazza della Repubblica 1, tel 055 239 8544. Of generally higher quality than COIN, but with less stock and a less inviting atmosphere.

FABRICS

Casa dei Tessuti Via de' Pecori 20r, tel 055 215 961. A staggering collection of sumptuous silk, linen, wool, and other fabrics.

FASHION

Most of the big fashion-designer names have stores on Via de' Tornabuoni or the nearby Via della Vigna Nuova. Here is a selection:
Armani Via della Vigna Nuova 51r, tel 055 219 041
Bulgari (jewelry and accessories), Via dei Tornabuoni 61–63r, tel 055 239 6786
Emporio Armani, Piazza Strozzi 16r, tel 055 284 315
Gucci Via de' Tornabuoni 73r, tel 055 264 011. The famous "double G" label, like Ferragamo (see p. 322), originated in Florence. Sells clothes, shoes, and accessories
Prada, Via de' Tornabuoni 67r, tel 055 283 439
Pucci Via dei Pucci 6 & Via della Vigna Nuova 99r, tel 055 287 622. With Ferragamo and Gucci, Emilio Pucci is one of the city's top designers, having made his name with signature silks and prints in the 1960s
Louis Vuitton Via de' Tornabuoni 24–28r, tel 055 214 344

FOOD & WINE

Dolce e Dolcezze Piazza Beccaria 8r, tel 055 234 5458. This store was started by cake and chocolate enthusiasts with no formal training. The results are superb—the cakes, pastries, and candies are, by general consent, Florence's finest.

Enoteca Murgia Via dei Banchi 55–57r, tel 055 215 686. Choice and excellent service are the watchwords of this wine store. Also sells olive oils, grappas, and other spirits and liquor.

I Sapori Via dei Servi 10, tel 055 238 2071. No time to visit Chianti? No problem! This store sells oils, wines, candies, and much more from the region. Ideal for gifts to take home, as most goods are well packaged.

La Bolognes Via de' Serragli 24, tel 055 282 318. Sells every variety of fresh and dried pasta it's possible to imagine. How about truffle or black squid's ink pasta to take home as a gift?

Pitti Gola & Cantina Piazza Pitti 16, tel 055 212 704. An inviting store with a selection of Tuscany's best chocolate, wines, oils, and artisan-made food. Also cookery and wine books.

Robiglio Via dei Servi 112r, tel 055 214 501. This *pasticceria* rivals Dolce e Dolcezze with its superb cakes and pastries and a rich hot chocolate drink.

GLOVES

Madova Via Guicciardini 1r, tel 055 239 6526. Look no further for leather gloves—this store has every size, style, and color imaginable.

HERBAL PRODUCTS

De Herbore Via del Proconsolo 43r, tel 055 211 706. Dried herbs, vitamins, soaps, health foods, silk flowers, and natural cosmetics. Come here for the extravagant product displays, even if you don't intend to buy anything.

JEWELRY

Torrini Piazza del Duomo 10r, tel 055 230 2401. Torrini registered its trademark in 1369. Traditional and modern designs, with an emphasis on gold.

KITCHENWARE

Bartolini Via dei Servi 30r, tel 055 211 895. One of Tuscany's best kitchenware stores. Everything from pots, pans, espresso-makers, and Alessi designer products to knives, corks, china, glassware, and much more.

LEATHER

Cellerini Via del Sole 37r, tel 055 282 533. Wallets, suitcases, shoes, belts, but most of all, bags: over 600 types to choose from.

Desmo Piazza de' Rucellai 10r, tel 055 292 395. A huge choice of leather goods under one roof.

LINENS

Caponi Loretti Piazza Antinori 4r, tel 055 213 668. Embroidery, linens, lingerie, and lace.

MAPS & GUIDES

Geographica Via dei Cimatori 16r, tel 055 239 6637. The only store in Italy where you can buy or order the full range of 1:25,000 Italian military (IGM) maps for hiking. Other Italian maps and guides also available.

MARKETS

Cascine Parco del Cascine. A weekly flea market held in a park west of the city center—buses 1, 9, 17 (Tues. 8 a.m.–2 p.m.).

Mercato Centrale Piazza del Mercato Centrale. Europe's largest indoor market is a must-see, even if you don't want to buy anything (Mon.–Fri. 7 a.m.–2 p.m., Sat. 4–7 p.m.).

Mercato delle Pulci Piazza dei Ciompi. Florence's flea *(pulci)* market has a predictable but still fascinating collection of junk, clothes, and inexpensive goods.

San Lorenzo Piazza San Lorenzo. Stalls selling clothes

and other general goods cram the square and its surrounding streets (daily 9 a.m.–7 p.m., closed Sun. in winter).

Sant'Ambrogio Piazza Lorenzo Ghiberti. Smaller than the Mercato Centrale, but with lots of small specialist food stalls (Mon.–Sat. 7 a.m.–2 p.m.).

Santo Spirito Piazza Santo Spirito. A flea market (second Sun. of each month) with used clothes, pictures, books, handmade jewelry, and other crafts, plus plenty of unsaleable junk.

PAPER & PENS
Giulio Giannini & Figlio Piazza Pitti 36r, tel 055 212 621. Founded in 1856, this company still handmakes marbled paper, books, leather desk accessories, and other stationery from its workshop at this address.

Il Torchio Via dei Bardi 17, tel 055 234 2862. Sells an enormous variety of marbled and other paper, plus boxes, books, and other stationery. Watch bookbinders in the workshop.

Pineider Piazza della Signoria 13r, tel 055 284 655 and Via de Tornabuoni 76r, tel 055 211 605. Pineider has branches around the world but was founded in Florence in 1774. It sells pens, paper, and writing accessories.

SHOES
JP Tod's Via de Tornabuoni 103r, tel 055 219 423. Prices for shoes and bags at this fashionable store are lower than you'll find in North America.

Salvatore Ferragamo Via de' Tornabuoni 14r, tel 055 292 123. Ferragamo made his name in the U.S., but his home base was Florence. Also sells clothing and accessories.

SOAPS & PERFUMES
Farmaceutica di Santa Maria Novella Via della Scala 16r, tel 055 216 276. A beautiful store selling soaps, perfumes, and

cosmetics, many made to ancient recipes created in monasteries and convents.

Farmacia del Cinghiale Piazza del Mercato Nuovo 4r, tel 055 212 128. A store that has sold natural cosmetics and other toiletries since the 18th century.

SIENA

Siena's main shopping streets are Via di Città and its two near neighbors, Banchi di Sopra and Banchi di Sotto. Food and wine are good buys, especially olive oils and *panforte*, a rich, dark cake flavored with cinnamon and other spices, made in the city since the Middle Ages.

BOOKS
Libreria Sienese Via di Città 6266, tel 0577 280 845. Siena has bigger and smarter book stores, but this family-run store has a good selection of guides, maps, art books, foreign newspapers, and English-language titles.

FOOD & WINE
Antica Drogheria Manganelli 1879 Via di Città 71–73, tel 0577 280 002 (closed Wed. p.m.). A treasure trove of the finest foods, wines, and spirits imaginable—all displayed in old wooden cabinets. Don't miss.

Consorzio Agrario Siena Via Pianigiani 5, tel 0577 222 368. The local Consorzio Agrario (a farmer's cooperative) sells the goods of its 4,000 members at this market. Good for olive oils, cheese, honey, and wine, sold at reasonable prices.

Enoteca Italiana Fortezza Medicea, tel 0577 288 497 (closed Sun. a.m.). Vaulted cellars in Siena's Medici castle hold about 750 of the best Italian wines to buy. Choose from 800 wines by the glass in the bar.

Gastronomia Morbidi 1925 Via Banchi di Sopra 73–75, tel 0577 280268. The second of

Siena's fabulous food shops, this is a superb delicatessen, in business since 1925. Ready-to-eat and prepared food are also available to take out in plastic containers, and there's a wine cellar downstairs, so it's great for picnic provisions.

MARKET
La Lizza Siena's main market is held every Wednesday morning at La Lizza, a large open area in the north of the city beyond Piazza Matteotti and Piazza Gramsci.

NORTHERN TUSCANY

As well as those described below, there are markets at the following northern Tuscany towns: **Barga** General market Fri. a.m. plus flea market second Sun. of the month; **Carrara** Mon. a.m.; **Castelnuovo di Garfagnana** Thurs. a.m.; **Colle di Val d'Elsa** Fri. a.m.; **Pistoia** Wed. & Sat. a.m.; **Prato** Mon. a.m.; **Viareggio** Mon.–Sat.

LUCCA

FOOD & WINE
Antica Bottega di Prospero Via Santa Lucia 13, no phone. This extraordinary shop sells every dried good imaginable, from pulses and dried herbs to daffodil bulbs and seeds for Italian staples, such as fennel.

Caniparoli Via San Paolino 96, tel 0583 53 456. Sensational handmade chocolates.

Taddeucci Piazza San Michele 34, Lucca, tel 0583 494 933. A beautiful, wood-paneled bakery: Try specialties such as *buccellato*, an old-fashioned bread flavored with aniseed and raisins, and *torta di erbe*, spiced vegetable pie.

MARKETS
Mercato del Carmine Piazza del Carmine (daily except Wed. a.m. and Sun.). There is a similar market in the east of the city in Via dei Bacchettoni (Wed. &

Sat.). An antique fair is held in the squares around the Duomo on the third weekend of every month. A craft market takes place in Piazza San Giusto over the last weekend of the month.

PISA

CRAFTS & GIFTS
Coltelleria Fontana Corso Italia 124, tel 050 41 369. High-quality kitchen and other knives, plus specialist kitchen equipment —wedges for splitting Parmesan, nutcrackers, traditional pasta cutters, and fluted pasta wheels.

Melani Corso Italia 44, tel 050 502 323. Silverware, glass, porcelain, and other ceramics. Also designer tableware and kitchen and cooking accessories.

FOOD & WINE
L'Altra Roba Piazza delle Vettovaglie 3, tel 050 598 987. One of several food stores on Pisa's market square. Sells pulses, oils, honey, fruit preserves, pasta sauces, fine bread, and seasonal fruit and vegetables.

MARKETS
Mercato Vettovaglie Piazza delle Vettovaglie (Mon.–Sat. a.m.). A general food market, held just north of the river.

Mercatino Antiquario Junction of Borgo Stretto and Ponte di Mezzo (second weekend of every month). Pisa's main antiques market.

SAN GIMIGNANO

CRAFTS & GIFTS
Bottega d'Arte Povera Via San Matteo 83, tel 0577 941 951. *Arte povera* means "poor art", or the craft of peasant tradition: Olive wood bowls and boards, chestnut baskets, baskets for drying figs, and terra-cotta ware.

MARKETS
A large market selling clothes, food, and crafts is held on Thursday morning in Piazza della Cisterna and Piazza del Duomo,

and a smaller one on Saturday morning.

Regular markets are held at the following towns in southern Tuscany: **Arezzo** Sat. a.m.; **Bibbiena** Thurs. a.m.; **Buon-convento** Sat. a.m.; **Castellina in Chianti** Sat. a.m.; **Cortona** Sat. a.m.; **Gaiole in Chianti** second Tues. p.m. of the month; **Massa Marittima** Wed. a.m.; **Montalcino** Fri. a.m.; **Monte-pulciano** Thurs. a.m.; **Pienza** Fri. a.m.; **Pitigliano** Wed. a.m.; **Poppi** Tues. a.m.; **Portoferraio** Fri. a.m.; **Radda in Chianti** fourth Mon. p.m. of the month.

ABBADIA SAN SALVATORE

FOOD
Pinzi Pinzuti Via Cavour 30, tel 0577 778 040. Crammed with wines, grappas, olive oils, honey, jam, pasta, herbs, and other Tuscan gastronomic treats.

AREZZO

CRAFTS & GIFTS
Abbraccio Piazza Grande 10, no phone. A unique little shop in the main square, which sells rare and extremely beautiful old fabrics and table linens. The store has no obvious name, so look for the linens displayed outside in good weather.

L'Artigiano Via XXV Aprile 22, tel 0575 351 278. A fine expo-nent of Arezzo's gold-working and jewelry tradition.

Busatti Corso Italia 48, tel 0575 355 295. Sublime cotton, linen, wool, and other fabrics, many of them handmade.

Morini Piazza San Jacopo, tel 0575 23 277. Perhaps Tuscany's best kitchenware shop. It sells pans, knives, and other essentials, but also fine china, crystal, and pieces by leading designers.

CAMALDOLI

CRAFTS & GIFTS
Antica Farmacia Eremo di Camaldoli, tel 0575 556 143. An old pharmacy that still has its original 1543 walnut paneling and sells herbal products, toiletries, honeys, and jams, many made by the monks of the Camaldoli Eremo, or monastery.

CHIANTI

WINE
Enoteca del Chianti Classico Piazzetta Santa Croce 8, Greve in Chianti, tel 055 853 297. A useful store that stocks wines by the Chianti Classico Gallo Nero consortium. Also other wines, olive oils, and vinegar.

CORTONA

CRAFTS & GIFTS
L'Etruria Piazza Signorelli 21, tel 0575 62 360. The best place in Cortona for terra-cotta tableware and other ceramics.

FOOD
Enoteca Enotria Via Nazionale 81, tel 0575 692 007. Drink or buy wine, along with meats, hams, and cheese.

Ristori Via Santa Margherita 9, tel 0575 603 571. Top-quality olive oil from around Cortona.

MONTALCINO

WINE
Fattoria dei Barbi Fattoria del Barbi del Casato, La Croce, 5 miles (8 km) southeast of Montalcino, tel 0577 848 277. Visits to most small Brunello vineyards are by appointment only (details from the visitor center, see p. 270). This lovely *fattoria* (estate), however, is open without reserving (closed Sat. & Sun. a.m.). You can tour the cellars and buy wine, cheese, and salamis made on the estate.

Fiaschetteria Italiana Piazza del Popolo 6, tel 0577 849 043. The co-op supermarket off Via

Ricasoli has a good selection of Brunello and Rosso di Montalcino wines at the best prices, but this bar-*enoteca* is a far prettier place to sample and buy wine.

MONTEPULCIANO

FOOD

Cugusi Via di Gracciano nel Corso, tel 0578 757 558. Store outlet for local cheeses made just outside Montepulciano by Silvana Cugusi. You can also visit the farm for direct sales (Via della Boccia 8, tel 0578 757 558).

Il Frantoio

Via di Martiena 2, tel 0578 716 305. The olive mill for a co-operative of 650 local growers. Oils can be bought direct from the mill or from the store in the town at Piazza Pasquino 9.

WINE

Contucci Via del Teatro 1, tel 0578 757 006. This is the most central of several direct-sale single estate outlets for Montepulciano's esteemed Vino Nobile red wine. Also try Avignonesi's estate store outlet at Via di Gracciano nel Corso 91 (tel 0578 757 872) and Fattoria del Cerro's (tel 0578 767 700) and Poliziano's (tel 0578 738 171) stores in Piazza Grande.

Enoteca Oinochóe Via di Voltaia nel Corso 82, tel 0578 757 524. A wine store that sells wine by most leading Vino Nobile producers, as well as Chianti, Brunello, and other superior Tuscan vintages.

PIENZA

FOOD

La Cornucopia Piazza Martiri della Libertà 2–3, tel 0578 748 150. Pienza is renowned for its pecorino, or sheep's cheese, and the village is full of stores selling this and other local foods. Much cheese is brought from elsewhere, however, so read labels. Buy from this excellent store, or visit small local producers.

LANGUAGE GUIDE

Italians respond well to foreigners who make an effort to speak their language. Many Italians speak at least some English, and most upscale hotels and restaurants have multilingual staff. All Italian words are pronounced as written, with each vowel and consonant sounded. The letter c is hard, as in the English "cat," except when followed by i or e, when it becomes the soft ch of "children." The same applies to g when followed by i or e—soft in *giardino* (as in the English "giant"); hard in *gatto*, as in "gate."

yes *sì*
no *no*
OK *d'accordo*
OK/that's fine/sure *Va bene*
I don't understand *Non capisco*
Do you speak English? *Parla inglese?*
I don't know *Non lo so*
I would like *Vorrei*
Do you have …? *Avete …?*
How much is it? *Quant'è?*
What is it? *Che cos'è?*
Who? *Chi?*
What? *Quale?*
Why? *Perchè?*
When? *Quando?*
Where? *Dove?*
Where is/where are? *Dov'è/dove sono?*
Where is the restroom? *Dovè il bagno?*
left/right *sinistra/destra*
straight on *sempre dritto*

Good morning *Buon giorno*
Good afternoon/good evening *Buona sera*
Good night *Buona notte*
Hello/goodbye (informal) *Ciao*
Hello (answering the telephone) *Pronto*
Goodbye *Arrivederci*
please *per favore*
thank you (very much) *grazie (mille)*
You're welcome *Prego*
What's your name? *Come si chiama?*
My name is… *Mi chiamo…*
I'm American (man) *Sono Americano*
I'm American (woman) *Sono Americana*
Mr./Sir *Signore*
Mrs./Ma'am *Signora*
Miss *Signorina*
How are you? *Come sta?*
Fine, thanks *Bene, grazie*
And you? *E lei?*
I'm sorry *Mi dispiace*

Excuse me/I beg your pardon *Mi scusi*
Excuse me (in a crowd) *Permesso*
Have a good day *Buona giornata*
No problem *Non c'è problema*

good/bad *buono/cattivo*
big/small *grande/piccolo*
with/without *con/senza*
more/less *più/meno*
enough *basta*
near/far *vicino/lontano*
hot/cold *caldo/freddo*
early/late *presto/ritardo*
straight away *subito*
here/there *quil/là*
now/later *adesso/più tardi*
today/tomorrow *oggi/domani*
yesterday *Ieri*
morning *la mattina*
afternoon *il pomeriggio*
evening *la sera*
entrance/exit *entrata/uscita*
open/closed *aperto /chiuso*
free (of charge) *gratuito*
free (unoccupied) *libero*
bathroom/toilet *il bagno/il gabinetto*
stamp *un francobollo*
postcard *una cartolina*
visitor center *l'uffico di turismo*

Help! *Aiuto!*
Stop! *Alt!/fermate!*
Look out! *Attenzione!*
Can you help me? *Mi puo aiutare?*
I'm not well *Sto male*
doctor *un medico*
Where is the police station? *Dov'è la polizia/la questura?*
hospital *l'ospedale*

road map *una carta stradale*
ticket *un biglietto*
train *un treno*
Let's go *Andiamo*

ENTERTAINMENT & ACTIVITIES

Florence and Tuscany offer a wide range of cultural and other entertainment, from world-class orchestras, opera performances, and music festivals to horseback riding, hiking, and art history or Italian language courses. Local visitor centers carry full details of forthcoming festivals and cultural events, plus contact information for other activities, such as rural horseback riding. They will also help with currently fashionable nightclubs and live music venues.

FLORENCE

For information contact Florence's visitor centers (see p. 52), or consult the listings section of the local *La Nazione* newspaper and monthly *Firenze Spettacolo* listings magazine, available from bookstores such as Feltrinelli (see p. 320). Tickets for events can be obtained from individual box offices or through Box Office, the city's central ticket agency, which has outlets at Via Alammanni 39 (Tel 055 210 804) and Chiasso dei Soldanieri 8r, off Via Porta Rossa on the corner with Via de' Tornabuoni (Tel 055 293 393).

Florence has several theater companies, but productions are invariably in Italian.

ART & LANGUAGE COURSES
British Institute Piazza Strozzi 2, tel 055 267 781. The long-established British Institute has short courses in Italian, art history, drawing, and cooking.

Dante Alighieri Via de' Bardi 12, tel 055 234 2984. Offers Italian language courses for varying levels of expertise. Also opera and literature courses.

Florence Academy of Art Via delle Casine 21r, tel 055 245 444. Summer art classes and life-drawing classes.

L'Instituto per L'Arte e Il Restauro Palazzo Spinelli, Borgo Santa Croce 10, tel 055 246 001. Regarded as one of

Italy's leading restoration schools, it offers courses on the restoration of frescoes, paper, furniture, ceramics, paintings, and glass. Courses last one to three years, but one month courses are also held in summer.

CINEMA
Florence has no shortage of cinemas, but most show movies dubbed into Italian. The only dedicated English-language cinema is the Astro, Piazza San Simeone-Via Isole delle Stinche (no phone). Some cinemas show movies in English (indicated by the words *versione originale*) one night a week.

PERFORMING ARTS
Amici della Musica Via G Sirtori 49, tel 055 608420 or 055 607440. Organizes a season of chamber concerts (Jan.–April & Oct.–Dec.), mostly in the 17th-century auditorium of the Teatro della Pergola (Via della Pergola 18, tel 055 247 9651).

Estate Fiesolana Venues around Fiesole, tel 055 597 8308. A major classical music and performing arts music festival held in Fiesole, usually between June and September.

Maggio Musicale Fiorentino Venues around Florence. Maggio Musicale (late April–early July) is one of Italy's leading music festivals. It has its own orchestra, chorus, and ballet, but also has concerts by international performers. Tickets from the Teatro Comunale (see below).

Orchestra Regionale Toscana Via de' Benci 20, tel 055 242 767 or 055 234 7355.

Tuscany's main regional orchestra is based in Florence, where it gives one or two concerts monthly in the season (Dec.–May). Performances are usually in Teatro Verdi (Via Ghibellina 99–101, tel 055 212 320).

Teatro Comunale Corso Italia 162, tel 055 27 791 or 055 211 158. This is the main city theater and hosts theater, music, and dance productions. It has its own chorus, orchestra (L'Orchestra del Maggio Musicale Fiorentino), and ballet (Maggio Danza).

NIGHTLIFE
Be Bop Via dei Servi 28r, no phone. The most central of Florence's major live music venues. Bands are mostly local and run the gamut through rock, jazz, and blues.

Dolce Vita Piazza del Carmine, tel 055 284 595. The Dolce Vita bar has been a fixture of Florentine nightlife for years, retaining its appeal through frequent decorative makeovers. Sit out on the piazza in summer.

Jazz Club Via Nuova de Cacciani 3, tel 055 247 9700. Florence's foremost jazz club has a sophisticated audience that takes its music seriously. Live music in a variety of jazz styles most nights. Closed Sun. & Mon.

L'Art Bar Via del Moro 4r, tel 055 287 661. A cozy and quite smart little bar that makes a good place for early evening cocktails or a late nightcap.

Meccanò Viale degli Olmi 1-Piazza delle Cascine, tel 055 331 371. The most celebrated club and disco in the city. Dress the part. Closed Sun. & Mon.

Space Electronic Via Palazzuolo 37, tel 055 293 082. Space Electronic has been around for years, but that hasn't dulled its appeal as a club and dance venue. Big, brash, and musically conservative. Closed Mon. in winter.

ENTERTAINMENT & ACTIVITIES

Rex Via Fiesolana 25r, tel 055 248 0331. Rex is a friendly bar north of Santa Croce, which comes into its own at night (busy on weekends).

FESTIVALS & EVENTS

Sfilata dei Canottieri Regatta of traditional boats on the River Arno on New Year's Day. *(Jan. 1)*
Diladdarno Three weeks of music, exhibitions, and street events celebrating the history of the Oltrarno. *(April–early May)*
Scoppio del Carro The "Explosion of the Cart" ends Florence's Easter Sunday ceremonies. A cart of flowers and fireworks is ignited at noon by a mechanical dove that "flies" along a wire from the Duomo's altar to the piazza outside.
Mostra Mercato dell'Artigianato A huge fair of crafts and artisan products such as glass, ceramics, and fabrics, held at the Fortezza di Basso. *(April or May)*
Maggio Musicale Tuscany's musical festival (see p. 325). *(May and June)*
Festa di San Giovanni The feast day of St. John the Baptist *(June 24)*, one of Florence's patron saints, is marked by a public holiday and "I Fochi di San Giovanni," a parade and fireworks display by Piazzale Michelangelo.
Calcio Storico Three fast and violent games are played in this famous soccer match, the first on the day after the feast of St. John. Teams are huge and play in 16th-century dress. Piazza Santa Croce or Piazza della Signoria. *(Last week of June)*
Festa delle Rificolone The Virgin's birthday is celebrated by a procession of children bearing lanterns to Piazza Santissima Annunziata. Also street parties and a parade of floats. *(Sept. 7)*

SPORT & ACTIVITIES
Golf
The nearest course to Florence is south of the city at Grassina. Circuito Golf Ugolino, Via Chiantigiana 3, tel 055 230 1009.

Gyms
The following Florentine gyms all

offer day membership rates: Indoor Club, Via Bardazzi 15, tel 055 430 275; Palestra, Via Palazzuolo 49r, tel 055 293 308; Ricciardi, Borgo Pinti 75, tel 055 247 8462. The Palestra Club is a women-only gym at Via Corelli 101, tel 055 430 202.

Soccer
Fiorentina, Florence's soccer team, plays at Stadio Artemio Franchi (Tel 055 507 2245) during the season (Aug.–May), but tickets sell out fast.

Swimming
Public pools in Florence are Le Pavoniere, Viale della Catena 2 in the Cascine park (Tel 055 333 979, closed Oct.–May), and Piscina di Bellariva, Lungarno Aldo Moro 6 (Tel 055 677 541, closed Oct.–May).

TUSCANY

ACTIVITIES
Hiking
Visitor centers in Arezzo (for the Casentino National Park) and elsewhere often have pamphlets detailing marked trails and hiking itineraries.

Many companies organize hiking vacations, either guided group or self-guided hikes. A long-established company for both types is the Oxford, U.K.-based ATG (Tel 0044 1865 310 399 from North America).

Horseback riding
For horseback riding holidays in Tuscany contact In the Saddle (Tel 0044 1256 851 665 from North America) or Equitour (Tel 0044 1865 511 642).

FESTIVALS
You may wish to plan your trip around some of Tuscany's larger events—notably the Siena Palio—but remember tickets and hotel rooms book up early. Virtually every village in the country finds an excuse to put on a show. Most smaller events follow a similar pattern: A

procession, often in traditional costume, followed by a special church service, fireworks, village marching bands, and lots of eating and drinking. Watch for fliers advertising a *festa* or *sagra*. Consult visitor centers for event details.

The selection of major events below is listed chronologically.

Carnivale Viareggio holds Italy's most lavish Carnevale (Carnival) celebrations outside Venice. Most towns have some sort of Carnivale festival or procession. *(Feb. or early March)*
Festa di San Ranieri Pisa. Candlelit processions, followed the next day by a rowing regatta in medieval dress. *(June 16–17)*
Gioco del Ponte Pisa. The "Game of the Bridge" is a tug-of-war in medieval costume held on Pisa's Ponte di Mezzo. *(Last Sun. in June)*
Festival di San Gimignano Opera, classical music, and arts festival. *(Late June–Oct.)*
Il Palio Siena (see pp. 202–203). *(July 2 and Aug. 16)*
Puccini Opera Festival Torre del Lago. Well-known festival of Puccini operas held near Viareggio. Tel 0584 359 322. *(August)*
Accademia Musicale Chigiana Siena. The town's leading musical association (Tel 0577 46 152) organizes concerts throughout much of the year.
Barga Opera Festival A concert series held in a pretty town north of Lucca. Tel 0583 723 250 or 0583 723 499. The Barga jazz festival is popular (Tel 0583 724 770). *(July–mid-Aug.)*
Bravio delle Botte Montepulciano. A barrel-rolling contest, plus processions, medieval drumming, and flag throwing. *(Last Sun. of Aug.)*
Giostra del Saracino Arezzo. Jousting knights and other events in medieval costume. Twice yearly. *(Sun. in mid-June and first Sun. of Sept.)*
Luminara di Santa Croce Lucca. Torchlit procession bearing the Volto Santo (see p. 257) around the streets. *(Sept. 14.)* ∎

INDEX

Bold page numbers indicate illustrations. Churches, museums, galleries, and other sights are in Florence unless otherwise stated.

INDEX

CREDITS

ILLUSTRATIONS CREDITS

Abbreviations for terms appearing below: (t) top; (b) bottom; (l) left; (r) right; (c) center.

Front Cover (tl) Corbis/Todd Gipstein. (tr) Pictures Colour Library. (bl) John Miller. (br) John Elk III. Spine Corbis/Todd Gipstein. 1, Chris Coe/Axiom. 2/3, AA Photo Library/Simon McBride. 4, Rita Pignato. 9, Owen Franken/Corbis. 11, Joe Cornish. 12/13, James Morris/Axiom. 14/15, AA Photo Library/Simon McBride. 16, AA Photo Library/Simon McBride. 17, AA Photo Library/Simon McBride. 18, AA Photo Library/Simon McBride. 19, Hubert Stadler/Corbis. 21, AA Photo Library/Simon McBride. 22/23, Scriptum Editions. 25, Farabolafoto. 26, Reclining man, room with Etruscan urns, Museo Guarnacci, Volterra, Italy/ Bridgeman Art Library. 27, Gold florin with a fleur de lys, Florentine, 1252-1303 (verso) (see also 83494) Bargello, Florence, Italy /Bridgeman Art Library. 28/29, Scala. 30, Lorenzo de'Medici, "the Magnificent". (1449-92), as one of the Three Kings, detail from the Journey of the Magi cycle in the chapel, c.1460 (fresco) (detail of 70619) by Benozzo di Lese di Sandro Gozzoli (1420-97), Palazzo Medici-Riccardi, Florence, Italy/ Bridgeman Art Library. 31, Apotheosis of Cosimo I de'Medici (1519-74) from the ceiling of the Salone del Cinquecento, 1565 (panel) by Giorgio Vasari (1511-74) (and workshop), Palazzo Vecchio (Palazzo della Signoria) Florence, Italy/Bridgeman Art Library. 32, Savonarola (1452-98) Burnt at the Stake in Piazza della Signoria (oil on canvas) by Italian School (15th centure), Museo di Firenze Com'era, Florence, Italy/ Bridgeman Art Library. 34/35, US Army Signal Corps. 35, Mrs Holly LaPratt/ National Geographic Society. 37, Scala. 38, Scala. 39, Scala. 40/41, Scala. 43, Joe Cornish. 44, Simon McBride. 47, Scala. 48l, Topham Picturepoint. 48r, Portrait of Niccolo Machiavelli (1469-1527) by Santi di Tito (1536-1603), Palazzo Vecchio (Palazzo della Signoria), Florence, Italy/ Bridgeman Art Library. 49, British Film Institute. 50/51, Gettyone/Stone. 53, © G Berengogardin// Contrasto/Katz. 55, AA Photo Library/ Simon McBride. 57, AA Photo Library/ Simon McBride. 58, AA Photo Library/ Simon McBride. 60, AA Photo Library/ Simon McBride. 61, AA Photo Library/ Simon McBride. 62, Rita Pignato. 63, Scala. 64, Scala. 67, Gettyone/ Stone. 68, Scala. 69, Chris Parker/Axiom. 70, AA Photo Library/ Simon McBride. 71, Scala. 72, © G Berengogardin// Contrasto/Katz. 73, AA Photo Library/ Simon McBride. 74, Simon McBride. 75, Scala. 76, Scala. 77, Scala. 78, Scala. 79 (t), Scala. 79 (b), Canto XXIII Dante and Virgil in the Circle of the Hypocrites, with

Caiaphas crucified on the ground, from the Divine Comedy (the Inferno), c.1313, Works by Dante Alighieri, (1265-1321), Vatican Library, Rome, Italy/ Bridgeman Art Library. 80/81, Joe Cornish. 81, Scala. 82, Scala. 83, Scala. 84, Scala. 85 (t), Scala. 85 (b), Scala. 86, AA Photo Library/Simon McBride. 87, Scala. 89, Joe Cornish. 90/91, AA Photo Library/Simon McBride. 91, AA Photo Library/Simon McBride. 92, AA Photo Library/Simon McBride. 93, AA Photo Library/Simon McBride. 94, AA Photo Library/Simon McBride. 95, AA Photo Library/Simon McBride. 96, AA Photo Library/Simon McBride. 97, Scala. 98, AA Photo Library/Simon McBride. 99, Scala. 100, Madonna and Child with Angels, c. 1455 (tempera on panel) by Fra Filippo Lippi (c.1406-69), Galleria degli Uffizi, Florence, Italy/Bridgeman Art Library. 101, Scala. 102, Scala. 103, Scala. 104, Scala. 105, Scala. 107, Joe Cornish. 109, Scala. 111, James Morris/Axiom. 112/113, Scala. 113, Scala. 114, Scala. 115, AA Photo Library/Simon McBride. 116, Scala. 117, AA Photo Library/Clive Sawyer. 118, Scala. 119, Bettmann/ Corbis. 121, Joe Cornish. 122, AA Photo Library/ Simon McBride. 123, Scala. 124, Scala. 125, Scala. 126/127, Scala. 129, Scala. 130 (t), Scala. 130 (b), Scala. 131, Scala. 132, Battle tournament, fragment of mural painting from the Sala del Pisanello (formerly Sala dei Principi) (sinopia) by Antonio Pisanello (1395-1455), Palazzo Ducale, Mantua, Italy/ Bridgeman Art Library. 135, Lorenzo de'Medici, "the Magnificent". (1449-92), as one of the Three Kings, detail from the Journey of the Magi cycle in the chapel, c.1460 (fresco) (detail of 70619) by Benozzo di Lese di Sandro Gozzoli (1420-97), Palazzo Medici-Riccardi, Florence, Italy/Bridgeman Art Library. 136, Scala. 136/137, Scala. 137, Scala. 138, AA Photo Library/Simon McBride. 139, David, detail of the head by Michelangelo Buonarotti (1475-1564), 1504 (marble) Galleria dell' Accademia, Florence, Italy/ Bridgeman Art Library. 140, Scala. 141, Scala. 142, AA Photo Library/Simon McBride. 143, Scala. 146, AA Photo Library/Simon McBride. 147, AA Photo Library/Simon McBride. 149, Massima Listri/Corbis. 151, AA Photo Library/ Simon McBride. 152, Lucy Davies/ Axiom. 153, AA Photo Library/ Simon McBride. 154, AA Photo Library/ Simon McBride. 156 (t), Scala. 156 (b), Scala. 157, Scala. 158, Scala. 159, Scala. 160, Scala. 161, Bedroom or Sala dei Pavoni with frescoed trompe l'oeil decoration of wall hangings and a frieze of birds, 14th centure, Palazzo Davanzati, Florence, Italy/Bridgeman Art Library. 162, AA Photo Library/Simon McBride. 163, Joe Cornish. 164, Hulton Getty Picture Collection. 165 (t), Mrs Holly LaPratt/National Geographic Society. 165 (b), Sunday Times. 166, Scala. 167, Scala. 169, Clive Nichols/

Fountain of Neptune, Boboli Gardens, Italy. 171, Scala. 172, Scala. 173, Scala. 174, Scala. 176, AA Photo Library/Simon McBride. 177, Clive Nichols/The Isolotto, Bololi Gardens, Italy. 178, Adam and Eve banished from Paradise by Tommaso Masaccio (1401-28), Brancacci Chapel, Santa Maria del Carmine, Florence, Italy/Bridgeman Art Library. 179, Scala. 180 (tl), Adam and Eve banished from Paradise by Tommaso Masaccio (1401-28), Brancacci Chapel, Santa Maria del Carmine, Florence, Italy/Bridgeman Art Library. 180 (tc), Scala. 180 (tr), Scala. 180 (bl), Scala. 180 (bc), Scala. 180 (br), Scala. 181 (tl), Scala. 181 (tc), Scala. 181 (tr), Scala. 181 (bl), Scala. 181 (bc), Scala. 181 (br), Scala. 183, Art Directors & TRIP Photo Library. 184, Joe Cornish. 185, James Morris/Axiom. 186, Travel Library. 187, Temperance, roundal from the Tomb of the Cardinal of Portugal, 1460's (glazed terracotta) by Luca Della Robbia (1400-82), San Miniato al Monte, Florence, Italy/Bridgeman Art Library. 188, AA Photo Library/Clive Sawyer. 190/191, Powerstock/Zefa. 193, International Photobank. 197, Travel Library. 198, Lucy Davies/Axiom. 198/199, Joe Cornish. 200, Scala. 201, Scala. 202/203, World Pictures. 203, EPA/P A Photos. 204, Art Directors & TRIP Photo Library. 205, AA Photo Library/Ken Paterson. 206/207, Rita Pignato. 207, Scala. 208, Scala. 209, Scala. 210/211, Scala. 212, Scala. 213, Scala. 214/215, Scala. 216, Scala. 217, Scala. 218, Scala. 219, Scala. 221, AA Photo Library/Clive Sawyer. 222, Rita Pignato. 223, Archivi Alinari ~ Firenze. 224, Scala. 225, Travel Library. 228, Art Directors & TRIP Photo Library. 228/229, John Heseltine Archive. 233, Joe Cornish. 234, Jill Swainson/Sylvia Cordaiy Photo Library. 235, Lucy Davies/Axiom. 236, Art Directors & TRIP Photo Library. 237, Joe Cornish. 238, Joe Cornish. 239, Julian Worker/Sylvia Cordaiy Photo Library. 240, Scala. 241, Scala. 243 (t), Joe Cornish. 243 (b), Joe Cornish. 244, Scala. 245, John Heseltine Archive. 246/247, Images Colour Library. 248, Travel Library. 249, Scala. 252, Robert Harding Picture Library. 253, Travel Library. 254, Julian Worker/Sylvia Cordaiy Photo Library. 254/255, Travel Library. 256, John Heseltine Archive. 258, Travel Library. 259 (t), Travel Library. 259 (b), Mary Evans Picture Library. 260, Travel Library. 261, Travel Library. 262, Simon McBride. 263, Joe Cornish. 265, Mick Rock/Cephas. 267, Mick Rock/Cephas. 268/269, Joe Cornish. 269, Chris Coe/ Axiom. 270/271, Lucy Davies/ Axiom. 271, Travel Library. 272/273, Gettyone/ Stone. 273 (t), Mick Rock/ Cephas. 273 (b), Mick Rock/ Cephas. 274/275, Joe Cornish. 275, Joe Cornish. 276/277, John Heseltine Archive. 277, Simon McBride. 278, Simon